# Be

### ABOUT THE AUTHOR

Sinclair McKay is the bestselling author of *Dresden*, *The Secret Life of Bletchley Park* and *The Secret Listeners*. He is a literary critic for the *Telegraph* and the *Spectator* and lives in London.

# Berlin

*Life and Loss in the City
That Shaped the Century*

## SINCLAIR McKAY

PENGUIN BOOKS

PENGUIN BOOKS

UK | USA | Canada | Ireland | Australia
India | New Zealand | South Africa

Penguin Books is part of the Penguin Random House group of companies
whose addresses can be found at global.penguinrandomhouse.com.

First published by Viking 2022
Published in Penguin Books 2023
001

Copyright © Sinclair McKay, 2022

The moral right of the author has been asserted

Typeset by Jouve (UK), Milton Keynes
Printed and bound in Great Britain by Clays Ltd, Elcograf S.p.A.

The authorized representative in the EEA is Penguin Random House Ireland,
Morrison Chambers, 32 Nassau Street, Dublin D02 YH68

A CIP catalogue record for this book is available from the British Library

ISBN: 978–0–241–99168–8

www.greenpenguin.co.uk

Penguin Random House is committed to a
sustainable future for our business, our readers
and our planet. This book is made from Forest
Stewardship Council® certified paper.

# Contents

# List of Illustrations

# Picture Credits

The majority of the photographs come from private collections. Others are from: 11, 14, 15, 16, 19, 21, 22, 26, 27, 31, 42, 45, 50, 53, 54, Alamy; 2, 5, 8, 12, 17, 23, 36, 41, Getty; 4, 9, 18, 38, 46, 48, AKG; 25, 33, 37, 51, 52, Topfoto; 1, Bridgeman; 43, National Archives. Every reasonable effort has been made to trace copyright but the publisher welcomes any information that clarifies the copyright ownership of any unattributed material displayed and will endeavour to include corrections in reprints.

# Maps

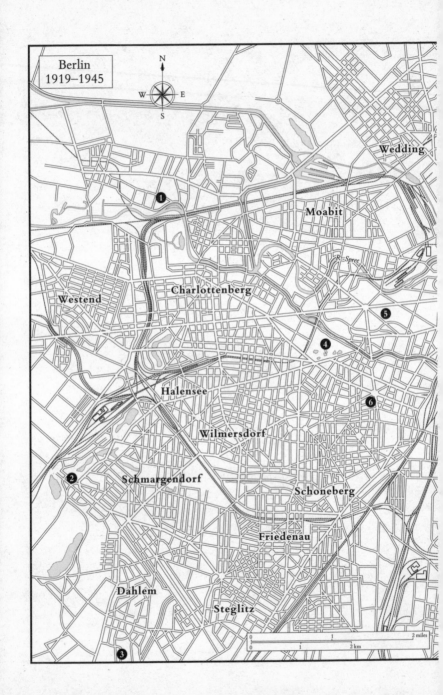

Berlin
1919–1945

N
W   E
S

Wedding

Moabit

R. Spree

Westend

Charlottenberg

Halensee

Wilmersdorf

Schoneberg

Schmargendorf

Friedenau

Dahlem

Steglitz

0         1         2 miles
0  1       2 km

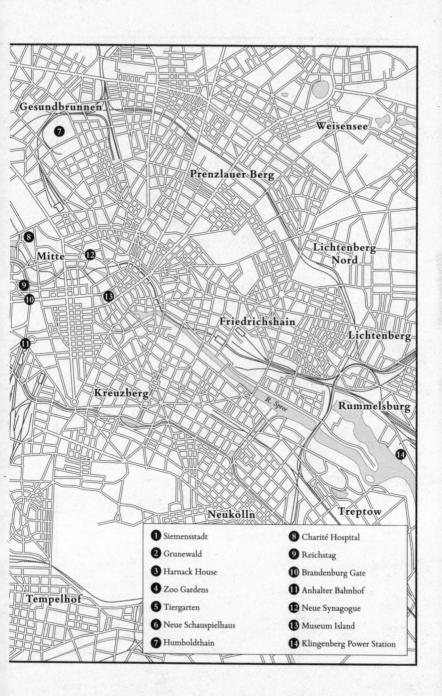

Gesundbrunnen

Weisensee

Prenzlauer Berg

**7**

**8**

Mitte

**12**

Lichtenberg
Nord

**9**

**10**

**13**

Friedrichshain

Lichtenberg

**11**

*R. Spree*

Kreuzberg

Rummelsburg

**14**

Neukölln

Treptow

Tempelhof

| | |
|---|---|
| **1** Siemensstadt | **8** Charité Hospital |
| **2** Grunewald | **9** Reichstag |
| **3** Harnack House | **10** Brandenburg Gate |
| **4** Zoo Gardens | **11** Anhalter Bahnhof |
| **5** Tiergarten | **12** Neue Synagogue |
| **6** Neue Schauspielhaus | **13** Museum Island |
| **7** Humboldthain | **14** Klingenberg Power Station |

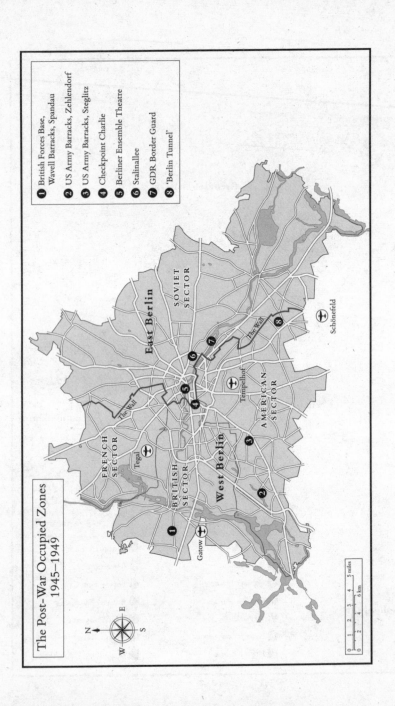

The Post-War Occupied Zones
1945–1949

1 British Forces Base, Wavell Barracks, Spandau
2 US Army Barracks, Zehlendorf
3 US Army Barracks, Steglitz
4 Checkpoint Charlie
5 Berliner Ensemble Theatre
6 Stalinallee
7 GDR Border Guard
8 'Berlin Tunnel'

East Berlin

SOVIET SECTOR

FRENCH SECTOR

BRITISH SECTOR

West Berlin

AMERICAN SECTOR

The Wall

Tegel

Gatow

Tempelhof

Schönefeld

N
E
W
S

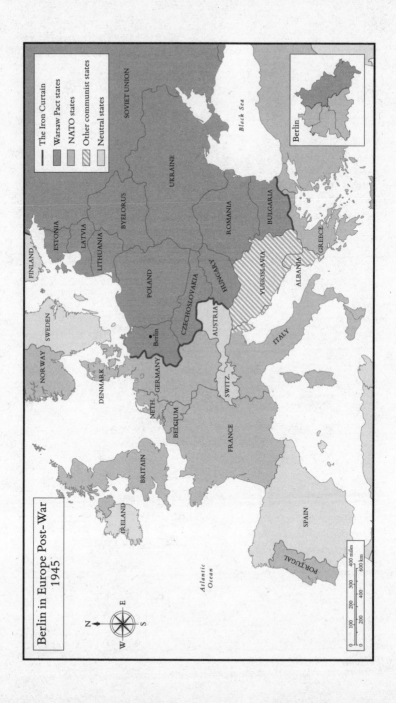

Berlin in Europe Post-War
1945

The Iron Curtain
Warsaw Pact states
NATO states
Other communist states
Neutral states

Berlin

SOVIET UNION

Black Sea

UKRAINE

BYELORUS

ROMANIA

BULGARIA

FINLAND

ESTONIA

LATVIA

LITHUANIA

POLAND

HUNGARY

GREECE

ALBANIA

YUGOSLAVIA

CZECHOSLOVAKIA

AUSTRIA

SWEDEN

NORWAY

DENMARK

Berlin

GERMANY

NETH.

BELGIUM

SWITZ

ITALY

FRANCE

BRITAIN

IRELAND

SPAIN

PORTUGAL

Atlantic
Ocean

N
E
S
W

0    100   200   300   400 miles
0    200   400   600 km

# Preface: 'Every city has history, but Berlin has too much!'

Berlin is a naked city. It openly displays its wounds and scars. It wants you to see. The stone and the bricks along countless streets are pitted and pocked and scorched; bullet memories. These disfigurements are echoes of a vast, bloody trauma of which, for many years, Berliners were reluctant to speak openly. In the shadow of filthy genocide, it was taboo to suggest that they too were victims in Hitler's war. The city itself is long healed, but those injuries are still stark: the old Friedrichsruhe brewery wall with a sunburst blast-pattern caused by heavy shelling; the bas-relief at the base of the nineteenth-century Victory Column, of Christ on the cross, pierced by shrapnel through the heart; the entrance portal to the bomb-crushed Anhalter railway station – Romanesque brick arches – now standing alone and leading only to empty air. In the Humboldthain, a rich park just north of the city centre, trees spring forth around a grim, vast, concrete fortress that, towards the end of the war, served as shelter, hospital and catacomb. Most famous is the shattered church tower, capped with metal, that stands over the busy Kurfürstendamm shopping street: the Kaiser Wilhelm Memorial Church. The tower is almost all that remains of the turn-of-the-century original; one night in 1943, it was hit in a bombing raid and engulfed in flames (and, after the war, a new hexagonal modernist church was constructed next to it). If you knew nothing of the history of this city, the initial sight of this strange tower would be disconcerting: what could be meant by this weird ruin preserved in the midst of an indifferent shopping concourse? Other European capitals acknowledge the dark past with elegantly aestheticized monuments; they seek to smooth the jagged edges of history. Not here.

Throughout the twentieth century, Berlin stood at the centre of a convulsing world. It alternately seduced and haunted the international imagination. The essence of the city seemed to be its sharp duality: the radiant boulevards, the cacophonous tenement blocks,

the dark smoky citadels of hard industry, the bright surrounding
waters and forests, the exultant pan-sexual cabarets, the stiff dignity
of high opera, the colourful excesses of Dadaist artists, the grim uniformity of mass swastika processions. And with the advent of the
Nazis came a steadily building drumbeat of death. Of the city's Jewish population, most of those who had remained in Berlin under the
Nazis – 80,000 people or so – were deported and murdered between
1941 and 1943. In addition, an estimated 25,000 Berliners were killed
by Allied action in the final weeks of the war in 1945. But there was a
continual proximity to fear, before and after, too: for anyone born in
Berlin around the year 1900 – and who was then lucky enough to live
on into the 1970s or 1980s – life in the city was an unending series of
revolutions; a maelstrom of turmoil and insecurity. This spanned the
reeling trauma of the First World War and the disease and violence
that immediately followed; the sharp, vertiginous inrush of modern
industry and the defiantly revolutionary architecture that mirrored
it, roaring through once familiar streets and workplaces; the nausea
of steep economic plunges, bringing destitution and hunger; then,
the Nazi supremacy, the psychosis of genocide and the fires of war;
and, finally, the heart of the city rent in two by competing ideologies.
At the centre of these traumas were those weeks at the end of the war
in spring 1945 when the devastation visited upon Berlin and its people was comparable to the infernal retributions of classical antiquity.

The city does not lack for heartfelt tributes to the dead: the exquisite and recent Holocaust memorial, a maze of monoliths that rise
further over your head the deeper you move among them, is one of
the few sites where the nervy pace of the Berliner is forcibly slowed.
A few streets away from here is the much older, pale-stoned neoclassical Neue Wache memorial, built in 1818 in the aftermath of years
of terrible European conflict. In recent times its purpose has been
widened, and it has been transformed into a striking hall of com-
memoration to 'victims of war and dictatorship', the light pouring
down through a circular hollow, or oculus, in the roof. But, for
Berlin, the singular cataclysm of Hitler's war and the destruction
wrought upon the city can never be easily memorialized. In the
spring of 1945, as the Americans and the British fought through
Germany, and as their bombers shattered ever more streets and

tenements, turning homes to ash, and the vast Soviet forces closed decisively around the city, their screaming projectiles piercing the air, ordinary Berliners were prisoners facing inescapable horror. It was carnage for which the world had no pity. The city became a battle-ground that spoke of the final obscenity of total war. The tokens of civilization were crushed into dust, and Berliners were forced into a scavenging existence that strained at the threads of human nature.

And there was a further element of anguish in 1945, one that tran-scended the bombs and the mortars that left unburied bodies beyond recognition, the epidemic of suicide as thousands of citizens chose to end their own lives rather than submit to an enemy that filled them with terror, even the wholesale rape in literally uncountable numbers that created decades of family trauma across the city. It was the fact that these violations and cruelties were regarded by the implacable wider world as being understandable – a final whirlwind of ven-geance as unstoppable as nature itself. The Nazi leadership had inflicted agony and death upon millions across Europe. Berlin's once-substantial Jewish community was terrorized for years before being expelled and exterminated. So how could their Berlin neighbours presume to tell the world that they too had suffered atrociously? This atoning silence left a bewildering cloud of moral ambiguity over the city. How total was the totalitarianism of the Nazis here?

The fall of Berlin in 1945 is one of those moments in history that stands like a lighthouse; the beam turns and sharply illuminates what came before and what came after. It was not just the squalid death of the man at the centre of the maelstrom, or the way in which his self-destruction in an underground bunker appeared to seep out and dissolve the foundations of the city itself. Nor is it a story that can be wholly understood as military history, since it is also a vast tapestry of ordinary civilian Berliners – greatly outnumbering the remaining soldiers who could no longer protect them – and their efforts to cling to their sanity as their lives were dislocated. It is also the story of those who had seen the warning shadows of this violence in the years beforehand. There were older Berliners in 1945 who had been there in the aftermath of the Great War and the failed German Revolution of 1918; who had already edged their way down icy streets trans-formed into sniper-canyons; who had already known chronic food shortages and unrelieved cold. In 1919, a poster appeared all over the city depicting an elegant woman locked in a tango with a skeleton. 'Berlin, stop and think! Your dance partner is death!' proclaimed its strapline. The poster, inspired by the poet Paul Zech, was about public health measures in the wake of war, yet it suggested a wider morbidity in the city's nature.

Similarly, the nightmare of 1945 threw its shadow far into the city's future. In the aftershocks of Nazism, those ordinary civilians faced new waves of post-war violence, of deprivation, of distress, and a whole new cycle of totalitarianism. The deathly grey of the Berlin Wall, upon which construction began in 1961, was itself part of the aftershock of 1945, as the city remained at the centre of global geopolitical anxiety, the potential flashpoint for a nuclear war. And yet even with this new iteration of duality, the wit and the art and the unselfconsciously defiant spirit endured.

People do not live their lives in fixed eras; an epoch ends, yet the people continue – or try to continue – much as they did before. The recent history of Berlin is often viewed through fixed prisms of division: Wilhelmine, Weimar, Nazi, communist, each period hermetically sealed. Yet the lives of its citizens formed an uneasy continuum through all these different regimes; these were people who always struggled hard to adapt to a city that changed with whiplash velocity. What must all of these violent revolutions have seemed like to Berliners who simply wished to live and work and love? Those who grew up in the Weimar era, who then felt the shadow of the Nazis fall, then in the years afterwards saw their city occupied and dominated by other powers – how did their mental landscapes, their memories of particular neighbourhoods, remain firm when the physical urban landscape around them was in a constant state of bewildering mutation and demolition, to the extent that even some born in the city could no longer find their way to once-familiar streets? Nor could these abrasively witty citizens ever be wholly defined by the nightmare of war; to explore their lives and their history now, it is important to acknowledge that their stories also encompass Berlin's extraordinary cultural hinterland: not just its wildly innovative and world-leading art and cinema and music, nor just its rich scientific endeavour, but also its tortured relationship with an ancient aristocracy and the constant grinding engines of class and street violence.

Before Hitler, this had been a cosmopolitan city, drawing fascinated visitors and immigrants from around the world. Among the smart apartment blocks and futuristic department stores of the 1920s moved artists with sensual and satirical visions of the new reality of city life. This exuberance would be almost completely (though never wholly, even under the Nazis) extinguished for a time. And immediately after May 1945, that flame jumped high once more, feeding on the oxygen of liberation. Then there was Berlin's pioneering pre-Nazi promise of personal fulfilment. For a time, women and men were relatively free to live according to their true sexual orientations. Here, unlike most other world cities at the time, they were not reviled; they could at last express the love that had been denied to them. Again, the Nazis did all in their power to smother this side of the city's life, and in the cruellest ways. A great many Berliners were sent to brutal deaths for this reason. Yet, out of the ashes, defiance reared, and the city rediscovered its taste for sensuality once more.

There was also a propulsion about the city's intellectual life. In science, as much as the arts, a range of new worlds were summoned in laboratories all over Berlin. Before Nazism, this had been Einstein's city, but he was not the only dazzling innovator. The mysteries of quantum physics were being explored here by minds that were operating in new and unimagined realms. The city's immolation in 1945 throws stark light on to the directions in which that science had travelled, and the lengths to which Stalin was prepared to go in order to steal its atomic secrets and make them his own.

The price of early twentieth-century innovation was insecurity and alienation; the sheer speed of the pace of discovery, and the pace of social, sexual and artistic change, was exhilarating for some, frightening for others. This gave Berlin a shifting identity that could not easily be defined. The city's unusual sensibility – apparent even amid the smell of death and the rubble of the Soviet invasion – had been noted previously. 'It has always,' wrote the poet Stephen Spender, 'been a city in which the psychology of the inhabitants was worn like hearts on sleeves.'[1] In 1930, the writer and satirist Joseph Roth wrote: 'Berlin is a young and unhappy city-in-waiting.'[2] He walked the streets of the east of the city, and said of Hirtenstrasse, a boulevard of severe apartment blocks: 'No street in the world is as sad.'[3] Yet, in 1920s travel advertising, Berlin was labelled 'the new city of light in Europe'.[4] It was noted in 1929 that 'there is no city in the world so restless as Berlin. Everything moves.'[5] The internationally renowned theatre director Max Reinhardt had observed, before the rise of Nazism: 'What I love is the taste of transience on the tongue – every year might be the last.'[6] Even in the pulsing neon lights that pierced the twilight autumn fogs, the possibility of darkness was always close. The artist George Grosz was preoccupied with 'the dark-walled tenements' and the imminence of 'riots and massacre'.[7] And after the war, when Berlin was racked between new occupying powers, that sharp sense of urban alienation was compounded, and artists such as Bertolt Brecht were among those who probed these tears and fractures. Both in the communist east of the city and the American-dominated western zone there was a resurgence of molten aesthetic energy. And, as with the period after the First World War, it was blended with something feverish and giddy and on the edge of ungovernability.

Berlin today is wonderful for the aimless walker; its apparent lack of any readily discernible centre makes it fascinating to explore. You might be inclined to see the heart of the city lying at the Brandenburg Gate, and the restored Reichstag that stands beside it. But no: there is no huge sense of occasion or pomp, merely a sense that it is here that the business of government is conducted without fuss. Perhaps that heart is to be heard among the grave museums and the cathedral to be found on 'Museum Island'; among those neoclassical colonnades and domes? Again no: while undeniably alluring and attractively landscaped, these grand nineteenth-century institutions seem almost self-consciously out of place: there to impress visitors but bearing no architectural sign that they are a part of the city's everyday organic life. Perhaps the key is to be found in the story of Berlin's hideously persecuted Jewish community. Not far from here, a little further to the north after a walk along the banks of the Spree, is an exquisite building: the New Synagogue, its Moorish dome glowing in the golden sun. Yet it is a revenant; in 1943, the synagogue was half-destroyed, and, in the wake of the war, the gutted structure decayed further until finally it was demolished. The building that we see today is a deeply felt reconstruction. It is an important part of the story – yet not the whole of it.

The same can be said of another vast replica: the Berliner Schloss – an eighteenth-century palace raised for the Hohenzollern dynasty, seized during the 1918 German Revolution, largely ignored by the Nazis, pulverized by Allied bombing and demolished by the Soviets in the 1950s – has been born anew by the Spree, or partially so. Three of its four vast exterior walls have been perfectly recreated in their baroque splendour; and the building now hosts the Humboldt museum. Yet this recreation has caused immense controversy too. Its passionate critics have argued that there is something sinisterly neo-colonial about the deliberate reconstruction of the seat of imperial power. 'Every city has history,' observed leading Berlin architect David Chipperfield, 'but Berlin has too much.'[8]

But there is a quieter, more working-class enclave in the north-west – streets of glum and dusty-looking apartment blocks where, in a sense, something of the city's essential historic heart has been captured. It lies in the offices of a remarkable endeavour. The Zeitzeugenbörse – a contemporary witness exchange – has been aiming to capture and record the voices of ordinary Berliners from right the way across the century: their lives and experiences through the traumas of the decades. The old sense that the German people had to suppress their own experiences of suffering had the unintended effect of creating a mass of historic dark matter: silence and obscurity when it came to certain epochal events. The wonderful academics and volunteers who run the Zeitzeugenbörse have been working in recent years to ensure that a generation of Berlin voices is never lost. It is these voices that can help guide us through a century both of terror and of stubborn fortitude.

And they can also bring vivid, haunting perspectives: for instance, from the memories of Helga Hauthal, a Berlin schoolgirl in the 1940s whose innocent obsession with the cinema brought her into conflict with unyielding authority; to Horst Basemann, a young Berliner on the eastern front in 1945 recalling his boyhood, and the intoxicating night-time forest bonfires of the Hitler Youth of the 1930s; from young office worker Mechtild Evers, who, in 1945, in her efforts to escape an oncoming army ran into even more appalling jeopardy; to Reinhart Crüger, a twelve-year-old boy in 1941 who witnessed with horror the Gestapo coming for each of his Jewish neighbours in turn; and Christa Ronke, a young teenager who, like so many others her age, had simply wanted to focus on her school studies even as the world around her disintegrated in 1945 and then, like her friends, somehow learned to suppress the trauma after the war as she sought to build a new life in this torn landscape.

While the reigns of the powerful are always closely recorded, the ordinary lives that were rocked and pitched by their actions and ideologies have a flavour and texture that perhaps tells us more about morality and human choices. And such matters have a particular resonance in Berlin: because of the close proximity of evil to all their lives, these citizens became especially fascinating. What happened in Berlin, and in the rest of Germany, might have happened anywhere, but how did those ideologies – the unyielding, cold-eyed brutality of fascism and the panopticon repression of communism – come to flower so fully here? And how did their repercussions continue to be felt throughout Europe and the West right up until that extraordinary night in the autumn of 1989 when the Wall – that final expression of totalitarian oppression – was at last breached?

In this sense, you cannot understand the twentieth century without understanding Berlin. Fundamentally, it was the moment of the city's fall at the end of the war in 1945 that encapsulated the nihilist horror: mass death without meaning on an unimaginable scale. Yet even in that miasma, it was still possible to discern sparks of the city's restless and impatient ethos. To walk the city now is to feel all those layers of the past. With great sensitivity in recent years, the authorities have made it possible to appreciate the different ideas of the city as it was. What the climactic darkness of 1945 teaches is that even as the shadows thickened, there were still Berliner lives and loves and dreams that spoke to the city's truer soul.

# PART ONE

# Dissolution

# 1. The Dwellers in the Dark

They were living their lives either beneath the ground or deep within concrete. They were buried. Somehow, this was endurable. Across the city of Berlin there were a thousand or so specially constructed air-raid shelters, but these could accommodate only a fraction of the city's population of just under three million. There were also the basements beneath apartment blocks, cellars beneath houses and the stations of the U-Bahn underground system. There were even slit trenches. Subterranean passages – prospects of rough concrete enlivened by angry propaganda posters – offered comfortless sanctuary. Civilians crammed too close together gazed up at curved ceilings or at one another; and they blinked at each muffled boom above that reverberated with a resonance that could be felt in the bones.

By the first week of April 1945, the rhythms of civilian life in Berlin had been sharpened to a point of terrible simplicity: the daylight quest to find rations – any food at all – with silent, near motionless queues that could last for hours. The weary walks through wrecked streets in thinning-soled shoes smothered with dust, entire districts deconstructed and rendered unfamiliar, with new views and prospects and disorientating absences: the cumulative effect of months of heavy bombing. The previous month had seen an especially frenzied raid, as though the Allied bombers had been seeking simply to smash the city into the earth. Even so, in the suburbs there were some factories that had not been shattered by high explosives – worked by huge numbers of forced labourers drawn from across Europe – and that labour continued, albeit with intermittent supplies of electricity and water. The city's still-functioning power stations continued to hum, tall chimneys exhaling white smoke; the vast and architecturally elegant generating station of Klingenberg, which cast its shadow over the River Spree in the east of the city, was itself kept alive by intelligent forced labourers who were making shrewd calculations about the future of the city and about which of the Allies would be

the first to claim it. The U-Bahn was still, somehow, broadly functioning, though only on the lines that had not received direct hits,
and strictly for those who needed it for work or military purposes.

With depressing frequency, the weary cry of the city's air-raid
sirens, low and throaty, would begin the race back down to the underworld. Since the autumn of 1943, Allied bombing raids had killed and
mutilated thousands, rendering entire streets and districts practically
uninhabitable, although there were those who stayed among the ruins,
unwilling to leave. Those citizens whose cellars and shelters had not
imploded would emerge each morning into days that looked like night;
the sky above grey and dense, sometimes 'smouldering yellow' with
the dust and the ash.[1] The air itself seemed burned: unextinguished
fires brought fumes from wood and paint and rubber. With handker-
chiefs over mouths, mothers and grandmothers looked on as the civil
defence authorities retrieved bodies – many in fragments – from
beneath the grey brick and stone. Any individual death had lost its
sanctity. Mass burials had been efficiently arranged, yet still a pervasive
sweetness in the air signalled decay. Clearly, not all the remains had
been recovered from the rubble. This was not for want of purpose; the
firefighters and the police and other civic workers remained dedicated.
Like the hospitals, though, they were overwhelmed. There were
instances when ideology dissolved amid destruction. The small Jewish
Hospital in the northern suburb of Gesundbrunnen – founded in the
eighteenth century and the sole Jewish institution to survive the war in
Berlin, chiefly because of its facilities and expertise – was, by the end
of the conflict, simultaneously hiding Jewish fugitives and treating
gentiles. By contrast, the central Charité Hospital, also founded in
the eighteenth century – some of whose doctors had been used by the
Nazis in the 1930s to carry out grotesque medical experiments and
to euthanize disabled and psychiatric patients – was now extensively
smashed; medical supplies and morphine were too sparse to minister to
the processions of the wounded. Many in the city, familiar with the
landmark of the Charité, did not comprehend just how close to their
own daily lives the true terrible eugenic horror of the regime had been.

At the beginning of April 1945 American daylight raids subsided,
but the nocturnal attacks by British bombers continued. Many Berliners who had lost their homes in these attacks were dwelling in

the shelters through the day and the night; for them, this life in the darkness must have seemed to be the limit of existence. The city's authorities had anticipated some years beforehand that Berlin might be in need of such sanctuary. Berlin is built upon sandy soil, so was always an awkward prospect for excavation, whether for sewers or for the underground railways that were constructed from the turn of the century onwards. In 1935 the Nazis stipulated that any new building in the city should be designed with a basement that could be used for shelter. The outrage of the first British bomber attack on the city in the autumn of 1940 prompted a 'Bunker Construction Programme for the Capital of the Reich'. By April 1945, and after eighteen months of sustained bombing from the Allies, a great many of those bunkers and basements had become sealed tombs. Entire streets had collapsed, punched through with thousands of pounds of heavy explosives, leaving infilled basements and passages beneath that rescue teams struggled to enter. One particular hazard that had faced shelterers was bombs hitting water mains; in that instance, their deaths would be caused by drowning, the waters rising to the brick ceilings too fast for them to escape. The U-Bahn stations were similarly vulnerable, the lines running only a few feet below the surface.

Despite such adversity, the keen edge of Berliner humour somehow remained present. The LS initials signifying *Luftschutz* (air-raid shelter) were said to stand for *Lernen schnell Russisch*, or 'Learn Russian quickly'.[2] The humour did not quell the fear. Since the beginning of the year, in days when the implacable Berlin frost gave the streets a metallic feel, the city had been teeming with exhausted and traumatized rural refugees. Some had come by rail; others entered the city wearily on roads, negotiating cobbles and icy tramlines, pointing westwards without final aim. They had fled their stolen farmlands in the conquered east, carrying with them the searing memories of those they had left behind who had not escaped the Red Army: the women who were raped repeatedly, many of whom had been later tortured and murdered.

Some Berliner civilians were aware – and fearful – that the vast Soviet forces now gathering in the distance and moving inexorably towards them had themselves witnessed Nazi-inflicted depravities and obscenities, keeping Soviet prisoners of war in open-air pens where an estimated three million or more had been deliberately starved to death under freezing skies. And by August 1944, as they pushed out of Soviet territory and towards Germany, huge numbers of those Red Army soldiers would have read in their newspaper *Krasnaya Zvezda* a terrifying account of a camp in Poland called Majdanek, written by the soldier and poet Konstantin Simonov. His agonized descriptions of its gas chambers, and of the 'thousands and thousands of pairs of children's footwear'[3] discarded there, had been among the first searing reports of these atrocities – so searing that some in the British and American authorities did not completely believe them. Rumours of what happened at the death camps had already reached Berlin. Brigitte Lempke, who was a schoolgirl at the time, recalled a classmate pulling her to one side and saying, 'I have to tell you something, but you must never repeat it, or something very bad will happen.' Slightly frightened, Brigitte agreed and her schoolfriend told her that her uncle, a doctor, had returned from the east. One night, when the girl was supposed to be in bed, she secretly listened to her uncle talking brokenly to her parents. He was crying, she said. He had seen ovens in which they were going to burn people. The girl offered a vivid simile: 'just how bread is pushed into the oven, people are pushed into it'.[4] It was an image Brigitte could never forget.

And for the Red Army, the nature of those they were seeking to defeat had found even sharper focus with the discoveries of Treblinka and then, in January 1945, of Auschwitz. 'Liberation' seemed too exultant a term for the rescue of living skeletons amid the obscene piles of dead bodies. They had also found several mass graves in haunted forests. These young soldiers needed little hardening against their enemy, although their Soviet superiors were initially insisting, through newspapers and radio, that these camps were the responsibility not just of a few Nazi officers, but of German society as a whole. They were emanations of the very nature of the Fatherland. The time would come as the Nazi regime collapsed when the Soviets would reverse this position, insisting that the German working people could not be blamed, but, until this monstrosity was defeated, the soldiers of the Red Army were left to wonder about the humanity of every German civilian they encountered.

The cycle of vengeance had a terrible velocity. In part, at the beginning of April, this was because of tensions between the Allies.

The American and the British forces, having fought their way through from the west, were poised to make the final swoop on Berlin. (The Allies had already long decided – with difficulty – upon the division of Berlin and the zones of the defeated capital that each would occupy; negotiations at the European Advisory Commission in London had been ongoing since the autumn of 1943, with figures such as US State Department diplomat Philip E. Mosely haggling with British and Soviet counterparts over 'hastily pencilled lines'[5] on maps.) Now, in the London *Daily Telegraph*, Lieutenant General H. G. Martin ventured that Hitler's forces still had some 'kick left in them' and that that would prevent Marshal Zhukov's Red Army getting close. He predicted that either the Americans under General Bradley or the British under Field Marshal Montgomery would be the ones to seize 'Fortress number 2 Berlin'.[6] The British prime minister, Winston Churchill, knew that the conquest of the city would finally extinguish the Nazi flame; but the Americans under the command of General Eisenhower had already silently ceded the race; and President Roosevelt, only days from his own death, and anxious about long-term US entanglement with Europe, was adamant that the race should go to the Soviets. This decision was communicated to Stalin through Eisenhower, and Stalin, perpetually paranoiac, had simply not believed it. He himself had deployed a double bluff to his allies, saying that he no longer considered Berlin to be the highest priority before, on 1 April 1945, telling his senior commanders, Marshals Georgy Zhukov and Ivan Konev, that they must reach Berlin first. Zhukov, forty-eight years old, had been born and raised in a village seventy miles from Moscow. His was a rural, turn-of-the-century childhood in a wide landscape of birch and fast rivers, where dusty poverty was endemic but where there were vividly recalled consolations of fresh-caught fish and summer berries. In this sense, even though Zhukov had been carried and raised by the tides of Russian history and revolution, he was similar to the younger men and women now under his command (although many of these younger people had known the hunger – in some cases famine – caused by Stalin's 1930s collectivization of farms rather than the oppression of Tsarist smallholdings). Latterly, Zhukov and his forces had seen their beloved lands devastated by the Nazis, and they were now fired by a dreadful, ineluctable energy that held an image of Berlin at its core.

As the news of the Red Army brought by those German refugees who had escaped the violent retributions seeped osmotically among Berliners, there was an understanding that their own idea and image of civilization were shortly to face an unknowable reckoning. In this sense, the impulse to stay burrowed in the twilight of the bomb shelters was a rational response to the terrors of the world outside.

Not all shelters were subterranean. There were striking structures to be found on some street corners, or nestled deep among the trees of the city's parks. Some were simply anonymous concrete cylinders with sloping roofs, while others took on the shapes of the buildings around them, like offices or flats, yet their rough texture and their blank, tiny windows made them faintly uncanny. Some rose out of the sandy soil of recreational spaces, their entrances simply angled slabs of concrete. Inside were tunnels that would come to a dead end. In the northern district of Wittenau were two concrete bunkers some fifty feet high, square in shape and with simple arched doorways, that evoked even more macabre associations: they resembled grand family mausoleums. In the central Kreuzberg area there stood one of the more ingenious shelters: a huge, round brick gas holder, originally constructed in the nineteenth century, had been converted into the Fichte-Bunker (it lay on Fichtestrasse): walls had been thickened and the unlit interior, reaching up to six storeys, had been divided into 750 small chambers. It was supposed to hold 6,000 people. By the beginning of 1945 it was sometimes holding 30,000. Local Kreuzbergers were joined by helpless rural refugees who had made their entrance into Berlin just as the menacing hum of the approaching bombers could be discerned.

Given their shallow depth, the shelters on the U-Bahn network gave only an illusion of impregnability. Even though at Moritzplatz station there was a further layer of tunnels to be found below the railway, in February 1945 any feeling of security was pulverized in a blink when the station above was hit and thirty-six people were killed instantly.

And across those last eighteen months of the war, it was estimated that some 30,000 civilians had been killed in air raids. The eyes of hundreds of thousands of Berliners had in that time grown accustomed to a world of catacombs, bare bulbs, rough wooden furniture, slop buckets. There were some, though, who could not contain their anger at what they considered the barbarous conduct of a bestial enemy, and the lives that they were being forced to lead. A little time before, photographer Liselotte Purper, who had worked with Goebbels's propaganda department, wrote to her husband Kurt Orgel, who was stationed east – one of the last letters he would receive before he was killed. 'Rage fills me!' she wrote. 'Think of the brutality with which we will be raped and murdered, think of the terrible misery, which the air terror alone is already bringing upon our country.'[7]

The majority of those taking shelter were women, many of whom had young children. Part of the exhausting dread inspired by the air-raid sirens was the speed at which unwilling children had to be hauled from their warm beds, dressed and hurried over to the nearest local shelter, sometimes in bulky prams. There was then the need to soothe frightened infants in the weird semi-darkness as the thunderous night rolled in. In the north of the city lay a grand landscaped park, the Humboldthain. It had been named in honour of one of Berlin's most distinguished historical figures, the pioneering eighteenth-century naturalist Alexander von Humboldt, who had sailed vast oceans in order to analyse the floral and geographic wonders of the world. In times of peace, this park had been a tranquil, flower-dotted contrast to the rough streets that surrounded it. Now it was a site that character-ized the city's deep unease. Despite the fires from ceaseless night-time bombing raids and the depredations of desperate citizens foraging for fuel, there were still rich trees growing here, high against the cold grey skies. But there were stretches of the park lawns that had been cut wide open, trenches zig-zagging like lightning bolts, and looming over all was a vast, square concrete tower, some 200 feet high and wide, crowned with octagonal gun platforms. At night, the tower roof would be manned by teenage boys, with the sparsest of training, pointing anti-aircraft guns impotently at the blazing skies. And inside was where the local citizens ran when the Allied bombers came.

The shape of the Humboldthain flak tower – one of three such structures in the city – was alien and yet disconcertingly familiar. The concrete was brutalist but the narrow windows were suggestive of a centuries-old fortress. Its gloomy interior was suffused with the common reek of humanity. Thousands had been gathering in these shelters on a daily basis across the last few months. Around twenty thousand at most should have packed into those grim storeys, but, in panic, many more pressed their way in. Familiar faces sitting on familiar benches and bunks were joined by strangers in dim, close-aired intimacy. The tower's low-ceilinged chambers and passages were lit with pale blue bulbs, which gave faces a ghostly pallor. The lavatorial prospects were basic and grim: composting efforts. In the keenest nights of that frosty spring, the vast walls, several feet thick, provided insulation but no ventilation, and the tiny windows were blocked off so that feeble lights might not be detected by the bombers. Along the walls were rows of basic, creaking bunks. To some, the very idea of unbroken sleep would have been satirical. And yet there were families here who had adapted to the new twi-light life, leaving the fortress only in order to obtain rationed food. Many had seen their homes demolished under ferocious Allied bomb-ing. The loss was not merely that of a secure roof and shelter but of the accumulated possessions that constituted family memory: the photo-graphs, the old mahogany furniture, the porcelain and the dinner services, all tokens of a certain kind of stability and continuity. Those threads that linked these shelterers to the past were snapped. And this dark concrete tower was now home. Others used it more spar-ingly, in the most extreme of emergencies, when the bombers were close to the city. They knew it was not a healthy place to be. 'When the guns on the roof were firing,' recalled Gerda Kernchen, who was sixteen years old at the time, 'the whole building would shake, which was very nerve-wracking.'[8]

The mere fact of the building's existence – it grew in the skyline of the suburb of Gesundbrunnen in 1943, constructed using forced labour – suggested to a number of Berliners that the course of the war had shifted. By the frozen days of February and March 1945, with Germany's borders penetrated from east and west, it was an increas-ingly grim symbol of siege. In this, it was joined by the stark visibility of another flak tower looming over the city's zoo. In some ways, this shelter had an even more urgent edge: its third floor – a similarly comfortless prospect of bare concrete – housed a field hospital. The facilities and the lights were sparse; one section was used as a maternity ward. Even in the spring of 1945, babies were being born into this cold, war-ravaged city.

A flak tower that stood within the Friedrichshain, in the city's east, held a ferociously guarded secret: a great mass of art and antiquities taken from Berlin's Kaiser-Friedrich Museum and other galleries, as well as those stolen from Jewish owners. The art that was hidden in the Friedrichshain tower included works by Caravaggio ('St Matthew and the Angel', 'Portrait of a Courtesan') and Botticelli ('Madonna and Child with Saint John') among others and was almost ludicrously vulnerable. There had been a plan by the start of 1945 to find more secure refuge for the collection of paintings and sculptures in Pomerania (on the northern coast of conquered Poland), though the mercury-fast advance by the Soviets destroyed that idea. A potash mine at Schönebeck (a town about sixty miles to the south-west of Berlin) was the next possibility, but with every available man engaged at arms, and with every able woman working elsewhere, the inclination disappeared. And just weeks previously, after another of the city's museums was engulfed in the searing flames of incendiaries, yet more works had been placed in the Friedrichshain tower. By March, various museum directors had coordinated a new plan: mines at Grasleben (an area to the west of Berlin and close to Hanover) and Ransbach (in the west of Germany, close to Frankfurt) were to be used. Some of the artworks were packaged carefully and taken out of the city, past vast craters, and into the countryside beyond. The last of these convoys departed on 7 April, leaving many works behind.

Civilians poked around these discarded masterpieces truffling vainly for stored food, for, while the art treasures were being evacuated, the citizens were not. There had never been a suggestion of any concerted effort to find Berliners temporary sanctuary in the towns and villages outside the city. They were effectively prisoners within the city bounds; there was nowhere else for them to go. Conversely, a number of families had, within the last eighteen months, actually returned to Berlin. Among them were children who had previously been spirited away en masse by the authorities to hostels in clear-aired mountain regions. Many were impatient to return to Berlin, as were mothers and grandmothers who pined for the familiar landmarks of home even as those landmarks were vanishing.

The city was defended, even though the Wehrmacht was lethally depleted; since 20 March, Army Group Vistula – there to fight the oncoming Soviet forces – had been led by General Gotthard Heinrici, a fifty-eight-year-old veteran from a family of Protestant theologians, whose powerful Lutheran faith was distrusted by his superiors. Earlier in the war, angry disagreements with the hierarchy had led to a period of forced retirement; now, with the Red Army fifty miles east of Berlin, the rehabilitated Heinrici was tasked with stopping this vast force from successfully crossing the River Oder and sweeping onwards for the capital. While there were urban whispers circulating among sheltering civilians concerning potential new wonder weapons even more powerful than the V-1 and V-2 missiles that had been streaking through the skies above the Channel and causing devastation in London, Gotthard Heinrici was perfectly aware that no such miracle was close. The previous commander of Army Group Vistula – Reichsführer-SS Heinrich Himmler – had allowed himself to be removed from the position having proved haplessly inadequate. The man who had devised the structure for the Holocaust and the obscene means for ending the lives of millions had withdrawn to a private retreat at the Hohenlychen Sanatorium some miles to the north of Berlin, suffering from self-diagnosed influenza. In the city from which he had withdrawn, there were exclamatory public pronouncements issued through street loudspeakers, written by the Minister for Propaganda, Joseph Goebbels. The minister was exhorting belief. In the early 1920s, Goebbels had understood Berlin as an 'asphalt monster' that made people 'heartless and unfeeling';[9] the asphalt had divorced the Berlin people from their true Germanness; the city had been 'asphalted by the Jews'.[10] By 1926, he was Gauleiter – or regional Nazi Party leader – of the city: a position he retained until his death. In a sly and brilliant analysis of his use of language, the contemporary philologist Victor Klemperer charted Goebbels's shifting attitudes to Berlin; how the conflict between 'soil and asphalt' became tempered and romanticized to the point in 1944 when Goebbels could declare that 'we have great respect for the indestructible rhythm of life, and the rugged will to live demonstrated by our metropolitan population'.[11] Their choice in the matter was limited.

It was also the case that many Berlin citizens were very quietly expressing their own doubts about the new wonder weapons. Behind

these seditious whispers – shared with care in a city where fierce
surveillance of public behaviour was still rigorously carried out by
resident block wardens – lay the leaden coldness of understanding.
There would be no reverse, no rescue. The teenage boys firing the
rooftop guns enthusiastically but uselessly at high-altitude bombers
were collectively known by the initials LH, which stood for *Lüften
Helfer* (air helpers). Those civilians sheltering beneath them inter-
preted the letters differently (in the manner of *Lernen schnell Russisch*):
they called them *Letzte Hoffnung*, or last hope. The joke had layers of
rueful bitterness. Paradoxically, the oppressively secular society that
had been fashioned by the Nazis since the mid 1930s itself stood on a
framework of para-religious faith: it required absolute belief in the
Führer, and in those who did his work. For this vision of Germany,
and Berlin, to cohere, it took faith to believe that the state had the
right to complete control over body and mind, and would then use
this control to nurture and protect the people. It took faith to believe
in miracle weapons. And in those shelters and cellars, the faith was
dissolving. There were those who, like General Heinrici, had held
on to their Christian belief despite all hostile government efforts to
marginalize the Churches and the laity. Theirs was a faith that it was
unwise to proclaim too loudly. If they prayed privately, it was in silence.

   And yet there were others in the city – underground both literally
and metaphorically – who were, despite the frenzy of extermination,
holding true to older beliefs and communities. Despite the method-
ical deportation of the city's large Jewish population to Auschwitz
and other death camps, there were a significant number of Jewish
people, possibly 1,700 or so, who contrived to remain in Berlin, hidden. Astonishingly, they had survived. These came to be known in
very closed, secretive circles as the 'U-Boats'.[12] Many of these Jewish
people had been taken in by gentile friends and associates. Some were
obliged to live much of their lives concealed in the almost permanent
darkness of basements. One such was Rachel R. Mann, who recalled
that she had been out the day the Gestapo came for her and her
mother. When she got home, she was taken in by a compassionate
neighbour; but in the winter and spring of 1945, as some Nazi functionaries grew ever more hysterical, she was compelled to stay in the
cellar. '[The neighbour] brought me something to eat every day and

sometimes she brought me up to her apartment so that I could take a bath. I was down there until the end of the war.'[13]

There was Marie Jalowicz-Simon, then Marie Jalowicz, who had been eluding the authorities since 1942, having dodged away from a Gestapo official one morning; later that day, when a postman attempted to deliver a letter to her, she simply told him that her 'neighbour' Marie had been deported east. This was scrawled on the envelope and seemed to seep through the city bureaucracy. She was soon to discover – wearing a jacket without a yellow star – that even though she came from a thoroughly middle-class background, the most kindness and generosity were to be found in the city's working-class districts as she sought factory work.[14] By the spring of 1945 she was sheltering in a small house in one of the city's northern suburbs amid her fellow citizens, a tiny number of whom knew her true identity. She regarded these working-class Berliners as her saviours, and as the true spirit of the city. They understood the enormity of the crime that had been committed by the state, unlike, in Simon's view, the middle classes, who had capitulated to Nazi philosophy. 'It was, above all,' she said, 'the educated German bourgeoisie who had failed.'[15]

There were numbers of those 'educated German bourgeoisie' who would have argued that they had had no choice, that they did not deserve to share the collective guilt and that their nights spent beneath buildings, waiting for bombs to plummet through, were a form of purgatory or penance.

Racism and enthusiasm for eugenicist theories were not unique to inter-war Germany; such beliefs were so widespread in some circles as to feel natural as well as respectable (King George V's personal physician Lord Dawson of Penn was just one of many British establishment figures who had an interest in eugenics, as did some prominent left-wing politicians). As these Berliners were forced underground by bombs, very few were reflecting on how their entire society had been poisoned by the obsession with racial superiority and degeneracy. It was still too close to be seen. For some, it would remain so, even after the war.

But as all these people, wealthy and otherwise, gathered their provisions – the tiny quantities of rye bread and meat, and carefully harboured supplies of alcohol, from Merlot to brandy – there was a subliminal awareness that their Führer had also become a permanent shelterer. While radio broadcasts shouted in various pitches of frenzy about the victory to come, and about the need for all citizens to defend their home, it was obvious that the Führer was not making public appearances. For so many who had seen their leader up close at rallies, there had been jolting moments of electricity when Hitler's eyes had met theirs – a sense that he somehow knew them, and had a strong bond with them. But, by spring 1945, the Führer's absence was breaking the mesmeric spell.

And very few Berliners would have imagined – even if they had envisaged a secret subterranean headquarters – the grim and extraordinary reality of the tunnels beneath the centre of the city. On the surface, in the garden of the Reich Chancellery, there stood a concrete cube with doors – one of several entrances to the complex. Once the visitor had got past the guards and the manically intrusive body searches, there was a circling descent down a spiral staircase into a world apart. At the bottom of those stairs, more guards, more doors: and then, within, a fuggy maze of tiny rooms and tiny passages, a labyrinth of rough concrete. Signs of hasty workmanship were everywhere: there were small puddles on the floor where water had dripped from the ceiling. To be found in that warren were sparse meeting rooms, kitchens, basic toilets and washing facilities, bedrooms and a telephone exchange. There were more stairs, descending to a depth of some forty feet beneath the ground, that led into an even more muffled underworld. This was where, on 1 April, the Führer had settled permanently along with his partner (soon-to-be wife) Eva Braun, their German shepherd Blondi and assorted puppies. His small study was carpeted, the walls hung with maps. The air conditioning whined noisily, like a vast trapped bluebottle. It wasn't especially effective. The atmosphere was close. Officials walked the corridors at all hours, and were summoned by their hunched leader at the most eccentric times. It was a world in which the Führer decided when was day and when was night; meetings with senior military commanders would be scheduled to start before midnight and sometimes would not finish before dawn. Amid all the concrete, time drifted without meaning. When these commanders and party officials slept, did they dream? In the privacy of these visions, did they share their Führer's waking delusions?

Elsewhere in the city, children were tormented with nightmares.

Nine-year-old Sabine K 'slept very poorly'[16] in her sheltering basement, as she confessed to her diary. She had dreamed that 'a Russian'
had entered the cellar, and asked her 'for water'. She had moved off
down a corridor, which twisted and then turned into an unfamiliar
passage whereupon 'a yellow light' shone and she was suddenly terrified to see a man with 'Chinese' features who tore off her coat and
'touched' her.[17] Was this nightmare the result of Nazi propaganda
painting the approaching enemy as 'Asiatic hordes'?[18]

Remarkably, in all those Berlin basements and bunkers and cellars
and underground stations and concrete towers that surrounded the
bleak labyrinth of the Führerbunker in great concentric circles,
the people did sometimes manage to find rest. The musician Karla
Hocker recalled that there was quite another way of absorbing the
atmosphere of the dank basement that she found herself in. 'Strange
atmosphere, a mixture of ski hut, youth hostel, revolutionary basement and opera romanticism.'[19] She and her companions were
suffused with the desire to sleep. For those out there under the open
skies – the ever more fanatical SS and Gestapo and plain-clothed
officers, gimlet-eyed for the smallest infringements of the Führer's
desires, poised to punish; and the very young teenaged boys upon the
roofs of those grey towers, manning the anti-aircraft guns that filled
the air with flashing fire – sleep was now a matter of submission to
exhaustion. Tiredness, like hunger, was a permanent condition. Just
a few months previously, all these Berliners – from the eldest shelterers to the youngest Hitler Youth army conscript – had been living a
life that might have looked to others to be wholly normal: schools,
cafes, concerts. They had accepted with remarkable speed the prospect of doomsday. Velocity was one of the key characteristics of
this city.

This new subterranean existence had been noted a little earlier by
a Soviet reconnaissance pilot, flying high over the east of the city. He
had learned of Berlin as being characterized by vivacity and light, by
the fires of foundries, by the seductive glow and modern neon of
consumerism. What he saw now was a winter city of darkness; he
saw trams motionless on empty streets; he saw vast factory complexes, shattered and blackened. He saw boulevards devoid of a single
soul. What had become of this city of light?

## 2. The Sacrificial Children

These boys had been moulded in darkness, yet their spirits had never been wholly smothered. The regime had sought to control not only what they learned, but also their interior realms of make-believe. None the less, there had always been some spark of childhood ungovernability and imagination that lay beyond the power of the Nazi government. By the spring of 1945 the regime in Berlin was simply seeking to bring childhood to a premature end. Young teenaged boys were being corralled (or, in some cases, eagerly volunteering) for adult military duties. All were aware that they were facing the prospect of their own mortality. It was not an abstract fear; for some of these young boys, the terror was insurmountable, discerned all too easily on their faces. Others, like Alfred Czech, who would find himself as a twelve-year-old being presented to the Führer in Hitler's final days to receive the Iron Cross, somehow, horribly, believed that his role as a boy soldier was natural. 'As a small boy, I didn't reflect much, I just wanted to do something for my people,' he told an interviewer decades later. 'I didn't think it was insane to send children into battle. It was war.'[1] He was now a part of the Volkssturm – the people's storm. This was the physical expression of the 'people's war' – the conscription of all civilian males who had until then been, for whatever reasons to do with either health or occupation, exempt from regular military service. By April 1945 that net had widened to include boys whose voices had not yet broken. Nor were young girls – members of the League of German Girls, and themselves sometimes no more than twelve years old – excluded from the urban battlefield. Theresa Moelle, aged fifteen, was taught how to use the hand-held Panzerfaust bazooka. In the days to come, she would have to deploy it. Just as with the boys of the Hitler Youth, the possibility of her death was ever present. The macabre abuse of children – their co-option as bodies to be hurled against the enemy – should have been one of the points at which natural Berliner scepticism hardened into resistance. And, for many, it was; mothers standing in queues looked at armed boys – the sons of other mothers – and could not quell their revulsion at the idea of child martyrs.

Yet the landscape of the broken city around them seemed to exhale nihilism. Just a few weeks before April 1945, the bombers had brought all-consuming fire to the district of Friedrichstadt, which – unusually, in what was always a broadly unpretty city – had once presented an attractive and historic prospect of a popular ornate theatre and two grand cathedrals in the classical style, as well as a large marketplace that had drawn visitors since the eighteenth century. On top of this was the vast Wertheim department store – a turn-of-the-century marvel that for a time was the largest of its kind in Europe. The thousands of lethal incendiaries dropped by American bombers in one of the largest daylight raids conjured an inferno that came close to turning into a firestorm. Berlin's firefighters could do nothing; the flames roared for several days, reaching eagerly from building to building and taking hold. The spread was stopped only by the murky maze of Berlin's waterways, and the distance between the buildings on either side. In the years to come, the district of Friedrichstadt would hold the attention of the world as a grim borderland. In 1945, its erasure was just another physical manifestation of the undeniable truth of the war, even as fantasies of secret weapons continued to be believed in some corners of the city and in some corners of the regime. One especially unhinged figure was German Labour Front head Robert Ley: he was convinced that German scientists had perfected 'death rays'.[2] There was something in this that chimed with the imaginations of ten-year-olds.

In those early days of April 1945, the teenagers of Berlin were being organized by the older members of the Volkssturm, some of whom, with their gaunt faces and Iron Crosses from the last war, had a haunted dignity. For a few of the boys, it did not matter that some of the uniforms procured for them were bathetically large; nor that some of these uniforms were those of the SS, rather than the regular army they revered. Their understanding of what lay ahead was necessarily limited by their ages. The boys who were posted to the flak-tower anti-aircraft guns were in some ways as insensible as those down on the streets below who were being taught how to load guns and bazookas, and who were being given swift training in the brutal realities of house-to-house fighting. It was not yet clear how long it would be before they were fighting to save their city, but it was understood by the boys that their own individual heroism would be called for. And there was little active resistance, because a generation of boys had become attuned not so much to the sinister nature of the Hitler Youth movement, but rather to the possibilities it had offered for escape, chiefly from the industrial poverty of Berlin's dreary suburbs. It had been this way since the early 1930s.

For Berliner Horst Basemann, who some years previously had joined his local Hitler Youth group, there had been something completely compelling about the weekends spent in the forests surrounding Berlin. It was more than simple bonding with the other lads; there was another element that reached rather further into his psyche. By the spring of 1945 he was a Wehrmacht prisoner of war, held east of the Urals, a young man in his early twenties blinded in one eye. It was at this point that he started thinking back over all that had seemed so natural to him, starting with his induction into the Hitler Youth in 1934. The mere act of being removed from the stifling, oppressive Berlin city streets had just been the beginning. As he recalled: 'In the evening we sit in a circle around the blazing fire. In front of us the lake is shimmering in the moonlight; behind us lies the forest.'[3] The leaders were only 'two or three years older' than him. But also sitting near that fire was a specially invited guest: a middle-aged man, a former First World War soldier. 'We hear his experiences . . . We listen eagerly to his words and hear the tragic end of his story. We boys are rested, moved and quiet inside. We look into the twitching flames of the slowly dying fire.'[4]

Basemann continued: 'This former officer picks up the fanfare trumpet and blows a tune that we don't know yet. Then he says: "If one day the call rings out to you, dear boys, to wipe out the shame of Versailles, I am sure that you will be ready to defend our Fatherland, if necessary also give your life." '[5] This seemed the very opposite of morbidity; to young minds, such heroism, framed by these flames in the silence of the dark countryside, instead sparked a form of inner exultation. The shame of defeat in the First World War and the manifold humiliations and consequences of the Treaty of Versailles – the

French and Belgian soldiers marching into the Ruhr in 1923 to seize coal and steel production, chronic nationwide poverty in part the result of reparations demands – could be overcome next to the bright fire, the sparks rising into the night. In addition to this were the songs that – at a distance – Herr Basemann recalled as being 'strange'. He remembered scraps of lyrics: 'If I should fall on strange earth – goodbye, that's the way it should be', and 'the most beautiful death of all is the soldier's death'.[6]

All of this took place far from parents, and from the watchful eyes of schoolteachers; and those who initially resisted their children's induction did so precisely because they were frightened of the quasi-religious feel of the movement. Throughout the 1930s some Catholic families stood firm against their sons and daughters being pulled closer to those fires. Across the country the Hitler Youth was also, in its earliest years, unpopular with a number of working-class parents, who loathed the strict authoritarianism of the philosophy. Broadly, those who had been drawn to the idea fastest were the middle and lower-middle classes. In Berlin, though, there was a difference that led to a greater working-class enthusiasm for the idea: the possibility of escaping, if only for a short time, from overcrowded tenements and grim, treeless courtyards. Berlin's poorer youngsters saw that the weekend camps on offer were free – good food, laughter, companionship and an unaccustomed sense of equality among boys from different areas and backgrounds.

Additionally, in Horst Basemann's experience, the movement's idea that 'youth must be led by youth'[7] did not seem to entail excesses. There was, however, a strong focus on military exercises. Quasi-parade drills were followed by intensive marches and runs across the leafy terrain of the city's outer forests. The boys were taught the principles of map-reading and orientation. There were also rough battle games: teams formed, camouflage adopted, ambushes staged, team ribbons seized – and 'any wounds were not cried over'.[8]

But the Nazis did not have complete dominion over these young urban imaginations: they found fuel elsewhere too. Hollywood westerns, and any film starring Gary Cooper, had been hugely popular in Berlin throughout the 1930s (as had Laurel and Hardy, also enjoyed by Hitler). There were also the science-fiction adventures of Flash Gordon (banned in 1941, just before the US joined the war, when in the syndicated cartoon strip Flash stopped fighting Ming the Merciless and turned his attention to fascism). Then there were the thrillingly sophisticated detective exploits of *The Thin Man* – a world of cocktails and daggers, brilliant deductions and gunpoint cliffhangers. But, most especially, there was a universal enthusiasm among these boys for the Wild West-based novels of a veteran German author called Karl May, whose cowboy hero creation was known as Old Shatterhand. The striking name came from this character's fierce fighting technique, which had damaged his own knuckles. Old Shatterhand's adventures, across a long series of novels, saw him righting wrongs and plunging into jeopardy across richly depicted prairies and deserts, together with his Native American sidekick Winnetou. It was fantastical, bloodthirsty stuff, packed with hazard and death – quicksands, crocodiles, hordes of hungry rats – and these novels held an all-encompassing grip on the German male imagination, even though their author had died in 1912 and had never set foot in America. Among Karl May's long-term fans were Albert Einstein, Thomas Mann and the artist George Grosz.[9] Crucially, another devotee was Adolf Hitler, who had read the books feverishly throughout his Austrian boyhood and returned to them frequently as an adult. Albert Speer, one of Hitler's inner circle, once observed that the Führer, when discussing military strategy, mentioned 'Napoleon and Old Shatterhand in the same sentence'.[10]

Yet, for the boys of Berlin, these stories, combined with their exciting war games, were simply a portal into another dimension, offering 'magic nights in the open, under a purple moon and amazing stars that have a so much wilder lustre than in European skies'.[11] Many of them came from Depression-hit homes: unemployed fathers, the abrasive anxieties and anger of poverty. There was nothing abnormal about daydreams of heroism, which were shared across the world, but the Nazis found, by instinct, the most direct means of turning those boyhood daydreams to their own purposes: the evocations of Siegfried in the forest, augmented with talks from real-life heroes who had fought in the last war and who had, as they saw it, been betrayed by real-life villains who now governed their affairs. It worked on the boys because the adults believed it too. In the years to come, these were the boys who would be sent, as men, to march across freezing steppes, and who would either witness or commit atrocities. The generation of boys who came immediately after them would still continue to read Karl May though, and US servicemen would find themselves looking on with bewilderment as the ragged German boys around them in 1945 played their games of cowboys and Indians.

All the singing and the marching of the Hitler Youth had been underpinned by a founding myth of youth martyrdom. In 1932, fifteen-year-old Herbert Norkus was living in the deprived district of Moabit, and his world had been circumscribed by the intense poverty of his parents. Although his schooling was good, everyday life for his family at that economically precarious moment was one of perpetual insecurity and hunger; and there was fear too. Norkus had joined the Hitler Youth, and like Basemann he had found intense escapism in those forest weekends, but the majority of teenagers who lived in his neighbourhood had pledged their allegiance to the Communist Party. The natural result of this – through all those streets of grey tenements and canals stagnant with iridescent oily water – was gang warfare. Mirroring the violent drunken clashes in bars between older communists and Nazis, the young men of Moabit considered themselves to be in a state of war. Herbert Norkus was a frequent target; often he would have to run in desperation, and hide out at the local cemetery until the danger had subsided. On one Sunday in January 1932, while he was posting leaflets for the Nazi Party around the neighbourhood, he was confronted by a group of local boys who were seized with a murderous anger. They had knives; Norkus was stabbed and beaten. He collapsed, dragged himself up and walked a little distance, then fell again, trailing blood. He died soon afterwards.

This was, for the Nazis, an even greater opportunity than that presented by the murder of twenty-two-year-old party activist (and thug) Horst Wessel in 1930 (even though Wessel's killing inspired a song that acquired global notoriety as the musical expression of Nazism); here, in the story of Norkus, was a boy cut down, as others looked on, while in the innocent service of the party that wished to save the country. The newspaper *Der Angriff* (The Attack) set no bounds to its nauseating reportage of the tragedy. 'There in the bleak, grey twilight,' wrote Goebbels in one propaganda piece, 'yellow tortured eyes stare into the emptiness . . . a frail child's voice is heard speaking as from eternity . . . "They killed me! They plunged the murderous dagger into my heart! And only because I – a child – wanted to serve my country."' Goebbels went further with the imagined voice of Herbert Norkus: 'I am Germany . . . my spirit, which is immortal, will remain with you.'[12] Then came the 1933 film *Hitlerjunge Quex*, a grim dramatization of the killing. It was shown over and over again, to successive cohorts of children, throughout the 1930s and throughout the war as well. In the early 1940s the Reich Youth Leader Baldur von Schirach invoked that 'immortal spirit' in a speech: 'This little comrade has become a myth of the young nation, the symbol of the self-sacrificial spirit of all the young who bear Hitler's name . . . Nothing binds us Hitler-Jugend together more closely than the knowledge of our brotherly link to this dead boy.'[13] Norkus was, in Nazi terms, canonized: 'Holy Flame of youth, you are the light in the darkness!' ran one wartime Hitler Jugend proclamation. 'You will show us the path which leads to the morning's dawning, the way of loyalty, the way of Adolf Hitler.'[14] This was intended to evoke para-religious inspiration in the young. By the spring of 1945, to those Berlin teenagers who had known nothing but a world dominated by Hitler, the Jugend hymn that was sung most frequently seemed unquestionable in its sentiments: 'Our flag leads us to eternity/ Yes, the flag means more than death!'[15]

When it came to the actual physical structure of Berlin, it was harder to see quite what the children and teenagers – no matter how inspired – could hope to save. Working amid the unstable wreckage of freshly bombed and demolished apartment buildings, the old soldiers gathered together under the banner of the Volkssturm began to teach Berlin's women and girls the brutal craft of war. Perhaps for some these tutorials had a useful distracting quality; a few minutes where it might be possible to imagine that these defences would work. The distractions were badly needed. Any activity – even

activity that seemed underscored with futility – was better than
enduring long, dread-filled days in semi-darkness. Even among the
hardier young, the smaller privations and minor setbacks of their
underground life were becoming harder to keep in perspective.
Christa Ronke was fifteen years old. She had been brought up in a
comfortably appointed and affectionate family home in one of the
city's suburbs. Some while back, that house lay beneath the bombers'
aim. A vast explosion, detonating in the garden, had destroyed the
home for which her parents 'had been saving for many years'.[16]
Christa's mother was helpless with tears; not just about the American
aggressors, but also about Hitler. Christa and her mother – her father
was fighting in the west – had managed to salvage some much-loved
keepsakes: there were antique porcelain cups, a porcelain ballerina
(now 'albeit without her right hand') and a few books. The 'beautiful
furniture' had been comprehensively destroyed. So too had the piano
upon which Christa had practised every day. She felt particularly
keenly the loss of the 'uprooted fruit trees, shrubs and pines'[17] that
had formed the landscape of their garden. Yet they themselves were
alive. By April 1945, however, the tensions were becoming almost
too much for Christa.

She and her mother had found new accommodation: a two-room
apartment in Dahlem, a wealthy suburb in the south-west of the city,
though at this stage there were few comforts to be appreciated. After
racing down to the cellar during a bombing raid, Christa had tripped
and badly injured her foot, but there was no prospect of receiving
medical attention. In addition, the rations were now so low as to
make hunger almost the complete focus of every day: a few grams of
meat, rye bread, butter. There was no milk to be had. In terms of
vegetables there were a few carrots and some beetroot, although the
real craving was for potatoes, and they seemed to have all but vanished. Another difficulty was that even if food could be obtained,
there was very little gas with which to cook it; supplies were pitifully
weak most of the time. The electricity was becoming intermittent –
four or five hours a day. The evenings were generally spent in
sepulchral candlelight before the sirens restarted the race to the shelter downstairs.

The moment in early April that seemed to Christa to encapsulate her helplessness came one afternoon when she had finished her day at school – the teachers were still attempting, in cold, unlit buildings, to at least give some semblance of structure – and went to get the family rations. At the grocery store she discovered that she had somehow lost all the family's ration cards. She was distraught and hurried home to confess. Her mother tried to comfort her, she recalls.

To her relief, however, there were still faint flickers of kindness in an otherwise flinty world: the lost ration cards, picked up by a stranger, were posted through the family's letterbox (albeit with a few missing – 'finder's reward!' she wrote ruefully). The next day Christa was able to acquire what, in relieved contrast to the lost cards, seemed like an abundance of bread and meat. This was one of the last moments of something approaching normality. The only world she had known was about to be upturned.

Other children had had their certainties violently wrenched away even earlier. Gerhard Rietdorff was a 'twelve-and-a-half-year-old'[18] boy in 1943 when, having been evacuated into the countryside, he was brought back by his family to Berlin, where they had moved to an apartment just off the 'very very busy Alexanderplatz'. He was enrolled at a mixed-sex school nearby where he was immediately smitten with 'the bright sweet eyes of a girl with blonde pigtails' whose name was Eveline.[19] Their mutual crush was innocent and heartfelt and tongue-tied; their 'fingertips accidentally touched on the table top' and Rietdorff was 'paralysed with happiness' by her voice. One day as they walked home, Eveline beckoned Rietdorff into the overgrown churchyard of the Marienkirche, where a quick kiss made both dizzy with elation. She ran off with the words 'See you tomorrow, my dear!' That night there was an infernal bombing raid; the school and many surrounding streets became glowing rubble. As Rietdorff recalled: 'I never saw Eveline again.'[20] By 1945, innumerable Berlin children were facing the prospects of their own shattering losses. For this reason, taking up arms might have seemed, for some, a form of escape or even liberation.

With the regular Wehrmacht in defensive positions in the country-side all around, the streets of Berlin itself were partly in the hands of increasingly deranged SS men determined to hunt out 'traitors' and partly in the hands of the older men of the Volkssturm, who, despite their glasses and the shabby, mismatched nature of their uniforms, could at least lay claim to the gravity of experience. These were men who had seen unholy, cataclysmic violence many years before. The Volkssturm had only been summoned into being months before, in the autumn of 1944. It had not been an act of desperation; rather, it had been believed by Hitler's lieutenants Martin Bormann and Heinrich Himmler that these men could bring a fire and a zeal which would have the effect of radicalizing the entire civilian population. There had been a time – after the famous 1944 assassination attempt on Hitler – when the elders of the Volkssturm had been viewed by the Nazi High Command with greater favour and less suspicion than some of the regular officer class. The Volkssturm was to be controlled not by the military but directly by the Nazi Party. It was to be fuelled not with military logic but by the thunderous and apocalyptic certainties of Nazi ideology.

Certainly, at the inception of the movement, there had been spectacle and rousing speeches as these middle-aged men, who by day were clerks and managers in suits and trilbies, were signed up and paraded through Berlin in their moss-green greatcoats and Volkssturm armbands. But there was also some reluctance. First, a number of the men did not want to wear the brown uniforms that signified Nazi, rather than Wehrmacht, status. There was another schism: older men who years before had been in the officer class in the First World War could see quite clearly the military deficiencies of the Nazi Party machinery, its incompetence and faulty weaponry. Instead, they would look to the regular army to supply equipment that actually worked, and training that would actually be effective.

The movement aimed to enrol all civilian males between sixteen and sixty; throughout Germany, this amounted to some twelve million men. By April 1945 the parameters had widened further, from thirteen-year-old boys to seventy-year-old men. Naturally, the Nazis knew that the Volkssturm could not compose a fully functional fighting force, but it was hoped they could hamper the enemy in more lateral ways: attack invaders, magnifying casualties, sapping morale until, after a long war of attrition and with the US and British forces exhausted, there would be a chance to shape the end of the conflict and the terms of the peace without complete German capitulation. The attitude towards the Soviets was different: this was *Existenzkampf*, a literal fight for the very life and soul of the country itself. Thus the Volkssturm had to engage in 'a relentless struggle everywhere that the enemy wants to set foot on German soil'.[21]

For these white-collar workers, the physical training itself – every weeknight after work, and for several hours each Sunday – was tiring; yet more tiring for some were the para-religious meetings in which the Nazi speakers would paint the world in terms of blood and death, soil and honour, extermination and survival. There were also outbreaks of faux medievalism: the Volkssturm were sworn to uphold high ideals of chivalry and courtesy towards women. And behind it all were the burning evocations of the Versailles betrayal. 'Never again 1918!' proclaimed the propaganda of Dr Goebbels. 'Our walls may break, but our hearts – never!'[22] By April 1945, the bubbling pitch of the lurid rhetoric was losing its power: perhaps among many Berliner men of a certain age, who had already lived through so much horror, it had never seemed especially authentic. There were a few canny others who simply wanted nothing to do with it. The father of Czech writer Peter Demetz was living in fragmented Berlin in the spring of 1945 and he knew that it would not be long before he was compelled to join the Volkssturm. His plan to avoid it – for he harboured no illusions about the forces that were coming to the city – was charmingly simple: wait until the thick darkness of blackout, find a shallow bomb crater and 'fall' into it, so invaliding himself out of any obligations.[23] He found a crater, but as he let himself drop into it he realized rather too late that it was very much deeper than he had thought. His crumpled frame landed on uneven masonry, and he managed to break not one but both legs. In that sense, he was very emphatically excused active duty.

The Nazis shrewdly realized that the civilian population harboured a quiet acceptance – and even regard for – the idea of American and British forces sweeping in. Culturally it was not difficult to see why: just before the war had broken out, one of Berlin's top-selling novels was the British author A. J. Cronin's *The Citadel*, set in the mining communities of South Wales and featuring idealistic, socially concerned doctors and class-based iniquities. Another was

Margaret Mitchell's lush American Civil War epic *Gone with the Wind*. There were many Berliners who at the last stages of the war could not resist tuning their radios to the utterly forbidden BBC. Not even all the icily ruthless bombing raids had wholly destroyed that belief in Allied decency.

The Nazis were keenly aware that this was the case, and one of the propaganda lessons shrilly recounted at Volkssturm meetings was the supposed plans that American GIs had for German women. There was a careful focus upon black GIs: naturally, the Nazis had no difficulty deploying one of the oldest and grossest racial slurs when telling the old soldiers what the American invaders intended. It was also underlined that the Americans and the British sought not only to defeat Germany but also to erase its culture: to make the very essence of Germanness disappear. It was around this time that other Berliners started hearing the rumours that the Allies were going to force a submissive Germany into becoming a wholly agricultural society (this was an echo of the real suggestions of the 1944 Morgenthau Plan, an American proposal to destroy Germany's ability to wage future wars by liquidating most of its heavy industry) with the sophisticated city stripped of not only its art but also its innovative technology. There may have been some among the Allies – notably Britain's head of Bomber Command, Sir Arthur Harris – who would not have disagreed with such an aim.

By early April 1945 the creak-jointed men of the Volkssturm could see very well – from their scant and aged weaponry alone – that their stand would be one of nihilistic futility. A few of the rifles issued were literally antiques, dating back to the Paris Commune of 1871. Others were in ragged condition, having been captured from French and other prisoners. The Wehrmacht soldiers either moving through the city or stationed there did try to make time for these amateur combatants. Men still in their office suits, their Volkssturm status denoted by a simple armband, were taught the finer points of loading and using the new weaponry. And for the children in their midst, there was guidance on how to use rifles that were rather too large even for the older boys. There were more insidious tutorials: local Volkssturm groups would be joined by SS officers, themselves behaving with the agitation of wasps in a jar. They were there to instruct the boys in quite another form of warfare: the suicide bombing of Soviet tanks. There was no compunction about invoking the sacrificial ritual of the Hitler Youth. Many SS men would themselves, some years ago, have been sitting around those forest fires with eyes wide, listening to stories of blood heroism.

By that spring, the hysteria of the Nazis was also made manifest with the advent of the Werwolf units; these 'Werewolves' were to be the final resistance to the fast-approaching Allied troops – a guerrilla force of closely organized terrorists who would attack through sabotage and close-quarter house-to-house fighting. They were there to prove that the Nazi regime would never submit. One figure who was drawn into that particular vortex was Oswald Mathias Ungers, later to find some fame as an innovative architect. Born in 1926, he had a boyhood fascination for aeroplanes and an ever greater aptitude for mathematics. He was pulled into the war aged sixteen in 1942 from the government workers service. Initially his job was to join teams building airfields; his weapon was a spade. He wanted to be a pilot but failed the medical and was drafted to Luftwaffe signals; as the conflict became ever more desperate, he was sucked deeper into the vortex. 'I thought that any decision I could make would be wrong anyway – that it would not be correct under any circumstances – and therefore it would be better to let myself drift,' he later told his interviewers from a specialist architecture magazine. 'Wherever I was sent, I went like a brave soldier.'[24] In 1945 he was nineteen years old: 'At the end – this is so strange – I was with the Werwolf. There were still some fanatics who believed that they could change the outcome of the war. We were assigned to a squad and hid ourselves somewhere in the dark forest.'[25] His enthusiasm was fleeting; soon afterwards, he would set out to get himself captured by the Americans.

For those few days at the beginning of April 1945 there might even have been a few Berliners left who could make themselves believe that a miracle was coming, and that the regime would strike back with a devastating force that would leave their enemies reeling. Though in Christa Ronke's view any such believers were by now being mocked by more worldly wise neighbours: and this in spite of the SS attempts to terrorize neighbourhoods with public hangings of 'traitors', 'deserters' and 'cowards'.[26] As she later recalled:

Mood of the people: the fight is madness. Everyone complains loudly at the government that it should finally call it a day. There's no point in fighting any more. The war is lost. Why the many unnecessary victims now: soldiers and civilians! Many are listening to enemy stations, including me. Of course, the Nazis are still talking about victory. We hope that the Americans are more likely to be in Berlin than the Russians. Goebbels and the newspapers believe that the Russians will murder and rape. The enemy station says the opposite. You don't know what to believe. The food situation is getting worse and worse; we're hungry, and, since no fields are tilled, things will get worse.[27]

There was no doubt that the men patrolling the broken streets knew perfectly well how much worse it was going to get. From the blackened empty apartment buildings and the burned churches to the once glamorous department stores that had now become forbidding unlit hulks, repositories of rumoured luxuries for the elites, the city that the older men had known – the city that they had been born into when Berlin and Germany were still ruled by a royal house, and a preening-peacock emperor – was being dismantled around them. It was impossible to envisage the city that was to come, or indeed the dazzling streets that had been. But the older men of the Volkssturm had long been accustomed to seeing those streets deranged by anarchy.

## 3. The Revolutionary Agony

Among the women and the men in those musty cellar-shelters were some who had been dedicated nudists in their younger years. The Berlin appetite for public nakedness, which had started before the First World War and became something close to a mass craze – *Nacktkultur* – in the 1920s, from parks to lakes to dance classes, had been an irrepressible impulse. Books on the subject by Richard Ungewitter had sold in their hundreds of thousands throughout Germany; a magazine called *Die Schönheit* (Beauty) was lavishly and tastefully illustrated with nudes. A former soldier called Hans Surén had written a guide called *Man and the Sun* about the benefits of exercising naked. (He and Ungewitter were also, as it transpired, profoundly anti-Semitic and fascistic, obsessed with eugenics and Aryan ideals of bodily perfection.) Public nudity – whether on the Berlin stage or by the waters of the Halensee – was broadly a metonym for the city's unselfconscious taste for extremism. Yet that extremism had also taken other forms, and brought with it turbulence and instability and insecurity. In many ways, the twentieth century had come fast – possibly too fast – to Berlin. Those citizens now facing the endless terror of bombing had seen destruction before. In the earlier eras of their youth, the turn-of-the-century city was in ruins of a different kind: the electrical industrial revolution had sparked late in Berlin, and, in the frenetic rush to catch up, areas were torn asunder to make way for vast modernist factories and foundries and chemical plants, as the poorest civilians – ever unsure about the security of their dwellings – found their lives becoming increasingly haphazard. Later, in the wake of the Great War, the monolithic tenement blocks in areas such as Wedding and Pankow were squalid, overcrowded, colourless and cold, and offered only tenebrous prospects in deep-shadowed court-yards or in the polluted grey skies above (one reason why – for some – trips to the city's forests to remove all clothing were a symbolic and cleansing liberation). With the poverty came violence – beatings and fights and assaults so frequent and so widespread that they were simply part of the grammar of the streets. In some senses, Berlin's elderly had never known true peace, and the city that the Volkssturm were now being told to defend with ancient weapons in 1945 had witnessed its streets made lethally dangerous through conflict before. As younger men in the winter of 1918, some of them would have seen or formed part of the large demonstrating crowds that gathered in the city's squares and in front of its government buildings, calling for the creation of a new world.

The end of the First World War had brought revolution to a nation that had come into unified being only some fifty years previously. When Germany swooped into the Great War, it and Berlin were under the constitutional rule of the House of Hohenzollern. The end, when it came, was dazzlingly fast. When the futility of so many millions of bloody deaths was combined with the bitterness of defeat, the start of rapacious reparations demands from the victors (the first of which was for twenty billion gold marks' worth of commodities) and with the vivid inspiration of the Bolshevik seizure of power in Russia, the anger came fast to the streets of Berlin. Kaiser Wilhelm II abandoned any idea of suppressing revolution and, mindful of the bloody and terrifying cellar-deaths of the Romanov royal family, bayoneted and shot by Bolsheviks in July 1918, sought sanctuary in the Netherlands. The middle and upper classes of the city were anxious that communism should find no place here, yet the socialist tide was rising. While moderate Philipp Scheidemann proclaimed the new republic from the balcony of the Reichstag, ardent communist (and anti-war campaigner) Karl Liebknecht addressed apparently bemused crowds from a rival balcony: that of the Kaiser's forsaken Berliner Schloss, the treasures of which had been plundered by enterprising looters. For a time, the unyielding starch of Marxist language came to the streets of Berlin. A Council of People's Representatives was formed, ratified by – among others – the General Assembly of the Berlin Workers' and Soldiers' Councils. Then, into this winter landscape of economic uncertainty and returning war-wounded, came violently right-wing former soldiers. By Christmas 1918, the pavements were increasingly speckled with blood. Skirmishes were ever more frequent.

In addition to the mutilations of war, the soldiers had also returned with disease: a strain of influenza dubbed 'Spanish Flu' that had mutated in the trenches and that was now spreading around the world. Its victims were, unusually, young and otherwise healthy. Across Berlin, as in other European and American cities, families and doctors looked on helplessly as patients, their lungs like sopping sponges, heaving with every drowning breath, developed heliotrope cyanosis: intense indigo colouring that spread from the cheeks to the rest of the face and the body. Sometimes there was bleeding from the eyes. The redness of the blood droplets on white cotton had a peculiar brightness. Death was inescapable and everywhere. These terrible symptoms would be seen again in 1945, due not to a virus but to the effects of self-administered cyanide, as many Berliners sought the most desperate form of release from fear.

Yet, as the aristocratic diplomat Count Harry Kessler observed in 1918, there was also a striking contrariness about the way that many other Berliners in that first post-war winter strove to ignore or minimize the crackling political hostility around them. They were determined to enjoy the festive season, even if it was only a simulacrum of normality, as Kessler recorded in his diary on Christmas Eve 1918:

The Christmas Fair carried on throughout the blood-letting. Hurdy-Gurdies played in the Friedrichstrasse while street vendors sold indoor fireworks, gingerbread and silver tinsel. Jewellers' shops in Unter den Linden remained unconcernedly open, their windows brightly lit and glittering. In the Leipziger Strasse the usual Christmas crowds thronged the big stores . . . In the Imperial Stables lay the dead, and the wounds freshly inflicted on . . . Germany gaped into the Christmas night.[1]

Yet on Christmas Day the socialists gathering under the radical Spartacist banner of Karl Liebknecht were back out in the centre of the city. They drew their inspiration from the Bolshevik Revolution in Russia; they wanted to see communism in Germany too, just as moderate SPD leader (and soon to be president) Friedrich Ebert was trying to cement the foundations of a new social democracy.

The Spartacus League had previously been an anti-war movement coordinated by the Socialist International; Liebknecht had been imprisoned for the last years of the war. His comrade Rosa Luxemburg, a brilliant polymath and political theorist who had moved to

Berlin in 1898 (and who had travelled to Warsaw to take part in that city's 1905 uprising, part of the revolutionary fire that had spread across the then Russian empire) had been in prison during the First World War too. She had learned of the 1917 Bolshevik Revolution from a sparse cell. Her confines could not dampen her exhilaration, although she did baulk at Lenin's rule through (by his own definition) terror: certainly, the masses had to undergo an immense spiritual transformation, but she believed that 'the elimination of democracy . . . is worse than the disease it is supposed to cure'.[2] Only socialism could bring true democracy, and equally it could not exist without it. By the time of her release in 1918, Luxemburg was forty-seven years old, a magnetic teacher for the eager young and perceived as an intense threat by conservative (and moderate) politicians. Luxemburg radiated an energetic optimism and hope; sensitive and sensual, she was as far from the emotionless stereotype of the chilly radical as anyone could be. Her former lover Leo Jogiches, with whom she remained close, could make her laugh so hard when they walked along the street that she had to sit down on the pavement to steady herself. She had a cat called Mimi; Lenin himself was among the creature's admirers. To the more conservative Germans, a figure such as Luxemburg – a Polish-born Jewish intellectual, and a woman on top of it all – was a premonition of the modern world to come.

Her Spartacist colleague Karl Liebknecht, meanwhile, was in rather different ways a foretaste of the sort of mesmerizing leadership that would in time prevail in Germany: a man whose charisma was not immediately obvious yet one who could exert great power over crowds. 'He was like an invisible priest of the revolution,' wrote Count Kessler, 'a mysterious but sonorous symbol to which these people raised their eyes.'[3] His speeches had a 'sing-song inflexion' and the enormous crowds that gathered to listen to him talk from the balconies of police stations seized by the Spartacists roared with approval and waved red flags while 'thousands of hands and hats rose in the air'.[4] For the poor of Berlin – the men who returned broken from war, the women exhausted with their unremitting responsibilities of work and family – anyone offering not just the bounties of socialism but the benefits of domestic security at a time when work and housing were continually precarious would have been cleaved to eagerly. Yet there were many other Berliners roused to hatred by Liebknecht's cause and his charisma. 'Berlin has become a witches' cauldron wherein opposing forces and ideas are being brewed together,'[5] wrote Kessler.

Those forces exploded in January 1919 with the Spartacus Uprising. In 1945, many of the middle-aged men in the Volkssturm would have remembered that earlier time when the machine guns, the grenades, the trench mortars had fired and blasted their way through the familiar streets of home. Liebknecht and Luxemburg had succeeded in inspiring a number of workers to arm themselves and to seize and occupy key points of Berlin: from the railway stations to the Brandenburg Gate to newspaper offices, there were gun emplacements on roofs and battles broke out between revolutionaries and national forces, bullets strafing windows and vehicles, red-flag waving parades caught in the sights of the government troops. Liebknecht declared that Friedrich Ebert's presidency was over, but it was very far from being so. Berlin was a battlefield; the SPD government unleashed the Freikorps – former soldiers, many of whom must have been psychologically scarred by the war, plus fanatical teenagers too young to have been called up for it – to suppress and destroy the communists. As with the army, there were officers and other ranks, but, in the wake of demobilization and defeat, the old structures of the real army had dissolved, and the way that they were re-formed in roaming packs of Freikorps groups was far removed from the old rules of engagement.

They were implacable and terrifying and pathological opponents. There was a song they favoured: 'Blood, blood, blood must flow, thick as a rain of blows.'[6] They were frightening misogynists too. Freikorps literature exulted in violence against women. One such Freikorps mercenary, having bludgeoned two Latvian women suspected of helping the Red Army in the Baltic, recalled the blood seeping from their heads as being the same shade as that of the roses outside the window.[7]

And that January, Karl Liebknecht and Rosa Luxemburg were eventually forced into hiding as the Freikorps murdered their way through the city, eliminating communists without any sense that there was a rule of law, or that they were slaughtering civilians (hundreds were killed). The streets of the centre of the city were whistling with bullets. And yet the cafes still served coffee, the tobacconists continued selling cigarettes, and, in the freezing January gloom, the city's trams showered sparks from their rails 'like fireworks'.[8] The city was finding a way to coexist with the state-sanctioned threat of violence. It succeeded.

Karl Liebknecht and Rosa Luxemburg were found and kidnapped by the Freikorps 'Guards Cavalry' division (so darkly suggestive of Prussian honour) and taken to the movement's base at the Hotel Eden. Liebknecht was 'interrogated'[9] – a euphemism for violent brutalization. He was subsequently shot in the back. Rosa Luxemburg was killed with equal brutality. The story was circulated that she had been spotted by a crowd of assorted right-wing opponents while she was being transferred by car from a hotel to another location; what actually happened was that she was bludgeoned fatally by the Freikorps and shot for good measure, and her body was then thrown into the Landwehr Canal. The whereabouts of her corpse remained a mystery for some months until, in the warm summer, her remains were found in the waterways, decomposed and bloated almost beyond hope of recognition, identified only after an autopsy carried out at the Charité Hospital.

The Spartacist Uprising was, over the course of the following weeks and months, quelled bloodily, the sounds of gunshots echoing off stonework, and there would be outbreaks of repercussive violence in the city between left and right throughout the decade to come. Even so, in the months before the inauguration of the new framework of German government – the Weimar Republic – in the late summer of 1919 (the historic and pretty town of Weimar a rather quieter proposition than febrile Berlin), the wider population of the capital had found a way of accommodating the irrationality, continuing to work, to shop, to drink. Theirs was a world that had been staring into an abyss of insanity throughout the war. There were mothers who were still mourning lost sons, and war-mutilated men who found that, on their demobilization from those foul, futile trenches, the state had little if anything to offer them.

The Freikorps itself offered nothing either, except further waves of bloodshed. There was an abortive coup in the spring of 1920, led by Wolfgang Kapp, that, with the streets around the government buildings thronged with paramilitary psychopaths, succeeded in making ministers flee. Kapp was a sixty-one-year-old former civil servant who cleaved with all his soul to the old militaristic, authoritarian, aristocratic Prussian Junkers. His followers were marching with swastikas before the advent of the National Socialist German Workers' Party. But even as he occupied government offices, the broader part of the Berlin population stopped the heart of his new fascist realm. A general strike against his putsch brought paralysis: no trams, no trains, no electricity, no gas. After just a few days, the coup was over, and Kapp fled the city for Sweden. None the less, the possibility of violence always remained; the social safety catch, removed by war, was difficult to put back in place. There were sporadic localized outbreaks of destruction; shops had windows smashed and goods looted so frequently that paramilitaries were granted a new privatized purpose: as vigilantes protecting businesses against anarchists.[10]

But there were those for whom even the jagged atmosphere of Berlin's streets were still better than the lands that they had fled. The end of the Great War had also seen an enormous influx of Jewish refugees from eastern Europe into the capital – displaced people. There was no proper system of asylum in the city, although bureaucrats did attempt to establish a framework of order, with papers that would allow poor refugees to pass through to other cities for work. There was an existing and long-established Jewish community in Berlin, often high bourgeois and Bismarckian in political inclination (conservative, intensely loyal to the state while also believers in social welfare) and leading in artistic and scientific fields. Nevertheless, there was anti-Semitism, even if it was more miasmic than perfectly visible, a set of attitudes never quite spoken aloud but always there. Even the large number of Jewish men who had fought in the trenches, and who had received lavish military decorations, were always aware, despite the earlier century's emancipation, of certain silent social and professional barriers that remained in the higher rungs of the society to which they had offered their lives. None the less, the Jewish community was an integral element of Berlin's soul. And there was perhaps an initial touch of uncertainty from it towards the incomers from the east. The satirical Jewish writer Joseph Roth – his own family having originally come from Galicia – could not disguise his ambivalence as he went to a boarding hostel in the east end of Berlin to report upon the new arrivals, who had fled Poland and Ukraine:

Many of the men arrived straight from Russian POW camps. Their
garments were a weird and wonderful hodgepodge of uniforms. In
their eyes I saw millennial sorrow. There were women there too. They
carried their children on their backs like bundles of dirty washing . . .
We know them as 'the peril from the East'. Fear of pogroms has welded
them together like a landslip of unhappiness and grime that, slowly
gathering volume, has come rolling across Germany from the East.[11]

Yet just a few months later Roth also observed that – free from
fear that local communities might turn upon them – great numbers
of Polish and Galician Jews established a fascinating realm for themselves within the city, near Alexanderplatz. Roth described it as a
'strange and mournful ghetto world',[12] although that was not quite
how it seemed to those who lived there. He entered one bar where
various men and women were setting up speculative business deals.
On offer were 'good bread, fish in various sauces and sausage from
Cracow', to say nothing of the schnapps. Elsewhere, on the Gren-
adierstrasse, 'there was a reek of onions, fish, fat, and fruit, of infants'.[13]
Poverty was widespread, among immigrants and locals alike. In the
early 1920s infant mortality rates across Berlin were shockingly
high – 322 deaths per thousand in some areas – greater than for any
other European city. Many were caused by gastric diseases, the result
of overcrowded and insanitary housing. A huge proportion of these
child victims were what was once termed 'illegitimate'; in that
period, some 20 per cent of Berlin's babies were born to unmarried
mothers, far higher than in other cities.[14] And these children, born
into the cold dust of poverty, were the most vulnerable to illness.

Elsewhere in the city, there were other arrivals from the east: White
Russians – those who opposed Bolshevism – fleeing Lenin's revolution. Among them was the young poet and novelist-to-be Vladimir
Nabokov (later to find a form of literary immortality with his 1955
work *Lolita*). In his novel *The Gift*, set in the 1920s, the protagonist Fyodor attends Russian poetry evenings and bad-tempered philosophical
debates in the smarter western suburbs of Berlin. He eats the hot
stuffed dough rolls that have migrated from St Petersburg to these
streets: 'He bought some piroshki (one with meat, another with cabbage, a third with tapioca . . .) in a Russian food shop, which was a

kind of wax museum of the old country's cuisine.'[15] Fyodor also has some snobbishly mixed feelings about the Berliners he jostles with on trams, disliking them for 'a love of fences, rows, mediocrity; for the cult of the office . . . for the lavatory humour and crude laughter; for the fatness of the backsides of both sexes, even if the rest of the subject is not fat'. Yet he also briefly throws himself into the city's cult of nudity, finding a glade in Grunewald to strip off and experience the unaccustomed 'freedom' around his 'loins'.[16] In broader terms, Berlin was a welcoming and accommodating home: an abundance of comfortably furnished rooms in respectable boarding houses run by landladies who were alternately fierce and protective, and who were occasionally observed (notably by the earlier British writer Henry Vizetelly) to have disproportionately large feet. This was just a couple of years after a war that was still sending shockwaves through society; the speed at which Berlin offered itself to new citizens from other countries was in itself a token of its modernity.

In a small way, the city's landscape had been changed by incomers, but the larger, more tectonic changes had been wrought by artists who even before the war had been looking at the aesthetics of architecture and seeing where Berlin might overturn all previous conceptions of what buildings and streets and housing estates should look like. Paradoxically, another of the long fuses that would begin to burn towards the advent of Nazism was Berlin's architecture.

Even before Hitler – who considered himself an architect and who dreamed of rebuilding Berlin to his own vision – had entered the city, its landscape had been violently unpredictable. Some of the factories that had arisen earlier in the century, like the 1909 AEG Turbine Works, designed by Peter Behrens, were more beautiful than the homes of the labourers who staffed their production lines. In the aftermath of the First World War, buildings fast became part of the cultural battle that would obsess Hitler until his death. Nor did that battle stop after the passing of the Nazi regime: the imposition of post-war communism upon almost half of the city would lead to further intense rearrangement of entire districts. To the people of Berlin, this was not some airy abstraction: architecture was an expression of the city's soul. It also symbolized the endless nervous twitching of public impatience: 'People had become accustomed at the time to seeing churches in the gothic style, synagogues looking oriental . . . and museums and civil service buildings in a kind of Italian Renaissance style,' said architect Hans Poelzig at a Berlin architectural event. 'Every attempt to make a stand against this has failed and industrial architecture alone represented the line of least resistance.'[17] And it was Poelzig in 1919 who demonstrated that the revolution could extend beyond industry. Even the interior of a theatre could suggest an entirely new world.

Berlin's great theatrical director Max Reinhardt was, in the aftermath of the war, set on creating a space that would draw in all of the city's populace, mass working-class audiences as well as the more rarefied middle classes. The location was to be the former site of a permanent circus, a grand enclosed arena. This would be the Grosses Schauspielhaus (Grand Theatre). Hans Poelzig stepped in and brought vivid disorientating expressionism to the city. The entrance hall featured vast arches, and huge light columns rising from the floor in organic, vaguely botanical shapes. More breathtaking yet was the central auditorium. Hanging down from the interior dome were Muqarnas – long, bulbous stalactites in serried ranks, which seemed to drip down the sturdy support pillars.

It might seem odd to observe that the shape of a theatre could form part of a deeply antagonistic battle over culture, yet in this case it did. The style of the Grosses Schauspielhaus came to be particularly loathed by Hitler, who – it later transpired – had fixed ideas on how a theatre should look: neoclassical, pillared, with velvet seating and boxes. 'He was especially fond of the numerous theatres built by Hermann Helmer and Ferdinand Fellner, who had provided both Austria-Hungary and Germany at the end of the nineteenth century with many late-baroque theatres, all in the same pattern,'[18] wrote Hitler's architect Albert Speer, of whom we will hear more later. But the point was not just about architecture: it was about the style of drama that would be performed in such places. The vision of Hans Poelzig would almost certainly be matched by ungovernability on the stage: radicalism, even obscenity. Shortly after the advent of the Nazi regime, the Grosses Schauspielhaus was rebuilt, the expressionist stalactites removed to create a more orderly space for the Nazi mind.

In contrast, there were other ferociously inventive architects in the city from 1919 onwards who had been anxious to remake it. Among them were young men who had studied under the lightning-flash creativity of Peter Behrens. Their names would find much greater worldwide fame than his. One of them was Ludwig Mies van der Rohe, who would later be acknowledged as one of the greatest influences on twentieth-century architecture and art. In 1921 Berliners were hypnotized by his extraordinary proposal for the city's first skyscraper block: his drawings depicted not a composition of brick and stone but rather a vast glass tower that rose high above all the city's roofs. It made Joseph Roth start daydreaming in wonder. 'What may have the appearance of a war against the elements is in fact union with the elements: man and nature becoming one,' he wrote. 'There is exhilaration in skyscrapers as much as on mountaintops . . . Clouds wander past the brows of mortal man as previously only around the brows of Olympians.'[19]

He also essayed a prescient prediction: 'Ten thousand people daily flow in and out of it,' Roth wrote: 'little office girls, emerging from the tight courtyards of the north of the city, quick tick of heels, black leather handbags swinging, filling elevators.'[20] It was swiftly rejected by the city authorities, but this vision of transparent glass and steel was one that Mies van der Rohe would later take with him to America; and one that, a hundred years on, would be replicated right the way across the world.

Mies van der Rohe also gave thought to the future of social housing; his creation of eighty-eight apartments later that decade in Afrikanische Strasse, in the working-class district of Wedding, pointed labouring Berliners to a cleaner and brighter life: sharply rectilinear, few rounded edges, interiors flooded with light from both vertical and horizontal windows and with the entire building faced in a pale lemon stucco, giving the faintest suggestion of the Mediterranean.

Mies van der Rohe was one of the founding members of a group of architects calling themselves The Ring, part of the aesthetic Neue Sachlichkeit movement. And this was not the only visionary housing project aimed at transforming both the material and spiritual welfare of the working classes. To the north-west of the city, just beyond the industrial zone that had been dubbed 'Fireland' because of the vast amount of glowing cinders and soot and smoke that it threw up into

Berlin's air, lay an even more ambitious site: a mini-city in its own right that had been established in the late nineteenth century. Siemensstadt was a vast complex devoted to the new illuminations of electricity and chemistry. Its factories and plants were vast red-brick structures, some elegant enough to resemble from some angles the new fashion for grand hotels; the housing for its loyal workforce was going to take a similarly novel form. At its outset, Siemensstadt was situated in a rather boggy wilderness far from local residences. By 1919, in the aftermath of the Great War, when it was the site of new plants for new technology, plus the first ever ten-storey factory, it was clear that the living arrangements of ever-growing numbers of employees would have to be carefully designed.

Hans Hertlein was the architect who drew up the revolutionary blueprints. The urban working classes had never lived like this before. There were to be 500 two-, three- and four-bedroom apartments. Instead of monotonous and filthy tenements, there were to be residential blocks with balconies and window-boxes, arranged to resemble a village, with green squares, wide arches and clocks in ornamental towers. Vitally, each flat would have proper plumbing, and most their own bathroom. The new homes were soon occupied, and by the end of the decade more were needed, for which an even more arresting style of modernism was employed. Among the architects this time was Walter Gropius, founding father of the Bauhaus institute, the manifesto of which was to gather art and design and architecture and crafts into a revolutionary aesthetic whole. The vision that he and other colleagues wrought in some 1,500 new apartments was that of sharp geometrical brightness and neatness; within, the flats were a symphony of different, unusual colours: walls of amethyst or emerald or dusty red. These were homes that felt young and invigorating and energetic. Remarkably, they not only would survive Hitler and the war, but also would continue their habitable lives long into the post-war age. There is no shortage of legacies to Walter Gropius, but these homes brilliantly symbolized the way that art could rise above even the most vicious and destructive ideologies. For Gropius himself, though, the path through the horror to come would not be easy to navigate.

This visionary – who had fought on the front line in the Great

War – simply wanted the world in which workers moved to be infused with beauty. Art and craft, he said, 'would rise one day towards Heaven from the hands of a million workers like the crystalline symbol of a new faith'.[21] His life, at the helm of the Bauhaus, would be dedicated to creating 'a new man in a new environment'.[22] A fresh aesthetic would envelop the factories, and thus 'breathe soul' into industrial mass production, giving even the plainest of commodities a joyous inventiveness. However, as with many visions of a new way of life, it was dismissed by several critics with something close to an angry impatience.

Indeed, the political response to the publicly funded Bauhaus – including its eccentric, avant-garde cocktail parties where guests sometimes dressed completely in metal, and the doubly eccentric magus-like artists who gathered young disciples and insisted upon garlic-infused vegetarianism – was almost always flinty. Gropius stepped down, and by the 1930s, with the advent of Hitler, he was eventually forced to emigrate. The last director of the Bauhaus was Ludwig Mies van der Rohe, and his job by 1933 involved spending ever larger amounts of time in police stations to secure the release of students who had been rounded up by the Nazis. (The complete aesthete, he could not help noting that the wooden benches in those police stations were very badly designed.) Mies Van der Rohe too was forced to emigrate. Both he and Gropius (the latter having first found a home in London's Belsize Park amid the exquisitely modernist white lines of the Isokon apartment building) established new lives in the United States.

Their revolution had set sail, and, as the 1930s dawned, there was a sense of more conservative visions pressing to the fore. The Nazis would soon find their ideal architects for the capital. Professor Heinrich Tessenow had been seduced by the forests and the lakes and the myths of Germany. His idea of architecture was all about drawing from the past. It was pathologically nationalist. Like his contemporaries, he was inclined to romanticize the working man, although his way of doing so was at a distinct angle, firmly rejecting the glass and the steel and the sharp edges of the future. 'Style comes from the people,' he told his students in the Berlin Institute of Technology. 'It is in our nature to love our native land. There can be no true culture that is international. True culture comes only from the maternal womb of a nation.'[23] He then went on to declaim in a nativist style that would find a terrible answering echo from the Nazis in the age to come. 'The metropolis is a dreadful thing,' said Tessenow. 'The metropolis is a confusion of old and new. The metropolis is conflict, brutal conflict. Everything good should be left outside of big cities . . . where urbanism meets the peasantry, the spirit of the peasantry is ruined. A pity that people can no longer think in peasant terms.'[24]

There had been a younger architect still learning his craft as the 1920s Berlin was dominated by the modernists; a man who knew that urban buildings were projections of power and of belief; that they reflected society and culture. Albert Speer, who had been born in 1905, was captivated by the words and work of Professor Tessenow. However, by the early 1930s, Tessenow was to find himself over-shadowed by the precocious success of his young admirer. Speer was pulled giddyingly fast into the personal orbit of Hitler. This was not by chance: Speer had been a member of the Nazi Party since the beginning of the 1930s. He and his wife lived in the Berlin suburb of Wannsee and he was especially popular with the local party officials – not merely because his profession lent their association a little gravitas, but also because he was the only local party member who owned a car. It was the district leader Karl Henke who first commissioned Speer to remodel the local headquarters; while the structure retained a conservative feel, Speer daringly suggested innovative Bauhaus wallpaper designs and strong primary colours – red and yellow – for different rooms. A visit from the party hierarchy elicited further interest from one of Hitler's henchmen in particular. Goebbels warmed to Speer's style and could also see the advantage of having a young, personable, cultured architect working to create dignified buildings that would give Nazism a visual badge of respectability. And in turn, following the Nazi assumption and seizure of power in 1933, Speer found that he was an object of fascination to Hitler himself. The Führer – he later claimed – did not lack for a certain raw architectural talent; he would sketch out concepts swiftly in pens of blue and red. But his induction of Speer into his most intimate circle had the flavour of seduction.

On one occasion, Speer found that he had arrived at a small event wearing an unsuitable jacket; Hitler insisted that he borrow one of his. This gesture of intimacy was noted with some surprise by others close to the Führer. On another occasion, a dinner for a small gathering of select guests, Speer was placed opposite the Führer; late in the evening, he found himself meeting Hitler's eyes, and then not being able to move his gaze away. He himself described what ensued as a staring contest. Speer determined not to move his eyes before Hitler did, with the result that the two men stared at each other in silence 'seemingly forever', as he wrote, before Hitler turned to talk to a woman by his side. Speer did not read anything into this contest, save for the faint and humorous discomfort. Yet he must have wondered: was this simply a display of power? An attempt to see deeper inside him? If that were the case, Hitler would have been disappointed, for, as Speer's own memoirs plus a long-ranging series of interviews (conducted after his twenty-year sentence at Spandau had been served) with the writer Gitta Sereny revealed, there was very little to be seen of Speer's soul.[25] There was simply nothing there. His capacity for reflection seemed wholly absent. Hitler kept him close, for Speer was to be the instrument of his grand dream for Berlin: to tear out its core of houses, apartments, offices, shops and factories, and replace it with avenues of neoclassical monumentalism, suggestive of ancient Greece. And in the years to come, late at night, amid discreet pools of light, the two men would meet in chambers close to the Chancellery office and converse secretly over Speer's ever-growing collection of scale models of his proposed regenerated city: Germania.

It was more than Hitler's obsession; when he was with Speer, gazing at the simulated buildings of marble, the sleek rectilinear facades, and, at their centre, the extraordinary bulk of the People's Hall, surmounted by a dome many times the size of St Peter's in Rome, there was a kind of tender passion there. He and Speer would discuss the minutest details – from the sources of the water that would fill the lake in front of the repurposed grand railway station to the way that the dome would be seen from different angles and perspectives. No one else – not even Hitler's partner Eva Braun – was allowed to see these scale models. They were a whispered secret between him and his young architect, a dream for the small hours.

At the core of Germania – the grand wide avenues lined with

governmental institutes, the dominance of the People's Hall dome and the projected space within it, so vast that the thousands of people within would seem ant-like – was a shuddering distaste for the apparently anarchic disorder of Berlin as it stood; not merely the tenement slums, with weekly washing flapping like cotton ghosts, but the rackety glamour of the grander department stores, the theatres, the factories and breweries. These did not befit a great city. Hitler expressed a desire for a capital that would dominate Europe, one that would inspire awe in all who saw it. This was a city that firmly rejected the future: there were no skyscrapers anywhere in Speer's vision (at a point when New York's fresh perpendicular skyline had caught the imagination of the world). Only the Führer could be permitted to gaze down from above upon teeming streets; that was not a seemly position for the ordinary man. Not one structure would interpose itself within the prospect of the great dome. This was also a manifestation of an older, darker romanticism: Speer wanted to build purely in stone because he was imagining his city as ruins in a thousand years. These ruins were to be entwined in ivy; the paintings of Tiepolo given substance. Not only was the presumption preposterous, but the idea – much liked by Hitler – also exposed a deeper truth threaded through their private daydreams: their fantasies were always, fundamentally, deathly. What Germania – in its scale-model incarnation – most especially lacked was any suggestion of a human presence amid its vast buildings, or visible on its long and wide avenues.

Later, as war came, and Speer was pulled away from architecture into becoming Minister for Armaments and War Production, standing at the helm of a ghastly, nationwide enterprise of slave labour, the vision of Germania started to recede, even if Hitler continued to visit his beloved model city in the night. The large-scale Allied bombing raids, starting in 1943 and escalating in intensity, saw Berlin being pounded into ash; no possibility of romantic ivy amid the crushed bone and pulped flesh. But cold and sociopathic though Speer was – a man who seemed genuinely bewildered by the idea that he should show real contrition – he could not be entirely dismissed. Although much of his architecture somehow contrived to be both pedestrian and oppressive at the same time, he did have moments of artistic inspiration, flashes of insight that allowed him to appropriate aesthetic effects to further glorify the Nazis.

Berlin had once been a dazzlingly nocturnal city; light – and its artful manipulation – was an integral element of its attraction. In the immediate aftermath of the German Revolution in 1919, it began to gather a global reputation as a city of rich illumination. 'Berlin is modern, modern due to its light,' declared the French artist Fernand Léger in the 1920s. 'Its fight against the night . . . I have now been in Berlin for eight days and have not noticed the night at all . . . Berlin is a single block of light.'[26] It was furiously competitive about it as well, and was widely described as having displaced Paris as 'the new City of Light in Europe'.[27] In the Weimar era, industry and science and commercial endeavour came together to make Berlin blaze so bright that all other European lamps would come to seem quaint and dull. There was even a term: *der lichtwirtschaftliche Gedanke*, which broadly meant 'the idea of the economics of light'. In 1922, neon came to the city, in its initial primary colours of red, blue and yellow; the discovery, made a few years earlier by British scientists, that neon gas in a glass tube produced an astonishing glow when subjected to an electrical charge was explored with particular zeal further in Berlin, with experiments bringing forth new shades of pink and green. Soon, the wet pavements of night were daubed in these reflected colours as hundreds and then thousands of electrically lit advertisements fizzed on commercial walls. The Osram lightbulb company, based in Berlin, meanwhile devised a range of new illuminations and there were plans in the 1920s for a spectacular architectural monument simply called the 'House of Electricity'.[28] But the hypnotic power of light in the darkness to seduce and ensnare, to tempt and persuade, found most vivid life in Berlin's newest art form: that of the department-store window display. As the city underwent its pulsating artistic revolution, 'it was the shop windows of Berlin that were most renowned worldwide'.[29] In the 1920s, the grand shopping streets such as the Kurfürstendamm were transfigured in the twilight by the most elaborate staged tableaux: haute couture set against moving landscape backdrops, or draped upon jerkily animated mannequins, or sometimes even modelled by real women standing behind the plate-glass windows, and lit with the art and care of a theatre production, from the gaudiest orange to the richest violet. The vast Wertheim store on Leipziger Strasse composed displays on the scale of Old Masters, one slightly macabre example featuring dozens of children's dolls dressed in white gowns, arrayed at different levels and sharply lit against a dark backdrop.

It was not just the windows, though. The buildings themselves were also sometimes luminous displays: the Karstadt department store on Hermannplatz had, by the end of the 1920s overtaken Wertheim as the largest of its kind in the world, standing nine storeys high and featuring two vast towers, the windows like vertical grooves in the brickwork, which at night were brilliantly illuminated; the entire structure seemed to pulse with glowing electricity. By the spring of 1945 Karstadt, which had once fused futurism with elegance, had a very different place in the imaginations of Berliners: the building, unlit and splintered with bomb shrapnel, was still in use but as a repository for emergency supplies of the most basic needs for the city. Under the steel skies, and drained of all its power, it resembled a sullen fortress. In either guise the Karstadt building, with its gaunt verticals and monumental scale, mimicked the buildings that were closest to the proud industrial heart of the city: its power stations. The echo was intentional, because when the streets of Berlin were flooded with light in the 1920s, many took a huge pride in those towering sources of that power.

The extraordinary and vast Klingenberg power station, built in the eastern quarter of Rummelsburg in 1925 – red brick laid out in expressionist style, not just in neat horizontal rows but also vertically and at forty-five degree angles, and containing offices with marbled floors – was a citadel of the future, a fortress with many towers, spanning some quarter of a mile by the banks of the Spree. Such a dominating structure might have looked intimidating and yet it was somehow softened by being reflected in the wide waters of the river. It brought not only light but also warmth; an outdoor swimming pool was opened nearby, heated by the plant's excess energy. Even the electricity substations had an astonishing grandeur. Using red brickwork again, some of these had the feel of church apses, but with innovative and strange angles and detailing. The structures that brought light themselves had a certain lightness of identity; architectural flair and flourishes, rich perspectives showing that industry did not have to be either ugly or soulless; that in a modern age, even the most functional of buildings were imbued with a delight in proportion and colour. (That these substations today not only survive but are in lively use as offices for technology firms and fashionable restaurants demonstrates that the artistic impulse was sound.)

Meanwhile, there was a gaudy and hypnotic import that found new and powerful life in the aftermath of the Great War: Luna Park, an American invention, a vast permanent fairground standing on the banks of the Halensee in the Grunewald forest to the west of the city and which brought vivid life and light into the night: here, under great lamps of glowing lemon yellow and deepest seductive red, pleasure-seekers immersed themselves in a world in which layered conscious thought was dissolved as it contended against pure sensation. This was also a 'hypermodern' realm, partly constructed again in an expressionist style by artist Rudolf Belling among others. Unlike more traditional German fairgrounds of the previous century – prospects of tents and braziers – this was a park in which different worlds and themes were summoned by means of facades, from gothic to oriental, and configured through distorted perspective. It was also filled with incessant, whirling movement: the writer Kurt Tucholsky found himself disorientated by one lurching carousel attraction which itself seemed a part of the 'cubist-expressionist' movement.

In addition to all of this was the extravagant quantity of beer sold and drunk. One bar area was fashioned to look like an old Bavarian inn, though extravagantly angled, and with a further twist: through it ran a gurgling stream of lager. Visitors who considered themselves a little more refined could take tea at the 'Luna Palace'. But the faintly feverish illusions conjured by the park worked best by night. So too did the increasingly exotic refreshments that could be found here and in other Berlin bars: a 'pink persico' was peach brandy with 'a shot of raspberry'; 'black and dash' was potato schnapps with 'a lump of sugar dipped in rum';[30] even the ordinary Berlin pale ale could be enlivened with 'a shot of raspberry'. Although the culinary tastes of drinkers remained quotidian – 'hot sausages, roll-mops, fried potatoes',[31] or even simply 'pea soup' served in 'tureen'-sized bowls and accompanied with hot rolls, or rye bread with caraway seeds, there was still the desire for visual novelty in terms of nightlife.

This was especially true of the Haus Vaterland, which opened later in the 1920s in the Potsdamer Platz; a six-storey phantasmagoria, its dome illuminated in moving neon, and filled throughout with restaurants and bars themed as different countries. Here was something more diverting than Berlin's old 'beer halls the size of railway stations'[32] with sausages served at central aisles; this was a dazzling pleasure palace, with cinemas and stages featuring dancing girls as well as bars. A restaurant area such as the Turkish cafe was an orientalist fantasy, rich in reds and ochres and ornamented arches. The building's exterior glow was intended to contribute to Berlin's architecture of light.

It was noted that the Berlin streets themselves shared this quality. 'The town was like a fairground,' wrote Erich Kästner. 'The house-fronts were bathed in garish light to shame the stars in the sky.'[33] Elsewhere, in the dance halls and nightclubs, there was often a 'red illumination' which, as one writer suggested, was partly about suppressing light as much as shedding it. In the Berliner Sportpalast, where epic cycling competitions were held in the evenings, spectators held their hands over their eyes against the intense glare of the spotlights trained upon the athletes. The aesthetics and the power of this light were noted by those who could see the political potential.

The expansion of the German air force, the Luftwaffe, and attendant defences in the mid 1930s brought another form of light to Berlin's darkness: the beam of anti-aircraft searchlights, vast columns of ghostly white piercing the blackness above. It was Albert Speer who, propelled into the orbit of Hitler, saw that such light could be used in quite a different way. In the spring of 1934 there was to be a mass party rally on the Zeppelin airfield. Such gatherings, intended to impress, were frequently edged with bathos, NSDAP officials attempting and failing to march in disciplined step, with their great paunches sagging over their uniform trousers. According to Speer, it seemed better to make them 'march out of the darkness'.[34] This would have the dual effect of disguising their preposterous appearance and also giving some dramatic lustre to what would otherwise be just a series of speeches:

I had occasionally seen our new anti-aircraft searchlights blazing miles into the sky. I asked Hitler to let me have a hundred and thirty of these . . . The actual effect far surpassed anything I had imagined . . . The . . . sharply defined beams, placed around the field at intervals of forty feet, were visible to a height of twenty to twenty-five thousand feet, after which they merged into a general glow. The feeling was of a vast room, with the beams serving as mighty pillars of infinitely high outer walls. Now and then a cloud moved through this wreath of lights, bringing an element of surrealistic surprise to the mirage.[35]

Here was the start of a distinct fascist aesthetic that would evolve and develop through the vast choreographed propaganda events of the Nuremberg rallies, and one that dovetailed with Hitler's preference for giving rousing speeches at night. He too understood the receptivity that the dark could bring. (This was an aesthetic that also – unconsciously – borrowed inspiration from the world of show business: it was noted years later that columns of light were a technique that had already been perfected for Berlin's sumptuous film premieres of the 1920s.) Speer, whose vanity was intense, assumed that the inspiration was his alone. 'I imagine that this "cathedral of light" was the first luminescent architecture of this type,' wrote Speer shamelessly in his memoirs, 'and for me it remains not only my most beautiful architectural concept but, after its fashion, the only one which has survived the passage of time.'[36] As an arrogant man devoid of irony, Speer would not have seen the bitter black comedy of that assertion, given that the Nuremberg rallies are scarcely the material for delicate art-gallery retrospectives. Yet, more broadly, the terrible drama inherent in the sharp contrast between glare and darkness was to define the visual memory of both Germany and Berlin. So too was the schism that existed between the city's historical tradition of mocking authority, and the speed at which people could be roused to violence.

## 4. Spilled Blood and Exultation

'An ability to appreciate the dubious side of things and a discerning sense of humour have always been fundamental ingredients of Berlin life,' observed the Jewish philologist Victor Klemperer (himself a Dresden citizen who miraculously survived the bombing firestorms of 13 February 1945), adding, 'which is why to this very day I fail to understand how Nazism could have thrived in Berlin.'[1] Laughter, however rough, was a measure of redemptive humanity; the enemy of rigid, hateful ideology. And yet, following the Great War and the German Revolution and years of economic desperation, its emotional corollary, hate, pulsed through Berliners' veins too. It was there as a palpable presence in the poorer streets. Sometimes, although the brutality took the form of allegiance to political cults, it seemed as though this was not enough to explain it; the rage and the bloody assaults were almost elemental. To an extent, this was true of many cities after the First World War; the pavements outside London pubs in certain districts were constantly spattered with blood, the vicious fights too frequent to even merit notice. But, in Berlin, the violence carried an extra edge that went beyond turf wars and strong drink.

'Certainly, it would be difficult to recall, in modern history, a happier hunting ground for cut-throats and other rogues than the German capital,'[2] wrote the Berlin correspondent of *The Times* in February 1920. Part of this, he acknowledged, was an 'after-the-war wave that also appeared to afflict New York and London'. Berlin, however, took it to a new level. '[I]t now takes a good deal to shock, thrill or even interest anyone who has grown accustomed to it,'[3] the reporter continued. Among the macabre cases: a fraught mother who crammed two of her children into a barrel and nailed down the lid, leaving them there until they had suffocated; a fortune-teller strangled for the sake of a few marks; and the serial killer of the Falkenhagen Forest who murdered so many people that, when he was at last caught, he confessed that he could not even remember how many victims there were. These sorts of cases, combined with the wide-spread availability of guns and outbreaks of gang battles in the working-class areas of Wedding and Moabit, made the streets seem unusually aggressive and febrile.

'All the principal defendants are callow youths, one of them a mere schoolboy, without experience in life or power of judgement,'[4] reported the *Daily Telegraph* of a Berlin political assassination in 1922 that had shocked a death-sated continent. 'They had intoxicated them-selves with crazy theories and senseless catchwords, by which the militarist elements in Germany try to console themselves for the loss of the war.'[5] There were conspiracy theories: not least of which was the recently published anti-Semitic hoax *The Protocols of the Elders of Zion*, which purported to prove that Jewish cabals were plotting to dominate the world. The crime for which one of these youths was standing trial – as an accessory, since the murderers themselves had either been shot or committed suicide – was the killing of Germany's foreign min-ister, Walther Rathenau. This was an act of violence where the city's blazing beer-hall bigotry came into furious collision with Berlin's ele-gant elite. Dr Rathenau was in some ways the embodiment of the city's early modernism: an industrialist as well as an essayist, an economist as well as an aesthete. And he was a key figure – politically and symbolically – in the fledgling Weimar Republic, desperately seeking ways for the country to find some stability amid the rapacious demands of the Versailles treaty, so that its economy could achieve its full mighty potential. Rathenau was the opposite of the old Prussian aristocratic stereotype; here was a fastidious fifty-four-year-old corporate techno-crat, leaning towards the left, Jewish although unobservant, envisaging a new workplace where management and workers could find harmony rather than being in perpetual opposition. Rathenau's family had been partly responsible for Berlin's innovative factories: his father Emil had seen the potential in electricity and had formed what would become the mighty AEG electrical company.

Rathenau was familiar with intense workshops, incandescent furnaces, the uncanny speed of automated production lines, the rich glow of innovative light, and he could also see what the demands for reparations were doing to the balance sheets of those factories. Rathenau, answering to Chancellor Joseph Wirth, attended solemn international conferences, and in 1922 could see only one way to ease Germany's isolation and strain: a surprise pact (actually more of a violent shock to France and Britain, among others) with Russia. Rathenau was rather admired by Lenin, who saw him as embodying an evolutionary step in capitalism that would point towards the certainty of socialism. The Treaty of Rapallo – which normalized diplomatic relations between the two countries, cancelled debts between the two and also secretly made military cooperation possible – caused uproar; there was fear of a new secret plan between Germany and Russia to dominate the European continent. Equally, there seemed little understanding that a cultured figure like Rathenau would not have entertained such an idea for a moment; this pact was more a symptom of Germany's economic desperation in the face of ever-increasing reparation demands from France.

Rathenau lived in a specially designed neoclassical villa amid the trees of Grunewald south-west of Berlin. Every morning, he was driven to the foreign ministry in a limousine. On this warm morning, the car's roof was down. Shortly after the chauffeur pulled away, the limousine was joined at traffic lights by a cheaper car, in the back of which sat two young men in leather coats. One opened fire with a machine gun, the other threw a hand grenade into the back of the vehicle. The explosion made the limousine rise into the air. Extraordinarily, Rathenau's chauffeur was only slightly injured, and, as he raced off to find help, a passing nurse comforted the dying foreign minister.

The young killers – Erwin Kern and Hermann Fischer, both in their early twenties – were already veterans of extreme political violence. They were members of the far-right and seethingly anti-Semitic Organization Consul (an offshoot of the Freikorps). They fled Berlin and attempted to find refuge at Saaleck Castle. Eventually trapped by the pursuing police, Kern was hit by a bullet and Fischer turned his own gun on himself. In the meantime, their getaway driver – twenty-year-old Ernst Techow – retreated to his uncle's house. Seeing his manic state – and having heard the news of the assassination – Techow's uncle in his fury bade his nephew to pick up a gun, go into the woods and shoot himself rather than face disgrace. Techow instead surrendered to the authorities and as an accessory faced the death sentence; this was commuted to fifteen years' imprisonment. Shortly afterwards, Rathenau's elderly mother wrote an extraordinary letter of forgiveness to Techow's mother – the only glint of redemption in an otherwise grim cycle of violence. The repercussions of the murder were equally serious: Rathenau's killing, which carried the sense of unstoppable anarchic bloodshed, shook the foreign stock markets and faith in Germany's economy, depreciating the currency, which contributed another wave swelling the approaching tsunami of hyperinflation; this in turn would destroy livelihoods and leave Berliners scrabbling in the humiliation of a worthless currency and panic buying.

It was in this period that a number of more elderly, wealthy Berliners – living off savings and fixed incomes – came to taste what it was like to be among the city's poor and desperate; with the mark losing its value by the hour, the accepted structure of civilization – the simplest act of shopping for food – simply melted. Family heirlooms replaced notes and coins, and all to acquire ever more meagre supplies of staples. There was urban scavenging, not just through bins but also the theft and consumption of pets. Those who had had little to begin with, meanwhile, were also left near destitute; what use were wages to steel-makers if the money was worth nothing by the end of the week? There were countless Berliner families for whom there was no possibility of restoration of faith in the political system thereafter.

And, even after economic stability was restored, there were still flames of political violence flaring unexpectedly. The bloody death of Rathenau was a continuing inspiration to other assassins, who loathed the Weimar regime, but who were perhaps impelled by deeper, primordial desires for violence. In 1925, a plot to murder foreign minister Gustav Stresemann was uncovered; the would-be assailant, Karl Kaltdorf, worked at the vast Siemens factory. Kaltdorf had been a devoted communist, but latterly had switched his allegiances and was now 'a violent Hitler-ite'. His intentions were announced in a letter to a friend: 'The swine must die.'[6]

There were cases of murder that were certainly not political but instead hauntingly nihilistic and which seemed also to have been part of the shadows of the last war. One such involved four middle-class teenagers in the Berlin suburb of Steglitz, all of them in their last year at school, who appeared to have formed a death pact: part murder, part suicide involving a gun. The case was taken to be proof of a kind of degeneracy in Weimar youth, resonating especially because there was a more generalized anxiety about what the children of Versailles had become. (A year earlier, there had been intense disquiet at a rash of killings committed by boys aged between nine and eleven – random knife attacks on adults and carried out with such frenzy that the blades were driven right through the bodies. Even more unsettlingly, these cases were unrelated, save for the fact that they appeared to be 'copycat' in nature.)

A general sense of disorder and malaise was reflected strongly in later Weimar literature. The most striking, in terms of both pungency and literary flair, was a 1929 novel of the city's underworld called *Berlin Alexanderplatz* by Alfred Döblin: the vinegary saga of a released convict, Franz Biberkopf, and his progress through an array of pornographers and prostitutes, gangs of thieves and the economically distressed middle-class people who agree to hide looted spoils for a cut, and the career criminals who exploit them. This vividly conjured world of freezing streets, cheap taverns ('beef cheeks and potatoes' are made to seem a luxurious treat) and frowsy apartments overlooking courtyards claustrophobic enough for neighbours to monitor one another's business closely, is suggestive of a city as maelstrom, its population caught helplessly in tides over which they have little or no agency. With the universality of harried poverty, transgression is ugly and inevitable. The structure and style of the novel reflected that chaos: as the well-intentioned but flawed protagonist progresses, the very air around him appears filled with random news items, conversation snatches, popular song lyrics.

This invocation of a city that had come late to modernity, and had done it in a very great hurry, was an immediate commercial success, not just in Berlin but internationally as well. Two years later, with Berlin now fully submerged beneath the economic tsunami set off by the Wall Street Crash – by 1931, some 25 per cent of the city's population was unemployed, and the same hungry percentage was wholly dependent on welfare payments that were slender and precarious at best – another, even less forgiving novel provoked not affection but rage. Its author was previously best-known for a hugely popular children's story called *Emil and the Detectives*. This new book, *Going to the Dogs*, was very much for adults. Erich Kästner brought sardonic wit to this account of a young, well-educated man, Jakob Fabian, finding himself adrift in a city where there is no secure work, a great deal of emotionally troubled promiscuity and a throbbing pulse of violence, which frequently threatens to overwhelm. Kästner caught that crucial moment in the city's life when working men and clerks alike split into rival groups – communists and Nazis – and began their ever more bloody conflicts.

Throughout the novel there are violent demonstrations, broken up by bloodthirsty police, and all this is combined with a sickly air of widespread poverty and ubiquitous sexual neuroses. The young protagonist Fabian is drawn irresistibly back to images of the Great War and the 'terrible photographs he had seen',[7] plus the human relics of that war haunting the streets of Berlin. There is a direct psychic connection between that carnage and the nauseating and brutal uncertainties of the city now:

> They said there are isolated buildings . . . still full of mutilated soldiers. Men without limbs, men with ghastly faces, without noses, without mouths. Nurses whom nothing could scare poured food into these disfigured creatures, poured it through thin glass tubes, speared into scarred and suppurating holes where once there had been a mouth. A mouth that could laugh and speak and cry aloud.[8]

These references to mutilation, on top of the brothels, the dance halls, the sleazy boarding houses where an infinitely interchangeable parade of sexual partners tiptoed up and down the stairs, caused immediate outrage: even in 1931, some months before the Nazis held political sway, the air was changing. Kästner himself had detected this – he was certain he would be denounced as 'a purveyor of filth' – and he had launched a pre-emptory defence of his work in an afterword to the novel which proved almost clairvoyant about the danger of another world war:

> To all of this the author replies: 'I am a moralist.' He discerns but one ray of hope, and he names it. He sees that his contemporaries, like stubborn mules, are running backwards towards a yawning abyss in

which there is enough room for all the nations of Europe. And so, like a number of others before and alongside him, he cries out: 'Watch out! Grip the handrail on your left with your left hand!'[9]

Surely only a sophisticated Berliner could have deployed the image of an escalator – a relatively new innovation largely the preserve of the smartest department stores – as the means by which reason might be restored.

So, were the city's younger 1930s generation – young men who had been boys when their fathers returned, silent and haunted-eyed from the trenches ten years previously – fighting their own war to make up for the one that had been lost? It was not so simple: the aggression on Berlin's streets by 1932 was in part due to two mutually uncomprehending factions, both of whom disastrously believed that history was about inevitable progress. Blood was shed with the most terrible ease, and in a variety of situations, frequently on marches and protests that either descended into brawls or invited the attentions of the city's armed police, some of whom had memories of the bullet-scarred anarchy of the German Revolution. Each death, on either side of the political chasm, was proclaimed a martyrdom; and yet those deaths seemed so frequent too. In addition to this was the inter-national dimension: Berlin's Young Communist League were seeking out active links with the Soviet Union, and included in their ranks were Russian émigrés who would preach the glories of socialism. Among the committed communists in 1932 was a fiercely intellectual schoolboy named Eric Hobsbawm – later to become one of the most influential historians of the century. He wryly recalled:

> Nazis and Communists were parties of the young, if only because young men are far from repelled by the politics of action, loyalty, and an extremism untainted by the low, dishonest compromises of those who think of politics as the art of the possible . . . the Nazis were certainly our enemies on the streets, but so were the police.[10]

One of the city's central rallying points was the Lustgarten, an expanse of landscaped open greenery adjacent to the grand museums and the Stadtschloss. By 1930, it had acquired a paramilitary feel when the Young Communists assembled. Their defensive quasi-uniforms

were at once curiously naïve but also a strong indicator to those Nazis –
whom they knew would be watching – that they were prepared to
fight. The writer Franz Hessel described the scene in his memoir:

> The Soviet standard is saluted with reverence. Long processions
> marched here from all corners of the city, led by strange instruments:
> trumpets with multiple bells, jazz tubas, African drums. These fight-
> ers are uniformed just like those they would like to oust. The grey shirts
> and brown tunics are belted in military style. And the processions are
> now orchestrated by the red armbands of the leading pivots.[11]

Hessel noted that a speaker positioned himself on the steps in front
of the cathedral. His fiery speech took on an unconsciously religious
element: the punchy slogans concerning the overthrow of oppression and justice for the poor were repeated by the crowd, almost as if
they were being led in prayer. The declaratory songs were like hymns.
And the movement was Manichaean; because theirs was the only truly
virtuous path, others who refused to follow it must therefore be
understood as malignant. Absurdly, by 1932, the greatest source of
evil, as the Berlin communists saw it, was not the obvious enemy of
the Nazi Party but the Social Democratic centrists, with their milky
deference to the malign forces of capitalism. They underestimated
the party's lethally wide potential.

There were other primal impulses in that drive to fight in the
streets. 'Next to sex, the activity combining bodily experience and
intense emotion to the highest degree is the participation in a mass
demonstration at a time of great public exaltation,' wrote Hobsbawm
lightly. 'Unlike sex, which is essentially individual, it is by its nature
collective, and unlike the sexual climax, at any rate for men, it can be
prolonged for hours.'[12]

This was also understood acutely well by the Nazis; the euphoria
that could arise through being part of a physically strong gang with
the passionate belief that they were fighting for decency and cleanli-
ness, for Germanic purity against the corrupting taint of foreign
Bolshevik influences. There was a profound cynicism in the young
Dr Goebbels, as he studied the means by which the young could be
influenced and suffused with bloodlust. He orchestrated the inflam-
matory news articles in *Der Angriff*; he and the party arranged Nazi

rallies in shrewdly chosen locations such as the vast Berliner Sportpalast – the indoor stadium that hosted Berlin's frenetic six-day cycle races. Franz Hessel again:

> The halls fill. The police patrol in front of the doors, because counter-demonstrations are to be expected from 'the Reds' outside. And the distance between walking past and throwing punches is no farther than that between biting one's thumb and drawing one's weapon for the Montagues and Capulets . . . If they weren't wearing their insignia, the Order of Reaction or Revolution, they could hardly be distinguished, these brash Berlin lads from both camps.[13]

Superficially this might have been so, but the fact was that the National Socialists held the promise of administering violence, and in every generation of young men in any country there will always be a faction drawn to the power and the ecstasy of untrammelled brutality. Goebbels himself – born into a lower-middle-class Catholic family in 1897 – was on the face of it quite the opposite of a thug: delicate-featured, he had been born with a club foot and his formative years had been marked by introversion. At school he had been so bookish and withdrawn that he later remembered himself as a 'solitary lone wolf'; an aspiring novelist attracted to all invocations of an essential Germanic soul. He attended university in Würzberg and it was in the immediate post-war years that he began to be drawn into right-wing student circles, among others who fantasized fiercely about national rebirth. Goebbels earned his doctorate in Philosophy and Literature, with a thesis focusing on the Romantic author Wilhelm von Schütz, which was also filled with this almost mystical *völkisch* spirit. At that point, he was not exceptionally anti-Semitic by the standards of the time. But he was soon to become so, and, crucially, he understood the hatred of those who were.

Dr Goebbels (he came to be known to colleagues as 'the Doctor' and never spurned an opportunity to flourish the title) was dazzled by National Socialism, and by the screaming rallies in which he suddenly felt himself part of a powerful community. That electric thrill of being conjoined – the ecstasy experienced on the opposite side by Eric Hobsbawm – was a phenomenon that came to absorb Goebbels. He was fixated by Hitler, and first met him after Hitler had served his prison sentence for the 1923 Beer Hall Putsch (an early attempted Nazi coup d'état in Munich that found its starting point in the cavernous Bürgerbräukeller). It was 1925, and Goebbels was convinced that he was in the presence of a man who would rule absolutely. By this stage, Goebbels's genius with media manipulation – the attention to detail with newspapers and posters, the impact of images of eagles and swastikas, even the shrewd use of humour – had commended him to the Nazi leader. By 1926, Goebbels was the Nazi Gauleiter of Berlin. At that point, the party's presence in the city was minimal, and those few members it did have got into ever fiercer clashes with communist supporters. Goebbels wanted to reach deep into the city's working-class districts and find not only seasoned street fighters – whose penchant for breaking faces came before ideology – but also more articulate followers who could be fashioned into 'political soldiers'.[14] He also needed what would now be termed a public relations campaign, not in any way to smooth or soften the image of the party, but to get it mentioned in the mainstream press.

In this sense, the National Socialist rallies being attacked by the communist Red Front could be useful in drumming up publicity; but Goebbels understood the Red Front better than he understood the carefully calibrated technocracy of the Weimar Republic. He himself had not recoiled in any way from the Leninist revolution in Russia; rather, he saw it in the Romantic terms of a rebirth or regeneration, and a brilliant loosening of the chains of capitalism. His fervour was directed towards effecting a revolution in Germany; it would take a different political form but it would still mark the triumphant ascension from the demands of international capital. The difference was that Goebbels had ascribed Germany's failings to a conspiracy theory, and in promulgating that conspiracy theory – the shadowy powers behind banking and the media – he was igniting the rage of ever-growing numbers of Nazi followers.

Yet Berlin's communists were essential to his plans, and, when Goebbels organized a public Nazi meeting in the working-class district of Wedding, his hopes were surpassed. The event took place at the Pharus Halls, and even before it had got properly underway communist fighters had burst in and swarmed onto the stage. This went beyond a brawl; the weaponry involved on both sides was deadly serious. There were 'heavy chains, brass knuckles' and 'iron rods' and large numbers of people received broken noses and bones, as well as other injuries requiring hospitalization. But, when the numbers were tallied, it appeared, at least according to Goebbels, that it was the Red Front who came off worst, with dozens hurt. It was this particular bout of carefully calculated violence that brought the party into the main Berlin newspapers. Goebbels did not require their approval; it was neither here nor there. What he needed was coverage of the fact that the Nazi Party was attracting working men, and that they – innocent pacifists all – were the victims of brutal attacks from Marxist terrorists.

Away from the headlines, these 'terrorists' were guided by leaders such as Walter Ulbricht, a young man with an intense gaze who in 1928, aged thirty-five, was elected to the Reichstag. Ulbricht was the purest of communist apparatchiks, having spent time at the International Lenin School of the Comintern in Moscow, and who declared that the aim of his party was 'the defeat of our own government . . . and to establish a Soviet regime'.[15] (The path he was to take through the maze of history would lead him in the years to come – via the International Brigade in the Spanish Civil War and Stalin's Terror in Russia, where he was based throughout the Second World War – ultimately back home to dominate both Berlin and, later, East Germany, exercising power to an extent that Goebbels could never have imagined.)

In the late 1920s and early 1930s Berlin was a city fluttering with multiple newspapers with large readerships, and in Goebbels's *Der Angriff* the focus of editorial anger was not communism as a movement but Jewish people, who could conveniently be identified with Bolshevism, as well as with high finance, publishing and the media. *Der Angriff* specialized in hideous caricatures of Jewish stereotypes, suggesting that, rather than forming an essential part of the city's organic spirit, they were infiltrating, seizing control, even directing international events. This was a fire that – in some quarters of the industrialized city – did not need a great deal of stoking. The fact that Goebbels himself had come relatively late to his own pathologically anti-semitic beliefs made his energetic promulgation of them all the darker.

## 5.   The Road That Led into Darkness

In the rich light of a bronze sunset, the flashing gold reflection had been visible from across the River Spree and the densely populated streets all around. Now it was dulled; a magnificent structure torn down not by Nazi malice, but by Allied incendiary bombs. The once richly detailed synagogue was empty and in wet ruins. In the first darkening years of oppression, it had offered the comfort of community; now it was a physical representation of the fact that comfort was illusory. The intention of the Nazis had been to make Berlin *judenfrei*, and the process had the quality of a slowly suffocating nightmare. From 1933 Jewish people were denied their professions, then steadily robbed of their businesses, then forbidden the pleasures, from park walks to concerts to favourite restaurants, open to all their fellow citizens; finally, in the blacked-out nights of war, they were forced from their homes for deportation by rail to destinations they could not envisage. Neighbours looked on silently as apartments were plundered, or occupied by low-ranking officials. By 1943 the authorities declared that Berlin was 'free' of Jews. And yet somehow, in those days in 1945, as the city awaited the gathering fury of the approaching forces, there were still survivors and fugitives moving lightly through the shadows. Even in the centre of Nazi oppression, there were some younger Jewish people doing all they could to evade the panopticon gaze of the Gestapo. The hollow synagogue on Oranienburger Strasse had once been a symbol of a city where this kind of horror had seemed inconceivable. There had been a time when Berlin itself had been a sanctuary.

Broadly speaking, the city had never really exulted in ornamentation; even the grander houses and palaces were dull neoclassical constructions that could have been placed in any other European city without raising either eyebrows or even any interest. But back in 1866, the novelty of this synagogue's great dome of glittering gold, flanked by two smaller domes on towers of rich terracotta colours, had proclaimed a fresh era of openness. The shape of this magnificent construction was almost a fantasia of orientalism, the domes deliberately suggestive of Mediterranean lands, and it was a spectacular counterpoint to the more dour, brown-bricked, twin-spired churches that otherwise rose above the city streets. It was the work of Eduard Knoblauch, replacing an eighteenth-century temple that was no longer large enough for the city's needs. The inauguration of this dazzling structure was attended by Otto von Bismarck, then prime minister of Prussia in this pre-unified Germany.

This was not the only synagogue, and perhaps nor was it even the most aesthetically pleasing. Just a mile or so to the north-east on Rykestrasse was a later, turn-of-the-century temple that – from the outside – seemed an echo of the city's modern industrial identity: intricate arrangements of red brick in arches contrasted with discreet flashes of gold in the lintels. The interior was calmer and more timeless: a prospect of cream and green, red and gold. In the years that were to follow the Nazi regime, it was the synagogue of Rykestrasse that would be at the centre of the efforts to come to terms with the existential horror that had been visited upon its congregants, and all their fellows across the continent. Before that darkness, these and the ten other synagogues that were constructed near the centre of Berlin should have been the most powerful sign that the city's Jewish population – steadily rising throughout the nineteenth century – was intrinsically woven into the fabric of the city's life.

Yet, despite that population growing to some 180,000 in the early years of the twentieth century, there was still in other quarters a constant sense of ambivalence. It was to do with the question posed by gentiles about belonging. Generally speaking, and as an example, if a family had lived for many generations in one country, or one city, then why would anyone think to ask if that family was 'assimilated' into the city's culture? Surely that family was as central a part of that city's life as anyone else, and not standing somewhere outside of it? Yet the term 'assimilation' echoed through Berlin's history.

On one level, this city was marvellously, conspicuously cosmopolitan, most especially in the years following the First World War. Additionally, and ironically, it has been observed that, even under the blackest skies of Nazism and the Second World War, that cosmopolitanism continued, if in a grimly different fashion, the city and its factories now filled with hundreds of thousands of forced labourers, prisoners drawn from right the way across the continent. Poles mingled with Russians and French on busy production lines and in spartan residential barracks. The conditions they lived in were a grotesque contrast to what had gone before. Broadly, Berlin's reputation for openness had pre-dated Weimar (notably, the eighteenth-century philosopher Moses Mendelssohn was gradually pulled into the embrace of Berlin academia and the court of Frederick the Great, thus inaugurating a new era of stability and acceptance for Jewish people). In 1866 the Neue Synagoge spoke of a burgeoning confidence – even though Jews in Berlin still did not have full citizenship. Here was a faith that was determined not to hide, rather to proclaim itself dazzlingly from all the streets around. This was at a time when, hundreds of miles to the east in lands under Tsarist tyranny, Jewish people were being terrorized by official decree. By contrast, this was a city in which a large community – in a variety of professions, from tailors to bankers, shopkeepers to scientists, clerks to philosophers, cafe proprietors to professors of literature – could prosper unmolested. 'I was so confident about being a German, a European, a twentieth-century man,' wrote Victor Klemperer of that earlier Berlin. 'Blood? Racial hatred? Not today, not here – at the centre of Europe!'[1] Religious life was centred on arguments about tradition and ceremony. Yet there remained the question, always asked by others: were they assimilated?

The term demonstrated that that historic image of openness had always had defined limits. For a long time throughout the nineteenth century, Jewish men were forbidden to join the army, still less to dream of belonging to the smart officer corps. By the time of the Great War they were finally welcome to enlist; but even after the sacrifices made in those trenches of blood, the question of assimilation was still being asked. Worse: there were non-Jews who in the aftermath sought to deny that Jews had fought and died at all. Some 10,000 Jewish men perished in the conflict, a huge proportion of the Jewish population; but although medals were issued and full honours bestowed, a number of resolute and bitter anti-Semites instead tried to insist that these soldiers had in fact shied away from the real fighting. The truth was that Berlin's Jews were very often more German in both sensibility and heritage than their gentile fellows, but by the early twentieth century culture was no longer held to be the chief indicator; instead 'race' became the new marker, with a continent-wide burst of enthusiasm for eugenics. Long before Heinrich Himmler had become obsessed with notions of Teutonic archetypes emerging from the chilly north, in opposition to desert-born Levantines, sections of Berlin society accepted their Jewish neighbours, bought their goods, employed their legal minds, rejoiced in their artistic and musical creativity, yet still never stopped seeing them as 'other'. Hannah Arendt piercingly identified the impossible positions that Jewish people had been placed in ever since the eighteenth century, even by gentile friends. 'Instead of being defined by nationality or religion,' she wrote, 'Jews were being transformed into a social group whose members shared certain psychological attributes and reactions, the sum total of which was supposed to constitute "Jewishness".'[2] This then stuck to every individual – a category other than German. As the storm of Nazism broke, even gentiles who were sympathetic to Judaism found it difficult to dissociate Jewish friends from malicious anti-Semitic caricatures and libels.

Thus, while the nightmarish speed with which the Nazis progressed from commercial boycotts to industrial mass murder could never have been predicted by a sane mind, the principle of anti-Semitism itself was not in any way a philosophical rupture: in the vicious days following the German defeat in 1918, one of the new novels flying off Berlin's bookstalls was an anti-Jewish potboiler titled *The Sin Against Blood*. It was not long after the Great War that – as well as the myth of the 'shirking' soldiers – the urban conspiracy theories began: that one of the reasons for the conflict was that it had been exacerbated by the powers of capitalism, Jewish 'profiteers' making money from armaments. Then there was another theory that, on examination, should perhaps have cancelled out the first – that the Russian Revolution of the Bolsheviks and the attempted German Revolution were masterminded by Jewish people seeking to spread the insidious doctrine of communism. This apparent contradiction – the ruthlessness and greed of capitalism, and the ideological fire of communism both being equally attributable to the Jewish people – is one that somehow persisted. Just as the pulp novels depicted Jewish villains as being fat, top-hatted cigar-chomping monsters of avarice, there was the equally shocking stereotype of the eastern European Jew: poor and dirty and the carrier of medieval diseases. This, plus the 1921 publication of the blood-libel hoax *The Protocols of the Elders of Zion*, and the continued belief that the press and academia were controlled by Jewish elites, meant that even a city as sophisticated as Berlin had pockets of anti-Semitism taking root in the darker corners. In some cases, the malevolence was murderous; even before the Brownshirts took to the streets, there were those whose hatred compelled them to plot bloody assassination.

Yet before, during and after the Second World War, right the way through to the division of the city between West and East, the story of the Jewish community in Berlin – its vertiginous rise, its systematic dismantling, its attempted obliteration and then the efforts in the years after the war for the city to rebuild and demonstrate atonement – is even more layered; for while brute anti-Semitism itself was predictable and common – the same stubborn stereotypes have continued to flare up elsewhere, all over the world, including in Britain – there were also bright outbreaks of philo-Semitism. These manifested even in the darkest of days, quiet and discreet at a time of spitting hysteria and cold-eyed mass murder. These acts spoke of citizens who were immune to vicious propaganda, preferring simply to see fellow human beings. Prejudice is rarely a surprise, but kindness can occasionally feel extraordinary. In the spring of 1945 there were still some Jews – a tiny number – left in Berlin; the vast majority had either been forced to the railway stations, there to board the trains pointing east, never to return or in many cases even to be heard of again. But a few, like Marie Jalowicz-Simon, had contrived to sink from the sight of the authorities with the aid of gentile friends. She and a handful of other young people around the city had shucked off the yellow stars on their coats and adopted non-Jewish identities.

Since the deportations had started in Berlin, there had always been whispers and rumours about where the Jewish people were being sent to. An entire point of the compass – 'the East' – became synonymous with death. Yet despite murder on an unprecedented scale, the Nazis had never quite been able to unpick the rich and complex

Jewish strands that were threaded through the life and culture of Berlin. There were Jewish people whose voices had helped form Berlin's understanding of itself, in ways that would prove much more lasting and durable than National Socialism. There had been the critic, essayist and philosopher Walter Benjamin, brought up in the west of the city in a prosperous household at the turn of the century, who observed the tiniest details of the streets and the parks (down to the innovative chocolate-dispensing machines), the students and the prostitutes, the dandies and the landladies, the salons and the rackety boarding houses, and gave Berlin a framework of urban philosophy. As a student in the days before the Great War, he and fellow scholars in the idealistic Youth Movement met in what they called 'The Meeting House' – rooms that Benjamin had rented, near 'the municipal railway viaduct' and 'the sluggish water of the Landwehr Canal'.[3] Benjamin was the exemplar of the Jewish Berliner who strove above all for *Kultur und Bildung* (culture and cultivation). He did not want revolution but desired dramatic social progress: 'It was a . . . heroic attempt to change the attitudes of people without changing their circumstances.'[4] And the aftermath of the war brought not revolution to Berlin, as he saw it, but something more like an unstoppable vortex: 'nothing remained unchanged but the clouds, and beneath these clouds, in a field of force of destructive torrents and explosions, was the tiny, fragile human body'.[5] Amid all this was a powerful sense of the 'last true élite of bourgeois Berlin'[6] within what seemed a solid foundation of civilization. He had a Proustian recall for the family and commercial networks of his youth: 'it was . . . certain that our suits would be bought at Arnold Müller's, shoes at Stiller's, and suitcases at Mädler's' and 'at the end of these commissions our hot chocolate with whipped cream would be ordered at Hillbrich's'.[7] (The contrast between that richly remembered world and the miserable end of Benjamin's life, by his own hand, in 1940 on the border between France and Spain as he sought escape from the Wehrmacht, intensified the poignancy of those recollections.) In those brief golden Berlin years of security, Benjamin's mother had favoured the Reform synagogue; his father the Orthodox. Benjamin in his youth showed a marked disinclination for either.

The same was true for many of his generation; but this did not mean that religious practice or feeling was overthrown. Lothar Orbach, born in 1924, remembered that his family and their friends believed in God and prayed, carefully observed the Passover table and the family Seder, and yet felt a distance from 'deeply devout Jews': 'We were Germans first, and Jews second, and disdained anyone for whom religion superseded national identity.'[8] Orbach's father had been among those Berlin Jews who had fought in the First World War, and, despite the anti-Semitism of some veterans' associations, he was not about to minimize the risks that he had taken for his country. 'He never went out without wearing his veteran's insignia, a black, red and gold ribbon, pinned to his lapel.'[9]

There was no such thing as a homogeneous Jewish community in Berlin, just as there was no such thing as a homogeneous Catholic one. But there were umbrella organizations, such as the Bund deutsch-jüdischer Jugend, which enfolded into itself an array of sporting, walking and political groupings. Within all these associations was a variety of voices: for instance, there were those who were passionately Zionist, and who campaigned for the establishment of the Jewish state in the Holy Land. Those who opposed them saw this as a form of romantic daydreaming; why would anyone wish to move to a landscape of desert antiquity when instead one could flourish amid the ever-accelerating modernity of Berlin? Orbach's parents were among a huge number of Jewish citizens who had reason to be grateful that the city was their home: in their instance, they had originally hailed from Pomerania in the east, which was suffocating by comparison.

'The self-deception of the intellectual Jews consisted in thinking that they had no "fatherland", for their fatherland actually was Europe,' wrote Hannah Arendt.[10] This was an observation made of Rosa Luxemburg, who herself had emigrated to Berlin from Switzerland; her intense linguistic skills – she was fluent in Russian, Polish and French as well as German – as well as her broader intelligence, gave her an immediate foothold in cities across the continent. The German-born Hannah Arendt was an example of a different branch of intellectual Jewish life. Born in Hanover, she had settled in Berlin and Heidelberg as a student in the early Weimar years. Leaning towards theology, she gravitated towards the philosophical seminars of the young Martin

Heidegger, author of *Being and Time*, who was articulating ideas of man being not merely a subjective observer but an entity inseparable from the world around him; a blend of existentialism and intense romanticism. Hannah Arendt, then seventeen, fell in love with the thirty-four-year-old Heidegger and they embarked upon an affair. Though the relationship soon ended, Arendt never left behind the influence that the philosopher had exerted upon her own method of thinking – despite the fact that, in 1933, he revealed himself to be a steadfast supporter of Hitler. He had not been furtive about this enthusiasm. 'Mankind is awakening,' he declared in 1931. 'Greatness is standing in the storm.'[11] During the course of their relationship in the mid 1920s, Heidegger and Arendt had discussed the *Augenblick* – the moment, the blink of an eye, the spark of spiritual rebirth when 'we shall all be changed'.[12] But that moment would seize them both at different times and in hideously different circumstances. None the less, Arendt's own academic fascination with German romanticism persisted. In 1929 she married Günther Stern and their Berlin apartment seemed in some ways the most perfect synecdoche of Weimar Berlin: thanks to the landlord's canny sense of making use of space, she and Stern had to make room for dance classes, which occupied the living room during the day; more than this, Arendt and the dancers also had to contend with a Bauhaus sculptor also working in the apartment – he just happened to be the son of the landlord.

Hannah Arendt, for whom an absolutely intrinsic aspect of Judaism was the life of the mind, was soon to see the viciousness of Nazism close-up when, in 1933, she was arrested by the Gestapo. She had argued in an essay that the new regime meant the absolute end of the idea of assimilation; and she began researching the extent of state anti-Semitism in the Prussian State Library, for a paper to be delivered in Prague. The Nazis had made such research illegal; Arendt was denounced by a librarian, and she and her mother spent eight days in custody being questioned. Upon release, they both fled for Switzerland.

Jewish families from all spheres were forced to hurriedly reframe their lives. There was a lavish department store on Friedrichstrasse called S. Adam, a family concern run by four brothers and famous for its rich range of luxury products – once the province of the aristocracy but now made available to wealthy middle-class Berliners. It also hosted grand charitable masked balls, a draw for the most refined layers of Berlin society. In 1930 the Adam business was caught in the first aftershocks of the Wall Street Crash; by 1932, it had been all but vaporized in the economic firestorm that hit the city. Then came the implacable Nazi campaign to boycott Jewish businesses, which meant commercial death (following which the Nazis would profitably step in to take over). It was soon clear to the Adam family that the new regime presented an immediate and terrible danger. Exile followed, and for one of the brothers, Fritz, an early death. His son and heir, thirteen-year-old Klaus, was sent to England and enrolled at St Paul's School. Very quickly, Klaus had to adjust to an isolated life in a strange land. He did so with intense energy, and indeed by 1939 was one of only three German-born pilots serving with the RAF, attacking the Luftwaffe with great courage. By the 1960s he had become Ken Adam, the hugely talented film production designer for the James Bond films, among others. He brought some Weimar architectural inspiration to those fantastical sets: using concrete, glass and fascinating angles, he created a world of heroes and villains that aesthetically would have been recognized in the Bauhaus. Years later, following the fall of the Berlin Wall, Sir Ken Adam returned to the city; there was, quite recently, a special film-museum exhibition focusing on his work.

There had also been a brief period before 1933 when Berlin offered solace to those who had been through trauma. This was the case for the orphaned Eric Hobsbawm, who had to leave Vienna, the city of his birth, with his sister. They came to live with comfortably off relatives. Like his recently deceased mother's, Hobsbawm's Jewishness did not extend to attending synagogue or observing ritual. Yet it was very much there as part of his identity as the historian-to-be surveyed his new home city. 'I came to Berlin in the late summer of 1931 as the world economy collapsed,' he wrote. 'The collapse of the world economy was up to a point something young persons of the middle class read about, rather than experienced directly.'[13] None the less, the consequences of that collapse were all too evident, like a series of volcanic eruptions. '[I]t dominated our skyline, like the occasionally smoking cones of the real volcanoes that tower over their cities . . . Vesuvius, Etna . . . Eruption was in the air we breathed. Since 1930 its symbol was familiar: the black swastika in a white circle on red ground.'[14]

Perhaps unusually for an intellectual, who would read everything that he could and at great speed, Hobsbawm was also intensely active; there was no aspect of Berlin that he was going to shy away from, even if it eventually meant confrontation. Away from the glittering modernism of the commercial centre, and in among the heavy nineteenth-century architecture of government, with its ponderous and pompous statues – not least those of the city's thirty-two rulers from 1415 to 1918 – he saw a city that had not quite managed to jettison its more reactionary Wilhelmine past. He understood that, elsewhere, pomp could have elegance; this was a quality that Vienna claimed. But, in Berlin, the effect was heavy and plodding. And, in any case, this was no place for teenagers. 'The Berlin in which the young of the middle classes lived . . . was a place to move about in, not stand and stare at streets,' he wrote. '[T]he point of those streets was that so many led to the really memorable part of the city, the rings of lakes and woods.'[15] Hobsbawm was a keen ice skater; conveniently, Berlin was 'notably' cold. Its citizens also had terrific vigour. 'It was a bullshit-detecting city,'[16] he wrote; even the local dialect and linguistic idioms were loaded with warm irreverence, and, unlike more fastidious Vienna, language was 'speeded up' and filled with wisecracks. He and his sister lived with their relatives in a large apartment in the smart Bavarian Quarter, but young Hobsbawm roamed around the entire city. How could one city contain him? He noted that his entire family lived in a 'transnational' world where movement was natural, especially when in search of career opportunities. His uncle, whose care he was now under, worked for Universal studios, an American company founded by Carl Laemmle, a German émigré who had never lost touch with Berlin.

There was no sense in Hobsbawm's education that his Jewishness marked him out as being exotic or 'other'. He attended the Prinz-Heinrich-Gymnasium, a solid, middle-class school that had appeared to have held on to a certain Prussian traditionalism: Protestant and conservative. 'Those of us who did not fit this pattern – whether as Catholics, Jews, foreigners, pacifists or left-wingers, felt ourselves as a collective minority, even though in no measurable way an excluded minority,'[17] he recalled.

As well as the rigorous teaching of Greek, Latin and mathematics, by teachers who seemed almost comically archetypical in their Prussian taste for tradition, the school also acknowledged that there was a wider world of physicality: the only time in Hobsbawm's life when he understood the point of exercise. Here, tradition loosened and freedom gathered momentum. The school had a long-established rowing club and, as a consequence, exclusive access to certain lake areas where the young people could meet on equal terms, and in the hazy warmth of summer evenings swim in the placid waters and talk. The schoolmasters – with their crew cuts and pale eyes – might have been irascible and impatient but they had hinterlands; they had fought in the Great War and now they were doing what they considered best for a new generation. They were good at encouraging their charges to head out of the city on youth-hostelling and hiking trips. And, even though they clearly did not care for youthful left-wing ideas, expressed with ferocity, neither were they closed to these intellectual avenues: in 1932, the shelves of Hobsbawm's school library contained copies of the works of radical dramatist Bertolt Brecht and *The Communist Manifesto* (any pupil expressing sympathy for communism was impelled by the teachers to actually go and read it).

Yet, as Hobsbawm wrote, it was very obvious that the country was the *Titanic* and that it was hitting the iceberg. The work of Hobsbawm's uncle with Universal Studios was threatened in 1932 not by the Nazis but by Chancellor Franz von Papen's desperate attempts to stabilize the economy. There was a new protectionist law compelling multinational firms operating in Berlin to employ mainly Germans. Hobsbawm's uncle was Polish; his job vanished. In order to make a living, he and his wife left Germany. The young Eric and his sister were now left in the care of another aunt, who lived in an apartment by a railway line, in a house filled with lodgers. The aunt would spend evenings with the tenants, beguiling them with horoscopes and tales of psychic phenomena (fortune-telling was popular in 1930s Berlin; in the last days of the war, Joseph Goebbels was similarly drawn to consulting horoscopes). By this time, Hobsbawm had been fully inducted into the Communist Party, and was receiving comfort from the sense of being part of a worldwide movement that would surely only gather in strength from its existing stronghold in the USSR. When Hitler was appointed Chancellor in January 1933, Hobsbawm remembered reading the headline in the paper; just weeks later, with parliament dissolved ahead of a new election, the Brownshirt squads were now auxiliary police, accompanying the officers to raid the Communist Party headquarters. The Reichstag went up in flames on 27 February, and, from this point, all freedom in Germany was stamped out. Free speech, a free press, even any opposition expressed in private telephone calls, would invite retribution. Communists were being arrested, detained, tortured. Before his own branch of the Communist Party was raided, Hobsbawm hid the apparatus for printing leaflets in his room at home. He was intensely alive to the danger; what had once been a matter of exultant marches through freezing winter Berlin streets had now attained the quality of a nightmare. The Berlin communists had never quite understood that others wanted power very much more badly than them.

Through the agency of Hobsbawm's uncle, the teenager and his sister were removed from Berlin in 1933 and sent to England, where they found sanctuary. For many other young Jewish people in Berlin, the possibilities were more frighteningly limited. While some families discussed the wisdom of emigrating – to either Britain, America or Palestine – others attempted to reshape their lives around the swiftly enacted aggression from the regime: not merely the boycott of Jewish businesses, but the extraordinarily painful expulsion of Jews from professional and academic positions. As well as the pain, there was the fear: the essential effect of the Nuremberg Laws (placing Nazi anti-Semitism and persecution within a newly drawn-up legal framework) was to strip away full citizenship, and this meant concomitantly stripping away the protection of the rule of law. The Jews of Germany, and Berlin, now faced the terrifyingly destabilizing prospect that the authorities could maltreat them without any legal constraint. They could be made, in essence, unpersons – no rights, no recourse to the law. In time, they would even have new names assigned to them, to further signify their Jewishness as their sole identifying characteristic, and thus their separation from free people. This was a road that led to a terrifying terminus.

There were also those in the city who had never given much thought to their Jewish heritage, but who now felt that atavistic aggression: the Nazis brought a note of hysteria to their cataloguing of previous generations in the search for 'impure' blood. In 1934 Ruth-Johanna Eichenhofer was a schoolgirl; her father was a vet. She was required by her school to join the League of German Girls (the female equivalent of the Hitler Youth). This involved a bureaucracy intended to ensnare. Eichenhofer's paternal grandfather was Jewish; her grandmother was Protestant. Eichenhofer's parents had to submit a form listing three generations of forebears, highlighting any who were Jewish. In her youthful innocence, Eichenhofer suggested to her father that they could simply change the names of the relatives – some of them Berlin bankers – on his side of the family. That way, no questions would be asked and she would be free to do what was expected of her in the League. Her father agreed, the forms were submitted and in the years that followed, she recalled, he was racked with ever-mounting anxiety. Eichenhofer was blithely certain that the forms would simply be stuffed into a cabinet somewhere and forgotten. But her father understood the sociopathically rigorous nature of Nazi anti-Semitism, and was tormented by the idea of his lies being exposed, and the retributions that might follow. When he died of kidney disease in 1941, his daughter was certain that the never-ending fear was a contributing factor to his illness.[18]

For Berlin's gentile children, the treatment of their classmates and friends as the 1930s darkened was a source of bewilderment; this was a time when parents considered it unwise to speak too openly or frankly about what was happening. Brigitte Lempke and her family lived in an apartment building, and one of her favourite neighbours was Herr Handke, a professional musician. In 1938, she recalled, he was suddenly 'no longer there'.[19] When his absence became prolonged, and the silence too curious to tolerate, Lempke asked the neighbours around the building if they knew where Handke had gone. She was told that he had been sent to perform the trumpet in some kind of camp in Poland. In that year, the dissolution of citizenship meant that those Jews who were deemed to be Polish were simply deported from Germany, east over the border. The Polish authorities (who had themselves been seeking to limit the numbers of Polish Jews returning to the country from Germany by demanding special passport stamps) were as stunned as those families who, with no notice, suddenly had to leave their homes and enter a dread-filled world where their passports and papers, their savings and their belongings, no longer had any kind of meaning. Refugee camps had to be established on the border. There was another unaccountable disappearance in 1938: Lempke's classmate Friedel Schneider. After the school holidays, Friedel had 'stopped coming to class'. Lempke was puzzled: she surely wasn't so unacademic that she had simply 'dropped out of school'.[20] Again, she asked around, and was told airily that Friedel and her family had now moved to Poland. At the time, Brigitte thought that in one sense her friend was perhaps better off over the border, for 9 November that year brought the terrifying pogrom that came to be known as *Kristallnacht*.

No ordinary person that night could have immediately comprehended the full scale of the carefully coordinated destruction and brutality that erupted in cities across the entire country. The pretext: the shooting in Paris of a German official. Throughout the day, preparations were made by the troopers and the Brownshirts for a premeditated assault on Berlin's Jews. Teenager Lothar Orbach, who lived with his family in the north-east of the city, watched the planned attack as it began on his street: lines of open military trucks drawing up, troopers leaping out screaming '*Jude verrecke, Juden raus!*' ('Jews should die, out with the Jews').[21] Across the road was a millinery business; the troopers not only smashed all of its windows but also dragged the petrified owners, the Sochachevers, out into the street. They were forced to wear placards around their necks that proclaimed that Germans should not buy from Jews. As Orbach noted, this injunction did not preclude looting, and within minutes fellow Berliners were rushing into the wide-open store and emerging 'wearing elegant new hats'. There was a chocolatier nearby called Friedlaender, whose business was 'destroyed'; as soon as the premises had been smashed, local children – amazed at the opportunity – ran into the shop and emerged with armfuls of sweets, and 'chocolate all over their faces'.[22]

The correspondent from the London *Times* hastened around the city as its synagogues faced desecration. He described 'scenes of systematic plunder and destruction which have seldom had their equal in a civilized country since the Middle Ages'.[23] He noted that nine of Berlin's twelve synagogues had been set ablaze. 'The synagogue in the Fasanenstrasse . . . was entered by a mob of young hooligans who destroyed the interior furnishings of the building and carried off the altar cloth. This was solemnly burned in the neighbouring Wittenbergplatz in the presence of a large crowd.'[24] The correspondent made his way into the centre of the city to the Kurfürstendamm, the elegant shopping district where many of the businesses were still – just – in the hands of their rightful Jewish owners. 'This morning,' he wrote on the day after *Kristallnacht*, '[on] the chief shopping street of Berlin, Jew-hunts were in progress. On two occasions I saw terrified Jews running before a small crowd of pursuers . . . in one instance a woman was in the hands of a crowd, who had her backed against a wall.' What had begun as coordinated destruction now took on a terrible flavour of frenzied anarchy. A smart cafe was smashed and its bottles of wines and spirits looted – by members of the Hitler Youth, among them 'little boys'.[25] The childish malice had also apparently possessed the old. 'An elderly ex-serviceman was engaged in battering his way into a Jewish dressmaker's shop by beating with a vacuum cleaner upon the handsome walnut screen which backed the window.' A furniture store was attacked: 'Powerful young men picked up the delicate satin covered chairs and sofas and dashed them against the walls until they were reduced to matchwood.'[26] Looting at least had some terrible greedy rationale: this was simply ungovernable hate.

For the correspondent of the *Daily Telegraph*, it was as though something had taken possession of the city. 'Mob law ruled in Berlin,' he wrote. 'Racial hatred and hysteria seemed to have taken complete hold of otherwise decent people. I saw fashionably dressed women clapping their hands and screaming with glee while respectable middle-class mothers held up their babies to see the "fun".'[27] And with the looting and the destruction came the killings. 'The caretaker of the synagogue in the Prinzregentenstrasse is reported to have been burned to death together with his family.'[28] Yet extraordinarily, in the midst of this violence, the torched Neue Synagoge was saved; it had found an unexpected and courageous defender in the form of policeman Wilhelm Krützfeld, who confronted the SA arsonists and – arguing that he was acting to protect surrounding buildings – bought time for local firefighters to quell the blaze that had been started (another act of defiance, since fire services everywhere had been instructed that they were not to intervene). The synagogue's more comprehensive destruction would come in 1943 at the hands of the Allies and their incendiary bombing campaign.

Elsewhere in the city that night there were lynchings, two reported in the east and two in the west. Amid the bloodshed, women were hurrying through the smashed entrances of fashion stores on the Kurfürstendamm and helping themselves 'to stockings and underwear'.[29] Although civil society itself seemed at that moment gossamer-thin, the bloodlust was not universally contagious. There were gentile onlookers who were shocked at seeing Jewish citizens terrorized by adolescent boys. Few dared to protest openly, but a number expressed a sense of shame as well as fear. One told the *Times* correspondent: 'One working man remarked to me that as a German he would not like to see the photographs that would appear tomorrow in the foreign papers.'[30]

Young Reinhart Crüger's grandmother lived on Sophienstrasse, just a few streets across the river from Museum Island and close to the Oranienburger Strasse synagogue. Crüger's grandmother was neither Jewish nor anti-Semitic; the area in which she lived had long been a Jewish neighbourhood. Even in 1939, at a point when large numbers of Jews had managed to emigrate, there were ever larger numbers who could not. Leaving Germany came at a substantial price: the Nazi government demanded money, valuables and property like some form of ransom. Those who could not leave Berlin were facing the inexorable tightening of the persecution: the seizure of businesses and the impossibility of finding a professional position (even highly qualified doctors were having to find ways of hustling for employment); the tightly restricted hours for shopping; the ban on using any form of public transport, from the underground to the trams; the ban upon walking through certain districts, squares and parks; the ever-shrinking rations, leading to continuous hunger. Soon all this would be followed by the compulsion into forced labour in Berlin's mighty factories. Little Reinhart Crüger had scant idea of any of this. The lives of gentiles, although conducted in the same streets, and in adjacent houses, might as well have been in a wholly separate dimension. But there were times when it was possible to see across that gulf.

Crüger's grandmother lived in a peaceful apartment house with a 'creaking staircase' and a view of 'chestnut trees' and the nearby Sophienkirche. 'Nazi-minded residents were less common here than in other parts of the city,' Crüger recalled decades later, '[but] the Jews tried to live as inconspicuously as possible because of the political climate.'[31] None the less, 'they got along well with their neighbours' and even by early 1939, in that small grid of streets, they were still treated as 'fellow citizens'.[32] The boy was taken shopping with his grandmother and one of the destinations was a department store formerly known as Wertheim; this smart and elegant Jewish-owned business, with branches across the country, was among those stolen by the Nazis and now traded under the name AWAG. The boy was only very vaguely aware that this was a primarily Jewish neighbourhood; he did not, he said, 'recognize the Jews among the passers-by'. There were exceptions: he was fascinated by those men he saw wearing 'double-brimmed hats, full beards and long black coats'.[33] His grandmother explained to him the customs and traditions of the Orthodox Jewish community. On subsequent visits, as the months progressed, the boy noticed that he saw fewer and fewer such figures.

With the war now thundering across Europe and the world, the boy, now twelve, returned to visit his grandmother in 1941. Leaving the U-Bahn at Hackescher Markt, he was instantly shocked by what he saw:

> The otherwise familiar area seemed somehow different to me. I stopped and looked around. Then it fell like scales from my eyes: the yellow Jewish stars on people's clothes! Wherever I looked, whether in the direction of Oranienburger, Rosenthaler or Dircksen Strasse, I could see passers-by with the Star of David. I was amazed and

horrified at the same time. So many Jewish citizens still lived in this part of the city. They crept along the pavement with embarrassed and frightened faces. This measure against the Jewish population was only a few days old.[34]

And it was clear to him what the stars meant: vulnerability to attack, the ever-present dread of denunciation. This was beyond robbing people of citizenship; this was a government branding a religious minority and making them targets for both official malice and random violence. The boy asked his grandmother what she knew about it, 'bombarding her' with questions: 'Is it right what the Nazis are doing to them?' 'Do you know any of them personally?'[35] His grandmother did, and she implored the boy to be discreet. She told him that of course she still greeted her neighbours, and still stopped for conversations in the street. But she also, quietly, and expressly against every regulation, helped out a few of her neighbours with extra rations, for even by 1941 the food available to Berlin's Jews was scarcely enough to avoid malnutrition. Large numbers of homes had already been appropriated, and Jewish people were being compelled to move into increasingly cramped shared accommodation.

Then the mass deportations began, conducted via meticulous bureaucratic principles:

> One day, at the beginning of October 1941, our neighbour Mrs Hohenstein received a form from the Jewish community in which she had to list her possessions . . . we didn't take these lists very seriously but Mr Hefter from the Jewish community seemed almost bewildered, saying that one thousand Jews would be picked from their houses and deported that evening. The one thousand people were those that had received 'the lists' . . . Just after eight o'clock that evening, two Gestapo officers demanded to be let into Mrs Hohenstein's room. No more than ten minutes later, Mrs Hohenstein came to us, face as white as a sheet, to tell us she was being taken away. The 'gentlemen' didn't know where she was going. Then the 'gentlemen' led her to the door. We heard it slam behind them and listened to the quiet little steps and the echo of boots stamping down the stairs. Then it was all silence again.[36]

An old lady on a night-time autumn street, flanked by two Gestapo officers, being walked to a holding centre in a once-familiar old-people's home; the faces of others, similarly torn from their homes; coats, scarves, light suitcases. Some men and women, wrapped up against the night, talked in tight tones of their forthcoming 'journey'; others exchanged prayers, blessings and farewells. From there, the military truck, the drive through the bomb-blackened city, then the arrival not at an ordinary railway station but at the crude and stark prospect of Grunewald freight depot. This, then, was the first steep slide into dehumanization; the old women and men who will have known that there was no possibility of making appeals to the young men who were supervising their removal from the city; no possibility of learning their destination. Even if they were treated at this stage with relative gentleness, there was the remorselessness too. They were now simply freight.

In January 1942, in a charming house overlooking the frozen Wannsee, SS-Obergruppenführer Reinhard Heydrich and other senior Nazis met for a conference to discuss 'the final solution to the Jewish question'.[37] This conference had emerged from discussions with Hermann Goering and others to do with the 'General Plan for the East'. The mass killing of Jews was already underway in Poland and in other territories. By the end of 1941, with the Wehrmacht pushing through Russia, bringing fire and death to towns and villages as they progressed, Hitler had reached the conclusion that all Jews had to be eliminated – not just the millions in the freshly occupied killing grounds of the east, but the Jewish populations from the entirety of Europe too. This vision of Hell – mass murder on a scale never before conceived, in addition to plans for slave labour and deliberate starvation – took the form, in this elegant villa, of a bureaucratic exercise (followed by a richly catered buffet lunch): the logistics of transportation, the railway capacity, the cataloguing of different age groups so that some people might be spared in order to carry out heavy labour. This was not a matter of intimidated underlings obeying orders: Heydrich and the others gathered in those warm rooms overlooking the lake were wholly convinced that the Jewish people as a whole had to be eradicated, as though they were a form of contagion. That this could be believed by a few monstrous fanatics was comprehensible, if terrifying: what was even more terrifying was that there were so many others, in Berlin and beyond, who could be made to believe it too.

And, by that January of 1942, Reinhart Crüger's grandmother on Sophienstrasse had found herself one evening being visited by the Gestapo. 'There had been a knock at my grandmother's door,' recalled Crüger. The Gestapo operative who stood there had said to her (as she later related): 'Heil Hitler, Frau Crüger, can I speak to you for a moment?' The old lady guided him through to the living room and he explained why he was there. He said: 'You know that there are still many Jews living on Sophienstrasse?', adding that 'a Jewish couple' were known to have an apartment in that very house. The Gestapo officer continued: 'We have an official list here detailing all the Jewish residents of the neighbourhood. So you can see that we are keeping a close eye on the Jews. And that's what we expect from you, too, dear Frau Crüger!'[38]

The woman stayed silent, allowing the officer to warm to his theme:

> All German citizens must defend themselves against these disgusting and inferior enemies of our Fatherland. For this reason, keep your eyes and ears open when it comes to the Jews. You must report any suspicious sightings – for example, if you see people moving around with suitcases and large bags – to police station 16 at Hackescher Markt immediately. I insist that you honour this duty! But the whole thing should be a matter of course for every German citizen, shouldn't it? Heil Hitler!

'When the visitor had left,' remembered Crüger, 'my grandmother simply stood petrified in the hallway. Those minutes when she had listened to all this must have been terrible for her.'[39] For this was the human consequence of the icy psychosis of the Wannsee Conference: men and women and children awaiting in terror for the ring of the doorbell. Some were told that they were being sent to special 'colonies'; others, more insidiously, that they were being removed from Berlin for their own safety from the Allied bombing raids – an innocent evacuation, nothing more. Crüger, once more staying with his grandmother, was witness one night to the cold horror of the round-ups: down in the street he saw a covered truck into which men and women with stars on their coats were being directed to climb. Then the noise of movement from downstairs: an apartment bell being rung. Crüger's grandmother, having warned her grandson to stay away from the window – if anyone saw him staring he could 'get into trouble' – now stood 'trembling' by her own apartment door, ear pressed against the wood, trying to discern what was happening below. The voices echoed up the stairwell. 'Is your name Heinrich Israel Lewin?' A fainter noise of assent. 'Show me your identification!' Again, the silence of obedience. 'You and your wife are to prepare yourselves to leave. Please pack no more than one suitcase and one bag. You will be ready within ten minutes.' As this chilling scenario was played out downstairs, Crüger's grandmother very gently opened her front door, sternly telling her grandson to keep absolutely quiet, but as she tried to take a look down the stairwell there came the noise of someone climbing up. In fear, she swiftly and softly shut her door again. She explained that the Gestapo and the SS never liked the sense that they were being watched. 'They don't want witnesses to their dirty work. Disgusting! Disgusting!'[40]

It is impossible to get a sense of how many of these deportees knew what lay before them in the forests of the east. Yet astonishingly – in the face of the Nazis' all-enveloping and all-seeing bureaucracy, cataloguing thousands upon thousands of people, and working through them inexorably – a few of Berlin's Jews seized rare chances to become fugitives: to change their names and become 'divers', or 'U-Boats', plunging deep into a shadow city of deception. A few months after the Sophienstrasse incident, the vast majority of Berlin's Jews had been taken from the city, and huge numbers of them had already been murdered. But for Lothar Orbach and his mother – who were extremely fortunate to have several intensely loyal gentile friends among their neighbours – there was just one mad, terrifying chance. The ring on their doorbell came on Christmas Eve, as traditional carols were playing on the radio. The visit had been prepared for. As the middle-aged Gestapo officers explained to the young Lothar that he and his mother were being removed from the city for their own good, Lothar's mother – pretending to be in the

bathroom – was readying their bags by the back door while Lothar
offered his would-be captors some ersatz coffee and fruit cake to
warm them up on this Christmas night while his mother got ready.
They accepted this hospitality. Leaving them in the living room, the
son and mother quietly stepped out of the back door and knew in
that instant that they could never walk back into their own world.

Their escape was far from guaranteed; they were in the block's
inner courtyard and the only way out was through someone else's
apartment. They thought they could count on the concierge, but
suddenly, even though her lights were on, she was refusing to
acknowledge their soft knocks. They tried other back doors of lit
apartments, but these too stayed firmly closed. Their neighbours
were terrified of endangering themselves. Eventually, satiated with
their coffee and cake, the Nazis in their apartment realized their victims had gone. The cry went up throughout the building: 'Anyone
caught hiding Jews will be shot!'[41]

And it was at that point that Lothar and his mother heard a thin
whisper from a balcony above; an old lady called Else Mueller
beckoned them to come up and conceal themselves under her bed.
The Nazis came to her door, but the old lady had taken the precaution of putting on a swastika armband and declaring, as they came up
to her landing: 'Did you catch those damn Jews?'[42] From their hiding place Lothar and his mother could see the jackboots, but the men
took Frau Mueller as one of their own. Later, in the silence of that
Christmas Eve, she told her neighbours that the Nazis had driven her
husband to suicide; everything about the regime was an abomination
to her. Over the next few days, the Orbachs adopted new names,
new identities. Elsewhere, the same was true of Marie Jalowicz-
Simon. They had all divined that they were at the edge of the abyss,
and that there was nothing further to be lost.

Apartments were ransacked; the grander houses in the suburbs,
which had once belonged to Jewish academics and industrialists, were
simply stolen by party officials. Valuables were looted, treasured keepsakes destroyed. As well as the annihilation of the flesh, the Nazis
also sought to erase memory; the officials who escorted the men
and the women and the children – with their single suitcases – to the
assembly point at the synagogue, and then on to the railway depot,

had long ago ceased acknowledging their essential humanity, their terror and their innocence. It had taken less than a generation for Berlin's Jews to be regarded as dangerous foreign matter that had to be expelled. Yet, while there seemed something icy and ineluctable about the propulsion towards homicide, the burning sadism at the heart of this hatred had been glaringly apparent even in the smallest of the sanctions taken against the community.

One of these had been the banning of Jews from cinemas. On its own, this was an edict with no logic or purpose; what conceivable harm to gentile Berliners could its Jewish people do in a cinema? Why could there not even be specially segregated Jewish cinemas, as there were with cafes and restaurants? But the cruelty was incandescently clear; the authorities understood very well that in ever more oppressive days, cinema was a psychic balm that people needed very badly. These comedies and musicals and thrillers were not merely simple pastimes, they were a chance to wholly immerse anxious minds in worlds that offered up different possibilities of compassion, laughter, excitement, love and justice. More than this, the Jews were specifically denied the rich artistic pleasure that they had played such a strong part in conceiving. There had been a time when Berlin – more than nascent Hollywood – had led with this new medium that had caught the imagination worldwide. After the war, it would be via film that the world would be forced to witness and confront the magnitude of the horror that had been visited upon the Jews. Long before that, the city had understood – and the Nazis in their own mirrored fashion had also grasped – that film itself could shape reality and the course of history.

## 6.  The Projection of Dreams

The gaunt young man, in his simple lodging room, stared with dread into the full-length mirror. His reflection gazed back at him, but with a different, unrecognizable expression. The young man was motionless, but, to his horror, his reflection began to move with a malicious deliberation. Then the reflection stepped forth from out of the mirror, at which the hearts of hundreds quickened with pleasurable fear. Did any of them also feel some subconscious tremor of recognition? *The Student of Prague* was a 1913 Berlin-made horror film so popular that it was remade twice; the city's audiences were always drawn to the uncanny. Yet how many who went to see the 1935 talkie remake – a production sanctioned by the Nazis – considered that this story of a reflected evil self might have been inspired by a normal-seeming society where abnormal violence was flourishing?

Ten years later, in early April 1945, the suburban Berlin picture houses that had not been burned by bombs (before the war, there were about 300 cinemas dotted throughout the city) were still showing their flickering phantasmagorias. Berliners were passionate about film; the medium in its earlier days had helped define the modern city. For many, like schoolgirl Helga Hauthal, it was an addiction: the great pale beam in the darkness. But unlike the other lights of the city, this, for her, was the evocation of better, more beautiful worlds. Within days, the surviving cinemas were at last forced by the authorities to close, and, to a great many adolescents, this was a source of almost physical pain. For Helga, any films starring the actress and singer Marika Rökk were as vivid as life itself.[1] Frau Rökk's speciality was romance and musical comedies, and her style was that of effortless glamour. She had been recruited by the film studio UFA in the 1930s in direct response to the concern of Joseph Goebbels that the ever-expanding Hollywood industry – if unchecked – would conquer and swamp the German imagination; the country – and the Nazi regime – needed stars who could match and outshine Ginger

Rogers and Carole Lombard. Marika Rökk, a trained ballet dancer of Hungarian heritage, brought elegance of movement and seductive lightness of touch to all her roles. She was frequently paired with the extremely popular actor Johannes Heesters, himself a matinee idol. For Helga, these sophisticated romances seemed a blueprint for life. She yearned to return to the cinema to immerse herself in these exquisitely calculated escapist stories.[2]

In broader terms, this desire to spend huge amounts of time in cinemas was common across the city; it was common also in the highest reaches of the Nazi hierarchy. There had been a point where Hitler had been attending private screenings of two films an evening. He never favoured anything too artistic or highbrow. In this, he and much of the Berlin population understood each other perfectly. It was in Berlin that the new medium of cinema had first been raised to a proper global art, in the earliest days of Weimar. And it was partly through cinema that the citizens of Berlin had come to frame their understanding of their home: in the 1920s and early 1930s there had been hugely popular social realist films chronicling the everyday life of the Berlin streets and the people moving through them. The city was fascinated with its own cinematic image. This continued under the Nazis, through films that were calculated to show the newly regimented people and the newly reordered streets, fluttering with swastikas, to the most impressive effect. And even by the spring of 1945, with the whirring projectors now silent, something of the extraordinary spirit and creativity of German cinema had – quite independently of the Nazis – managed not only to survive but also to thrive.

It was there in the young actress Hildegard Knef, who only months beforehand had been signed to a major studio; yet by March 1945 – preparing to disguise herself as a male soldier in the defence trenches around Berlin in order to escape the violent sexual attentions of the Red Army – Knef was summoning a resourcefulness that far exceeded the imaginations of most screenwriters. An enigmatic form of that creativity was still to be found in the thoughtful actor Paul Wegener, who had in 1920 earned worldwide fame with his haunting and beautiful cinematic vision of a Jewish folk tale, and yet who had found himself later co-opted by Goebbels into Nazi historical epics. In March 1945, Wegener was still living in his exotically decorated home in the south-west of the city, and preparing himself for atonement. And the spirit flickered elsewhere in one particularly sparky and engaging writer – so engaging that, even with his obvious antipathy to Nazism, Goebbels had sought out his imaginative talent for a 1943 cinematic fantasy epic in full colour: *Münchhausen*. That writer was Erich Kästner. His had been among the first novels to be burned in intimidating pyres in 1933. Yet in the spring of 1945, Kästner had somehow not only survived the regime but was devising a means of escaping Berlin via the ruse of a cinematic screenplay.

These figures, in their own way, pointed to the vast importance of film in the wider German imagination, and would very much shape it after the war as well. One reason the medium held such a particular hypnotic hold on Berlin was that this was the city where by the 1920s film – and its production – had become luxuriant and legitimate art, as opposed to simple, gaudy, carnival attraction. Throughout the First World War, money had been channelled to the film-makers whose studios lay in the wooded southern suburbs of Berlin for the purpose of creating propaganda. But, as the war ended, this investment then went into an industry that might in part help redeem the German nation on the international stage.

In 1919, film was still silent. This, for Berlin's auteurs, was quite the reverse of a limitation. Rather, it offered them the possibilities of the world. Language is local; but an appealing image is universal. Directors and producers, such as those gathered in the huge Babelsberg studios of UFA, saw clearly how their dramas and comedies and fantasies might transcend borders, reaching not only into continental Europe but also to Britain and America. The Weimar era brought forth actors like Conrad Veidt, Marlene Dietrich and Emil Jannings; directors such as Ernst Lubitsch and Friedrich Wilhelm Murnau; productions such as *Faust*, *The Last Laugh* and *The Blue Angel*. Later in the decade, a young Jewish screenwriter drawn to this city from Vienna began his career observing the social interactions of young Berliners: his name was then spelled 'Billie' Wilder.

Wilder's earliest contribution to Berlin film remains fresh and modern today, even though it was one of the last silent productions. *Menschen am Sonntag* (People on Sunday), made in 1929–30, was both socially realistic and also pleasingly comic – a tale of four young

Berliners, two women and two men, who decide to spend a sunny summer Sunday messing about flirtatiously beside one of the city's lakes. The city itself was lightly drawn: busy streets drenched in sunshine, poky rented rooms with busy wallpaper, thriving cafes and shops, and great numbers of people flocking to the lakeside pleasure resort. The production – greeted with great critical and popular acclaim – was the result of Wilder and directors Robert Siodmak and Edgar G. Ulmer throwing ideas back and forth in the intensely fashionable Romanisches Café: swift jottings on paper napkins. None of the three seemed to have a sense at that point that their Berlin was disappearing, or that they would find themselves forced to emigrate and make new careers in America. *Menschen am Sonntag* portrayed a city and a youthful population at ease with itself. This was in the immediate aftermath of the Wall Street Crash; the resulting economic firestorm had yet to reach Berlin but it was approaching fast. Here was a moment of urban harmony captured indelibly: no swastikas, no Young Communists, no street fights, no slums. Wilder had recently come to Berlin from Vienna and was besotted with it. He loved dancing, as did millions of his fellow citizens. For a short period he had worked as an *Eintänzer* (taxi dancer) – a term used interchangeably for paid dance partners and gigolos – in one of Berlin's grander hotels. 'The women were very light on their feet,' he recalled later. 'I was very light on their feet as well.'[3]

By 1945 Wilder was an American citizen who had already begun to make a distinct aesthetic mark on Hollywood. (The scene in his 1959 comedy *Some Like It Hot* in which Jack Lemmon in blonde wig and cocktail dress tangos through the night with Joe E. Brown might be relished as an inversion of his *Eintänzer* days.) And by the time Wilder's intense noir thriller *Double Indemnity* had opened in 1944, he had been drawn into a very specialized branch of the US Army, that of psychological operations. Wilder was promoted to the rank of colonel, and in early 1945 Berlin was once more foremost in his thoughts as the US Army fought its way through the freezing flatlands of western Europe. The prospect of victory for the Allies was certain, even if the timing of it could not be predicted. But Colonel Wilder was starting to think about how film might be used among the gothic ruins of Berlin. He was thinking about how he might once more seduce German audiences, but this time with the aim of coaxing them away from the Hitler cult. Yet there was also a private trauma in his prospective return to Berlin. When he had emigrated in 1933, travelling via Paris before arriving in the US, he had left his mother, his grandmother and his stepfather behind in Austria. The 1938 Anschluss (union) with Nazi Germany brought Austria under direct Nazi rule, with the immediate removal of fundamental rights from Jewish citizens. By the outbreak of war, it was intensely difficult for Jews to leave Austria; the authorities refused to recognize previously legal documentation. By the early 1940s, the deathly transportations had begun. Wilder's mother and grandmother were not even taken to the same death camp: they were murdered surrounded by strangers. At the beginning of 1945, he had no information at all on what had become of them. And yet, even facing that unfathomable horror, he was thinking about the people of Berlin, and about how his cameras might repair their damaged minds.

It was fitting that one of Berlin's young auteurs should be returning in such a role: the city had also taught the world how film could envelop the senses like a dream. This latent Berlin talent first became obvious shortly after the First World War in 1920 with *The Cabinet of Dr Caligari*, directed by Robert Wiene. This was an uncanny horror thriller with disorientating layers – a sleepwalking murderer, a fairground mountebank later revealed to be the demonically possessed director of a lunatic asylum – with grotesque expressionist sets, where rooms were distorted and shadows took the shape of daggers. The film seized the imaginations of audiences worldwide who just a year earlier had regarded Germany itself as the font of a demonic force. Some years later, the Berlin critic Siegfried Kracauer theorized that the mad Dr Caligari was a premonition of Hitler. Yet those warning foreshadowings in German cinema were more like fever dreams – not exact political analogies, but evoking a wider social sense of growing dread.

There was another macabre and hugely popular film tale that perhaps more acutely evoked the latent duality in Weimar culture. The first remake of *The Student of Prague* (1926), the second silent version, also starred Conrad Veidt, this time as the man who unwittingly sells his reflection to an emissary of the Devil. This was not an old folk tale but rather the conception (partly inspired by the E. T. A. Hoffmann story 'The Lost Reflection') of the actor/director Paul Wegener. When it was remade in 1935, with Anton Walbrook, the unease was ironically real for the actor. Walbrook's mother was Jewish and he was gay. In 1936, after travelling to Hollywood for a film, he returned not to Germany but instead made for England, where he settled and went on to star in a great number of productions. Meanwhile, the creator of *The Student of Prague* stayed; the Nazi regime held Paul Wegener in a close embrace. He did not return this warmth.

If the regime had studied his earlier career more closely, it would have seen that Wegener was some distance away from their anti-Semitism. In 1920 he had explored Jewish myth on an extraordinary scale in *The Golem: How He Came into the World*. The vision of the medieval ghetto of Prague was reimagined in a Berlin studio; a visually fascinating and lavish maze of stone and slate, with madly pointed rooftops and windows and archways weirdly angled. This was the work of the architect Hans Poelzig; it did not seem incongruous to him that he should be conjuring a fairy-tale fantasy for the screen while helping to shape Berlin's modernism in the real world. The story was one of persecution: Prague's Jewish community threatened with expulsion from their homes by the emperor, whose decree accused them of 'crucifying Our Lord' and 'coveting the wealth of Christians'.[4] Rabbi Loew, in a laboratory of twisting stone, consults ancient texts in search of a means of protecting his people. They prescribe fashioning a man from clay, animated by means of a magic word placed in an amulet in his chest. At first the creature – as incarnated by Paul Wegener with clumping movements and sensitive facial expressions that would go on to influence Boris Karloff's haunted Frankenstein monster – is a benevolent force: cutting wood, running errands and then, spectacularly, at the emperor's palace, saving both the emperor and his court when the roof collapses. But the creature has a capacity for evil too, and when Loew's manservant conceives a thwarted passion for Loew's daughter Miriam, the Golem is manipulated into an outbreak of murder and fiery destruction. In the end, it can be stopped only by the innocent intervention of a child. More interesting yet was that this Jewish community, while inhabiting a dream-like landscape of intensely exaggerated angles, was not presented as being threateningly 'foreign' to the film's mass audience; instead, there was intimacy and warmth.

No matter how well-intentioned, however, there was also another undercurrent in the film that might have been subconscious – the association of a rabbi with hermetic mystical powers. We see Loew studying the stars, but to gather their supernatural portents. His laboratory is dark and alchemical. Fairy story though this was, the Jews of Prague, while sympathetic protagonists, were also portrayed as fascinating exotics. They were the heroes, yet they were still 'other'. None the less, *The Golem* was a huge hit: the premiere itself, complete with celebrities and floodlighting, was among those that set a later Hollywood template for star guests, and Berlin's cinemas were packed for weeks.

So, while Wegener certainly went on to produce and star in Nazi-sponsored films in the 1930s and 40s, and was personally honoured by Goebbels by being made an Actor of the State, there was always – as some observed – an element of reluctance or ambivalence. He never made any public pronouncements of support for the regime. It was possible that he accepted the work and the honours because to have refused them would have provoked the wrath of the Nazi hierarchy and, like everyone, he only wanted to survive and to protect his family (and, in his case, five former wives). By the beginning of 1945, Wegener's face was to be seen in every Berlin cinema that remained open under the bombings and the blackouts. Goebbels had commissioned an historical epic called *Kolberg* – the story of a town under siege in the Napoleonic Wars. The citizens resisting this assault were the heroes; Berliner audiences might have been bemused by the crushingly obvious weight of the propaganda parallel. Wegener – a resident of Berlin himself – might also have been struck by it. His apartment, in the south-west of the city, quite close to the lakes and trees of Grunewald, was noted for its rich Asian furnishings and also for its pair of Buddha statues. Wegener's fame was international, and come the final days of the Nazi regime in Berlin his apartment would find itself being used in one of the more surprising Soviet interventions.

The propaganda possibilities of the new medium of cinema had been obvious since the Great War; but it had also seized Hitler in the Weimar years much the way that he had been transfixed when first hearing

Richard Wagner's operas. One particular film seemed to him not only a masterpiece but also a work that exulted in the nobility of Aryanism. It was near the lakes in the south of Berlin that, under the vast roof of a studio in 1924, a mythological and misty German forest was created. Through these mighty trees rode the blond warrior Siegfried; in among these groves there was also a quite extraordinary dragon, breathing real fire; there were elves too, blacksmiths and magic swords, castles and aristocrats: the seemingly unselfconscious retelling of the saga of the *Nibelungenlied*. With astonishing confidence the young director Fritz Lang conjured an entire world existing outside of time, and conveyed the gathering sense of tragedy, with a young hero's death foretold. This was not simplistic escapism: the scale and the depth were operatic. It also ran to the epic length of five hours, in two instalments; here was a film that asked audiences everywhere not merely to suspend disbelief but to give themselves wholly to the experience.

What made *Die Nibelungen* so truly remarkable was not just the lavish production values – an extraordinary feat at a time when the nation was only just beginning to emerge from the nightmare spiral of hyperinflation – but the intensity of its intention to capture, as its screenwriter Thea von Harbou said, the essence of Germanness.[5] (She was, for a time, Lang's wife, and later a Nazi Party member.) She also suggested that the decision to make the film was a form of unconscious bidding; that the story chose her 'in order to remind Germany of a glory that it had almost forgotten'.[6] The assertiveness of this Wagnerian vision – just six years after the most devastating conflict that had left the nation humiliated – was registered even at the time. A young Aryan hero, riding through a haunted landscape, towards his prophesied violent end: if this was intended as some kind of 'balm'[7] for the wounded nation, as some suggested, it was a curious and morbid one. And yet it clearly had tremendous resonance.

The film's 1924 premiere – held at the 1,770-seat UFA-Palast am Zoo cinema – attracted, among others, a government minister and the president of the Reichsbank, as well as many other dignitaries. It also mesmerized the young Joseph Goebbels and Adolf Hitler. They both held it to be an extraordinary work of art in its own right, but also one of the most important films ever made: a production that chimed deep within the German soul. For many years afterwards

Fritz Lang insisted that he had intended almost the complete opposite: that his depiction of this fairy-tale aristocracy was focused
especially upon its decadence and decay and dissolution and that
theirs was a world that could, and should, never last. But Goebbels
was determined to appropriate Lang's vision.

Three years later, Lang's imagination found new and amazing futuristic form in *Metropolis*: a near-future fable, featuring an extraordinary
robot woman and set in a fantastically realized Berlin – towers of
light, the air filled with bi-planes and monorails and, down below,
labourers enslaved to demonic engines that powered the city above.
This was also to prove inspirational to the Nazis. The story and its
message, in truth, were garbled; a muddy semi-Marxist allegory featuring the novelty of an android doppelgänger posing as a beautiful
and innocent woman. But none of that mattered; the key was the rav-
ishing spectacle of strikingly angled architecture and the play of light.
And, again, it was those close to Hitler who seemed most enraptured.

Even as the growing radiance of Hollywood lured contemporary
directors and actors, from F. W. Murnau to Marlene Dietrich, Fritz
Lang continued to work in Berlin; among other compelling productions (such as *M*, starring soon-to-be émigré Peter Lorre as a child
murderer), he was heavily immersed in the fictional creation of a
criminal mastermind called Dr Mabuse. In 1933 *The Testament of Dr
Mabuse* – in which the mastermind, now committed to an insane
asylum, continues to project his will by preternatural means through
the Berlin underworld – opened, and then closed almost as quickly.
In January 1933 Hitler had become Chancellor, instantly giving the
Nazis power that extended into every sphere. They did not care for
the film's suggested allegory – that the violent denizens of Berlin's
underworld were analogous to the Nazis, and that the satanic Mabuse
was akin to Hitler. With the film's prohibition, Fritz Lang was now
alive to the danger the new regime posed to him and his family: his
mother, who had converted to Catholicism, had been born Jewish.

Yet even *Mabuse* could not dim the admiration of the new Reich
Minister for Propaganda for Lang's work. Goebbels and Hitler often
discussed *Die Nibelungen*, and, with film now in a new era of sound,
were anxious to see it remade on an even more lavish scale. Here, as
they saw it, was a story and a spectacle that could project the glories

of the new Nazi era out into the world. Thea von Harbou was approached about the possibility of writing a screenplay for this mooted new production and was carefully guarded in her response. Lang's instincts, however, when he was summoned to a meeting with Goebbels, prickled with anxiety, and even though he kept the appointment – Goebbels telling him that he was 'the man to make the Nazi film'[8] – the director knew that he would have to leave Germany to avoid compulsion. Lang first went to Paris and thence to the United States. By spring 1945, when his old city was encircled by the forces that were about to move in to crush it, Lang's latest critically acclaimed Hollywood noir – *The Woman in the Window* – was thrilling his American audiences.

The Führer's intense love for film, of any genre, coloured the years of Nazi cinema. (Conversely, there were films that were hated by the regime too; even before they came to power, the Hollywood-produced anti-war film *All Quiet on the Western Front* had seen its Berlin screenings in 1930 sabotaged by the Nazis, who destroyed equipment, threw stink-bombs and released mice into the auditoriums. The production was subsequently banned.) The archetypes of film were deliberately projected into all areas of life under Nazi rule. Berlin itself seemed to become, in one sense, a vast film set for the regime's cameras: the elaborate stagings of the city's May Day festivities, or for the public celebrations of Hitler's birthday on 20 April – swastika flags as tall as the buildings they were draped over, crowds gathered before vast maypoles – were captured as cinematic spectacles. 'If the Nazis were movie mad, then the Third Reich was movie made,'[9] as one academic later expressed it. The most famous and egregious example of the use of the medium to cement the regime's hold on the popular imagination was through Leni Riefenstahl's *Triumph of the Will*, the documentary that recorded the 1934 Nuremberg Rally. Except the terms 'documentary' and 'recorded' are absurdly inert; what she did, through montage, tracking shots, low angles and stirring music, was to create a propagandist spectacle of her own. To have been part of that rally would have been one thing; for Germany's cinema audiences, gazing in wonder at the symmetry of the crowds shot from above, or the power of their Führer, his image captured from below to heighten his presence, there was the extra adrenaline and emotion summoned through the strange intimacy of cinema; the faces of ordinary people and their leader alike, enormous on the screens, gazing out into the silvery blackness. Riefenstahl in later years tried to deny that she had set out to produce a work of triumphalism, that all she had done was capture a moment for history. But she hadn't. She had actively helped to create it.

The main shows in the Nazi period were sometimes – though by no means always – nakedly intended to stir up hate. Among the viler propaganda efforts was the 1940 production *Jud Süss*, starring the actor Werner Krauss; twenty years previously, he had mesmerized the world as the titular Dr Caligari. Before the war, his tremendous skill as a character actor prompted a co-star to remark that he was a 'demonic genius'.[10] Like Anton Walbrook, the young Krauss had been spotted by the famed theatre director Max Reinhardt, to whom, the actor later declared, 'I owe everything in my life'.[11] Unlike Walbrook, or indeed his *Caligari* co-star Conrad Veidt, who had left Germany as soon as he could, Krauss was content to declare his fealty to this new Nazi regime. As a classical actor, his work extended beyond film. In 1943, as the Wehrmacht was struggling from east to south, Krauss took to the stage for a production of a play that had already found great favour with Hitler. Shakespeare's *The Merchant of Venice* gave Krauss an opportunity to essay an account of Shylock that met with popular and critical approval. He was, one reviewer wrote, 'a pathological image of the Eastern European Jewish type, expressing all its inner and outer uncleanliness'.[12] (Oddly, amid the general ban on British playwrights on the German stage throughout the war years, Shakespeare was not only exempted but actively exalted by the Nazi leadership. The Hitler Youth were encouraged to take part in 'Shakespeare Weeks'; Goebbels had said of Shakespeare: 'What a huge genius! How he towers over Schiller!' And Hitler himself had remarked of the *Merchant* that it presented a 'timelessly valid characterization of the Jew'.[13] The only other English-language playwright permitted in Nazi Germany was George Bernard Shaw.) Werner Krauss and Paul Wegener were to be among the actors resuming their art amid the dust and death of the immediate post-war Berlin years, and Krauss himself was to be the subject of furious protests. Even throughout the war years, he had the occasional critic who told him that his Jewish characterizations in *Jud Süss* seemed calculated to generate hate. Krauss responded furiously that this was no concern of his; he had simply been doing his job as an actor.

Among the obvious propaganda films, there were also huge numbers of genre pictures that by contrast seemed simply to be competing with the frothy escapism of Hollywood. It was for this reason that the actress and singer Marika Rökk – the heroine of schoolgirls like Helga Hauthal – came to occupy such dominant positions on the screen. Rökk specialized in uncomplicated musical romances – *Light Cavalry*, *It Was a Gay Night at the Ball* – that would involve elaborately staged dance routines. The Nazis made a close study of the films emerging from Hollywood, and especially the screwball comedies and sentimental melodramas, but the directors and producers at UFA and other studios had been given an immediate guide by Goebbels in March 1933 when he addressed them at a specially convened meeting at the Hotel Kaiserhof. Film, he told them, had to be shaped to 'the contours of the Volk' and all productions had to have 'roots' deep in 'the bedrock of national socialism'.[14] UFA was swift to jettison all of its Jewish employees; most were fired in the first several months of the Nazi regime. Even though it now meant a serious dearth of talent – around 1,500 Jewish and gentile German artists and technicians were instead to find fresh flowering in Hollywood – the studios were eager to be seen to be conforming.

In some ways, as a prototype student of film, Goebbels was keenly analysing Hollywood not just for straightforward propaganda purposes but also because he understood that cinema could provide an invaluable emotional release; this became vitally important throughout the war, as those left behind at home were suffering acute anxiety for the men who were now scattered across the world's continents and oceans in various theatres of conflict. Following the calamitous military reversals in North Africa and on the steppes of Russia, Goebbels – as well as appearing at the Sportpalast in 1943 to tell the citizens to prepare for total war – commanded his film-makers to provide ever more diverting spectacle. This was vital for morale, and he believed that cinema had a crucial role in propelling Nazi Germany to victory. One genuine aesthetic curiosity that withstands viewing today is the full-colour production of the aforementioned fantasy epic *Münchhausen*, made in 1942 but not released until 1943. Given that Nazi control of the cinema was so absolute, here was a film shot through with a curious ambivalence; a story that alternated feverish exhilaration with sudden, iron melancholy. It was based upon the folk tales featuring the legendary liar Baron Hieronymus von Münchhausen; there are interludes involving magic telescopes, a romantic affair with Catherine the Great, an encounter with occultist Alessandro Cagliostro (who confers immortality upon our hero), a ride through the air on a cannonball, an extraordinary arrival in eighteenth-century Venice and a voyage to the moon via hot-air balloon, where the baron and his manservant discover that it is inhabited by flowers with talkative human heads that are detachable.

All of this – with artful special effects – was filmed in the richest colour; the sequence filmed upon Venice's Grand Canal in 1942, where the Baron sails in during Carnival, watched by hundreds of extras in full costume – was an astonishing extravagance. So too was the use of genuine (stolen) gold and porcelain for the tables in the Russian banqueting scenes. Yet one vital figure was alive to the strangeness of it all: the man who had written the screenplay. At the end of the film, Münchhausen, now in the present day, sitting in a gazebo talking to his young house-guests, intimates that he has had enough; that he will forgo his immortality and die. But, one of them cries, you are a demi-god. 'Yes,' replies Münchhausen, 'but a demi-god is only half a man.'[15] This line seemed precisely the reverse of Nazi triumphalism; it took the cult of death and sacrifice and made it instead something weary and sad and autumnal. Münchhausen had seen not only this world but also worlds beyond, and through the centuries. And none of it was enough. What was such an ending supposed to convey to Goebbels and the Nazi leadership? Only Goebbels knew the secret identity of the film's screenwriter, Erich Kästner, for his work had been banned for years. Remarkably, the author had elected to stay in Germany even as its rulers demonized both his work and him. He had been aggressively interrogated by the SS on two occasions, yet even this did not intimidate him into leaving Berlin. Throughout the late 1930s and early 1940s, he had survived partly by publishing in neutral Switzerland. He focused on books for children, taking some care that his pacifist, anti-Nazi leanings did not show through too obviously. A film like *Münchhausen* required an artist with his prodigious imagination to bring the spectacle to life. Goebbels took the risk in allowing Kästner to proceed and agreed that the screenplay should be written under a pseudonym; it would not do for a banned author to be seen to be involved. But what was Kästner really saying with the film? Münchhausen as a character is genial and energetic and infused with comic spirit, but the weight of sadness seems always there too. Unlike Lang's *Die Nibelungen*, here was a myth exposed to the reality of human feeling.

The film was extremely popular, and Hitler was delighted with it and its exultant set-pieces. Then, somehow, he discovered that Kästner was the writer and his initial response to this was molten rage; he ordered that Kästner be given no further screenwriting work. By 1944, with Berlin being bombarded mercilessly day and night, cinema was an ever more important sanctuary, especially for those in the suburbs a little distant from the obvious targets. By the spring of 1945, Kästner himself had suffered his own material losses when a bomb destroyed his Berlin home – a smart apartment in a four-storey house on Roscherstrasse, just off the Kurfürstendamm, filled with books, typewriters and 'the perennial bone-hard sausage in the pantry'[16] – as he sheltered underground. He knew, in those final days as the Soviets approached, what horror lay ahead. Kästner had also picked up frightening rumours that the remnants of the SS roaming through Berlin planned to murder him before the Red Army could take the city. He and several film friends began planning for their escape. The idea was to make for a tiny village in the Tyrol. If they were challenged they were going to claim that they were scouting locations for a new film called *Das verlorene Gesicht* (The Lost Face).

And, as all this was unfolding, another key figure in German cinema, this one right at the start of her career, was about to adopt a startlingly different means of survival. In years to come, Hildegard Knef would be internationally famous (and infamous), but in 1945 she was a nineteen-year-old film actress who had only just been discovered. She was in some ways emblematic of the modern Berlin. She had been brought up in the broadly affluent, artist-favoured district of Wilmersdorf in an apartment next to an elevated railway line, which obliged everyone to suspend their conversations as trains passed. Her father died young, her mother was eccentric and at times manic. Her stepfather was a cobbler and she attended a school where the early embrace of Nazism had been eagerly accepted by some of her teachers, if not by all of the pupils. Frau Knef found herself repulsed by the shouting ferocity. But she had enjoyed the summer of 1936: the Berlin Olympics under the strong sun that everyone termed 'Hitler weather' and her glimpse in the distance of the Führer himself. A few years later – and under the bomber-laden skies of war, which constantly resulted in a 'windowless bedroom' and 'glass splinters in the bed'[17] – Knef had found work in 1943 in the animation department of UFA. Almost as tradition demands, she was spotted while eating in the canteen by one of the studio's executives, who saw the cinematic potential of this green-eyed blonde. She was awarded a scholarship for acting training (strikingly, even as total war began, such things were still considered of sufficient importance by the Nazi regime).

It was while playing a role in a Berlin theatre in 1944 that she was to meet Ewald von Demandowsky – a Nazi propaganda-film producer and SS officer. They began a relationship; Knef had by this time won her first film role in a bucolic drama called *Journey into Happiness*. This was one of the last Nazi productions. And by February 1945 she was among those countless Berlin women listening to the news of Soviet advances and trying to weigh up what the future held. One of her female friends was addicted to fortune-telling and Tarot cards; all she could say was that the coming days were 'horrorful'.[18]

Knef and Demandowsky (now conscripted into the Volkssturm) were, by March 1945, uncertain what to do. 'We are bombed continuously now, by the Americans, the English, and sometimes the Russians,' wrote Knef.[19] The film offices that first employed her were burned to the ground in a raid and now she, along with her fellow citizens, was trying to navigate a life that swung wildly between moments of pure panic and long hours of silent tedium. Even the simple act of shopping for groceries was a blend of suspense and boredom. 'They say you can get marmalade in Dahlem [a neighbouring city quarter to Wilmersdorf],' wrote Knef. 'I join the queue; we shuffle forward, take cover in the doorways, peep out, line up again. Trucks full of women and children rattle past, refugees from Frankfurt on the Oder, from Strausberg, from Spindlersfeld.'[20] And it was the refugees who appeared to bear the starkest message. 'They shout, "Clear out, the Russians'll rape you, beat your brains out!" One of the women rants, "They crucified my husband, nailed him to the door, and cut off my sister's breasts; clear out!" '[21]

It was at this time that the notion of an escape plan from the city began to form for Knef, a strategy founded upon her life-long love for acting. Knef was going to disguise herself as a man. She was tall and statuesque and had confidence that in a greatcoat, sweater, trousers and cap she could look and move like a man. This was not a madcap whim but inspired by the very real and pressing fear of rape. And across the city, as the Red Army drew audibly closer, a great many other women dwelling in cellars would hit upon the same idea to repel attackers. But Hildegard Knef was going to take it further (and not entirely by design). In dressing like a man, she was also going to join a group of men – Volkssturm, SS and teenage boys – suddenly caught up in the street-by-street battle for the city. Knef would find that the pretence was initially successful, but, in the days to come, the act would create unexpected repercussions and unanticipated danger. After the war, Hildegard Knef would establish an extraordinary – and sometimes scandalous – niche for herself in the cultural life of the divided country. (Her lover Demandowsky, conversely, would be captured and executed.) In the meantime, though, her desperate flight and quirky stratagems seemed to blend the fiction of Erich Kästner with the wry eye of Ernst Lubitsch. Even at the fall of Berlin, one of its young performers was holding true to the city's anarchic artistic spirit.

Elsewhere, though, to the south of the city, there was an institution – heavily damaged by bombing but still standing – dedicated to the opposite. As well as film and fantasy, Berlin had for many years seen pioneering work carried out by the most visionary of scientists. In that cold, wet spring of 1945, three of those scientists, well aware that the world was on the edge of the atomic age, were making their own plans. Even though all the nuclear research carried out under the Nazis had long since been removed to quieter parts of the country, the laboratories in Berlin still contained secrets, knowledge and material that would be of inestimable value to whichever side seized them first. These scientists knew that they faced capture either by the Americans and the British, or by the Soviets. They appeared to have made their choices.

## 7.  The Uranium Club

The stars in the skies above were no longer quite what they seemed. Even the darkness that enveloped them was different. Einstein had changed the shape of the universe. There were some, in the immediate aftermath of the First World War, who thought that the new general theory of relativity – that space and time were intertwined, and could be distorted by gravitational forces – was itself a by-product of the mind-distorting horror of the trenches; that the greatest intellect had become unmoored by the atmosphere of war, and in doing so inverted the world's natural laws. Among them was Joseph Goebbels, who, hostile to Einstein's Jewish heritage, subscribed instead to the ludicrous notion of a specific 'Aryan Physics', and who later – by the desperate bunker days of April 1945 – came to believe that the movements of the stars might really hold the mystic secrets of the future, which could be unlocked by horoscopes. By that stage Albert Einstein was a long-time American citizen, and his former home district in Berlin had itself been so intensively targeted by bombers that it too had become an inversion of all that it had been. But, years before all that, his theory of relativity had, for a time, placed Berlin at the centre of the scientific world.

In the first week of April 1945 some of the scientists who had been inspired by Einstein in earlier days were now gazing upon what remained of their work and reading through the findings of their own dazzling research in a daily state of advancing fear. Many of Berlin's laboratories were now simply shattered glass and powdered brick; as with the city's industry, so the lights of its remaining science were being extinguished. Many of the more sensitive research programmes had already been evacuated from the city, but there were a few physicists who had remained behind – men who had navigated various moral tightropes throughout the war and who now understood that their knowledge of nuclear physics would make them targets. Among them was a professor who had once seemed destined for a dehumanized death in the camps of the east. Gustav Hertz was, in the official terms of the time, a 'second-degree part Jew'.[1] His grandfather had been Jewish; in the mid nineteenth century, the entire family had converted to Lutheranism. For the Nazis, this was insufficient purity; Professor Hertz had been the Director of Experimental Physics at the Berlin Technical University. The betrayal of his so-called tainted blood saw the authorities casting him aside from that role.

That Professor Hertz had won a Nobel Prize for his pioneering work with electrons was dismissed, for this was a branch of scientific inquiry that the regime did not trust (like the work of Einstein, this was a field that was regarded by the Nazis as Jewish invention). That Hertz had been a demonstrably proud citizen meant nothing. That he had also worked throughout the First World War to help develop chlorine gas as a terrible battlefield weapon did not impress the Nazis either. Yet perhaps a glint of that brilliance, the idea of international prestige and respectability, had helped preserve him, and, although he was exiled from academia, Professor Hertz was welcomed into the vast Berlin electricals firm Siemens. The complex had – inevitably – been seriously damaged by bombs throughout the intense campaign of 1944 to 1945. Yet some of the laboratories housed in these battered buildings still survived. And in the chilly days of April 1945, Professor Hertz was – together with two scientific contemporaries – envisaging the possibilities of surviving the future. One of his companions was an amazing young physicist called Manfred von Ardenne, an expert in wireless and early television technology. In the hermetic world of atomic and quantum physics, all the scientists in this tight group – who met and discussed their work frequently – either knew or had calculated how atomic bombs might be made a possibility. In the intense vulnerability of the ruined city – institutions gaping open to the rainy sky, the enforced nightly home of underground shelters – there was now no possibility of escape. The scientists were also sharply aware that they would be sought after by the enemy and that – thanks to Soviet intelligence gathering – the Red Army and Stalin's NKVD would know exactly where to find them. The extraordinary, pioneering leaps in understanding the raw structure of the cosmos that had taken place in Berlin over the past thirty years now meant that their minds would be beyond value in any geopolitical conflicts to come.

The irony that the Nazi regime could not grasp the scientists' understanding of nuclear physics – and the possibilities of nuclear weaponry – in the way the Soviets and Americans did cannot have been lost on these men. The fact that some of those crucial advances in atomic science had stemmed in part from the imagination and the philosophy of Albert Einstein was something that the Nazis could never accept. Even in the early 1920s, when Einstein – living in Berlin – had become famous worldwide, and was feted by fellow scientists and journalists and society figures, and even the film comedian Charlie Chaplin, there were significant numbers of nationalists and agitators who loathed the new universe that he postulated. Einstein insisted that the general theory of relativity was not a revolution. He had not usurped Isaac Newton; instead, he had applied his laws to a universe that the seventeenth-century mathematician could never have conceived of, and, by doing so, caused them to evolve. Newton's gravity could not explain the greater forces at work in the galaxy; Einstein imagined the bending of light and the slowing and speeding up of time. There were those who hated him for it because they felt that he was deliberately destabilizing solid reality. Even in the early 1920s, feverish anti-Semitism led German nationalists into believing that Einstein could only have postulated such ideas because he was Jewish.

As a Swiss-German, Albert Einstein had made his home in Berlin before the Wilhelmine regime had thrown the nation into a war that itself had loosened the foundations of rationality. And after that war, in the German Revolution, communists had fought with Freikorps in the street beneath the window of Einstein's office.[2] The battles had extended to the University of Berlin, with the communists occupying the campus and demanding that in future only socialist academics and socialist students would be admitted. They looked to Einstein, expecting his support; instead, he expressed his fears for freedom of thought, and did what he could in official circles to have order restored. Order in Weimar Germany could frequently feel illusory. Over the next few years, as this painful harmony was rocked terribly by poverty, grinding reparations and hyperinflation, Albert Einstein became a true international celebrity, a man with an image every bit as recognizable as Berlin's film stars. He was invited to Britain and America, there to address packed audiences comprising not just scientists, but eager followers across a great many disciplines. Brash journalists treated interviews with Einstein almost as jocular contests: could this wayward-haired figure – the apparent embodiment of eccentric boffinry – be caught out in any way or indeed be made to look foolish? He could not, largely because he had a lively comic spirit and a wry self-awareness about the impact that he made.

Einstein and his wife lived in Berlin's quiet and well-to-do Bavarian Quarter; a street of slightly overbearing apartment blocks with plush interiors, just a little south of the Tiergarten, the city's richly landscaped central park. The intellectual and social salons of the city relished all opportunities to grasp his ideas; Count Harry Kessler recalled that Einstein encouraged him to see that the general theory of relativity was essentially simple; and drew an analogy between a glass ball with a light on the top, and flat beetles moving around on its surface: a realm both finite and yet limitless. At a dinner party, one guest was thrilled to hear that Einstein was 'deeply religious'. Could it really be so? 'Yes, you can call it that,' Einstein told him. 'Try and penetrate with our limited means the secrets of nature and you will find that, behind all the discernible concatenations, there remains something subtle, intangible and inexplicable. Veneration for this force beyond anything that we can comprehend is my religion.'[3]

The opposition from many scientists – who could not accept that gravity was not merely just a force, but actually formed part of the infrastructure of the universe – was in those early days dismissive, as though Einstein had been discussing supernatural phenomena. Some of these scientists still believed in such manifestations – namely, 'the ether' – themselves, and perhaps understandably, since this was an extraordinary period of challenge and questioning where the newest theories might as well have been supernatural: the Danish scientist Niels Bohr and Max Born were exploring the sometimes uncanny quantum realm where, on the atomic level and smaller yet, the universe appeared to start behaving in inexplicable ways: particles defying measurement, electrons acting and reacting differently when observed. The University of Berlin's most senior academic, its rector Professor Max Planck, had himself led the way in this quantum field while researching thermodynamics. Like his younger friend Einstein, it had never been his intention to undermine the classically formulated laws of physics, but there were now observable phenomena, involving radiation and heat, that could otherwise not be explained. Planck's research was affected grievously by the terrible economic earthquakes of the 1920s; his laboratories sometimes could not operate, owing to lack of funds or resources.

This rising generation of physicists, soon joined by a young Werner Heisenberg, were spending much of their time in deep, abstracted thought. Einstein frequently descended into trance-like states. On one occasion he had spent so long in the bath that household members called through the door in alarm. He came to and answered sheepishly that he'd thought that he was sitting at his desk.[4]

Yet Einstein was also piercingly clear-sighted about the world around him, and the increasingly poisonous political atmosphere. In the early 1920s, there was a public meeting, billed as a debate about relativity, which he could not resist attending. In order to enter the hall, however, he had to pass a range of swastikas that had been hung up. In this debate – and in other public arguments with hostile scientific colleagues – he asked pointedly whether they would object so strongly to the very idea of the theory of relativity if he wasn't Jewish.

Einstein was ceaselessly courageous in the sense that he knew he should never shrink back from the thugs, but by the early 1930s he was also very aware of the chill that was breathing through the city. He understood Hitler to be in part a product of economic catastrophe. 'I do not enjoy Herr Hitler's acquaintance,' he proclaimed from Pasadena, California, where he had been invited to teach and research at Caltech. 'He is living on the empty stomach of Germany. As soon as economic conditions improve, he will no longer be important.'[5] Yet this was to ascribe pure rationality to the nation's wealthy middle classes. Among the millions of desperately poor people, either unemployed or on short hours, both communism and Nazism seemed in their extremes to offer answers. But Hitler and the NSDAP were, if not loved by the middle classes, then not especially feared by them either; those families who had seen their life savings disappear in the hyperinflation of 1923 could no longer trust any branch of the Weimar regime to guarantee economic security. Hitler's appeal, grotesquely, was that of stability.

By early 1933, Hitler's ascension to the Chancellorship having been followed almost immediately by the burning of the Reichstag, enabling the Nazis to blame and whip up rage against the communists, hold a heavily freighted election and swiftly impose iron-gripped totalitarianism, Einstein understood that if anything he had underestimated the terrible forces at play; the dark matter exerting such strange effects across the nation. The night after the Reichstag fire, Einstein told his mistress: 'I dare not enter Germany because of Hitler.'⁶ But this did not mean that he would keep his silence. Einstein sailed for Belgium, where he delivered this ringing statement: 'As long as I have any choice in the matter, I shall live only in a country where civil liberty, tolerance and equality of all citizens before the law prevail. These conditions do not exist in Germany at the present time.'⁷

And so it was that Berlin's greatest mind was sent into exile: the response of the Nazi regime was furious. One popular newspaper declared: 'Good News About Einstein – He's Not Coming Back', continuing in its editorial that he was a 'puffed up bit of vanity [who] dares to sit in judgment on Germany without knowing what is going on here – matters that forever must remain incomprehensible to a man who was never a German in our eyes and who declares himself to be a Jew and nothing but a Jew.'⁸

The pain experienced by the exile was quite different from that suffered by those who stayed and sought vainly to make accommodations with the regime. Einstein's great friend Max Planck had to live not only with his absence but also with the subsequent cruelty of the Nazi clampdown upon Jewish people in academia. In one sense, he did for a time successfully resist the regime; *Gleichschaltung* (coordination) came a little later to the Kaiser Wilhelm Institute than to other official bodies and he did what little he could to shield its Jewish members. One such was Professor Fritz Haber, who had – throughout the First World War – developed both chemical weapons and agricultural fertilizers: laboratory-created instruments of death and life (his first wife committed suicide; it was said by some that she had been driven to it by her husband's development of gas warfare. Conversely, his fertilizers – though toxic – resulted in much-needed bountiful harvests. That nauseating duality persisted. Some years later, Haber's laboratories developed the cyanide gas Zyklon A, originally intended for farmers to use against crop-eating insects but which would later be adapted by the Nazis as a means of exterminating human life on an unimaginable scale). Professor Planck defended Haber to the Führer himself, but Hitler was monomaniacal about, as he put it to Planck, Jewish people 'sticking together like burrs'.[9]

Eventually, the viciousness of the regime, and the war to defeat it, would come to devour Max Planck whole. In 1944 his beloved home in the smart suburb of Grunewald was completely wrecked on one of those nights of incessant bombing. Very much worse came when his younger son Erwin – a Weimar politician who had been levered out of office and into commercial work – was arrested by the Gestapo for his suspected involvement in the 1944 plot to assassinate Hitler. Erwin Planck was eventually brought before the People's Court in January 1945; simply to stand before this sinister tribunal was a guarantee that violent death was coming. Professor Planck had sent a desperate letter to Hitler, asserting his son's innocence. The silence was implacable. Erwin Planck was hanged that month. Professor Planck had already lost his eldest son in the First World War. This final grief – the last savage act of a sociopathic state – ushered the old man towards the grave. Not even the cascade of warm honours that fell upon him in the immediate aftermath of the war – all the proper respect that he had been denied throughout Nazism, including an enthusiastic welcome to London unique among German scientists at that time – could heal those terrible wounds.

Another luminous figure at the Kaiser Wilhelm Institute – one whose talent had been recognized and appreciated by Max Planck before the First World War – was also ironically someone who might have been able to give the Nazis the knowledge necessary to produce atomic weaponry. As a woman of Jewish heritage, however, Lise Meitner was in danger from the moment that the Nazis grabbed power. Born in Austria, Meitner had studied at the University of Vienna; her field was physics, which was profoundly unusual for a woman at that time, but it brought her to Berlin, where women in science were not quite so rare. The then middle-aged Max Planck was conservatively resistant to the idea of a woman working in the new field of radioactivity and atomic research, though that resistance soon dissolved in the face of her tremendous ability, energy and effervescent imagination. She was teamed with another brilliant chemist and physicist, Otto Hahn, and together, throughout the 1920s and 1930s, they made some of the most extraordinary leaps in understanding.

'Radioactivity and nuclear physics were making incredibly rapid progress at the time,' Meitner recalled years later. 'There was an amazing, surprising new discovery almost every month in one of the laboratories working in this field. We developed very good scientific and personal relationships with our young colleagues.'[10] By the early 1930s she was being invited to give prestigious lectures, and for a time her career seemed almost to have its own gravitational field that enabled her to rise above the new Nazi regime. Despite the expulsion of Jewish colleagues across the professions, Meitner's Austrian citizenship – the two states had not yet been welded together – afforded her some temporary protection, and at a point when she and Otto Hahn were daily unlocking more atomic enigmas. It was not that she was oblivious to the threat, but her work was of all-encompassing importance to her, and she would not be deflected by the hatred of grubby political opportunists. In the institute's laboratories, she was bombarding uranium with neutrons in a bid to create very heavy artificial elements called transuranics. Through these experiments involving isotopes of uranium-238, she and Otto Hahn were on the brink – unwittingly and unintentionally – of changing the entire course of world politics and history by bringing the prospect of the atomic bomb closer.

The Nazi annexation of Austria in 1938 was the point at which the threat to Lise Meitner from the regime became active and proximate as she immediately lost the protection of her Austrian citizenship. Otto Hahn and other colleagues begged her to leave Germany at once. The speed at which she did so was remarkable; she had only time to pack two small suitcases. With the aid of friends, she wove her way to the Netherlands and thence to Stockholm, where she was welcomed at the Nobel Institute.

Her frustration at having to abandon her work was intense; she and Hahn continued corresponding and it was clear that they had – in the course of their latest experiments – discovered atomic fission. 'There is something about the "radium isotopes" that is so remarkable that for now we are telling only you,' Hahn wrote to her in December 1938.[11] Those isotopes were behaving in ways that Hahn and his colleague Fritz Strassmann simply could not interpret conclusively. 'Perhaps you can come up with some sort of fantastic explanation.'[12] Had the uranium nucleus 'burst apart'? Meitner told him that it had; confirmation of Einstein's posited formula 'on the conversion capacity of mass to energy'.[13] There, within Berlin, was one of the first steps towards the possibility of producing nuclear weapons. Nazi Germany had a commanding head start over the Allies. That the road to that destination was to twist and distort so violently was the equally fascinating phenomenon of the forces of morality and science combining and failing to coalesce.

Professor Hahn stayed in Berlin; when war came, he had little choice but to remain. And, among the country's leading physicists, there was to be a new programme, simply referred to as the 'Uranium Club'.[14] It was around this time in 1940, in America, that Einstein was making direct representations to President Roosevelt warning of the possibilities that the Nazis could develop nuclear weaponry. The secret was out there; it could not be unlearned. In Germany, the extraordinary young physicist Werner Heisenberg, already famous for his uncertainty principle (to do with the momentum of particles that could be neither predicted nor accurately measured), was quick to understand the potential of fission. Yet its full devastating possibilities lay outside the strict borders of the Nazi imagination. The scientists in Germany – although under orders to advance the war effort – were hampered by the very nature of the regime itself. Many of their most brilliant colleagues were Jewish, and had been forced to flee a state that in any case had disavowed their work 'Jew science'; additionally, the various scientific institutes were not efficiently centralized; and, on top of all that, they were relatively underfunded. The creation of an atom bomb would require vast industrial facilities, such as those that were later implanted in the desert at Los Alamos for the Manhattan Project. The laboratories in Berlin, some within the Siemensstadt factory complex, were not enough. If the Nazis had not had such a disdainful lack of curiosity about this field, they would have provided more.

Hahn and Heisenberg saw close up the baffled failure of the Nazis to grasp what Churchill and Roosevelt could; in 1942, they were summoned to a meeting with the Minister for Armaments and

Munitions, Albert Speer, and various military figures, held at the Kaiser Wilhelm Institute in Harnack House. The purpose was for the scientists to give lectures to the military about 'atom-smashing and the development of the uranium machine'.[15] Afterwards, Speer asked Heisenberg how 'nuclear physics could be applied to the manufacture of atom bombs'.[16] According to Speer, Heisenberg told him that, theoretically, such a bomb could now be built; but that it would take Germany at least two years to develop one. Speer was not encouraged. Hitler in the meantime was also hearing back from the young inventor Manfred von Ardenne about nuclear possibilities. He, like his generals, appeared to have some difficulty envisaging atomic weaponry; if used on a battlefield, could it blow men out of a car two miles away? If used on a city, what would be the guarantee that the fission could be in part be contained – or would there be the horrifying prospect of a chain reaction that could come to devour the earth?

After the war, Professors Hahn and Heisenberg both asserted that they were vehemently opposed to the regime, and Heisenberg suggested that he himself had actively sabotaged the nuclear research programme. There is still some ambiguity about this; his 1941 meeting with fellow physicist Niels Bohr in Copenhagen, and the possible meanings of what he discussed, are today as opaque as quantum propositions. Was Heisenberg pleading with Bohr to make the Allies stop developing their atom bomb? Was he soliciting technical intelligence? Or was he taking a fantastic risk, betraying his own country by letting Bohr know that he too understood the theory necessary to create such a weapon? There was, for so many Germans, an extra dimension of moral agony that their Allied counterparts often could not understand: even though the scientists detested and feared the Nazi regime, they were also fearful that their country and their people might be destroyed. The German physicists who had a strong intuition that a programme such as the Manhattan Project was underway, knew that the cities in which they and their loved ones lived might some day simply be obliterated by the vengeful Allies. The heavy bombing campaigns from the RAF and the USAAF – the infernos rising into the skies, the thousands of shrunken, charred civilian corpses – were indicative of a driven ruthlessness. The capability was always there.

The German aim to develop atomic weaponry – if such a disorganized push might be described as an aim – came to an effective halt in 1942. There might have been an element in the Nazi hierarchy that yet again smelled something of Einstein and his 'Jewish science' behind nuclear physics. In any event, imaginations were fired by a 'wonder weapon' of quite a different nature. It was the work of a young man – an engineer – who as a boy had gazed up at the vast night skies above the forests of Berlin and dreamed about the day when it would be possible to fly to the moon and walk on its surface.

Wernher von Braun had a boyhood obsession with the science and mathematics of rocketry, and of flight. He came from an aristocratic family background – his father was a Junker baron – but in Berlin and in the countryside thereabouts he had received his education in a series of progressive boarding schools that were a feature of both the Wilhelmine and Weimar eras. His family home was in the extraordinarily smart Tiergarten, and, despite the mingled snobbery and anti-Semitism that were such a distinctive feature of the city's high society, the young boy invited Jewish friends from his first school home for tea.[17] His mother, who herself could have been a scientist were it not for the traditional constrictions of home and family, gave the boy a telescope; and, at that point, the obsession with reaching the stars overwhelmed him like a tide. His sense of mathematical form and structure was instinctive but, unlike Einstein, his experiments were wholly physical rather than abstractions.

As a boy, he pursued knowledge outside of laboratories, sometimes to the rage of neighbours. Early rocket experiments resulted in panic in a greengrocer's shop, and pedestrians scattering off a pavement as a runaway projectile on a trolley, sparking wildly in all directions, fizzed past. Von Braun's monomania about rockets led him to a youthful engineering apprenticeship in a metalworks – practical 'dirty hands' work, as it was known, was part of the curriculum for gaining an engineering degree. The family chauffeur would take him at dawn each day from his luxurious family home to a vast factory in the north-western district of Tegel. The older workers there regarded this young aristocrat with amusement; one, a mentor figure, set him the challenge of fashioning a perfect cube out of a shapeless lump of metal. Each time von Braun presented the older man with the finished article, it was waved away as being substandard, and he would have to return to the chore of filing it. He was taught patience, but he had no need of lessons of hyperfocused perfectionism.[18] The young man was also becoming part of an exclusive rocket-technology circle of specialists; even the UFA film director Fritz Lang had approached them. He wanted spectacular footage for his new epic, *Woman in the Moon*. Von Braun moved to the University of Berlin; all those boyhood notebook theses concerning fuel and thrust and trajectory were finding life.

Wernher's father, Magnus, had, in 1932, been elevated to the role of Reich Minister in Franz von Papen's doomed government; by now, national unemployment was touching six million and the streets of Berlin were filled with symptoms of distress, from Great War veterans begging to the vicious armies of 'blond bulls' (as one observer described them) in the brown and black uniforms of the SA and the SS, hunting communists to assault. The Weimar government had attempted to ban both Nazi groups, but not their communist counterparts. The resulting outrage led to the ban being lifted, and the violence sharpening. Yet, for the von Braun family, all of this was mere politics; when Magnus was dismissed after Hitler became Chancellor it made no impact upon the family's security or wealth. Indeed, the rich young Wernher – whose extensive academic work on rocketry led to him and a handful of other experts being granted a piece of wasteland in the north of the city to pursue their experiments – would claim later that he hardly paid any attention at all to the change of regime, such was his financial insulation.

In the early 1930s, when he was barely twenty years old, his work caught the attention of the military. Von Braun and colleagues later suggested that working for the army was not a matter of ideology or a desire for conquest but simply a means of securing good funds to pay for pure scientific pursuit. He received his doctorate in 1934, aged twenty-two, but, in the years that were to follow, his rocket research would itself follow a very singular trajectory. First, he and his team strove to perfect liquid rocket fuels. Then there was the matter of orientation: how might such a projectile be guided? By 1937, work had begun in Peenemünde, in northern Germany, on what was to become the V-2 rocket – a weapon that would soar into the stratosphere, touching the very edge of the planet's atmospheric boundaries, before its descent upon city streets and civilians, instantaneous violent death striking without warning from the clearest skies.

Hitler had been astounded by the youth of the scientist; he could not believe, after an early face-to-face meeting, that this young man was the genius who could devise these weapons of vengeance. Von Braun would later claim that he himself did not subscribe to Nazi beliefs. The fact that he happened to be a member of the Nazi Party and – during the war – an SS officer were details that were brushed aside on the grounds that, in those times, it was standard practice. Yet it was equally clear that something at the centre of Dr von Braun was dead. Late in the war, retreating from Allied bombing attacks, he was overseeing the conversion of the Mittelwerk, a tunnel complex in the Harz mountains in the south of the country, to create more V-2 rockets. These works used slave labour from the Mittelbau-Dora concentration camp to hew out wider, deeper caverns from the existing tunnels to run rails through them. The slaves slept in the tunnels, in bunk beds. There was no running water, no sanitation, little food. Daily, the slaves would wake beside corpses; there was typhus and dysentery and unending, unrelenting violence. Any slip on the production line and bony backs would be lashed. There were scaffolds up to the tunnel roofs, enabling more exhausting pick-work; the men would die as they stood, falling to the rocky ground below, and would be replaced instantly, their bodies taken to the ovens of Buchenwald. Those who died quickly were estimated to have numbered around 3,000 people. Some 17,000 more were to suffer slower and even more terrible deaths. However much he would later elide such details, or profess limited knowledge from his own position as a scientist and technician, von Braun must certainly have understood exactly what was happening on this site; in a terrible and curious way, the sadistic guards who beat the prisoners to death might be easier to fathom than this man.

And, as the war neared its end, von Braun calculated that the Nazi regime would fall quickly. He knew that he would be captured, and so ensured that those who seized him were American. The past twelve years of this aristocratic son of Berlin were then carefully veiled by the US authorities, the Americans allowing him to find fame as the pioneering rocket expert of the National American Space Agency that would in 1969 land a man on the moon. The deaths of so many slave labourers that resulted from von Braun's earlier employment were conveniently ignored.

By the spring of 1945, the wider world was aware of the full obscenity of Nazi evil. Film footage of the piles of bodies had revealed the true deathly logic of the regime: human life reduced to diseased refuse. Although such images were as yet unseen by German citizens, they could not have been wholly unaware of the murderous truth of their rulers: the whispers of Auschwitz had circulated in the capital. Yet the streets were still being patrolled by ever more neurotic SS men eager to make examples of those they deemed guilty of defeatism.

In the 1945 ruins of Berlin, four scientists in particular were preparing themselves for its final collapse – the nuclear physicists Gustav Hertz and Manfred von Ardenne and two of their colleagues, Peter Thiessen and Max Volmer. Like von Braun, von Ardenne was a young aristocrat – thirty-eight years old – whose mania for physics had propelled him into funding his own research laboratory with a vast family inheritance. Von Ardenne's realm of expertise was wide, but he focused especially on electron microscopy (illuminating and magnifying impossibly tiny samples with beams of electrons, rather than the visible photons of light) and also on wireless communication and television; in 1932 he produced the world's first public electronic television broadcast (an image of scissors – a striking and clear shape) and by 1936 was televising parts of the Berlin Olympics to the few existing TV receivers (some set up for public viewing).[19] He had been friends with the physicist Otto Hahn, and he was acutely aware of the nuclear insights of Werner Heisenberg. Von Ardenne had conducted experiments in his own private laboratories and had also been consulted by the Nazi hierarchy for his views on the viability of nuclear warfare. Yet, even under totalitarianism, he had managed to keep a little distance between his work and the greedy demands of the state.

In April 1945, as the Soviets massed to the east of the city, von Ardenne, Hertz, Thiessen and Volmer formulated a plan. It was certain that Soviet agents would be coming for them. It was equally certain that what remained of their laboratories would be ransacked. The quartet would have had a shrewd idea that, just as the Americans were advanced in their development of atomic weaponry, the Soviets would have been working hard on these problems too. The wider assumption among physicists for the last few years was that vast industrial facilities would be required to process the necessary uranium, but it was von Ardenne who believed that the uranium might be enriched with much smaller centrifuges. To von Ardenne, his work was all-consuming, irrespective of governmental politics, be they Nazi or communist or indeed liberal and democratic. And as much as he seemed resigned to the idea of being spirited away to Russia, along with his most valuable technical equipment, to continue his work, he did not anticipate doing so under duress. He, Hertz, Thiessen and Volmer agreed between them that whoever was first seized by the Red Army should immediately tell their captors that the other three were indispensable to the work to come. Remarkably, given the scale of indiscriminate destruction all around them, and the ruthlessness of the coming conquerors, the scientists were to find their new masters receptive to their request. Von Ardenne was one of those Berliners who had swum through the tides of history, and he would live long enough to see the collapse of communism and the reunification of Germany in 1990. In 1945, perhaps he would have understood better than anyone that history never ends.

Meanwhile, as the shape of future global geopolitics was being formed in those apprehensive hours, other Berliners yearned for means of escaping their own fears. They wanted to lose themselves in symphonies. Between the wars, the city had pulsated with the richest variety of music, from the classical lieder of Richard Strauss to the verve of jazz. Even Nazi efforts to ban this and other forms of what they considered degenerate music were ultimately to fail, as among soldiers and young people in the darkness of 1945, there were certain rhythms and melodies in the air that somehow could not be constrained.

## 8. The Prophecy of Flesh

The young of Berlin craved jazz, with all the force of a narcotic addiction. The lengths to which they would go – even in war – to defy the Nazi ban on this music were ingenious. Before the war, bands visiting the city from Belgium or Sweden, getting together with their German counterparts, found sometimes hilarious ways of subverting the strict rules: they performed forbidden American tunes by means of changing the original titles. The popular number 'Whispering', for instance, was announced instead as 'Lass mich dein Badewasser schlürfen' – 'Let Me Drink Your Bathwater'.[1] There was an official Nazi report regretting the activities of some youths in Berlin taverns; they were 'so plainly opposed to the respectable light music conforming to German taste, and are demanding jazz bands, sometimes in no uncertain terms, that the bands are gradually giving in, and the wilder, "hotter" music they play, the more unrestrained the applause they obtain from young people of this type.'[2]

Berlin had been suffused with music before the Nazis; and it was suffused with music throughout their regime, and after it as well. In the sensual life of the city, it was absolutely key. 'My parents gave me my gramophone on my fourteenth birthday in 1941,' recalled Manfred Omankowsky.[3] Despite its weight, he used to carry it down on summer days to his boat at the Tegeler See, where he would meet with friends and, under the strong Berlin sun, hidden in the reeds, they would listen to 'forbidden Swing'.[4] Elsewhere, even amid the later miasma of death, the city's notorious cabarets would be among the first startling resurrections in the post-war world, and the wider appetite for classical concerts never abated. The Nazis understood instinctively that music had power; but they were less certain about how that power might be harnessed for their own advantage. Unlike the imagery of film and art, or the singing of popular anthems or hymns, classical music spoke to the interior mind and soul. The most totalitarian of governments would never quite know the blend of individual emotions and thoughts that might be conjured through-out the course of a symphony. There were early efforts in the Third Reich to establish a steely control over the sorts of music that the population listened to: the famous bans on jazz, the loathing for the unsettling atonality of Schoenberg's compositions. There was even, later in the 1930s, a display of 'Degenerate Music' in sheet form, intended as a companion piece to a 'Degenerate Art' exhibition, filled with the compositions that the Nazis considered grotesque. But musical taste was never wholly controllable, especially in a city like Berlin, which was well supplied with concert halls and opera houses and in which – through records and radios – the unstoppable tides of new musical oceans had flowed into the ecstatic ears of younger lis-teners. Broad assumptions were made about 'Nazi music' after the war by the Allies occupying Berlin – that there were specific pieces that would be forever identified with flickering-torch rallies or goose-stepping parades – but these were too simplistic. In fact, after the war, Berlin's conductors and musicians and impresarios resumed with programmes that in some ways were not dissimilar to those of the 1930s or the 1920s. It was through music that the genuine spirit of the city and its people persisted, even as political thugs sought to suppress or capture it.

Back in the 1920s, Hitler had mused in *Mein Kampf* about the propa-gandist possibilities of music: 'symphonic genres could so easily be used for the purpose of ideology',[5] he wrote. But after attaining power, he seemed to realize that it was not so simple as that. At the 1938 Nuremberg Rally, he declared that music of itself could not express political values; that a symphony could not convey the firm beliefs of National Socialism. Mixed in with this was a faux humility; an idea that politicians should not lean upon the German genius for music, for fear that such pressure might cause this genius to warp and go 'in the wrong direction'[6] (though if there was no 'right' direction, this argu-ment seemed to be contradictory). None the less, it has been observed that the emphasis of the Nazi Party was not so much upon direct anthemic sloganeering as upon a concentration on the nature of Ger-man music; that young composers should emulate musical forebears such as Wagner and – to an extent – Beethoven, who had captured within their works something of the essence of Germany's soul.

This appeared to be a sincere belief; so much so that, throughout the 1930s, the world-acclaimed Berlin Philharmonic Orchestra was used not merely to add cultural prestige to the Nazi regime, but also to tour European capitals with performances of the prized German composers. This was music as soft power; used to impress upon other nations the fact of German exceptionalism. But it also had the purpose of demonstrating to these nations that German superiority was also natural and should be accepted. The orchestra travelled to France, and to Austria just before the Anschluss in 1938; so rather than simply expropriating the music, the Nazis sought instead to become associated with it, and with harmony and beauty. Wilhelm Furtwängler, conductor of the Berlin Philharmonic, was dismally aware, though, of the ugliness of the regime that he was dealing with. Almost as soon as the Nazis introduced Aryanization (the forced expulsion of Jewish people from the professions, as well as the acquisition of their property) he was forced to sack some of his Jewish musicians, including the cellists Joseph Schuster and Nikolai Graudan. The concertmaster that he himself had appointed – Szymon Goldberg – was similarly forced out in 1934, and travelled the world with the Goldberg Quartet. And, in hideous contrast, there were other members of that orchestra who proudly flaunted their fierce Nazi loyalties, including the violinist Hans Woywoth, who attended rehearsals in full SA uniform.

The persecution of the Jews right from the start of the regime was an immediate source of anguish to the middle-aged conductor, who himself had been garlanded with honours by the new rulers: in swift succession, Furtwängler had been appointed Prussian State Councillor, Reich Senator of Culture and Vice President of the Reichsmusikkammer. These ornate titles were soon stripped from him as Goebbels began to sense that Furtwängler was not politically reliable. Meanwhile, it was not only musicians who were suffering. The acute distress of his secretary Berta Geissmar was a terrible thing for Furtwängler to see; she too was Jewish and she too was being forced out from the Philharmonic. The appalling velocity of this Nazi wave of hatred made her mind up for her quickly: she felt she had no choice but to leave her own home. Frau Geissmar travelled west across Europe and eventually sailed for London. Before long,

she was the much-appreciated assistant of conductor Thomas
Beecham.

Furtwängler himself had never – until February 1945 – felt sufficiently threatened by the regime to consider emigration. After the
war, there were those who asked him why – if he loathed his new
leaders so much – he could not have at least contemplated it. 'It was
my task to help German music,' he said. 'The people who, once upon
a time, produced Bach, Beethoven, Mozart, Schubert and others live
on under the surface of the National Socialist Germany. I could not
leave Germany in her deepest misery.'[7]

Yet his relationship with the National Socialists was one of constant conflict. From the start, in 1933, he was perfectly open with
them about his feelings. He had written to Goebbels in that year protesting about the harshness and the self-defeating effect of driving
the nation's finest artistic talents into chilly exile. 'Men like [Bruno]
Walter, [Max] Reinhardt and [Otto] Klemperer must be able to play
their part in the Germany of the future,'[8] he wrote. Yet in that open
letter he had also expressed his support for any 'struggle against Jewishness directed primarily against those artists who are rootless and
destructive, who wish to achieve their effect through kitsch and dry
virtuosity'.[9] Furtwängler's passions were deeply rooted in what he
himself frequently referred to as 'blood' and 'soil'; like the Nazis, he
often invoked images of an essential German folk spirit. He believed
that spirit soared through German music. In 1930, Furtwängler wrote
that it was 'the greatest artistic achievement of all peoples of modern
times'.[10] He was a profound cultural conservative, and also a profoundly gifted one. He was a conductor of international renown
(recordings of his works are still sought after). This placed him in an
unusual position with the regime. He knew that he could appeal
directly to either Goebbels or Hitler. He also knew that he could
afford to demonstrate his distaste for their all-enveloping aggression;
Furtwängler largely absented himself from the triumphalist 1936
Berlin Olympics, and he was reluctant to conduct in vanquished cities like Vienna – part of the Nazi strategy to impose undiluted
German culture on Austria – agreeing to do so only if he could not
find means to avoid it.

Part of the Nazis' cultural vision was a sentimentalized and

1. The deathly winter of 1918–19 – defeat and disease – brought near civil war in Berlin. As communists and government-backed Freikorps fought, other civilians sought to restore normal lives.

2. Rosa Luxemburg, an unusually warm and charismatic communist, and figurehead of the Spartacus movement, was murdered by the Freikorps in 1919. Her body was thrown into a canal.

3. The restored Neue Synagogue, which glitters across the city's skyline. The building survived the fires of *Kristallnacht* but not Allied bombing. It lay in partial ruins until the late 1980s.

4. Modernists sought to bring beauty to the industrial everyday: the 1920s Karstadt department store, which glowed at night, was an exemplar of how Berlin – home of pioneering electrical firms Siemens and Osram – was bathed in light.

5. For international visitors, Weimar Berlin of the late 1920s offered unusually sensuous pleasures. For the wealthier of them, venues such as the Hotel Adlon were at the centre of the Jazz Age.

6. Chemist Otto Hahn and physicist Lise Meitner, here photographed in 1912, were to become Berlin's atomic pioneers. Professor Meitner, one of the first women in this field, was forced to leave the country in 1938 because of her Jewish heritage.

7. The extraordinary electrical laboratories of the young inventor Manfred von Ardenne (including his Van der Graaff generator) in the early 1930s; his expertise would eventually be sought by Stalin's Soviet secret services.

8. Throughout the Weimar years, Berlin was very much Albert Einstein's city. Smart society competed for his presence (and the chance to hear him explain Relativity), and his appearances throughout the 1920s and early 1930s prior to his US emigration attracted large crowds.

9. Berlin cinema blazed a global aesthetic trail in the 1920s. Fritz Lang's epic *Die Nibelungen* (1924), featuring doomed Siegfried in haunted forests, was intended by its writer to evoke the German soul.

10. Lang's *Metropolis* (1926) was an extraordinary science-fictional vision of future Berlin. The film, with its dazzling contrasts of darkness and vast beams of light, captivated the Nazi leadership.

11. Hitler's architect Albert Speer – who in the late 1930s produced scale models for a rebuilt future Nazi Berlin called Germania – shared his designs with the Führer in the dark small hours.

12. Paul Wegener as the avenging man of clay. *The Golem* (1920): a redemptive Jewish folk tale from an actor/director who was – amid Berlin's wartime ruins – called back to the stage by admiring Soviet officials.

13. The philosopher Hannah Arendt (pictured here in the early 1930s), who later wrote of the origins of Nazi evil, was obliged to share her rented Weimar flat with an avant-garde dance class.

14. The young Crown Prince Wilhelm, heir to the Kaiser, and his wife the Grand Duchess Cecilie had once been met with adulation in Berlin, but following the Kaiser's abdication in 1918, this swiftly changed to scorn.

15. Before he found literary immortality with *Lolita*, novelist Vladimir Nabokov and his wife Vera were part of Berlin's 1920s Russian community. He was beguiled by the city's taste for public nudity.

16. In the 1930s, many of Berlin's working-class tenement blocks – with dark, damp, cold courtyards – were in dreadful condition, becoming breeding grounds for anger.

17. Some of the city's modern factories – such as the AEG Turbine works, designed by Peter Behrens in 1909 – were brighter and more beautiful than many of their workers' homes.

18. Berlin's taste for velocity found expression in metro systems that soared and dived above, below and through streets, and occasionally buildings.

19. Street violence became commonplace during the 1920s and 1930s; pitched battles between Nazis and communists frequently resulted in serious injuries and deaths.

condescending idea of the working classes gasping with joy at being introduced to the beautiful music to which they had never previously been exposed. In this, the Nazis had much in common with other totalitarian societies that had no inkling that members of those very working classes might just have made their own way towards this music without paternalistic guidance. There was a photogenic occasion in 1942: Wilhelm Furtwängler conducting the Berlin Philharmonic under the vast industrial roof of the city's AEG works to an audience of workmen. They were given the prelude to Wagner's *The Mastersingers of Nuremberg*. In other wartime efforts, Furtwängler was extraordinarily unbiddable, pretending to be ill to avoid conducting Beethoven for Hitler's birthday and refusing to take part in propaganda films about the Philharmonic and Beethoven. An angry Goebbels wrote in his diary: 'Furtwängler has never been a National Socialist. Nor has he ever made any bones about it, which Jews and emigrants thought was sufficient to consider him as one of them . . . Furtwängler's stance towards us has not changed in the least.'[11]

There was one way to threaten this proud man, though, and that was by favouring a younger rival. An Austrian prodigy called Herbert von Karajan conducted a performance of Wagner's *Tristan and Isolde* in 1938, aged just thirty; the Berlin press hailed him as the 'wonder Karajan',[12] and printed his relatively youthful photograph next to that of the bald Furtwängler. He was given a recording contract with Deutsche Grammophon. Von Karajan commended himself in other ways. Unlike the older conductor, he was a member of the Nazi Party. He was always happy to begin recitals with a performance of the 'Horst Wessel Song', the anthem of the Nazi Party. There was also the frisson of his more modern methods of conducting, an energy that Goebbels found attractive. He was appointed director of the Berlin State Opera. He elicited a performance of Carl Orff's *Carmina Burana* in 1942 that was so exceptional, the composer himself pronounced himself thrilled.

But, following that lethal pattern of old, this prodigious talent was none the less destined to disappoint the Nazi leadership. There was a performance of *The Mastersingers* staged especially for Hitler; von Karajan conducted from memory without a score, the baritone was drunk and made mistakes, and the entire interpretation was deemed a failure by the Führer, who furiously took it personally. Then there was the matter of von Karajan's second marriage in 1942: his new wife Anita Gütermann, heiress to a textile fortune, had a Jewish grandfather. In the implacable tests of purity set by the Nazis, this meant that she herself was Jewish, and that von Karajan was now tainted by association.

Both conductors, such intense rivals in many ways, stayed loyal to the city that had given them fame. By the early days of 1945 both Furtwängler – his own home hit by incendiaries, and subsequently given a bespoke bomb shelter by Albert Speer – and von Karajan were separately contemplating not only their futures but also the future of the music for which they shared such passion. Furtwängler was already an old man; for von Karajan, though, these Nazi years in Berlin were merely the shadowed prelude to a more extraordinary and golden period in the city. For, in the end, the Nazi instinct about the difficulty of seizing music, bending and controlling it for political purpose, was absolutely right; there were always compositions and melodies there, beneath the surface of the regime, running like underground rivers, unstoppably, and always certain to rise up once more.

Certainly, the types of music that the Nazis had sought to stamp out were more persistent than they could have imagined; even those they had striven hard to demonize. In 1928 the Nazi newspaper *Der Angriff* as well as the city's more legitimate journals had reported on an extraordinary street battle at the Silesian station in Berlin, which had begun as a tavern tussle between two sets of gang members (one group dressed rather strikingly in top hats). This fight had burst out into the street and had soon sucked up to 200 more men into the whirlpool of the melee. The violence was very serious; one casualty died of his wounds in hospital several days later. Surely only the Nazi Party could have drawn a parallel between this 'degenerate' behaviour and a new 'play with music' by Bertolt Brecht and Kurt Weill that had recently opened.[13] This production, *Die Dreigroschenoper* (The Threepenny Opera), was the apogee of all that the Nazis loathed; here was a piece about prostitutes and murderers and protection rackets in Victorian London, searing, cynical and sympathetic, with its music infused with the subversive vibrancy of jazz. But, more than this, it was intended as the modern age's riposte to old opera, which was the province of 'aristocracy'.[14] This, by contrast, was opera for the working man; and it – and Weill and Brecht – were swiftly lauded in Britain and America before the Nazis were in any position to suppress their work.

For all Jewish artists and songwriters, it was understood that there could be no reasoning with the National Socialists. After 1933, any of their works that continued to find an audience were swiftly stamped upon. The hugely popular Swedish singer and actress Zarah Leander – who was herself extremely comfortable with Nazi rule – had a huge hit in 1938 with her recording of a song called 'Bei mir bist du schön' ('To Me, You are Beautiful'). The melody was everywhere. Then it was revealed to be a Jewish composition. The Nazis promptly banned it. Meanwhile, the Nazi prohibition of jazz (which had in fact begun rather earlier in the Weimar era in the state of Thuringia in 1930) was explicitly a racist decree: the musical form was linked on posters with horribly caricatured black men. This meant that Berlin's main radio station was under immediate orders to censor its playlists. The official guidelines on the limits placed upon bands were preposterously detailed and almost comic in their pomposity. Pieces 'must consist of a natural legato movement devoid of the hysterical rhythmic reverses characteristic of the barbarian races and conducive to dark instincts alien to the German people (so-called riffs)',[15] ran one injunction. Another declared that 'Strictly prohibited is the use of instruments alien to the German spirit (so-called cow-bells, flexatone, brushes etc.) as well as all mutes which turn the noble sound of wind and brass instruments into a Jewish-Masonic yowl (so-called wa-wa) . . . Musicians are likewise forbidden to make vocal improvisations (so-called Scat).'[16] Meanwhile, the Reich Chamber of Music declared that 'jazzified, judified dance music'[17] was an affront. Yet to great numbers of Berliners, it was no such thing; rather, in the immediate aftermath of the Great War, and the years that followed, it had been an almost transcendental means of turning away from the ubiquity of death. 'Music plays in hundreds of locales,' reported the *Berliner Tageblatt* on New Year's Eve in 1918, 'dance after dance: waltz, fox-trot, one-step, two-step. Legs race across the floor, shirts fly, hearts jump . . . and New Year greetings resound in the exact same streets where the steps of demonstrators had just echoed.'[18] One writer openly likened the revolutionary music to Einstein's theory of relativity.

And, like a hidden spring, it kept gushing out; not least because it became apparent in the late 1930s and early 1940s that members of the armed services – and in particular the Luftwaffe – were frustrated that they were forbidden to listen to swing. Their complaints grew louder. The regime had to compromise: and it did so in a baroque manner. In Berlin, in January 1940, a new band was formed: Charlie and His Orchestra. This curious ersatz orchestra – which, as observers of the band noted, featured some extraordinarily good musicians, the best of their type in Europe at the time – would purvey swing with a Nazi varnish in live radio shows broadcast not only to Germans but also across to Britain, where there was apparently a small audience for their performances. The nucleus of the band had been a very fine saxophonist – and enthusiastic Nazi – called Lutz Templin. Sensing that there had to be some kind of pressure valve for musical demand, Goebbels enjoined Templin to assemble musicians who could perform numbers that would be acceptable to the ears of both senior fighter pilots and the Nazi hierarchy. The hook was plagiarism; very often, the band simply took American hits and gave them Nazi lyrics. In one song, 'Charlie', singing as 'Winston Churchill', crooned (in amusingly accented English): 'The Germans are driving me crazy/ I thought I had brains/ But they shot down my planes.'[19] In another, the American Cole Porter hit 'You're the Top' received a fantastically unsubtle rewrite. 'You're the top/ You're a German flyer/ You're the top/ You're machine-gun fire/ You're a U-Boat chap/ With a lot of pep/ You're grand.'[20] Mixed in with all of this were songs involving Wall Street capitalists and the machinations of international Jewry.

Yet, as the German singer Evelyn Künneke observed, lightly rather than disapprovingly, the band itself was composed of 'half-Jews and gypsies . . . Freemasons, Jehovah's Witnesses, homosexuals and Communists'.[21] It offered its own rather tilted form of sanctuary. The enthusiastic drummer Fritz Brocksieper (known as 'Freddie' and famed for 'his inordinate noise'[22]) had a Greek mother. His grandmother was Jewish. There was a laconic and rather brilliant Czech accordionist, Kamil Běhounek, summoned to join the ensemble in 1943 as others were drafted into full military service, who was bemused by the slick professionalism of the entire enterprise. He recalled years later:

> I wondered what sort of village band I was going to be working for. But orders is orders. I got to Berlin in the evening. In the darkness I could make out the ruined buildings which bore witness to the devastating air raids. Next morning I went to the huge broadcasting centre on the Masurenallee . . . I felt like Alice in Wonderland. Here was this big dance orchestra with three trumpets, three trombones, four saxes, a full rhythm group. And they were swinging it! And how! Lutz Templin had got together the best musicians from all over Europe for his band.[23]

'Charlie' himself – Karl Schwedler – was, as far as anyone could discern, a faithful Nazi; he certainly sported SS-monogrammed dressing gowns. He was also a risk-taker with a silkily amoral approach to the war (including trips abroad that would result in bounties of black-market specialities such as stockings and luxury soap). And it is faintly possible that his attitude to the Nazi Party as a whole was a little layered. The over-the-top repurposing of American and British hits for German audiences may have been entirely free from irony; but the borderlands of comic intention are extremely difficult to police. And the question of aiding a regime they found poisonous was, for the band members, simply too abstract to worry about. As Běhounek put it so succinctly, it was either this or joining a forced labour production line in an armaments factory.[24]

Elsewhere, across the Atlantic, under the wide, cold skies of an affluent New York suburb – white-boarded villas, cool green lawns, dainty shopping parades and a pebbled shore overlooking Little Neck Bay – there was an exiled Berlin visionary and sensualist who understood that, in spring 1945, ordinariness was itself a form of paradise. All about him was American abundance: food, warmth, alcohol, the fundamental security of home; the powerful comforts that he knew had been completely stripped from the fellow citizens he had been forced to leave behind. Here was an artist who had been among the first to see directly into the heart of the Nazi movement; who had been the first to detect, in the early 1930s, the relish of sadism in its restoration of torture to the public realm. This artist, born in 1893, had also produced the most vivid visual chronicle of Berlin's Weimar years: canvases rich in satirical nakedness and sexuality. From 1916 onwards he had bathed his visions of the night-time city – haunted by prostitutes, mutilated soldiers and the fat, complacent bourgeoisie – in lurid reds. He understood the human impulse towards transgression, and Berlin's tremendous appetite for decadence. George Grosz was hardly an ascetic soul himself; before he was forced to flee to America in 1933, and make a new life as an art teacher, he had been a dandy, a firebrand communist, a very committed drinker and the most uncannily acute observer of his age. Most particularly, he had understood the extraordinary sexual energy of Berlin: the plump brothel eroticism, the preposterous indignity of lust. He revelled in the more perverse, violent corners of the city's unconscious soul too; he and his wife Eva Peters posed for a photographic portrait in which she stood in her underwear by a full-length mirror while her husband was positioned behind it, leering and gripping a large kitchen knife: an arresting burlesque on sex crime.[25] Grosz also understood how the men of the SS had sought to harness and distort the city's transgressive energy. Yet if he could have seen Berlin in the war years, Grosz would have been amused by the more straightforward outbreaks of sexual rebellion on the production lines of the war factories in the 1940s: working-class women laughingly colluding to fondle the backsides of young male forced labour colleagues, and persuading them to meet in oily factory corners for furtive sexual congress. ('I was a sixteen-year-old virgin and was uncomfortable – but also aroused – by the advances these women made,' recalled Lothar Orbach).[26]

Life in 1940s New York (George Grosz lived in Douglaston, an area about ten miles east of Manhattan) had dimmed his former ferocity. But as the city that was once his home was disintegrating, Grosz summoned his old powers for an intensely unsettling composition. Entitled 'Peace I (Frieden)', here was a painted nightmare that matched the reality of his old home. Black skies lit red and gold with ferocious fires, the heat swirling in whorls, vast uprooted trees and exposed orange brickwork, and at the centre of it all, moving through these ruins, a hooded figure in robes carrying a rough satchel. The figure has frighteningly piercing eyes: red, seemingly accusing, staring directly at the viewer. It could be a man or a woman, and it could exist at any point in time. (It has been suggested that the figure might have been his mother, who had not emigrated with him, but stayed behind in Berlin, and had been killed in an Allied bombing raid.) In terms of its apocalyptic weight, the painting was in one way an eerie premonition: a year later, Grosz would remark of Berlin, 'It's all gone. Only dust remains. Tree stumps, filth, hunger and cold.'[27] Yet in time he would return.

Grosz's Weimar art had itself been viewed by unfriendly eyes as unacceptably transgressive: he had been a special object of loathing to the Nazis because of what they considered his obscenity, as well as his intense socialist beliefs. He was, they declared, 'cultural bolshevist number one',[28] and his paintings were the first centrepieces of their 'Degenerate Art' exhibitions in the nation's major cities. In turn, though, he had always painted what he considered to be the fundamental truths of his fellow citizens; his opprobrium was universal. 'To be German is always to be tasteless, stupid, ugly, fat, stiff,' he said. 'To be unable, at the age of forty, to climb a ladder; to be badly dressed. To be a German is to be a reactionary of the worst kind.'[29] Art had always been a threat to the Nazis, not merely because of extreme innovation that induced nausea in conservative eyes but also because it could evoke laughter and pity and fellow feeling for those who might otherwise be shunned. Grosz's pencil-and-paint chronicle of the Weimar and early Nazi years could never be wholly extinguished; and the remarkable openness that he detected in his fellow citizens was soon to find expression once more even amid the dust and the sexual violence.

In an age of extraordinary art, Grosz was an exception from a very early age; having studied in Dresden and at the Berlin school of arts and crafts, his nascent career – delayed by the Great War – began when he was temporarily invalided out of that conflict, rejoined it in 1917 and was invalided out once more with what would now be recognized as post-traumatic stress disorder. Even before the Wilhelmine era imploded, Grosz – through the medium of jarring-angled expressionism – was portraying Berlin as a conflation of bare breasts and buttocks, luxurious interiors, balloon-headed plutocrats, poverty-stricken streets and suicides. With the German Revolution came the awakening of Grosz's political consciousness. He joined the Spartacist League and was a spirited proselytizer for communism. He was a pioneer in montage, creating savagely satirical art through the juxtaposition of pictures and headlines found in ordinary newspapers. Yet there were also layers here; he was no garret-dwelling puritan. The man who fought for class justice was himself a fastidious dresser, with silk suits and an ivory-topped cane. He was also obsessed with westerns (an enthusiasm he shared with many other Berliners, but which he took rather further by occasionally dressing up as a cowboy), and his taste in alcohol leaned towards the baroque. One favoured cocktail was the Green Minna, a striking blend of potato-derived schnapps and vivid peppermint liqueur.[30]

As a Dadaist, he performed startlingly obscene tap-dance routines on stage, yet during the day he could sometimes be found in the smart and fragrant salons hosted by Count Harry Kessler. Grosz spent some months in Soviet Russia in 1922, and had the chance to meet Lenin, though, strikingly, the artist upon his return was to disavow the Soviet revolution, having seen the effects upon the cold and hungry population close-up. None the less, his loathing of corpulent capitalism – and the damage it wrought upon the poor of industrialized Berlin – did not dim.

Invited to the US to teach in New York for a semester in 1932, Grosz realized upon his return to Berlin a few months later that he and his family could not possibly be safe under the National Socialists, and by the time of the German election in March 1933, and the subsequent speedy dismantling of basic freedoms, Grosz was in New York. His interest in the Nazis as a subject for his corrosive art was intensified. In the 'Interregnum' series of pen drawings from the mid 1930s, Grosz illustrated the darkening city of Berlin with a perceptiveness that was unmatched; he was the first to identify artistically what was happening in the new-built camps that were being established near Berlin and around the country in 1933.[31] Old friends and associates of his – playwrights, socialist politicians – were being arrested, taken to these prison camps and subjected not only to tooth-breaking interrogations but also to punishments that were random and entirely sadistic: ritualized whippings, for example. Grosz drew this world in all its starkness, showing cells dominated by leering SS men. There were very few in Berlin who sought to draw public attention to the truth of what was happening to the Nazis' political opponents far from the eyes of any objective judicial system.

In 1944, Grosz gave a frightening interpretation of Nazism's ultimate destination: in his canvas 'Cain, or Hitler in Hell' the artist depicted the dictator sitting amid the sulphur pits, head lowered, mopping his brow, the skies of damnation copper with flame. Beneath his feet lay great numbers of emaciated corpses and skeletons, some clinging to his boots. Months before the Red Army's horrifying discovery of the death camps, Grosz seemed to have foretold the central obscenity of the Nazi cult, and the only possible destination that it could reach. (After years in the private collection of the Grosz family, the painting was finally unveiled in Berlin in 2020.)[32] Grosz's artistic career had begun with an intense preoccupation with trauma and sex and, although frequently cruel, his paintings and drawings had throbbed with fleshiness. This, however, was different: a world of horror stripped of all sensuality and indeed all hope. In time, Grosz would return to Berlin, and he would sit upon piles of rubble, sketching. His later work too would come to express the personal losses and traumas that the Hitler cult had inflicted upon him.

Grosz additionally identified one aspect of Nazism in its earliest form that had long preoccupied its communist opponents: a perceived culture of homo-eroticism among its ranks – a transgression that might be leveraged by the left for political advantage. By itself, there might have been nothing remarkable about it; military homo-eroticism had also been a (well-publicized) feature of a number of the aristocrats who gathered around Kaiser Wilhelm II at the beginning of the century (exposed in a bitter round of lip-smackingly scandalous newspaper exposés and libel cases). Then, in the wake of the Great War, as in so many other aspects of life, Berlin actually became pioneering as a city in terms of acceptance and understanding of

homosexuality, even if intercourse between men remained techni-
cally illegal under Paragraph 175 of Germany's judicial code drawn
up in 1871. (Female prostitution, for comparison, was legalized by the
Reichstag in 1927; the profusion of brothels in fiction and on screen
was reflective of Berlin reality.) The city had had a thriving subterranean gay culture since before the Great War, and it became more
visible during the Weimar era. In the 1920s, even Hitler seemed
relaxed about the sexual orientation of his sociopathic SA lieutenant
Ernst Röhm. A bulky man who had suffered terrible facial injuries in
the First World War, and who had been brought close to death in the
Spanish Flu epidemic that followed it, Röhm was among the earliest
members of the NSDAP and was friends with Hitler at the very
beginning of the movement. He saw nothing transgressive about his
own homosexuality. The war and the military had defined the shape
of his future life, and he was perfectly at ease with his orientation.
'Only the real, the true, the masculine held its value,' he declared of
the cataclysm of the war.[33] But this for him meant a form of hyper-
masculinity, which he saw encapsulated in Nazism. There was a
wider male phenomenon in Weimar Berlin of *kalte persona* – cool personality, or, in another sense, coldly detached – following a conflict
that had torn men down. To Röhm, communism and Bolshevism
were embodiments of feminine anarchy and 'indiscipline'.[34] Hitler
made him chief of staff of the SA. As the decade progressed, Röhm
dedicated himself to the paramilitary assertion of brutality on the
streets. Enemies were maimed in alleys. Weimar was itself, as he saw
it, an embodiment of the decadent feminine. Röhm argued that
modern men should be free from 'prudery'.[35] 'The struggle against
the pretence, deceit and hypocrisy of this society must take its starting point from that which is most basic in life, the sexual drives; only
then can it be led generally with success in all human life. If the struggle in this area is successful, then the masks can be torn from the
illusions in all areas of human social and legal order.'[36]

And at the start of the 1930s, the SA was to take on an even more
vividly terrible life, fomenting assaults and fights outside Berlin factories and pubs. Those who sought to exploit Röhm's sexuality as a
weakness were broadly his socialist enemies; a number of intimate
letters written by Röhm were handed to a journalist who proceeded

to expose him. Yet the exposure was in part redundant; Röhm saw no reason to hide the truth about his sexuality. This in part said something about the intense modernity of Berlin. But, by 1934, it was used against him by his former friend, now firmly in power. Concerned that the prodigious numbers of SA auxiliaries under Röhm posed a threat both to the standing military and potentially to his new dictatorship, Hitler approved the liquidation of its key personnel. When what turned into a mass murder – the 'Night of the Long Knives' – became common knowledge, the Nazis explained the vicious purge partly as being a reaction to the decadent homosexuality of the SA's leadership. This was simply an excuse, yet one that Hitler exploited energetically, proclaiming in the Reichstag: 'The life which the Chief of Staff and a certain circle around him began to lead was intolerable from any National Socialist viewpoint.'[37] The Nazi persecution of all gay men accelerated from this point onwards; they became undesirables to be identified, named, then purged from public view, and sent to concentration camps. Röhm himself was offered the possibility of suicide, and was left alone in a cell with a gun. He refused, declaring that if he was to be shot, then Hitler should pull the trigger. That trigger was pulled, although by someone else.

Yet, while his life had been filled with relentless fascistic violence, Röhm was never wholly predictable. In the 1920s, he had shown some curiosity about a new organization in Berlin which at the time was unique in the world: the Institute of Sexual Science. Based in a handsome house near the Tiergarten, decorated throughout in the elegant Biedermeier style, this establishment – part clinic, part meeting place, part museum and part lecture hall – was the culmination of the work of Dr Magnus Hirschfeld, who, since the beginning of the century, had sought to have all shades of human sexuality explored, researched and understood – a direct challenge to more old-fashioned ideas of erotic morality, seeking to remove the taint of shame. A prolific writer of widely read books and pamphlets on the subject of homosexuality throughout the early years of the century, Hirschfeld had already been tremendously influential in persuading the Berlin authorities to relax their policing of the city's underground gay culture. Hirschfeld himself was gay, and, by the 1920s, he was living with the institute's secretary, Karl Giese. And the institute was a source of some wonder – and in many cases reassurance and succour – for those anxious about a range of issues, heterosexual and homosexual, from impotence to STDs, from reviving marriages to helping those who wished to transition. (Though it might seem in some ways a relatively modern issue, Dr Hirschfeld was a compassionate campaigner for gender recognition and what he termed 'sexual intermediaries'. 'Love is as varied as people are,' he declared.) The institute campaigned vigorously on matters of sexual health, and also for sexual tolerance. It was prominent in the promotion of feminism: psychiatrists such as Dr Mathilde Vaerting argued about the 'natural equality between woman and man' and that 'sexual dominance' was related to 'political dominance', a social artifice, rather than being a matter of differing male and female psychological attributes.[38]

And, for Hirschfeld, it was beyond dispute that homosexuality was innate. 'What is natural,' he wrote, 'cannot be immoral.'[39] But he also had a fascination for all the different impulses and desires of human nature. The novelist Christopher Isherwood, who became semi-resident at the institute, described how, in the quieter parts of the building, there were informal displays of ladies' lace underwear, as sported by ferocious Prussian generals, and various whips and rods, speaking to Berlin's thriving subculture of spanking (a recurring leitmotif in Erich Kästner's *Going to the Dogs*).[40] That Ernst Röhm and other hard-right figures, including Nazi Party members, had initially noted the institute, not to destroy it (at least, not at that point) but to learn more was a remarkable commentary on Berlin sophistication; such an establishment – certainly one so wide-open to the public and broadly advertised – could not have been conceived of in Paris or London at the time. (In fact, it also had scientific antecedents: in 1869 the Royal Prussian Scientific Commission for Medical Affairs had argued that same-sex relations should be decriminalized since they were 'no more injurious' than 'fornication or adultery'.[41] The recommendation was ignored, but, in the coming years, the growth of cities such as Berlin offered gay people new possibilities of anonymity and discretion that could not be found in villages or small towns.)

Dr Hirschfeld was a prominent and passionate campaigner against Paragraph 175; under this legal ruling, across the years, huge numbers of gay men had been prosecuted, and huge numbers had committed suicide. In his studies, Dr Hirschfeld had found that a hidden gay culture was present in all strata of German society, from the loftiest and flintiest aristocracy, to those living amid the ash and dust of industrial poverty. He understood the law as forbidding people to fall in love; the inhumanity was starkly obvious to him, and he fought to make it so to the wider world as well. To an extent, this was successful in Berlin throughout the 1920s; while the city had long had bars and clubs that appealed – discreetly and secretly – to almost exclusively homosexual clienteles, the Weimar years brought a new and occasionally fashionable frankness. It was not only sophisticated English writers such as Isherwood (giving that world a form of immortality with his 1939 novel *Goodbye to Berlin*) who were making these discoveries; rather more ordinary tourists, from across the continent as well as America, were now enjoying a new nocturnal demi-monde of bars where sex and gender seemed endlessly fluid and changeable. On the streets, the police had been persuaded not to hunt down men who were making assignations. Dr Hirschfeld's simple thesis that human sexuality – and, more importantly, human love – held many possibilities appeared to have been accepted.

The atmosphere within the Institute of Sexual Science was not that of a medical practice; instead, it was restfully and elegantly furnished in the manner of an exclusive retreat. And it was also a powerful draw for a range of other scientific and psychiatric voices; Dr Hirschfeld had made it an abiding principle that this was an arena not for rivalries, but to pool knowledge of hitherto unstudied areas.

Of course, this was before the Nazis had attained power; and Dr Hirschfeld was always acutely aware of their threat, but his lover Karl Giese was swift to take the first and most vital precaution against state violence. In 1932, while Hirschfeld was engaged in international speaking tours as the shadow fell across Germany, he had the institute's confidential records – patients and clients – gathered together, secured and sent abroad for safe keeping. He knew that such acutely sensitive information could be used with devastating effect. He was also correct about the malign intentions of the new regime. In the first few days after the Nazis' ascension to power, the institute was placed under continual state surveillance. By March 1933 the violence had begun. There was a raid by the Nazi authorities and the institute's extensive library was torn apart; thousands of scholarly volumes were taken outside and burned in vast fires. The institute's administrator, Kurt Hiller – a gay Jewish communist (the courage required in that intersection of persecutions must have been extraordinary) – was arrested and imprisoned in a series of concentration camps, including Oranienburg, near Berlin. After suffering horrendous beatings, he was released in 1934 and was eventually able to leave Germany for London. Many other gay men were never afforded that opportunity.

None the less, throughout the increasingly bleak 1930s – and even in the 1940s, as Berlin's nights were wrapped in the total darkness of blackout – there were men who simply could not bear the loneliness, and who risked death in search of companionship. For this reason, blackmail – which had been so prominent a feature of Wilhelmine gay life, as Kaiser Wilhelm II's circle knew – was given a new and terrible strength. In Lothar Orbach's extraordinary memoir of life as a young fugitive Jew living in Berlin throughout the war, there is a sad episode in the wake of a 1943 bombing raid where his associate Tad explains how they can make much-needed money very quickly. 'Answer me one question,' he says to his friend. 'How badly do you want to get through this?'[42] They meet at the station by Berlin's zoo and Tad indicates a men's public lavatory. 'I watched the men across the street furtively making their transactions,' wrote Lothar, 'and saw the naked fear in their eyes as they huddled nervously on the corners.'[43] Tad's plan is to pretend to be a male prostitute; once he has made a pick-up, Lothar is to follow them back to the intended victim's apartment. He is to then pose as a police officer, coming to arrest the pair of them. In this pitiless world, the ruthless scheme must have seemed irresistible.

Tad succeeds in enticing 'a well-dressed middle-aged man';[44] Lothar tails them back through the debris-filled streets and thence to a smart residential block where, by some miracle, the stained-glass windows illuminating each landing have not been shattered by the bombs. The victim's apartment is also unusually well appointed and preserved: with 'heavily flocked fleur-de-lis wallpaper in pale blue and gold' and a 'gold Persian rug'.[45] The victim has money; the scam is perpetrated, with Tad, trousers artfully unbuttoned, begging mercy from the 'officer' and then offering a bribe which will, of course, come from the victim. The middle-aged man is in tears; he proffers the cash; the young men leave. Afterwards, they can barely speak to one another out of guilt; their victim had done neither of them any harm. Yet there is an unspoken shadowy layer beneath even that: that their victim actually escaped very lightly, parting only with a few hundred marks. Under the Nazi regime, other men, similarly entrapped, were destined for the camps. Young Orbach himself – in different circumstances – was to be betrayed after years of precarious invisibility, and in 1944 he was transported to Auschwitz. Yet that was not where his life was to end, and, remarkably, he would in time elect to return to the ruined city.

In one way, the Nazi approach to homosexuality – as cruel as it was – also fed into the regime's singular focus on heterosexual relations, and a preoccupation with procreation. One prominent Berlin artist in particular – the polar opposite to George Grosz – gave voice to these views, both in his speeches and in his paintings. For Adolf Ziegler, the purpose of the image of a naked woman was not merely to evoke arousal in a man, but also to fill that man's head with the prospect of patriotic reproduction. The woman was there as a vessel – the means by which the Aryan bloodline might be promulgated. Under the Nazis, this idea was intended as orthodoxy, even normality. The same was true of Ziegler's art, which was the encapsulation of everything that the Nazis wanted from painting in the public realm: representative, realistic, with acknowledgements to both classical art and more folksy rural historical portraits. Ziegler's output ranged from tastefully arranged nudes to family groupings to portraits of apparently timeless women in the country gathering fruits. It was not completely unsensual – there was life in those oils – nor was it unaccomplished, for these were paintings of immense technical skill. Yet the intense ideological seriousness pulsed through. Ziegler also occupied a central place in the story of Berlin's artistic life because it was he who made the pioneering suggestions as to which works of art should be publicly shamed under the Nazis. As the Reich Chamber of Arts president, it was Ziegler who wanted to see the work of George Grosz consumed by flame.

The styles of Weimar art that had led to Berlin capturing the attention of the world had been abominated very early on by Hitler; he regarded the Dadaist movement and cubism not as glittering innovations in sensibility, but as active conspiracies against German identity: a Jewish or Bolshevik plot to undermine the nation by reducing its artistic foundations to 'insanity'[46] that could not be comprehended by the ordinary man. The work of the middle-aged Adolf Ziegler, by contrast, had a much more *völkisch* feel: ordinary German people and family scenes, capturing moments of grave reflection in homely kitchens or parlours. There were Aryan boys looking similarly grave; women in fields, staring either at one another or into the distance. (The odd thing about these neat and impeccable portraits – aside from the sense that they could be showing us people from decades or even centuries earlier – is that all the subjects look notably melancholic. Certainly they seem healthy and Aryan but there is apprehension in all of their eyes. For this reason, these paintings cannot be counted as pure Nazi kitsch; there is something more complex at work, suggestive of authenticity.)

Ziegler, as mentioned, also specialized in a certain kind of neoclassical female nude, intended partly to suggest the roots in antiquity of the German soul but also – given their startling realism in the areas more normally covered with gauze – to announce a weirdly strident sexuality. When Ziegler pulled together the first exhibition of 'Degenerate Art' in Munich in 1937, he declared: 'You see around us monstrosities of madness, of impudence, of inability . . . What this show has to offer causes shock and disgust in all of us.'[47] The 'degenerate art' was in itself a source of degeneracy: Grosz's perverse men in suits and shameless harlots in their lurid world were triggers for debauched behaviour in those who beheld them. The exhibition, touring Germany, proved genuinely popular with a great many people. Hitler and the Nazis were not alone in their intense dislike of these manifestations of modernism. Other works, from artists such as Paul Klee and Emil Nolde (who had shown some initial sympathy with the Nazi regime but found his vividly colourful expressionist works spat upon anyway), were not understood and were resented fiercely.

By way of contrast, Ziegler – Hitler's favourite artist – provided smoothly accomplished reassurance, and his work took prominent positions in that same year's 'Great German Art Exhibition'. One particular painting, a triptych entitled 'The Four Elements', was soon to hang over Hitler's fireplace. In this work, which deliberately harks back to the style of the Old Masters without a hint of the required subtlety, four naked models – Fire, Earth, Wind and Water – are seated on a marble bench, with props such as silk and ears of corn. It is not so much kitsch as deliberately anachronistic, but the aim was explicitly to give praise to the fecundity of German womanhood. If it had been produced under any other regime, and at any other period, this work might have been regarded either as a sly satire on the classical style or as a sophisticated post-modern appropriation of it.

That Hitler regarded himself as an artist was widely known even before he seized power. Bertolt Brecht wrote a mocking poem about his painting, deliberately conflating it with house painting and likening the state of Germany to a rundown property that he is attempting to beautify. 'O Housepainter Hitler/ Why were you no mason? Your house/ If the whitewash gets into the rain/ The dirt underneath comes out again.'[48] In 1937, the boys of the Hitler Youth across the nation received a striking present from the organization's leader: portfolios containing reproductions of the Führer's rustic watercolours, with the exhortation 'These . . . from the hand of our Führer reveal to you the artistic personality of a man who has become more and more of an embodiment of the creative genius to his young people.'[49] Creativity was another form of virility; as the artist sought to promulgate his ideal of true beauty, so too was that beauty partly intended to inspire the young women and men of Germany to reproduce their own bloodline purity.

The reality in Berlin could never have begun to approximate the sickly romanticism of the art; even without war, even without the cloying, pervasive scent of death amid half-demolished dwellings, the young people always had very much their own idea of what constituted a satisfactory approach to love. Helga Hauthal was still at school in 1944 and her own sense of romance was – ironically, as it would transpire – moulded entirely by the Nazi-approved films that were still playing in Berlin's cinemas. 'Most of the films were not suitable for minors because there was kissing on the screen,' she recalled many years later.[50] On top of this, some of these films carried a frisson that the directors – if not the regime – had been fully aware of. There had been a reissue of Fritz Lang's silent epic *Die Nibelungen*. Helga was enthralled. Young (doomed) Siegfried was the epitome of young Aryan manhood. He also happened to be very handsome and muscular, and the Siegfried imagery was also ubiquitous in magazines and newspapers, right into the war.

More pressing, though, was the modern sophistication of the current screen actresses. The look of beautiful performers like Marika Rökk was irresistible, and to emulate it became a matter of some urgency. This meant that Helga had to have a perm at any cost. The chief difficulty was that the Nazis had decreed that hairdressers were not allowed to create this hairstyle for girls under the age of sixteen. Helga, however, had a family friend who was willing to circumvent the rules in this. When she got home 'after the procedure', as she put it, she augmented it with an extra 'frill' at the front of her fringe with a comb – a style that had been carried off by Marika Rökk. Unfortunately, she was called up for duty in the League of German Girls shortly after this. In the first parade, she was told to drop out of line and turn round so that her fellows might inspect this forbidden hairstyling. The group leader told them all that Helga 'looked as German girls should not look'.[51]

This innocent transgression was one that she simply could not resist. 'Asserting oneself and learning independence,' she remembered. 'These are important.'[52] It would continue to be so after the last guttering flames of Nazism had been extinguished: even in 1945, many of the young people of Berlin were more than ready to transgress further than even the previous generation. But first the old foundations of the society that their parents had known had to be destroyed.

# 9.   The Ruins of Palaces

The imperious old woman, tall and stout, moving through the antler-hung panelled rooms of her vast home, seemed for a time determined to resist the temptation to flee the city. In previous years she had seen branches of her aristocratic family amputated in bloody slaughter, and it was obvious to her that the possibility of violent death was approaching her own home fast. She had already had to flee her country Schloss in rural Silesia in order to return to this gladed retreat on the fringes of Berlin. But where else was there to go now? She was a duchess; she had once been a crown princess. Had history pivoted a different way, she would have been the Empress of All Germany. Her husband was the former Crown Prince Wilhelm. His father had been the last Kaiser. Wilhelm II had abdicated swiftly at the end of the Great War, and fled with little dignity to the Netherlands. The monarchy in Germany was terminated. But some spectre of hope haunted the life of his heir. The heir's wife, Cecilie, was more sourly realistic.

The Duchess Cecilie of Mecklenburg-Schwerin had once been a figure at whom the people of Berlin stared as she went about her charitable works and state duties. Staring is not the same as defer-ence; Berliners of all classes were especially swift in the wake of the Great War to throw off the habit of genuflection. The walls of her life, and that of her husband, had closed in dramatically in the inter-vening years. The former crown prince and the duchess were by the start of 1945 holding out within the woodland palace that had been built especially for her in Potsdam, a few miles to the south-west of the city. Duchess Cecilie was in some ways an emblem for the city's extreme divisions of social class that, despite all – the formation of the republic, the appropriation of lands and property – had somehow survived. Even the title 'duchess' seemed like a jewelled anachronism. This, though, was the end.

In the watery quiet of Potsdam, a prospect of lapping lake and gardens, landscaped in the English style, was their sanctuary; at night, under the cover of blackout, its remoteness from the city centre protected it from the trajectory of the bombs. This wooded fastness was a most singular palace that had been designed, before the Great War, in part as a tribute to English architecture.[1] It contained 176 rooms, and yet by means of a brilliant illusion of brick, timber and Tudor detailing, it contrived to look very much more modest and, in places, even homely. The trick was that it had several courtyards, which meant that beyond the galleries and the dining halls and the smoking parlours were yet more of the same, obscured by rambling corridors. Viewed from some angles, and from the distance of the gardens that surrounded it, this eccentric tribute to British domesticity seemed to make a virtue of understatedness. And so the fifty-eight-year-old Duchess and her unwell husband sequestered themselves in the house that had been named after her: Cecilienhof.

The bombs dropped by Allied planes did not discriminate between the social classes. The grander houses of Berlin were, in theory, as vulnerable to the searing fires as the most ill-built tenements, although, unlike poorer citizens, the aristocracy as a rule had the advantage of a number of roofs to choose from to live under. But though inherited wealth and extended titled connections brought material security, the nobility of Germany had since the end of the Great War been vulnerable in other ways. In one sense, these once regal families with their ancient names remained in Berlin only on sufferance. Many had been trying to make accommodations with the regime's monsters. Many had joined the more brutal wings of the regime itself. And yet they still found belatedly that the monsters held them in contempt. By the end of the war, in 1945, that sufferance had become open suspicion and hostility.

A few months previously, in July 1944, it had been a conspiracy of aristocrats that had attempted to kill Hitler at his Wolf's Lair by means of a bomb planted in a briefcase. This was not to be just an assassination but a full-blown coup: as soon as it could be confirmed that Hitler was dead, the military in Berlin would be coordinated to seize power from the Nazi hierarchy. The chief mover in this plot was Colonel Claus Schenk Graf von Stauffenberg, a thirty-six-year-old officer who had frequent direct access to Hitler. The injuries he himself had sustained in the war were very visible: he had lost one eye, his entire right hand and two fingers on his left. His anger and anguish had been building while serving in the east (he had spoken out in horror at SS atrocities perpetrated against the Jews), but his broader sense of patriotism and duty and his work ethic were unchanged, and to this extent he was impossible to distrust. He was not the first to conceive of removing Hitler in a bloody coup; one of his chief associates, General Henning von Tresckow, also from a socially exalted family, had been connected to previous conspiracies to kill the Führer, including one scheme involving a boxed package of Cointreau containing explosive.[2] But although many others were involved in this 20 July plot – a tight social circle of Prussian and Bavarian aristocrats – it was, in the end, von Stauffenberg who tried to implement the plan personally. With terrific nerve, he had planted the bomb briefcase – and primed it – in a meetings hut where the Führer was due. The bomb exploded; but the Führer escaped, his life largely preserved by the obstruction of a table. Von Stauffenberg, believing none could have survived, raced to Berlin and tried to set the coup in motion, contacting fellow conspirators. As well as its extraordinary audacity, what made the plot even more remarkable was the number of non-military and aristocratic figures who had known all about it from the start.

On the day of the attempted uprising, Countess Marie Vassiltchikov – a Russian exile living with her friend Aga Fürstenberg near the Duchess Cecilie in Potsdam – was at work in her Berlin office when another friend, Gottfried Bismarck, burst in, 'bright red spots on his cheeks'.[3] Why was he in such a state? Was it 'the *Konspiration*'? Her colleague Loremarie whispered, 'Yes! That's it! It's done.' Then the two women held each other by the shoulders and 'went waltzing around the room'.[4] That euphoria drained swiftly as the day's radio news bulletins – increasingly strident and hysterical, and reconfirming Hitler's escape – continued. Back amid the trees of the Grunewald, in a vast, smart villa, the countess and her companions gathered with a sense of increasing dread. 'We found the Bismarcks in the drawing room . . . Gottfried pacing up and down, up and down. I was afraid to look at him. He . . . kept repeating: "It's just not possible! It's a trick! Stauffenberg *saw* him dead." '[5]

A number of the military conspirators were soon in cells; among those who weren't, General Henning von Tresckow was swift to commit suicide. For Count von Stauffenberg, his final sight of the world was lit by the beams of car headlights as a firing squad raised their rifles the following evening. In one sense, this was a kindness. Some of his associates, far from any prospect of help or mercy, faced an atrocious ordeal: death by slow strangulation, brought to the edge of oblivion and then revived, only to have to go through it all again. This nightmare procedure was carried out in front of a film camera and under stage lights: a fresh evening entertainment for the Führer to view in his private cinema.

It was for this reason that the aristocratic plotters later attained a form of near martyrdom: the men who rebelled against the unfolding horror of the Holocaust and sought to exorcize the root of that evil. Yet these men were not saints, and in some cases their views of the world were infused with a moral ugliness that differed from the Nazi regime only by degrees. Von Stauffenberg had joined the army aged eighteen and came to the Berlin Military Academy in Moabit several years later in 1936 to study modern warfare. In common with the scions of most gilded German society, his passion for horses was unquenchable; he had an anachronistic and romantic view of their use on the modern battlefield. He also had a loathing for the nature of Berlin, and of large modern cities generally.[6] In his youth, he and his brothers had been part of the German outdoor movement the Wandervogel, which placed a deep emphasis on escaping the evils and squalor of industrialization out among the lakes and forests and mountains where the pure German spirit might be found. But they were also drawn into the exclusive circle of the poet Stefan George, who after the First World War surrounded himself with a select group of aristocratic young men. He held a paramystical belief that the ideals and beauty of ancient Greece might be reincarnated in German manhood, preparing the way for their destiny: to lead Europe. Occasionally, George would address his meetings of 'Secret Germany' dressed in a draped toga and looking, as one critic observed, like an old crone.[7] (Stauffenberg's mother discreetly removed her sons from these events.) In those post-war years, there was nothing especially unusual about the grander Catholic families recoiling from

Germany's hyperactive industrialization and finding succour in both the vigour of the young and the mystic landscapes through which they rode.

To this extent Stauffenberg's circles subscribed to that strange and paradoxical view of the Jewish people, associating them with corrupting wealth and influence on the one hand while on the other regarding the impoverished eastern European Jews as an equal threat; and his own earlier years in the war as an officer in Poland were most certainly not marked with any kindness or pity. Many of his co-conspirators had elements of toxicity in their hinterlands; General von Tresckow had, without qualms, organized the mass kidnapping of Polish and Ukrainian children to be shipped west as forced labour.[8] When Hitler and his deputies had gazed into the eyes of those who were to become conspirators, they did not see treachery.

Yet there was always ambivalence on both sides of the relationship between the Nazis and the older clans. The grander elements of the old Wilhelmine German social order in Berlin – to be seen dining at the Hotel Adlon or Horcher's – were never wholly to the Nazi taste, despite the ostentatious efforts of Hermann Goering to acquire some of their luxurious ease and style. And nor could they ever, in Nazi eyes, be understood as wholly trustworthy. Paradoxically, one of the chief drivers of anti-Semitism – the hatred of 'rootless cosmopolitans' who moved with apparent ease through every nation – was also one of the key characteristics of the royal Hohenzollerns, and all the other households with castles and seals and emblems. For, at this level of society, the aristocracy transcended all European borders, to an extent that they could never truly share the purity of Nazi nationalism. Even in the aftermath of the Kaiser's deposition – one of the founding principles of the new Weimar Constitution was that the power of all inherited titles was abolished – families such as the von Stauffenbergs and the Schleswig-Holsteins periodically wafted from Budapest to Oxford, Norway to Belgium: for them, in this hermetic upper-class dimension, all these lands were owned or had once been owned by their kith. The branches of these families spread across the entire continent, and it was all alike to them. Stauffenberg himself had in the inter-war years spent a great deal of time in England, on large estates, and on horseback. For people such as he and the Countess Marie Vassiltchikov, Berlin was a noisy, dirty convenience; sophisticated restaurants and theatre, but with a repellent underbelly.

Class tension had always been one of the city's leitmotifs; the visible inequality of the 1920s and the early 1930s, when upper-class flâneurs sipped coffee outside the most exclusive cafes while, just feet away, men with filthy clothes and amputated limbs stood silently in the hope of alms, had been briefly dissipated by war but not forgotten. In the burnished bars of the Hotels Adlon and Excelsior – silk, glass, velvet and the high laughter of moneyed youth – aristocrats and tourists (many of them English) drank and danced. Yet even here there were unexpected social layers. It was said that among the *Eintänzer* – male private dancers – of the Hotel Adlon were titled men who had lost everything after the Great War.[9] By 1945, privilege was less visible near the centre of Berlin; the once-affluent middle and upper-middle classes joined the same queues as the working classes for their meagre supplies. Yet, even despite the plot against Hitler, a particular stratum of the upper classes continued to exist in a parallel realm; and among the older men and women with titles were those who had never accepted the idea that their time had passed. For them, the restoration of the old Wilhelmine social order still seemed as though it might be a possibility. In the rich tranquillity of Grunewald and Potsdam, some of these gilded creatures by 1945 managed to maintain a few of the old lustrous trappings of life; but they were never free from dread.

The emblem of this ever-shifting social uncertainty was the House of Hohenzollern itself. By the early days of 1945, the very formulation of that title seemed a Ruritanian throwback. Wilhelm, the former crown prince, had dreamed of restoration; his father died in 1941, making him the head of the family. Instead of the exultation of power, his empty days were spent in echoing panelled rooms, largely avoiding his estranged wife. At the turn of the century, theirs had been one of the greatest of European dynastic matches, the engagement photographs depicting a young, good-looking and apparently modern couple. The infidelities and the unhappiness began very soon afterwards. Duchess Cecilie of Mecklenburg-Schwerin was descended from nobility (her mother was the Grand Duchess Anastasia Mikhailovna of Russia). On the occasion of her wedding in

1905, Duchess Cecilie – notably tall, as well as beautiful – had arrived in Berlin by train to be greeted with red roses; it was reported that Unter den Linden was 'strewn' with them in her honour.[10] She was taken by carriage through the Brandenburg Gate, and there was a vast gun salute in the Tiergarten. The marriage made her Germany's crown princess. Gathered for that wedding were all the royal houses of Europe; among the guests was Archduke Franz Ferdinand of Austria, whose assassination would spark the Great War less than a decade hence.

In those days before that war, the young duchess had taken to what she saw as her obligations in the city. There were the official duties; she was among those who encouraged the growth of football in Berlin, and she was adept at state matters. She formed a strong bond with the British royal family, and a friendship with Queen Mary, wife of George V, that would endure. When war came, her husband went off to fight. He was noted, some years later, as being the sort of officer who lightly gave orders for men to march to their deaths while he wore tennis flannels.[11]

And defeat for Germany in that conflict brought an immediate dissolution of fortune for the whole family. In the wake of the Kaiser's abdication, his son had little choice but to leave Germany as well. Though he would be permitted to return within a few years, his wife the duchess had already made her own arrangements. Would she join him in exile with their six children? It seemed not. Although descended from Russian aristocracy, Cecilie regarded herself as wholly German now. And so she divided her time between the Oels estate in Silesia and Cecilienhof.

In the space of just fifteen years, an entire way of viewing society, and hierarchy, had been inverted. By 1920 a baroque spectacle such as a carpet of red roses to greet a duchess in Berlin would have been comically, grotesquely inconceivable. And, broadly, the new modernity of the city – the hard dazzle of the commerce, the stylized industry, the frequently violent extremity of the art – did not fit the world of the aristocrat. This was not their Germany. The many branches of the Hohenzollerns, and Schleswig-Holsteins, and the numerous interlocking dynastic combinations of royalty and nobility that could be traced through the *Almanach de Gotha*, continued to spend much of their time in nineteenth-century pursuits, their lives an ever-moving diorama of hilltop castles and diamond-flashing balls, royal weddings and funerals, hunting lodges and feasts, manoeuvring and intrigue. This existence, seemingly hovering outside time itself, persisted for a remarkably long time.

Wilhelm, meanwhile, found himself in careful negotiations with the Weimar Chancellor Gustav Stresemann. The exile could end, though only if the former crown prince conducted himself with care: the political arena was intensely fissile and there were those on the right who might have sought to use the Hohenzollern heir as a totem to gather around. More potentially dangerous, though, was the former crown prince's gnawing sense that his destiny had been stolen from him. He did return to Germany in 1923, and finally rejoined Cecilie at the Oels estate. In 1926 they came back to Cecilienhof, but it was no longer theirs. The house that his father had had built especially for the duchess had been expropriated and was now owned by the government; Cecilie and her husband were merely allowed to live there. That privilege, it was agreed, would end after three generations. There were other properties and estates that had been seized. The former crown prince and his wife were now merely ornaments. That, in turn, lent their lives a sense of fragility; a revolution, once started, may never stop. It might be for this reason that by 1926 Wilhelm was seeking to make a terrible alliance.

In that year, an honoured guest to the Tudor fantasia of Cecilienhof was Adolf Hitler. The Crown Prince had identified the NSDAP as a possible medium through which the honour and status of his family might be restored; he mistook Hitler for a conservative. This was to be the first of many humiliating approaches made by Wilhelm. He sought the society of the Nazis, rather than them seeking his. His need for them was very much greater than theirs for him.

Wilhelm and Cecilie were by 1930 part of Berlin's sometimes ironical pageant of high society, objects of curiosity – and sometimes scorn – to those who observed them. At a Max Reinhardt production of Hofmannsthal's play *Hard to Please* at the Komödie Theatre, the former royal couple were there, and not in one of the grand boxes, as Count Harry Kessler observed:

In the first row of the stalls sat the former Crown Prince and his wife. He has gone quite grey, almost white; the Crown Princess is a fat, elderly woman. Nevertheless, he has retained all his junior officer mannerisms, standing among the audience in the intervals with a cigarette hanging from his mouth . . . The hereditary Hohenzollern lack of taste reaches in him almost monumental proportions.[12]

But Cecilie had adapted to this chilly new world – celebrity without power – better than her partner. This fleet-minded, flame-tempered woman had understood since 1918 just how close she and so many of her extended family stood to the edge of the abyss. Nor had she felt for many years that she could rely upon her husband. He had never been faithful; his numerous affairs had once brought her to the brink of suicide. They were together, but she was alone.

Wilhelm persisted with his abject efforts to please Hitler. In 1932 he had briefly considered standing in the presidential elections: his horrified father, still in exile, forbade him. His son then publicly gave his support to Hitler instead of the aged president, Paul von Hindenburg. Hitler gave an unctuous interview to the *Daily Express* in which he stated: 'I value the ex-Crown Prince's action highly. It was an absolutely spontaneous action on his part, and by it he has publicly placed himself in line with the main body of patriotic German nationalists.'[13] There was more spontaneous help from Wilhelm. In 1933, just weeks after Hitler had taken hold of the power offered him by another aristocrat, the penultimate Weimar chancellor Franz von Papen, the Nazi leader staged a curious ceremony labelled 'The Day of Potsdam'. The idea of it was to confer legitimacy upon his new regime by aligning it with the past, and specifically with the House of Hohenzollern. The crown prince played his part gladly: military and SS ceremonials took place at the Garrison Church in Potsdam; President von Hindenburg was there to shake Hitler's hand. On another occasion that year, Wilhelm was happy to pose for photographs outside Cecilienhof wearing the swastika armband.

The hope flickered on that, as Hitler consolidated his hold on power, so the Führer might restore some aspects of the old monarchy. Yet as it became plain that the National Socialists had no intention of returning German society to that particular form of hierarchy – there could be no room for any figurehead other than the Führer himself – the former crown prince's campaign of flattering letter-writing cooled. Perhaps mercifully, he would not hear what Hitler was saying privately within the chambers of the Reich Chancellery. 'How glad I am that we have no monarchy and that I have never listened to those who have tried to talk me into one,' he was reported to have said after returning from a visit to Italy in the 1930s (Mussolini's fascist state had not dispensed with its own king). 'Those court flunkies and that etiquette!'[14] Hitler had his own court flunkies and etiquette; why should he have to observe a rival ritualism? Wilhelm was regarded by others as little more than a 'parade pony'.[15] His enthusiastic support for the regime granted him no privileges. Nor was there any serious danger that, in the event of a coup against the leadership, he could be a plausible new figurehead for Germany.

The subsequent distress endured by the once royal couple could scarcely be compared in any way to the freezing nightmare of horror that was visited upon so many of Berlin's citizens. Yet whatever flickers of happiness they might have had were sluiced away by the conflict. Their eldest son – also Prince Wilhelm – met his death in France in 1940. The extraordinary turnout in Berlin for his funeral – some 50,000 members of the public lined the route of the cortège – was a source of intense vexation to the Nazis. To them it suggested an immovable veneration for an older form of aristocratic authority, and so from that point it was decreed that the more socially exalted members of the services should no longer be allowed to serve anywhere near the front lines. Countess Marie Vassiltchikov observed that the Nazis did not want any more of these 'glamour deaths'.[16] None of this could have mattered to the grieving mother.

Meanwhile, the humiliations involving the seizing of property had not ended under the Nazis. In the inter-war years, Wilhelm and Cecilie had had the theoretical use of an extraordinary property once owned by the Hohenzollerns in the centre of Berlin on the banks of the Spree, the Monbijou Palace, which was in part a residence and in part a vast museum of treasures and antiquities acquired over the decades by the family, exhibited as a means of celebrating its history and the various illustrious princes and Kaisers it had brought forth. Yet as war came – and even before the skies were filled with the bass hum of Allied bombers – the palace had been deemed expendable; in another of his seemingly innumerable megalomaniac architectural schemes, Albert Speer had planned for it to be moved stone by stone so that he might erect in its place a new Reich Museum more fitting to the regime. Even this delicate plan was halted when the Allied incendiaries were released, the fires rose, and in a single night the Monbijou Palace was hollowed out and rendered wholly uninhabitable.

By that stage of the war, it had been some time since the couple had tasted the palace's splendour. They had removed themselves from the city to one of their final bastions: Oels, a rambling castle-fortress in German-occupied Silesia. By the end of 1944, it was grimly obvious that there was to be no sanctuary on that country estate either: the approach of the Red Army brought whispers of dread before it. And so the former crown prince and his wife returned to Potsdam.

By this stage, Wilhelm was under constant watch by the Gestapo. He may have been bewildered by the twisting currents of history that had led to his becoming almost a prisoner. By the winter of 1944/45 the future seemed filled with little but the prospect of violence and death. He was also gravely ill. The once golden prince had serious problems with his gall bladder and with his liver. As the snow lay on the Potsdam ground, he was removed from Cecilienhof and taken to a small mountain town in Bavaria, at the very southernmost tip of Germany, called Oberstdorf, there to receive medical attention. There was no further need for the attendance of Gestapo agents. And his wife was left behind amid the frozen lakes and the woods of Potsdam. By February 1945, with the Red Army scything through Silesia and Pomerania, Cecilienhof was no place of safety; equally, she must have had a sense when she finally fled her mock Tudor palace that she would never see it again. She too would become a displaced person, though with none of the harrowing discomforts that common fugitives were made to suffer.

Naturally, Wilhelm had not been alone among the German aristocracy in pledging fealty to fascism. There were others who went a very great deal further. An especially striking case was George V's cousin and Queen Victoria's godson Charles Edward, the former Duke of Saxe-Coburg and Gotha (the bonds with the British royal family were multitudinous – Queen Victoria had also been the great-grandmother of Crown Prince Wilhelm). Charles Edward was brought up and educated in England but fought for Germany in the Great War; his English titles were removed at around the time that the Saxe-Coburgs became the Windsors; and after the war he was immediately attracted to the intense violence of the Freikorps in Berlin, and thence to the NSDAP. He became an Obergruppenführer in the Brownshirts. By the mid 1930s, he was president of the Anglo-German Friendship Society, a sinecure approved by Hitler, and in this position he moved freely through English society, attending the funeral of George V. This former duke might not have felt that he was a marionette, but his purpose – to exert influence and persuasion in the highest social and political circles – was none the less rigidly controlled.

And it was an aristocrat who perhaps more than anyone was responsible for the Nazis managing to seize control of the country: more than that, a nobleman who prepared much of the ground for the advent of their kind of totalitarianism. Franz von Papen, very briefly the Chancellor of Germany in 1932, was a Westphalian aristocrat; a raptor-faced, steely-eyed authoritarian who had been installed in that office by President Hindenburg, partly as a means of countering the surge in support for the Nazis and Hitler but partly also as a means of satisfying General Kurt von Schleicher, who was close to placing the country under military rule. This was a point at which terrifying economic insecurity was once more roaring through the country, and through Berlin, like a firestorm. The aftershocks of the 1929 Wall Street Crash were causing bank failures, a collapse in confidence and the vertiginous rise of unemployment and intensely cruel poverty for millions. Out on the streets, ever-increasing numbers were swelling the Nazi vote. The young Weimar Constitution, barely more than a decade old, was melting like wax in the flames. Von Schleicher was the defence minister in von Papen's 'cabinet of monocles'.[17] Elsewhere, there were other aristocrats, such as Baron Ferdinand von Lüninck, who were convinced that Germany might be saved only if it abandoned its experiment with democracy;

for him, Weimar was 'the logical culmination of the French Enlightenment and Revolution'.[18] His subtext was fear of conspiracy: that the country was as a result being steered by Freemasonry and Jewish capitalism. This was a view shared by the Cabinet of Monocles.

Von Papen had the same flintiness. He looked at the suffocating nightmare of urban unemployment – hundreds of thousands in Berlin – and he decided to intensify the pain of it, creating a new obstacle course of means tests before dole payments would be made. Meanwhile, those industrial workers fortunate enough to have retained their jobs had their wages frozen. At the same time, the largest businesses found their share of the tax burden reduced. The attitude towards the poor was unyieldingly hostile. Von Papen ruled by presidential decree. He was an enthusiastic censor of Berlin's formerly exuberant free press – at one point shutting down ninety-five publications. He was in fact the breathing archetype of cold-eyed militarism; when aged just eleven, he had specifically asked to be sent to a cadet school. During the First World War, as well as fighting on the Western Front and in the Middle East, he spent a period as a diplomat in the United States, where his time was frequently devoted to blockade-thwarting plots and schemes of furious sabotage. He was expelled. After the war, and in the violent roil of the German Revolution, he briefly enlisted in the Freikorps in the Ruhr, and relished leading his little unit, intimating that he was protecting the traditions of Catholicism against a communist onslaught. It was here that von Papen acquired a taste for politics, but as it was conducted in a previous age. He was later described by an American journalist as 'gentlemanly';[19] von Papen would have viewed the term with disdain. Nobles were finer than gentlemen.

His family's branch of the aristocracy was Roman Catholic; and, although his friends and associates would be treated with ruthlessness and extreme violence by the Nazis, he himself was to find an accommodation with Germany's new rulers. In the gathering gloom of the world's economic depression, von Papen's authority had collapsed by November 1932 and his former ally General von Schleicher was moving against him, once more threatening the possibility of a military dictatorship. Furious and humiliated by being forced to relinquish office to von Schleicher (whose chance to savour it, amid lurching instability, was vanishingly brief), von Papen had already established a warm social relationship with Hermann Goering, and in January 1933 agreed to an arrangement whereby President Hindenburg would assent to Hitler assuming the chancellorship with von Papen as his vice-chancellor, with like-minded conservatives joining him in the cabinet. The aristocrats were bestowing power, without thinking of consulting the voting public, but their calculation was that this power would be toxic. To lead the government at this point was seen as taking the wheel of a boat during a howling storm: by making Hitler assume full responsibility, navigating the maelstrom, he and the Nazis – it was thought – would have their extremist impulses constrained as they met the cold reality of office. Then, as they weakened, von Papen would once more be able to take charge. This was more than an epic miscalculation; it was also based upon a fundamental distaste for the Weimar Constitution. The aristocrats not only made Hitler's rise to supremacy possible but did so at a point when there was nothing completely inevitable about his ascension. The economic gales, devastating though they were, would soon abate. The economy would recover. The centre parties could have rallied. In the late 1920s, the Nazis had surged and then had been cast out into the fringes. There was no reason why this might not have been the case again. But the older German elite did not care for the multiplicity of voices in the Reichstag. Franz von Papen was not a Nazi; much about their taste for violent rhetoric – and physical violence – he found repellent. But it was also for this reason that he underestimated them.

He thought he had his own power base: his vice-chancellery office and team were moved into the grandly named Borsig Palace in 1933 – an Italianate sandstone edifice which had been the headquarters of a Prussian bank. Though hardly a pacifist, von Papen wanted to steer the Nazis away from their addiction to street violence, and their predilection for having political opponents detained and tortured. Some months later, von Papen made a speech, without consulting Hitler, expressing his desire that the common brutality be brought to an end. He imagined his voice would have the influence to humble Hitler. Instead, the speech brought death to his closest associates. It was here that von Papen was finally to understand the bloody sociopathy of those he had considered vulgar upstarts.

The Night of the Long Knives – Hitler's murderous purge of the SA, including the cold-blooded killing of his old friend Ernst Röhm – was widened to swoop in on what was known as the Papen Circle. The SS and the Gestapo marched into the Borsig Palace. Herbert von Bose, von Papen's press secretary, was manhandled into a conference room. He was invited to take a seat. As he did so, an SS man positioned behind him raised his gun. Von Bose was shot in the back ten times. Von Papen's lawyer, Edgar Julius Jung – who yearned for the government of Germany to revert to a more traditional Wilhelmine autocracy – was led away. Later that day, he too was shot in cold blood. The floors of the Borsig Palace were stained red; when working on an immediate rebuild of the site, Hitler's architect Albert Speer found himself staring briefly at the bloodied marble, and then looking away quickly, troubling himself no more with the spectacle.[20]

In the midst of this sudden horror, von Papen himself was placed under house arrest in his Berlin villa, with the telephone cut off. The SS men guarding him subjected the vice-chancellor to subtle sleep-deprivation techniques; after several days of this, with the attendant disorientation and dread, he was suddenly summoned to the Chancellery, where he found that in the new, all-Nazi cabinet, there was no longer any chair for him at the table. He begged for a private audience with the Führer; and he declared finally that he would no longer serve his Fatherland. Hitler was satisfied; all he needed was the removal of this aristocrat from government. Almost immediately afterwards, he asked von Papen to be the German ambassador to Austria. Von Papen swiftly accepted, and indeed performed his new duties with zeal. He was one of the figures who worked to create the conditions under which the 1938 Anschluss could be effected successfully.

Life became more fraught for von Papen when he was then made ambassador to Turkey just before the outbreak of war; the conflict would see him struggling to pressurize the Turks into softening their wholehearted support for the Allies. Added to this, the Soviet secret service, the NKVD, made an attempt on his life with a bomb. Nor were his own feelings about the Nazi regime entirely unambiguous; in 1943 he formulated a mad and vainglorious effort to convince the

Americans, through the Office of Strategic Services in Turkey, that when Hitler was vanquished – as he was certain that he would be shortly – von Papen himself should be installed as Germany's new leader. The interesting suggestion was relayed to President Roosevelt and the instant response was an order to the OSS to cease all communication with von Papen. Not long afterwards, Turkey severed all diplomatic relations with Germany. In 1944 von Papen was forced to return to Berlin. He was rewarded for what were seen as his splendid efforts: Hitler presented von Papen with the Knight's Cross. By this stage, von Papen had calculated that his communications with the Americans – in the course of which he stressed he had tried to help pockets of Jews – would perhaps ease post-war consequences. But like all senior figures in the regime, he had very good reason to fear the vengeance of the Red Army and the Soviet High Command. He was allowed to retire to his family estate of Wallerfangen in the Saar, in the far west of Germany, and beyond the reach of the Russians.

By April 1945, the Cecilienhof Palace was empty; the duchess had known that she could stay no longer. Yet, unlike the streets of shattered stone that lay a few miles to the north-east in Berlin's centre, this palace and its wooded surrounds, and the luxurious villas that lay close by, were still broadly untouched. In just a matter of weeks, Cecilienhof would be the stage for a meeting that would command the attention of the entire world, a conference where vast and terrible decisions about the future of the continent – and the world beyond – were made. But the majority of citizens in Berlin were, by April 1945, denied the luxury of speculation about the future. Their city was suspended in time; an unending midnight, between one era and the next. The three weeks that were to follow – through which they were to face bombardment and conquest and unimaginable trauma – seemed to have neither day nor night; yet somehow, these Berliners retained an extraordinary obdurate toughness, and a keen sense of their own identity. In those three weeks, the entire world was once again watching their city.

## PART TWO

# Necropolis

## 10.  Suspended in Twilight

The fear pressed silently on all their hearts, though it took different outward forms. Some sought to master it through routine or regularity, even in the most grotesque tasks. To the north of the city centre, near Siemensstadt, there was a sixteen-year-old boy who in the morning following each Allied bombing raid would step out amid the glowing, smoking wreckage, and, with tenderness, turn over the fresh corpses that lay face down in the streets to assure himself that they were not members of his own family. Among the soldiers either passing through the city onwards towards their implacable enemy, or temporarily pausing at makeshift bases by the larger railway stations, there were outbreaks of displacement activity – wholly needless errands, suddenly remembered bureaucratic chores. Other soldiers simply – and in ever greater numbers – dodged away from their units, hoping to disguise themselves as civilians. Among those civilians there were strained arguments in queues and upon what remained of public transport, sometimes sparked by loudly voiced opinions about the soon-to-be demonstrated superiority of German forces and countered by those who quietly expressed scepticism. Around them were the signs that said everything about that superiority: once-elegant terraces of apartments, seemingly sliced in half; tall hills of collapsed brick and concrete, the air dense with the dust of ruins; the frequent glimpses of bloodied flesh amid the weeds. By 12 April 1945, the people of Berlin found themselves stuck fast in a cycle of daily dread; the heart-pulsing business of waiting.

They were unmoored: unprotected, bare and defenceless. And they had lost the most crucial privilege of their social contract: the sense that their government existed above all to protect their lives. Certainly what could be mustered of the Wehrmacht was engaged in trying to create feasible, calculated defensive positions under Lieutenant General Hellmuth Reymann; the city had some sixty tanks within its bounds, as well as optimistic trenches on sandy plains and camouflaged artillery near woodland a few miles on the outskirts. Then there were layers of more extemporized defence being prepared within the city boundaries too, using the topographical advantages of canals and rivers, and all the possibilities they brought of slowing an ineluctable advance of enemy tanks and troops. But the point of these concentric layers of defence was that they were protecting the heart of the regime at the Reich Chancellery, not its people. That regime had never seriously planned for this moment; the people were by this stage an abstracted detail. Even if there had been any impetus towards evacuation, the critically damaged nature of the railways around the city, and the increasing attacks from Soviet bombers and strafers above, would simply have redirected death and panic.

General Alfred Jodl and other Wehrmacht commanders would have known that the Soviets had flown reconnaissance photography missions over Berlin, and they would have had a calculated suspicion that Soviet High Command had – through this, and interrogation of prisoners – formulated a street-by-street plan of the area. In fact, the Red Army had gone further. 'Our engineers had built a precise scale model of the city,' wrote Marshal Zhukov, 'which was used in studying questions relating to . . . the offensive, the general assault, and the fighting in the centre of the city.'[1] To capture a vast tract of land was one thing; to conquer a city, with its innumerable sniper positions and secret passages, was another. Berlin would have to be smashed with bombs; it would have to be seared with flame. Streets would have to be pounded until they collapsed. The Soviets would have to tear the city apart with even greater explosive power than all those months of Allied air attacks. The Nazi hierarchy understood all of this. The result was that the civilians who remained within what the Red Army termed 'the lair of the fascist beast'[2] were themselves potential targets; there was no alternative. This was the final reality of total warfare. Nor was there any possibility of escape other than to pack a bag and set off on foot into a countryside that – for all they knew – was teeming with Red Army soldiers. A few Berliners still genuinely believed that Heinrich Himmler was masterminding a new wonder weapon that would vaporize the enemy lines instantly, though a great many more knew that this was simple pulp-fiction fantasy. Meanwhile, property, savings, jobs – nothing could be counted upon. And the children and the infants? Not one life could be guaranteed. All they knew – from relatives, from refugees and from gothically expressed Goebbels communiqués – was that the approaching Red Army was quite without mercy.

The nights in Berlin – in the intervals between the booms of flak guns – now had periods of silence, yet in some streets where the rubble lay chest-high on the road – sharp and uneven beneath unsteady feet – there were always cracks and reports to be heard as bombed houses and apartment blocks buckled further on their foundations. In the early days of April 1945, the life of Berlin citizens had a focused intensity on simple subsistence: days spent in queues outside the blackened hulk of the Karstadt department store, or in even longer lines around local greengrocers and bakers. At the beginning of the month they had been told in official proclamations that 'dandelions and stinging nettles' were to be used as a means of supplementing more orthodox vegetables.[3] They were also told that their gas supplies were soon to be shut off. This was a life of cold water and candlelight and never-satisfied hunger.

Startlingly, during the day there were still signs of a functioning city. Those who walked the streets of elegant Charlottenburg and the less salubrious Moabit could still very occasionally hear the deep roar beneath the pavements; U-Bahn trains were still running on those lines that had not been bisected by bombs. The general public was told that they were not allowed to travel underground; the trains were there strictly only for military work purposes or official use or in cases of dire emergency. Above ground, tram routes in many districts had been disrupted or disabled by the anarchy of shattered stone. Yet those who set out on foot – willing, perhaps, to walk miles across the city simply to spend time with relatives or friends – found that in other respects, extraordinarily, there was a form of normality. Even by that late stage of the war, those cinemas in the suburbs that had not been reduced to glowing embers by the bombing raids were continuing with their screenings. The lush colours of the historical epic *Kolberg* must have greeted Berliner eyes with fresh potency: the blues and reds of the uniforms, the luxuriant green of the landscapes, contrasted with the ashy grey of reality. Such escapism must have been dreamlike. There were other modest diversions as well: some of those who had office jobs – the older men, the young women who were their secretaries – continued to present themselves for work, although often there was not much to do except speculate about wider matters. And, despite the closure of many restaurants and bars, the world-renowned Hotel Adlon, near the Brandenburg Gate, partly converted to a military hospital, still contrived to cater for senior party officials with a thirst; for those with the influence, it was still possible to procure fine wines and subtle brandies. Elsewhere, the factories in neighbourhoods such as Wedding and Tegel continued with their manufacture of gun barrels and tank parts. The polyglot workforce of prisoners toiling on these production lines saw no let-up, and, even in those days of intense fuel scarcity, smoke rose from the tall factory chimneys. These workers also speculated among themselves. For some, the oncoming Red Army would mean untrammelled liberation; for others, the Soviet approach meant a whole new world of danger, for the Stalinist regime had already ruthlessly exterminated so many of their east European countrymen.

There were still the refugees too; the terrified and exhausted farmers and labourers from Silesia and Pomerania, arriving disorientated in the vast metropolis and reluctant to stop, moving inexorably across the city from east to west, as though they did not mean to rest until they had marched all the way to the North Sea. A few weeks earlier, Goebbels – inspecting the city streets from his official car – had shuddered at the sight of these tired, filthy people, who did not fit his idealized image of German children of the soil in the slightest.[4] There were practical difficulties too: in a city where many hundreds of thousands of homes had by now been lost, and where the food supplies were uncertain, how could it be possible to accommodate yet more desperate and helpless people? The city's grimly overcrowded shelters were barely sufficient to give sanctuary to the present population.

All Berliners were acutely aware of the lengthening shadow; that only a few miles away, telephones in German homes in small towns were being answered mockingly by strangers speaking Russian,[5] and that escape was increasingly inconceivable. How did they cope with the unceasing anxiety, these exhausted Berlin civilians, as the daylight air-raid alarms began and factory workers such as sixteen-year-old Gerda Kernchen ran for the rough concrete entrance of the Humboldthain flak tower, jostling with so many dozens of other girls? Nor was their dread misplaced. The storm was just days away. Some fifty miles to the east of the city, a vast, implacable Soviet force under Marshal Georgy Zhukov was daily, patiently, amassing along and behind a wide horizon-encompassing line near a plateau called the Seelow Heights, the 'Gates of Berlin'. The 'heights' were scarcely mountains – this was an area of sandy heath rising some 150 feet over the banks of the River Oder – but the slopes on either side of the ridge were steep, and the terrain before them became swampy when inundated with rain. The extraordinary numbers of Red Army forces gathering in the region – along miles of tents and dugouts – had their eyes firmly fixed beyond these seemingly trifling topographical obstacles, however, and their commanders were ensuring that they were looked after: there was an abundance of hot strong tea (plus, unofficially, torrents of alcohol), and special 'Sanitary Instructors' on hand to inspect wounds and give advice on treatment.[6] Finally, at this late stage, there was – after lengthy gaps and stutters – the succour of constant supply lines. 'We made quite sure the troops would experience no shortage of ammunition, fuel or food,' wrote Zhukov.[7]

Conversely, under General Gotthard Heinrici, over 100,000 German soldiers – frequently young, hopelessly inexperienced – were gathering on the defensive lines without any of the comforts of certainty. Many had only heard reports and hearsay about the war on the eastern front, and about what had been wrought upon eastern Europe. Many had themselves served only in France, or in other western theatres. So in some cases their preparations to face this very different enemy were as much spiritual as physical. Elsewhere, some eighty miles to the south-west of the city, the US 9th Army had reached the banks of the Elbe, a little outside Magdeburg, after a fantastic spurt. There was still the eager expectation among some US personnel that they would be permitted to advance upon Berlin at speed. Within days, this permission would be denied.

For many Berliners, the question of which forces would reach the city first was more than mere speculation: there was a heart-hammering weight of dread about it. At night, the terrible Soviet guns could be heard – or imagined – in the distance. Gerda Kernchen had known no other rule than that of Adolf Hitler. How did she account for the daily dissolution of ordered existence? By day, she had been sewing uniforms in a clothing factory that had once been used to supply the popular department store Peek and Cloppenburg. The work was congenial (or at least became so once she had mastered the machinery – upon volunteering, a couple of years previously, Gerda had fibbed to the authorities about her experience in the trade).[8] The previous winter, her supervisor had noticed that she had no proper overcoat, and had discreetly allowed Gerda to take some material used for naval clothing to make herself one. In broader terms, her schooling had been curtailed but the factory work had brought the satisfaction of making a tangible contribution to the war effort. Her older brother Heinz was in the Wehrmacht, and had been drafted out to the eastern front. He had observed to his sister with studied nonchalance that he preferred to have a chance of actively fighting the enemy than to wait passively in Berlin for the enemy to come and bomb him.[9]

Heinz perhaps was not aware that the Berlin authorities had no intention of allowing their citizens to be passive. For Gerda, the hours over the past eighteen months had almost become scheduled around the Allied bombing raids. Every night, when at home with her parents in the suburb of Wittenau, there was the trek to the local bunker, which was equipped with bunk beds, benches, a kitchen and toilets. The teenager had some sympathy for the families who had taken to living in that concrete twilight permanently, either rendered homeless when RAF bombs had shattered their homes or simply through the abiding and unceasing fear that the bombs would target them next.[10] Nights of fractured sleep among stirring, restless neighbours; the morning check to see whether her own home had been hit; the clocking-on at the textile factory; and, at any point, the sirens and the mechanical rush to the nearest bunker from the works. The Humboldthain flak tower, designed to shelter thousands of people, would in the days to follow hold hundreds more on top of that, many hideously wounded, crying out into its unsettling blue-lit darkness.

Eight miles to the south-west, in a small lakeside town called Werder, a film and sound technician had arrived, having sailed her rather smart yacht down the River Havel to the Grosser Zernsee. In the days to

come, Marion Keller would be an extraordinary witness to the changing tides of history.[11] The yacht had become a sanctuary for Keller
and her husband after their Berlin apartment had been bombed out.
More than that though, for friends and associates, the six-berth vessel
was a valuable place to air dissenting views far from hostile ears. Frau
Keller's husband, Kurt Maetzig, had Jewish heritage in his family line;
only his work had spared him. The couple were naturally and passionately anti-Nazi, and so too were many in their circle. Even those who
had party badges, she recalled, were only 'brown' (i.e. Nazi) on the
outside. The boat 'had been a refuge for new and old friends' in that
April of 1945; fugitives not from bombs, or from the Red Army, but
rather from a newly resurgent and vengeful Gestapo meting out
deadly punishment to anyone guilty of damaging morale. There were
citizens still being captured and tortured. Frau Keller herself recalled
that she represented a subliminal object of suspicion to some: a fine
ancestry that she claimed she could date back to Charlemagne, combined with the kind of intense red hair that in other times could have
led to her being 'persecuted as a witch'.[12]

A combination of oversight and favours granted years earlier
meant that she, her husband and two assistant technicians were still,
at that point, deemed key workers; she was in 'an officially recognized professional niche', as she recalled.[13] In Werder, Frau Keller and
her team had set up 'our own research laboratory for radio and sound
technology', a 'mini operation' comprising just her, the assistants and
a 'glass washer' to deal with the chemical equipment for film process-
ing, at a sufficient distance from the vulnerable city.[14] They established
a laboratory in a partly disused brewery; an historic structure of
sturdy dark brick with an impressive view over the lakes and woods
towards Berlin, reached by means of an epic outdoor stairway that
trailed up the hill. The makeshift laboratory was in what had been an
echoing beer hall. 'Our test equipment was placed upon the former
bar tables.' They had been joined by the owner and some of the
workers from a jam factory that occupied neighbouring buildings;
Frau Keller knew the owner, who at that time was employing
'foreign workers' amounting to a hundred or so young women
from Russia and Poland. But 'hardly anyone thought about work
any more'.[15] All were aware – most acutely the foreign forced

labourers – that the Red Army was approaching 'in a wide arc' and would soon embrace the city 'like an iron clasp'.

Out in Werder, news-sheets were difficult to procure; there was still the radio though. The official radio broadcasts with their roaring rhetoric seemed to Frau Keller and her team increasingly separated from reality. As well as being tiring to listen to, this kind of propaganda was of no practical use, unlike 'enemy transmissions'. It was strictly forbidden to tune in to Allied stations and frequencies, and the danger of being denounced was still high, so the team had to drape a woollen blanket over the receiver and lower its volume in order to listen for updates. Frau Keller remembered that among her team, the general feeling by mid April 1945 was one of 'ambivalence'; they all recognized that the only way of 'getting rid of Hitler' was by 'losing the war'. But they also understood that this too would carry grave repercussions; that it would 'come to an end terribly for everyone and everything'.[16] It was impossible to discern a future beyond the Nazi regime; some of that pervasive cultural nihilism had fogged the vision even of those who yearned for the return of stability and sanity and kindness.

Despite such depredations, music could still be heard in the benighted city. On that 12 April, the city's central radio station played host to an upbeat performance of popular romantic hits from the Nazi-approved jazz band Charlie and His Orchestra. Berlin's young were still listening to records, even if they were ersatz swing. Eighteen-year-old Brigitte Eicke had slightly more elevated tastes though: from 1943, when she was taken on an outing with the League of German Girls to a production of *Madame Butterfly*, she had an ear for opera.[17] Frau Eicke lived with her mother in the north-east of the city, in a working-class suburb called Prenzlauer Berg. Her father, who had once been a pig farmer, had died in 1939. Now the teenager, having assiduously studied shorthand, was working in the offices of a firm called Koster.[18]

Life for the last few months had been filled with fear by the nighttime sirens, and with relief by the greetings to surviving neighbours the following day; yet even though the landscape of her childhood city was being violently deconstructed around her, with every possibility that one of those bombs or incendiaries might finish her, Frau Eicke somehow held on to some tokens of quotidian normality. She had taken up smoking, despite the faltering supplies of tobacco; it was ubiquitous in all the films that she watched so raptly. In the Koster offices, her boss always seemed to have access to a supply of cigarettes. He was also – despite the city's daily slide deeper into ruin – unusually and vocally optimistic at a time when so many other ordinary Berliners were apprehensive. He expressed confidence in 'Heini' – Heinrich Himmler – devising a stunning reversal that would repel the Soviet forces.[19]

There were also still a few classical musicians in the city, dutifully preparing a fresh repertoire. On that April afternoon, under the cold steel sky, there could be heard, from within the Beethoven Salle concert space, fragments of epic symphonies as the city's Philharmonic Orchestra rehearsed a performance to be given that evening for the Nazi hierarchy, commissioned by Albert Speer, the Minister for Armaments. That the musicians were still in the ruined city was striking. After the orchestra's own hall had been bombed and reduced to fragments in January 1944, it had relocated to the City's Opera House. That in turn was rent apart and burned in February 1945, its plush boxes, the velvet seating, burning bright and fast. The Philharmonic's conductor, Wilhelm Furtwängler, had left the city some weeks beforehand; the musicians had been offered the opportunity to move south to Bayreuth, home of the Wagner festival, where at least if the Reich were to fall they would be facing American victors. Yet these players had elected to stay in Berlin.

The concert that Speer had commissioned was touched with bathos, although it is extremely unlikely that the vain and unreflective Speer would have seen that. The programme featured as its centrepiece the final aria of Brünnhilde from Wagner's *Götterdämmerung* (*Twilight of the Gods*); in this, standing at the pyre of Siegfried, she calls for the gods to visit fire upon Valhalla. Then, as the pyre itself is set ablaze, Brünnhilde mounts her horse and rides directly into the inferno. The audience consisted of 'golden pheasants' – senior party officials – and family and friends, who listened in darkness. The only illumination was from the lights for the musicians' stands. The hall was unheated, and so they were obliged to keep their overcoats on.

There were several other pieces, the most notable having been written by Germany's greatest living composer. Richard Strauss's *Tod und Verklärung* (Death and Transfiguration) was also a grim and pre-posterous choice on the part of Speer. Here is a piece concerning a dying artist and his final torments and ecstasies. 'Is this – speak, soul – is this death?' Strauss himself had had the most jagged of relationships with the Nazis; his daughter-in-law was Jewish and, for years, he had had to take care not to anger the regime in order to keep her and the family safe. And, ironically, as the Berlin Philharmonic performed this piece for Speer and those senior Nazis, Strauss himself was in Bavaria on his estate, having that very day finished another compos-ition, called *Metamorphosen* and having just committed to paper his own pure loathing of Hitler. 'The most terrible period of human history is at an end,' Strauss was to add a few weeks after completing this score, 'the twelve year reign of bestiality, ignorance and anti-culture under the greatest criminals.'[20]

Strauss could see on 12 April what Hitler, even then, could not. It is said that as the Philharmonic took their bows that evening, boys from the Hitler Youth passed among the audience with wicker baskets filled with cyanide capsules, offering them out. The image is almost too gothic to be believed. And yet death had, from the very start, been at the heart of the Nazi cult. As the concert ended, and meagre light-ing was extinguished, Speer returned to the Reich Chancellery, down into those grim and ever more rank bunker corridors, and made his way directly to Hitler's private apartment, where he found the grey Führer frighteningly transfigured and electric with euphoria. Hitler had at last been delivered the miracle that he had yearned for, the blow that would make his victory certain and possible. President Roosevelt was dead!

## 11. The Screaming Sky

For those who had lost their faith in the quasi-religion they had been brought up in – the swastika their totem, the forest fires their communions – how could sleep have been possible in the cold dugouts on the slopes of the Seelow Heights? Tents, tarpaulins, rotting leaves, freezing wet mud and grass, light kept to a glimmering minimum; those on this plain who allowed themselves to speculate as their eyes fixed on the bare damp branches must have feared this was their last night on earth. For many, this was to be the case. Even eight decades later their lost corpses would still be discovered periodically, bones emerging from that bloodied soil.

Among those tens of thousands of young German soldiers encamped in the darkness, heads low in silence, there was a very small number who had held fast to the older religion that the Nazis had – in their jealousy – worked so hard to suffocate: the Wehrmacht still had chaplains. They were few, but even youthful recruits turned to these 'German Christian' pastors for comfort.[1] A night such as this, awaiting the roar and the inferno of an unstoppable enemy, was when, for some, simple prayers and even quiet hymns were necessary. The Wehrmacht chaplains were not compassionate about all men; theirs was a branch of Protestantism that was as fervidly anti-Semitic as the Nazi High Command. They had worked hard, since the rise of the Third Reich, to eliminate any echoes of Judaism from biblical teaching: this meant that the Old Testament was thoroughly ignored, and even terms such as 'Hosanna' and 'Hallelujah' were rejected as Semitic.[2] Instead, soldiers might ask for a copy of the New Testament (by 1945, even these were vanishingly rare: a couple of years previously, the Nazis had ordered the cessation of printing, citing paper shortages). Hymns had been rewritten. 'Holy God We Praise Thy Name' now had a new final stanza which ran: 'May our slogan ever be – loyalty to the Führer, the Volk and the Reich!'[3] There could be no mention of Christ without – somewhere – a mention also of Hitler. But what the Church still offered – and which the Nazis never could – was the prospect of Heaven, and the life beyond. Wehrmacht chaplains, who had accompanied the armies out in the east, and had seen the charnel houses that they had created, had a specific understanding of why God would ultimately stand with them and forgive the ordinary soldiers: this was a war being fought against not only the Jewish people who had sought Christ's death – in their view, Judaism would be shattered against the cross – but also the godless Bolsheviks.[4] Yet, if there persisted a small minority among German troops who sought out pastors for both solace and communion, for most of the young soldiers, gathering together near the Seelow Heights, indoctrinated into the beliefs and passions forged in the fires of the Hitler Youth, little certainty remained. Their commanders too seemed to have lost all conviction that victory was still possible.

The fifty-eight-year-old general who was directing their fates – himself a devout Lutheran, from a line of theologians – had had his own convictions on this matter shattered in the last few days; Heinrici had at last understood that the Führer he had fought so hard for was now a shrunken effigy inhabiting a spectral world, lost in a wilderness of his own pagan beliefs. Now the German troops assembled to face the Red Army were soon to discover the limits of their own faith and experience. Many were barely sixteen years old. The sky above them was a blanket of sullen cloud. Visibility was rendered ghostly by drizzle. Hours before the first grey suggestions of dawn on 16 April 1945, the German troops must have been filled with nauseous apprehension. They knew that, in the distance, the Red Army had been gathering for the last few weeks, establishing bridgeheads over the River Oder, bringing through ever-increasing volumes of ordnance and supplies. There had been a hiatus – the Red Army's forces elsewhere were securing Pomerania – but, amid the fields and woods and villages, the Germans were intensely aware of the waiting presence of those armies. What many of these men could not have known was how horribly that force outnumbered them. Stretching across that wide plain, and reaching back for miles, were now some one and a half million Soviet soldiers.

Army Group Vistula – the banner that the defenders of Berlin were gathered under – had been drawn from other theatres of war around the country. Open questioning of the regime and its decisions was lethal, a bullet piercing the back of the skull with scarcely the suggestion of a trial. But the SS could not see inside men's hearts. Save in the very north of the country, there was no corner of Germany in which it was anything other than plain that the advance of the Allies was inexorable. Here at what was termed the 'Gates of Berlin' was to be the battle that would precipitate the final collapse. It was to be one of the largest armed confrontations in history. The number of casualties on both sides would be breathtakingly high. And yet – as with so many savage battles – the landscape that was to receive this blood and flesh was itself gentle.

Seelow itself was a tiny and dignified town that lay above the River Oder. The defensive German forces mustering outside it would only have had the most expressionist sense of the vast armies building a few miles to the east near the village of Reitwein, on another spur in the land, where Zhukov would position his command post. The domestic and miniature delicacy of the small villages and settlements in this area (stretching down many miles north to south) was now subsumed by populations of Soviet men and women. Even before the outbreak of the battle, there was no silence; there couldn't be. The sheer uncountable and unthinkable multitudes, the engines and the horses, the ceaseless movement, all generated a distant aural effect akin to the waves of an approaching ocean. In the evenings, among the Red Army forces, there were outbreaks of traditional dancing. Proximity to Berlin brought confidence and euphoria. Marshal Zhukov had arranged for each man and woman to be handed a leaflet exhorting them to one last great effort. 'The enemy will be crushed along the shortest route to Berlin,' it read. 'The capital of fascist Germany will be taken and the banner of victory planted over it.'[5]

The man whose responsibility it was to stem this roaring tide was a rare realist. General Heinrici had served in many theatres of war and had always been broadly sympathetic to the politics as well as the military aims of the Nazi regime. He later suggested that the only aspect of it all that he loathed and opposed was the murderous anti-Semitism. (This was not an unusual post-war proclamation for many former authority figures to make.) Now he had his eyes firmly fixed upon the terrifying reality. This he had discussed with the armaments minister, Albert Speer. There was no possibility, he thought, that Berlin itself could be held; if the Red Army broke through the defensive lines into the city, then that was it. Heinrici had argued with some force against a plan for the Wehrmacht to blow up all of Berlin's bridges to impede Stalin's forces. The suicidal futility of the idea seemed to him staggering. Heinrici at least wanted some roads and railways left unmolested so that civilians might have the tiniest chance of escape.

The Belorussian and Ukrainian armies gathering under the command of Marshal Zhukov on the Oder–Neisse front held the keys to the future. If they could not be defeated outside the city, they most certainly could not be defeated once they were within its boundaries, progressing along the Reichsstrasse 1 trunk road and along other entry routes. And with the end of Berlin would come the end of the Third Reich. Barely sane bunker talk about resistance continuing in the north of Germany even after the city's fall was beyond futile. There was unfathomable pressure on both sides; Stalin had told Zhukov that it was vital that the men and women under his command conquer the capital by 22 April; the date was Lenin's birthday and thus had a secular sacredness. He had been pitted in competition against Marshal Konev and his forces, which were approaching Berlin from the south, creeping around like an embracing arm. Zhukov had been key to the defence of Stalingrad; he had, in the words of Macbeth, 'supp'd full with horrors'. And now here, on this moist plain through which rivers and their tributaries flowed, an area in which tiny towns had been half reduced to rubble, he was assessing an unknowable enemy. That the Nazis were defeated seemed obvious, yet their defence retained a wild fury and bite. The Wehrmacht commanders were intensely aware of the atrocities they had inflicted upon the Soviet people over the last four years; they had no doubts that the same pitiless butchery was now intended to be visited upon them. And there were still sharp tactical minds at work within the German ranks.

In front of the Seelow escarpment, mines were laid; anti-tank ditches were constructed. Near the slopes of the heights, artillery had been wheeled in, facing the plains below. There was an extra layer of defence too, behind all this: more tank obstacles, designed to slow movement to a near halt. The thousands of German men who were being brought to the area – among them wholly inexperienced draftees from the Luftwaffe and the Kriegsmarine – were not positioned permanently on the heights themselves, but a mile or so back down the reverse slopes, in patches of woodland. The reason for this was that Heinrici understood what form the Soviet assault would take. There had to be some distance or his forces would be reduced by the shelling to blood and bone within the first few minutes.

One quiet act of preliminary sabotage had already come off quite successfully: channels and waterways and a reservoir that ran around and through the rich agricultural land were altered and diverted and opened, together with some of the local water supplies; this had the effect of saturating the soil, turning the large flat fields into foot-sucking swamps. In addition to this, the positions that the German forces had taken in the wooded escarpment overlooking the fields and the rivers had a certain medieval advantage about them; the Red Army and its tanks would be faced with the dual obstacles of flood and gravity.

For many of the teenagers in their ill-fitting uniforms, squatting in dugouts among the trees, the coming confrontation with the Red Army was to be their first taste of war. Heinrici and others had argued with some anger against High Command about the use of boys; there was an obscenity about the sacrifice of children. Some of those boys – the assiduous readers of the Karl May adventure novels – might have jibbed at the idea that they were too young for this patriotic adventure. But the more sensitive and alert among them would have given thought to a future in which the Red Army could not be stopped, and their hearts would have drummed accordingly. If any of them managed to fall asleep that night, their dreams would have been brief, for the Soviet attack was launched at 3.05 a.m., in the heart of the darkness.

The still-black sky started to echo with a thousand terrifying screams. The explosions, orange and molten, came split seconds later, swift and random, trees uprooted and bodies flung aside. Against the dark air were meteor-streaks of light; and with them came further alien screams, a noise that could not be likened to anything natural on earth. These were the Katyushas – the Soviet slang term (a diminutive, like 'Katy') for rockets mounted on truck beds. They were hopelessly inaccurate, but that was not the point of them; when fired in vast numbers, they could turn the world into a disorientating and petrifying anarchy. The repercussions from their blasts caused distant shelters to quake; German soldier Friedhelm Schöneck recalled the nauseating illusion of the ground itself undulating under the ceaseless bombardment, 'like being on a ship in a Force 10 gale'. 'A deafening noise fills the air,' he wrote. 'Compared to everything that has gone before, this is no longer a barrage, it is a hurricane that tears everything up above us, in front of and behind us. The sky is glowing red, as if it were about to burst. The ground wobbles, shakes and rocks.'[6] The screaming missiles would not stop, and as they detonated in thick wet soil and amid trees and leaf cover, the sheer weight of the onslaught began to ripple outwards across the land, the echoes thrumming through the air of the early hours. In Berlin, citizens and military alike awoke to what at first sounded like a 'rolling' thunderstorm,[7] distant hollow booms pulsing through the night. In small towns near Berlin, this uncanny storm began producing poltergeist effects: pictures and mirrors started shuddering on walls; the bells in household telephones began to ping and jangle. By now awake in the blackness, these townsfolk and villagers understood that this was the beginning of the battle, yet there must also have been something atavistic about the way that those relentless solemn booms resonated against already quickened hearts.

The initial assault had been anticipated – even though the Katyushas created a vortex of confusion, the vast majority of the German defences had been pulled back just out of their range – but it was merely an overture. 'Our men . . . are realizing that a new phase of this gigantic war, and one of the hardest trials, has begun,' wrote German war correspondent Lutz Koch. This was, he said, 'the hurricane of the Russian artillery'.[8] It was to be followed by a Soviet weapon that seemed torn directly from the imaginations of Fritz Lang and Albert Speer: projected light. Using 143 vast searchlights positioned around the plain, the Red Army turned the intense beams on the Seelow Heights, and at the German artillery angled on the escarpment. This projection was intended to pinpoint enemy targets with a sharpness that made them easier to aim at, the dazzling light conveying power and superiority calculated to to induce panic in those caught in its unsparing glare. 'Over one hundred billion candle power illuminated the battlefield,' wrote Zhukov some years later, still affected by it.[9] 'It was an immensely fascinating and impressive sight, and never before in my life had I felt anything like what I felt then.'[10] The combined glow reached high into the sky. Lieutenant Colonel Pavel Troyanovsky described it as 'a thousand suns joined together'.[11]

In normal circumstances the ploy might have been effective, but the conditions that night were far from normal. Because of cloud and mist, and the dust thrown up high in the air by the explosions, these intense beams seemed to be caught, muffled against a fine fog of matter, and thrown back, creating a near Brocken spectre effect around those who were casting the light. As climbers on mountains, dazzled in icy mist by the sun behind them, sometimes see grey ghost or 'spectre' figures – the illusion created by their own projected shadows – so the Red Army forces began, under that baffled light, to attain their own silhouettes in the murk of that blurred morning. The great beams that had been intended to transfix the enemy had instead bounced back and betrayed the projectionists, turning them into easily identified targets. The Soviet 8th Guards Army had started its advance towards the heights when the initial barrage had stopped by 4 a.m., but the intense light and the fog, combined with the fact that heavy vehicles and armoured personnel alike found themselves being slowed almost to a stop by the boggy swill of the drowned soil, led to a wholly unanticipated disaster. The Germans were able to launch a grim defence and those slogging through the plain were helpless. The air roared with German artillery, and very soon the Soviet death toll beneath the heights was appalling, blood streaming into the viscous mud. What made it worse for Zhukov was the concentration of his forces in this ghastly open arena; while Konev proceeded with his own forces from the south, Zhukov, who had been convinced that he would capture the heights on the day, was forced to report back to Stalin that he had been delayed. Quietly, Stalin asked him if he expected success the following day. Zhukov sought to assure him that this would be the case, and that it would be easier to 'smash the enemy troops on an open battlefield than in a fortified city'. Stalin concluded the conversation with a curt 'goodbye'.[12]

For General Heinrici, this was the last day that it was possible for the regime to imagine – even if only in an abstract sense – that the Wehrmacht had any sort of chance in holding back the Red Army; the last day when a certain skill and experience could be deployed effectively, wreaking damage upon an otherwise utterly impervious adversary. He had no doubts that, despite that resistance, the Soviets would break through within hours. He had been confiding in Albert Speer, who that morning had been driven to a high point not far from the Seelow Heights to witness what he thought would be the inevitable Red Army breakthrough. All that could be seen, however, was a dense mist. Speer withdrew to 'Goering's animal paradise, the lonely woods of Schorfheide'.[13] The woods teemed and rustled with deer and wild boar; these had been hunting grounds for centuries. And amid the trees, the lakes and the boggy ground, Speer 'dismissed his escort', found a tree stump, sat down and began writing a speech.[14] A few days earlier, he had intended to defy his Führer's orders for a 'scorched earth' destruction of Berlin's infrastructure but had had his original speech censored by Hitler. Now he was recomposing it, as he later claimed, and going further: this speech, as a Reich minister, was not just going to explicitly ban the blowing up of bridges and factories, railway lines and waterways, as Heinrici too had advocated: it was also going to forbid 'Werewolf activity' – fanatical Nazis intent on fighting to the death, even if all around them died too. More than this, he claimed that he intended to order that all prisoners – Jewish and political – should be surrendered to the forces that would come to occupy the land. Sitting in that silent forest, Speer was writing of an 'unshakeable' faith in 'the future of our nation'.[15] Later that day he was conferring with General Heinrici, who was patrolling the heights. Speer thought that he could deliver this speech from a radio station with a guaranteed electricity supply in Königs Wusterhausen; Heinrici told him that, by the evening, that radio station would be under the control of Soviet forces. Perhaps the best option, the general told the architect, would be to record the speech on a 'phonograph record' and 'leave it with him'.[16] Speer was not aware that Heinrici already had his own plans.

For many of the women of Berlin, the very idea of planning for survival seemed an unattainable luxury; it was scarcely possible to anticipate the next loaf of rye bread. Yet they were not docile; quite the reverse. Even as the city's wider defences began to creak and crack, large numbers of women – from factory hands to office workers and mothers with small children moving from shelters to dilapidated damaged homes and back – were showing courage, adaptability and endurance. Electricity could no longer be counted upon even for short periods, and the task of obtaining ever-depleting rations – even though small children were granted extra calories – was still a prospect of cold lines on threatening streets. On some lamp-posts, loudspeakers were beginning to broadcast harsh exhortations to do with fidelity to the Reich, and watchfulness for treachery. A very few women – such as the journalist Ruth Andreas-Friedrich – were actively (if invisibly) resistant to the regime (she and her partner, the orchestra conductor Leo Borchard, had been secretly and bravely helping a number of Berlin's 'underground' Jewish people) . Others practised their own form of mental defiance: women on production lines and in the outskirts of the city openly proclaiming to one another that they now had nothing but contempt for the Nazi hierarchy. What underlined every dissenting voice was a more broadly unspoken fear. The women of Berlin had been betrayed by men; the soldiers and the SS were supposed to have held back the hordes, and had clearly, horribly, failed. This is why a number of women took with such alacrity to the idea of arming themselves. Despite its vulnerability, Berlin did not lack for weapons; its wartime factories had, despite the most intense bombardment, been able to turn out large numbers of guns and rocket launchers. Many women were being taught the use of Panzerfausts. These anti-tank projectiles – which could be fired by hand from a tube mounted on the shoulder – had proved dramatically effective for the Wehrmacht; the idea of their use on once familiar streets of shops and flats seemed to have been accepted as part of a broader changed reality. The Panzerfaust was a single-use weapon, loaded with a hollow-charge bomb. It had a sight, so that a broad aim could be taken, and it was devised in such a way that there was little recoil from the fired explosive, which allowed it to be used by those with smaller, slighter figures without hurling them backwards. There is footage of one elegantly dressed woman, complete with smart hat, taking aim and firing the Panzerfaust, the training target exploding satisfactorily. This was a weapon that might be used by mothers. In the east of the city, which had suffered grievously in the Allied air roads, the fragments of walls and the dark-eyed shells of bombed-out tenement blocks could hardly be damaged any further, no matter how many Panzerfausts were fired; and the idea of a weapon that could burn out a tank must have brought a kind of fleeting comfort to many.

There were a very few women who – knowing that the scarce escape routes from the city were fast closing – had the agency and the material means to leave Berlin. Office worker Mechtild Evers – who had made up her mind a few days previously when she, her boss and several of her colleagues had availed themselves of the office safe to take three months' salary[17] – still kept a very specific destination in mind: a port called Stralsund a little over one hundred miles to the north, where she knew that her soldier husband was stationed, and thence to a small island called Hiddensee, which in pre-war years had been popular with bohemian middle-class holidaymakers. The prospect – gorse, sand, a lighthouse and the cold, clear Baltic beyond – filled her dreams.[18] By mid April, there was no prospect of catching a train out of Berlin; the only realistic possibility was walking and hitchhiking. Very soon after she left the city's outskirts, Evers found herself diving for cover behind a truck as a British plane swooped in low. Even in the wide open countryside beyond the city there was no likelihood of safety: she was a lone woman on a hostile road. But she had no intention of stopping.[19]

The wider point was that one of the abiding ideological principles of the Nazis – that German women should reject modern notions of equality and instead focus upon the home and children – was finally and completely eradicated. In Berlin, the principle had never really gained much traction in any case; from the 1930s, women contin-ued to have an ever-strengthening presence in office jobs; during the 1940s, many of Berlin's women were on the factory floors, on intensive production lines, supervising the sort of advanced machinery that in previous years had been the exclusive province of men. The deployment to them of explosives was a natural progression.

Yet amid the women were the children; members of the Hitler Youth and the League of German Girls who were being pulled into the city's defences with no apparent qualms or compunction from party authorities. There were teenage girls who had joined the Werewolf movement. Heidi Koch recalled how each day brought an ever more pressing weight of fear. 'We spent much of our time digging holes, making walls of rubble and upturning motor vehicles and trams,' she recalled. 'There were many members of the SS in the city. I kept asking questions until one turned and shouted at me: "Do you know what will happen if the Russians get here? They will probably f★★★ you and shoot you, do you understand?"'[20]

And, for the citizens of Berlin, there was the public broadcast of deranged rhetoric issued as an 'order of the day' from the Führer. Only the most devoted of the Werewolves by that stage may have drawn energetic inspiration from it. 'For the last time, the Jewish Bolshevik arch enemy has hurled his masses into an attack,' the communiqué ran. 'He is trying to pulverize Germany and exterminate our people . . . The old men and the children will be murdered. Women and maidens will be debased to the level of barrack-room harlots. The rest will be packed off to Siberia.'[21] Meanwhile, the Führer declared, 'everything has been done to build a strong front line . . . Bolshevism . . . must and will bleed to death in front of the capital of the German Reich.' Yet there were also words and exhortations here that Albert Speer and a number of other senior Nazis knew were simply suicidal nihilism. Hitler's order continued:

> He who in this hour does not do his duty is a traitor to his people. He who gives the order to retreat . . . is to be arrested at once and if necessary to be shot on the spot, regardless of what rank he holds. If in the days and weeks to come every soldier does his duty then the last onslaught from Asia will collapse as in the end the breakthrough of our enemies in the west will collapse. Berlin remains German. Vienna will become German again. Europe will never be Russian . . . Russian Bolshevism will drown in a sea of blood.[22]

He ended with a curious reference to the death of President Roosevelt: that all this was happening 'at the very moment when destiny has taken away from the earth the greatest war criminal of all time'.[23] The flicker of a belief in the possibility that somehow Roosevelt's death might precipitate some form of collapse in morale among the Western Allies, averting inevitable German defeat, was still there. Of the many delusions that whispered through the concrete corridors of that claustrophobic bunker, this was among the most puzzling.

Anyone who left that bunker in the hours afterwards and glanced upon brickwork elsewhere in the city might have noticed several walls painted with a singular message: the word 'Nein'. This was the regime-defying work of the journalist Ruth Andreas-Friedrich, who had gone out at night with paint, stealthily avoiding the darker figures patrolling the blackened streets.[24] At this stage of the city's hastening slide into the vortex, a single word would have been sufficient to have a middle-aged woman hanged or shot.

At Seelow, although the initial Soviet deaths on that flood plain were in the tens of thousands, there was no possibility that the advance of all those many more behind them could be resisted for long. General Heinrici conferred with his senior commanders as the sun progressed through the misty sky and as the foul air continued to ring with explosions and the shriek of rockets. 'They cannot hold out much longer,' he said of his own forces. 'The men are so exhausted that their tongues are hanging out.'[25] The plain and the hills of Seelow were now a prospect of twisted steel, bone and pulped flesh. This was the sort of mass slaughter most associated with the Great War. The hours to come would see a great deal more blood, but there was no stasis. Terrified of Stalin, and in his own blazing drive to be the conqueror of Berlin, there was no prospect that Marshal Zhukov would consider more pragmatic possibilities; his army had to be driven on.

The number of dead can even now only be an estimate: somewhere between 30,000 and 33,000 Soviet soldiers were killed in the ensuing three-day battle, and some 12,000 Germans lay dead. As the sky darkened at the end of the first day, and complete blackness stole over the land, the advance was stealthily made by Soviet tanks moving beyond the main battlefield. In Seelow itself, three houses were captured by Red Army troops before midnight. More fissures would be found, and explored, and then torn wide open by the invaders. General Heinrici, in the meantime, knew his own mind, and it was no longer in any kind of accord with his Nazi superiors. He knew that the Gates of Berlin were buckling under unprecedented pressure, and that nothing he or thousands of defenders could do would prevent that Soviet tide rushing through.

## 12.   The Tears of All Mothers

Time had once stretched illimitably; the Germany that the Nazis had shaped was founded on the rhetoric of a thousand years, and this was to have been expressed not just in conquest, but in architecture and art as well. Albert Speer had fantasized that his vast neoclassical Germania landmarks would stand for centuries, only to decay finally amid green weeds in great beauty. Now, on the morning of 20 April 1945 – the fifty-sixth and final birthday of Adolf Hitler – ordinary Berlin streets to the north and north-east edges of the city that had not already been mutilated and broken by the Allied bombs were being targeted by Soviet artillery. The vast forces commanded by Zhukov had flooded through the Seelow Heights and had swept to the green, leafy outer fringes of Berlin with nightmarish speed. The air of these northerly suburbs was filled with the unearthly howls of Soviet projectiles; the walls of tenements and apartment buildings were pierced, some collapsing like wounded giants forced to their knees, exhaling dust. The Nazis had laid claim to a millennium to come; instead, the city now seemed robbed even of the ordinary passing of time. For the citizens not entombed, breathing in the ordure and the filth of the concrete fortresses and shelters, the impact of the distant artillery registering as a deep pulse that could be felt as well as heard, there was no longer any sense of the hours. 'No one knows what time it is any more,' remarked one woman, complaining that the city's clocks were all too damaged to tell.[1] Time 'slips by like water' wrote another in her diary, adding elsewhere that this was a 'timeless time'.[2] For the ordinary people of Berlin, time's landmarks had vanished: birthdays, for them, if not for their leader were meaningless. And with the loss of a sense of time came a related sense of having become unmoored from life.

In the forests outside the city, however, on one particular country estate in the north-east, close to the advancing Soviet line, time was accelerating; deep in the woods was a vast and preposterous wooden palace – roof of dense thatch, exterior walls punctuated with trophy antlers – which was being emptied at speed. This curious house was, for the last few years, where a vast collection of Europe's finest art had been held: Van Gogh, Rubens, Tintoretto, Botticelli. Here were some 1,350 paintings of almost inestimable value, all of which had been ruthlessly expropriated and stolen since 1933. Again, the idea had been that, as the Nazi future stretched out, so these works of extraordinary beauty would at last once more be displayed before an appreciative German people, perhaps on the occasion of their curator Hermann Goering's sixtieth birthday in 1953. Goering's sensuous greed had found its most compulsive form in his journeys across Europe to help himself to the most exquisite art. Much of it, by 1945, was crammed into the extensive cellars of Carinhall, his vast hunting lodge-cum-palace in the woods, there being insufficient room to hang so many treasures on his baronial walls. And by 20 April 1945, as he prepared to leave this palace for the last time, so the artworks were similarly being evacuated: packed up, parcelled, scheduled for rail journeys to the south of Germany. Carinhall was to be wholly abandoned, along with the remains of Goering's beloved first wife, Carin, after whom the house had been named.

She had died young in 1931; and, when the palace had been completed, Goering had had her body exhumed and brought there to lie in a specially built tomb in the grounds. (Goering had married again in 1935, and his new wife, Emma Sonnemann, an actress, became regarded as the 'First Lady' of Nazi Germany because the Führer himself was not married; his partner Eva Braun could not, with any sense of Nazi propriety, play that role. By April 1945, Emma Goering was in the south of the country.) Goering had envisaged his own future reaching into the distance, and the prospect of his death too: he had long planned to have his own body interred in the same tomb at Carinhall. Now that future was a blank fog; it no longer existed. On 20 April, Goering's plan was to travel to Berlin, to the Reich Chancellery, to mark the Führer's birthday. Beyond that, his thoughts and intentions were fugitive. He certainly understood that he would never again return to Carinhall. He had had the entire house threaded and studded with explosives, intending that, in the event of the Red Army drawing closer, the house was to be utterly destroyed. Now, that time had very suddenly arrived. Many sculptures and other pieces of art that could not be packed up fast enough were to be consigned to the lake, or simply buried in the woods. And the spirit after whom the palace was named? The body of Goering's first wife was abandoned in that tomb in the grounds, for where else now could she be taken or reinterred? That morning, the bones in the mausoleum trembled as Goering himself fired the first of many detonations and the walls of Carinhall crumpled inward.

There was a larger forest – some miles to the east of the city, lying between Berlin and the Seelow Heights – through the trees of which were moving haunted, desperate men in retreat; some who belonged to the 18th Panzergrenadier Division, others – boys – who belonged to the Hitler Youth. The budding springtime canopy must have seemed to offer temporary shelter and sanctuary in the warming air. Yet this thick maze of tall pine, with its narrow paths and roads, springy and needle-strewn underfoot, was to prove just as dangerous as the wide-open plains. This was Märkische Schweiz, near Buckow and Strausberg, an area once said by a nineteenth-century physician to have such pure air that lungs would turn to velvet. Here, in peacetime, was a rich prospect of lakes and woods, of walking trails and swimming jetties, and small towns and villages with centuries-old churches. Now there were the approaching thunderclaps of artillery, and the intimations of distant scorched air. One local village, Waldsieversdorf, had been in part evacuated as its people fled, though a few had stayed, intending to kill themselves. The surrounding forests, always solemn, were now funereal.

It was to areas such as this that special buses were commissioned to carry the older men of the Volkssturm out of Berlin city centre, so that they too might face the oncoming enemy. Zhukov had calculated some time earlier that the German plan would be to replicate the circumstances under which the Wehrmacht itself had been vanquished in Russia; that they would aim to bog down the Red Army and bring it to a standstill in the hope that it might then be bled white. The difference now was that the Red Army supply lines were inexorable; train after train, carriages with flat beds carrying camouflaged materiel, moving east to west. In addition to this was the psychology of proximity: the centre of the Nazi web was just a matter of miles away. On top of this was the evidence of human collapse. Among the German forces so violently ejected from the Seelow Heights, the survivors unable to disguise their disarray, there was no sense that there was the strength for the vicious slog of attrition.

Here, amid the paths of slender tall trees, fallen branches and shallow trenches of slippery mud, one particular party of Hitler Youth found that they were, in essence, trapped. Soviet tanks had been progressing along wider nearby roads, the soldiers of the Red Army intensely aware that their enemies were hidden in the forests. And those same soldiers knew how those enemies might be lethally attacked beneath those canopies: tank fire aimed at the tops of the trees. The horrifying effect was a rain of fire, searing wood splinters shooting through the air like bullets, filleting flesh, and inescapable bright orange embers, cascading from above, producing gouts of flame on clothes and burning exposed skin. These were boys whose only knowledge of armed combat had come largely from films, and from the adventures of Old Shatterhand.

Nor did the forests to the south-east of Berlin offer any form of sanctuary. Near the village of Halbe, deep in the Spreewald, a romantic landscape of pine, red alder and marsh oaks, richly veined with waterways, thousands of men belonging to the German Ninth Army, on shadowed forest roads and in makeshift encampments, were under orders to hold the defensive line. But they too were hemmed in within that vast labyrinth of trees, and it soon became apparent that attempted breakouts by units were being met bloodily by Marshal Konev's ruthless forces on the ground and also from the Soviet Air Force. For huge numbers in the coming days there would be no escape from fierce, choking fires, nor from the tree-bursting explosions, nor from the continual bombardment from screaming rockets. Their tanks and vehicles became unwieldy in the loose, sandy soil; in the thick, burning haze, and with the sun difficult to discern, whole units became hopelessly disorientated, moving in wide circles; and, after some days, the scale of the slaughter amid these once-silent groves was astonishing. Some 40,000 German soldiers were killed, the roads through the woods becoming a prospect of scorched metal and blackened tissue and the crying wounded. Many of these casualties were barely more than teenagers. Even now, the soft floor of that old forest yields up remains. Remarkably, there were still those in the SS who retained their crystalline faith in the Führer, averring that it was Bolshevism that brought death; there were many men closer to the Führer who had lost that luxury of unwavering certainty.

In previous years, 20 April had been a day of ostentatious celebration in Berlin, marked with a holiday, the street furniture garlanded with ribbons. It had not seemed unnatural to citizens across Germany to mark their leader's birthday. Younger people would daydream of the gifts that they might present personally to Hitler, to let him see how much he was loved. On his fiftieth birthday, on 20 April 1939, soon after the conquest of the Czech territories, Berlin was transformed into an ecstasy of martial spectacle: as well as the goose-stepping parades staged by the services, performed for a Führer standing before a throne, the dais and the area around him festooned with flowers, public buildings were hung with vast banners proclaiming 'Führer, we thank you'.[3] And the Führer indeed received extravagant gifts: cars, paintings, and one present that he appeared to value above all the others – the original manuscript score of Wagner's opera *Rienzi*, which had been signed, many years back, by the composer himself.

Now, in the sterile, dusty light of the Reich Chancellery bunker, this was the one gift that Hitler had chosen to keep by his side; the musical score and libretto that always moved him to rapture. It was after hearing *Rienzi* performed for the first time, he had told an associate, that his life had been transfigured. 'In that hour,' Hitler said, 'it all began.'[4] Did he, by 20 April 1945, have a conception of the hour it would end? While he instructed his subordinates that he did not want to see this birthday celebrated publicly, Hitler had also started to convince himself – or at least so it seemed to those around him – that he could devise a means by which the Allies could be made to collapse. 'He gave the impression of a man . . . who was continuing along his established orbit only because of the kinetic energy stored within him,' observed Albert Speer.[5] But that inner force was in marked contrast to his outward appearance, the decay of which was in part the result of drug dependence:

Now, he was shrivelled up like an old man. His limbs trembled. He walked stooped, with dragging footsteps. Even his voice had become quavering and lost its old masterfulness ... His complexion was sallow, his face swollen; his uniform, which in the past he had kept scrupulously neat, was often neglected in this last period of his life and stained by the food he had eaten with a shaking hand.[6]

In this sense, the Führer continued to be the perfect emblem of the destroyed city and nation.

Also in attendance on that ironic birthday were Nazi figures who had wielded an unremitting power of death over millions, but who were now bathetically diminished. Foreign affairs minister Joachim von Ribbentrop was there; Himmler too. The official who had condemned uncountable men, women and children to cold and terrifying deaths had – with true sociopathy – met with a representative of the World Jewish Congress (and agreed to the release of 7,000 prisoners from nearby Ravensbrück women's concentration camp) as part of an effort to negotiate a surrender to the Americans. If it was true that Himmler genuinely believed that any negotiators would agree that the mass exterminations were a technocratic detail of war, then it was also the case that he was truly, genuinely empty. With that sense of time slipping away, Himmler, like Goering, did have the survival instinct, and he too was formulating the means by which he might leave the city and take refuge in another corner of the country.

Later that day, the Führer would rise from those depths to walk under the sky one last time, giving a glimpse of the human ruin that he had become, but, before this startling appearance, Berliners in the west and south-west of the city, who were as yet just beyond the range of mortars, were told that the Führer's birthday would be marked by a gift to his people: a small boost in that week's rations. In truth, these were actually emergency rations, issued in anticipation of a forthcoming siege. The weary mothers who emerged from basements into that grey world could expect to see a little extra butter, a few vegetables to augment an occasional potato, a tin of fruit or a serving of jam and a small amount of genuine coffee (as opposed to the acorn-based ersatz variety). There were reports in other corners of the city that small supplies of sausage, rice and lentils were suddenly available.

Twenty-nine-year-old mother Dorothea von Schwanenfluegel remembered the beneficence, but that time spent outside patiently queuing also brought for her a glimpse of the horror that was falling upon the city. Across the street from the shop she saw a boy, no older than twelve, slight and small. He was sitting in a 'self-dug trench' and appeared distrustful of any approaching adults.[7] None the less, she got closer and was startled to see tears running down his face. Beside him lay an anti-tank grenade. Gently, she asked the boy what he was doing there. He told her his instructions were to wait there until a Soviet tank rolled into view. Then he was to take the anti-tank grenade, run under the tank and detonate it. He had been persuaded – or forced – into the prospect of sacrificing his own life.

Frau von Schwanenfluegel looked at the boy, and at the explosive, and wondered if he even understood how to work it properly. She knew that, whatever happened, his suicide would be doubly futile: Red Army soldiers would simply shoot the child dead before he could reach the tank. Yet, at the same time, this mother could not act upon her instinct, which was to take the boy home with her and hide him. The SS were patrolling the streets and enforcing their will with a new and ever-more irrational frenzy; if the boy deserted his post, he would become another of the figures (there were now many of them across the city) dangling lifeless from lamp-posts, having been pulled up there on ropes by hand, the suffocation slow, the noose tightening. And if she took him in and hid him, they might hunt him down; and, in that instance, not only he, but Frau von Schwanenfluegel and her own children would be murdered as well. She collected the special birthday ration, and gave him some; then she left the boy, who remained in that trench, 'sobbing' and 'muttering'.[8] She returned the following day, out of a ghastly curiosity; the boy and the anti-tank grenade were no longer there. Her hope was that the boy's mother had found him and that he was safe. The bitterness of this daydream lay in the suspicion that this had not happened; this was no longer a world in which children were rescued by their mothers. It was likely that the SS had taken the boy and placed him in a more forward position.

Any sense of time further dissolved and lost clarity for those who sought sanctuary under the surface. The U-Bahn had never been an especially aesthetically pleasing metro system; even the fanciest stations, with outbreaks of decorative tiling, were still impatiently functional. Yet these dim, echoing spaces were, for some, greatly preferable to the close-smelling twilight of the concrete flak towers. Although, unlike London, where many underground stations were deep tubes, hundreds of feet down, the Berlin U-Bahn system was broadly composed of stations that lay no more than one or two storeys beneath the surface, the psychological sense of protection was still strong, and, while the city authorities had originally tried to discourage Berliners from using them as shelters, it was tacitly allowed in the spring of 1945 as the Allied bombs fell in ever more intense clusters. Now there was increasing danger from the Soviet Air Force as well. Safety was never certain; tunnels could become tombs instantaneously at worst, nerve-wracking sanctuaries at best. Gesundbrunnen station was a shelter with bunk beds, properly functioning lavatories, and some other rudimentary items of furniture, these comforts offset by the continual clangour of ventilation pipes. To sit here was to exist in a state of permanent dusk, never knowing what the world above would look like the next time you emerged into the ashen air. By April 1945, over three-quarters of apartments near the centre of the city had either been rendered uninhabitable or simply obliterated. Those who had sheltered in the underground darkness near platforms and rails were frequently obliged to return to that uncanny limbo, eyes flickering constantly to the concrete ceiling above.

On 20 April the U-Bahn municipal director Fritz Kraft had a meeting with Ludwig Steeg, the city's mayor; before them was a question about what would become of the city's tunnels, and how they might be used in the struggle ahead (mirroring the arguments to do with the city's bridges, and other infrastructure). Higher authorities had quietly made the suggestion that if it looked as though the American and the British forces were to be the first to arrive in central Berlin, then the network should be transferred untouched to their administration. If, alternatively, the Red Army were to push forward hardest, then the aim would be to destroy the miles of tunnels to hamper their takeover. With those tunnels still emphatically inhabited – and with infrequent trains continuing to carry factory workers – decisions were deferred. Kraft will have known that there was one sure way to make the tunnels unusable: explosives triggered close to the city's rivers and canals would have the effect of causing sluice-like floods. But he would also have known the risk to countless lives if the plan were carried out. And while these agonized discussions continued, there were those who were finding other uses for the trains that were standing in depots or at line termini; the Volkssturm, together with the SS, were picking through each carriage in order to wrench out metal poles that might conceivably be used as weapons.

One substantial part of the city centre that had once stood outside of the usual eddies and currents of time was the Berlin Zoological Garden. But the war had turned many parts of it into a charnel house, and now, with the repercussive noise from the guns placed on top of the nearby flak tower, the few remaining specimens were being driven mad with stress and terror, imprisoned and helpless within cages and enclosures. And, as Hermann Goering made his own plans for departure from Berlin, one of his more unusual friends was desperately trying to find ways of looking after these traumatized animal charges.[9] Dr Lutz Heck was the director of this historic institution, established in 1844. It was one of the largest zoos in Europe, its orientalist entrance famous across the continent, and even on 20 April 1945, after years of bombardment, it was still open to the public. There was little in the way of remaining wildlife for that public to see. The Ibex rock garden had been pulverized; the aquarium had been comprehensively demolished in one night. Two years of repeated Allied bombing raids had destroyed a number of other structures and wildlife. In the wake of the raids that were carried out in the autumn of 1943, there were urban rumours and some panic: lurid talk among Berliners of escaped tigers and panthers that were now prowling the streets in the blackout, and on the hunt for human flesh. The sad truth was that many of these creatures lay dead. On Budapester Strasse that same year, Berliners were both distressed and bewildered by the spectacle of large alligators lying lifeless on the pavements, having been hurled from the zoo by bomb blasts.[10] By 1945, dead species were being surveyed in quite a different way, hunger-maddened Berliners speculating on what various sorts of wild meat would taste like.

The surviving animals that were in Dr Heck's care, from Siam the elephant to a baby hippopotamus called Knautschke, were becoming ever more difficult to tend to, and Heck was becoming ever more agitated. Despite this concern for helpless creatures, the doctor was very far from being either a saintly or indeed an especially kind man. Instead, fifty-three-year-old Heck was a figure who loathed a great number of his fellow men (while simultaneously believing that animals had an essential innocence that could touch the soul).[11] And he was friends with Hermann Goering because, some years back, the two of them had discovered a mutual interest in what they saw as the unsullied purity of Germanic nature and wildlife. Goering had become interested in the ideas of naturalist Heck early on in the Nazi regime, and they shared a passion for hunting wild game, and for roaming deep in forests. Heck was a dedicated Nazi; a party member and a scientist with strange ideas about resurrecting extinct species. He and his brother Heinz had, in the 1930s, conducted eugenic-type experiments on various breeds of cattle in an effort to reintroduce the aurochs: a large horned beast. There was also an attempt to regenerate a species of Eurasian horse called the tarpan, using its modern descendants: the result was called the Heck horse.[12] Strikingly, his brother Heinz was implacably not a Nazi; indeed, his early opposition to the regime had seen him consigned to Dachau for a short time, after which he remained an object of distrust to the party. Lutz Heck, by contrast, had been especially at home amid the pines and the oaks around Goering's residence: the two men had frequently discussed the means by which national parks might be created across the nation. The Reich Nature Protection Law had come into force in 1935; in their own way, sections of the Nazi Party were strident environmentalists. Yet it was an ecological sensitivity that was suffused with xenophobia: a distaste for and fear of the idea of the natural realm being invaded by foreign strains. Lutz Heck and Hermann Goering shared a vision of *Heimat* – a homeland where native Germanic wildlife and plant species might flourish.

Heck was also a passionate anti-Semite. With the ascension of the Nazis, he had been swift to purge Berlin Zoo of its Jewish staff and board members. Those members of the Jewish public who owned shares in the zoo had them ruthlessly expropriated. Dr Heck took this malice a stage further in 1938, even before *Kristallnacht*, by banning Jewish families and children from even visiting the zoo; if animals could touch the soul, he had no intention of allowing Jews this beautiful moment of communion. This hatred oddly formed part of his conservationist philosophy. The Jewish people, linked so inextricably in the Nazi imagination to capitalism, were accused of being the despoilers and exploiters of the natural world. The fact that that natural world was abused every bit as badly by Nazi industrialists as by their imagined foe seemed not to make a difference. As the Germans invaded Poland, and then started pushing further east, Heck was fascinated by the idea that the lands themselves would be remodelled to suit the Germanic soul: from the soil to the trees to the waterways, nature itself would be under the command of the *völkisch* spirit. 'For the first time in history,' Heck mused in 1942, 'a nation is undertaking the modelling of a landscape in a conscious way.'[13] Like Goering, he believed in the idea of the *Dauerwald*, or the eternal forest. There was a Nazi guide to forestry published in the late 1930s that had offered this thought: 'Ask the trees, they will teach you how to become a National Socialist.'[14]

The first Allied bomb to fall on the zoo came in 1941, and, in the years that followed, the destruction became ever bloodier. The zoo had been landscaped in stone and grass, as a means of creating a semi-natural environment for the larger captive species, but, like the Tiergarten itself, bombing raids left terrible craters and intense anguish for the animals that survived (the young hippopotamus – Knautschke – lost his fellows in one such raid; remarkably, the creature lived in the zoo for many years after the war, as the environment around it was painstakingly rebuilt). By April 1945, Berlin's electricity supplies had become so erratic that the power to the zoo was cut; and this in turn meant that the zoo's water supplies could not be made to function. In a fog of helplessness, unable to think what to do with his few surviving animals, Dr Heck wandered blankly out of the zoo; it would not be long before he, like his friend Hermann Goering, would be formulating escape plans. Dr Heck was soon to abandon the zoo altogether, taking from it whatever money he could find; and his retreat from the city would be on a bicycle.[15]

Just outside the fences of the Berlin Zoo lay the once grand and green acres of the Tiergarten park. It currently resembled, in some respects, a desert: treeless (those that had stood there either uprooted by the endless bombing or exploited by inner-city Berliners with axes and saws on the search for any kind of fuel), pock-marked with craters, the once rich grass now a prospect of dull, sandy soil. The city's children had used those depressions and blasted tree stumps as a playground, for even this shattered landscape had afforded possibilities for new iterations of favourite games involving cowboys or detectives, but by 20 April a thicker silence had fallen over the area, broken only by the distant crackles and deep reports that seemed to echo from all around. And, that morning, the skies above the Tiergarten were again filled by hundreds of British bombers, flying over that vast haunted space that could not have more clearly delineated the heart of the city, and thus the remaining governmental buildings all around it. Berliners had no warning of this raid: the alarm systems had broken down. Later, to many, it barely registered as an occurrence: so integral had the raids become in the fabric of everyday life that they scarcely touched the consciousness.[16] But as the planes approached, the boys manning the guns on the tall flak tower were ready to begin blasting ineffectually once more; and, once more, the violent noise that they created sent the few surviving zoo animals below into a delirium of distress.

By the large railway stations – Silesian, Anhalter – there was the same sense of the years being displaced; an unstoppable stream of rural refugees, with horses and handcarts and unkempt beards and frayed clothes, navigated their way through what looked like military encampments, with makeshift outdoor kitchens and fires, so that civilian Berliners might have imagined themselves somehow transposed to the Napoleonic Wars. Bathroom facilities were non-existent; refugees and soldiers alike were compelled to relieve themselves in corners, further polluting the already pungent air. There was also a sharp change in the countenances of the soldiers: young men who had aged, and whose eyes now seemed dulled. The structure of the

Anhalter Bahnhof was skeletal and the arches that had once supported the vast glass canopy were bare; the station through which so many of the city's Jews had passed, ordered on to the trains that would take them to Theresienstadt, had been hit repeatedly by Allied bombs, most recently in February 1945. In the absence of trains, the platforms and the rain-exposed concourses made makeshift muster points for the regular Wehrmacht and for grey-haired Volkssturm alike. In the streets immediately around, there had been threaded a tangle of telephone wires to facilitate urgent communication. Yet these wires brought no news of miracle weapons, or of mighty German divisions storming to the city's defence. There were also a few *kneipen*, or bars, that had escaped bombing, and which were still serving beer to those men who were able to sidle away from their commanders and stand in darkened saloons. Soldiers and civilians alike still had recourse to the consolation of alcohol; those breweries on the outskirts of the city that had not been hit had slowed production but held voluminous stocks. Nor was it too difficult to find civilians who had stashed supplies of everything from fine red wine to brandy in cellar shelters. In the absence of any recognizable daily civic rhythm, pleasure had to be taken where it could be found. The soldiers and their commanders around these makeshift headquarters, it was observed, were filling the minutes and the hours with empty activity that spoke of fear: pointless messages, deliberately repetitive errands. Time for these fighting men was now measured in the frequency of reports concerning the approach of the enemy.

For civilians, the one other means of keeping an anchor on the passing days and hours, retaining a sense of ordered time, was through what remained of Berlin's media. Those who knew where it might be possible to get hold of a copy of the two-page daily newspaper *Das Reich* were, on the morning of 20 April, facing a grim new prospect: not merely the hills of rubble that had been homes, or the suggestions, amid the dust and shattered glass, of fragments of bodies; nor even the posters from the authorities, appearing like rashes on the sides of walls that held, with the legend 'Die Vergeltung kommt' – Vengeance is Coming.[17] Now they also faced the repetitive heartbeat boom that pulsed through the air; this was the Soviet heavy artillery aimed at the northern suburbs of Berlin, and the barrage began at

11.30 a.m. It did not sound like liberation. Meanwhile, the newspaper itself continued with its defiance of reality. Extraordinarily, there was still a great demand for it – not because it was universally believed, more that any news at all was better than a frightening silence from the city's authorities. To mark the Führer's birthday, Joseph Goebbels had composed an editorial intended to revive the flames of faith in his people:

> He will be the man of this century, who was sure of himself despite terrible pain and suffering. Who showed the way to victory. He is the only one who remained true to himself, who did not cheaply sell his faith and his ideals, who always and without doubt followed his straight path towards his goal. That goal may today be hidden behind the piles of rubble that our hate-filled enemies have wrought across our once proud continent, but which will once again shine before our burning eyes once the rubble has been cleared.[18]

Berliners like Dorothea von Schwanenfluegel had learned to detect the subtexts in these proclamations. This was on a day, she recalled later, that bodies 'were hanging everywhere';[19] and boys like the putative sacrificial tank bomber that she had encountered were being murdered by hysterical members of the SS. The Goebbels line intimated that only the Führer had managed to keep to 'the straight path'; the implication was that weak and foolish elements in the military and in the civic authorities had faltered in their faith, and that this doubt had brought the nightmare barbarian forces to their gates. Yet even at this late hour, insisted Goebbels at the conclusion of this diatribe, the people still had their chance; redemption could be theirs. His appeal to Christian imagery was beyond cynical:

> As he has done so often before, God will throw Lucifer back into the abyss even as he stands before the gates of power over all the peoples. A man of truly timeless greatness, of unique courage, of a steadfastness that elevates the hearts of some and shakes those of others, will be his tool. Who will maintain that this man can be found in the leadership of Bolshevism or plutocracy? No, the German people bore him. It chose him, it by free election made him Führer. It knows his works of peace and now wants to bear and fight the war that was forced upon him until its successful end.[20]

Balanced against this irrational rhetoric, issued from a concrete catacomb, the inner-city streets above – many of which were now mazes of piled-up tank barriers and planks over fresh ditches, all in the shadows of surviving apartment blocks, shops and factories – were busy with elderly men and women; the Volkssturm militia – overcoats, caps and hats, makeshift armbands – were milling and shuffling around the barricades, and their female relatives were venturing out from shelters carrying baskets of rationed food for their lunch.

There were women who insisted upon taking super-active roles; any passivity in the face of the approaching destruction seemed agonizing. The young film actress Hildegard Knef, driven almost mad by the combination of the Allied bombing and the deep, distant 'murmuring' of Soviet artillery, demanded to stay by the side of her lover (and SS officer) Ewald von Demandowsky, who had been called up to a makeshift military headquarters in the suburb of Schmargendorf; this, in parts, was an industrial prospect of vast railway marshalling yards and brick warehouses and depots. Knef – notably attractive, green-eyed, blonde and statuesque – adopted the first of her disguises. She 'put on a beret, tin helmet, turtle neck sweater, training-suit trousers' and new boots that belonged to her stepfather.[21] Suitably deglamorized – and ignoring all objections from her lover – she persuaded him to cycle with her along the cracked roads. 'The streets are quiet, empty, dead,' she wrote. 'People are sitting in their cellars, waiting. The murmuring is clearer, nearer.'[22] The headquarters was near the marshalling yards. 'They give me a tunic, a battered Italian cap, helmet, belt, machine gun, ammunition, hand grenades, pistol.'[23] And it was clear that this like her earlier disguise was already working. She was approached by a 'bloated, beery' soldier, who demanded a name and age. She told him nineteen. He began screaming at her, still having not realized her sex. Why, he demanded, was she not at the front? She removed her helmet, then the beret. 'His face stretches, dissolves, he slaps his thigh, howls with glee. A gal, he howls, wanna join us? Yes, I answer. How about that for guts, he whinnies.'[24] But there was no mockery: Frau Knef was instantly draped with ammunition belts, taught the mechanism of safety catches, given a target test and from that point was inducted.

Her Schmargendorf HQ was a ground-floor flat with 'no

windowpanes' and 'closed shutters' and a bed-frame without a mattress. In her first few hours there, listening to the incessant distant artillery, Knef's party was joined by a 'pimply' fifteen-year-old boy, armed and frightened and ready to pull the trigger at the slightest noise.[25] There was also a soldier there who had fought at Stalingrad, and who now seemed like the wise – if gruff – counsel of the group. Before long, yet more men marched in. 'The cellar's bursting; privates, young-old, very young reserves, SS,' she wrote. 'Uniforms have been crossed with each other, it looks like a carnival. There is a smell of sweat, cabbage, unwashed bodies. No one speaks.'[26] Frau Knef had joined these men because she – like huge numbers of women across Berlin – had listened to the stories emerging from the east about the Red Army and the threat of rape. The fear of sexual violence was pervasive.

Elsewhere, even in the leafy far west of the city, a little further from the Red Army rockets, teenage schoolgirl Christa Ronke found her imagination filled horribly with the idea of Berlin's defences being torn down. Her father was out there, fighting, even though he himself had let it be known to his wife and daughter a short while back that he now considered it 'pointless'; Christa had no possibility of knowing where he was as she listened to those Russian guns. 'We can hear the artillery from afar,' she wrote. And yet life – even in this immiserated and minimalist form – somehow had to continue.

In their part of the city, there was now 'no electricity, no telephone and no more newspapers'.[27] 'We cling to the hope that maybe the Americans will be here before the Russians,' she wrote in her diary. 'In addition, there is talk of a "Wenck" army that is supposed to free us. But I don't believe in it.'[28] General Walther Wenck – at forty-four the relatively young commander of the Twelfth Army ordered to hold off the British and American forces – was at that moment further west of Berlin, helplessly penned in but at the same time trying to make life tolerable for huge numbers of civilian refugees fleeing the city. Rather than shooting or hanging them, Wenck was attempting to avert a human calamity by feeding them. He was seemingly alone in understanding, even if it was too late, that the priority was not to save the regime but to save lives, although by that time it could not be said who was in the better position: the refugees starving in the city's outer forests or the people like Christa Ronke and her mother who were still joining queues at allotted times for sparse groceries as the air around them echoed to the sounds of gunfire.

Some Berliners from the eastern suburbs had become refugees within the bounds of their own city; gripped by the infection of fear as they watched neighbours pack only the meanest of essentials in their haste to leave, and overwhelmed by the sense that they too must escape before it was too late. The journalist Erich Schneyder recalled happening across an old acquaintance who was – or until very recently had been – a corporate lawyer. This man was now wandering the avenues carrying a heavy briefcase full of banknotes. He had been preparing for this emergency for some time. But now that time had come: and where was there to go?[29]

All the while, the flags and notices proclaiming the Führer's birthday were in the sight of parents and children who were either moving through the city towards the western suburbs, where it was imagined the Americans might arrive, or standing helplessly in those queues, looking up at every intimation of a distant explosion, or the echoes of gunfire. There were still, even amid the disintegration, some youngsters who retained a simple adoration for their leader.

German children had dreamed about meeting the Führer. Even before he became Chancellor, there was a charisma about him that left an imprint on growing imaginations. Hildegard Dockal was eleven years old in 1929 when a visit from the NSDAP leader was planned for her neighbourhood; her father and mother, listening to his speeches on the radio, had become enthusiastic supporters, and the radiance of his projected character began to inspire the young girl. On the day of the visit, daughter and mother positioned themselves hours beforehand at the outdoor lectern in readiness; there was a delay as the leader's motorcade had been held up by a vigorous protest, and – as the girl heard later – the leader himself had been forced to leap out of his car and strike at his opponents with 'a dog-whip'.[30] Eventually, he made it to the appointed public space and moved among the large assembled crowd, shaking hands with supporters and pausing for a few words with lucky chosen ones. He stopped to greet the man who was standing beside Hildegard Dockal,

and the girl gazed upon 'his shining eyes'.[31] She was in a state of rapture; but when the leader moved on without acknowledging her she
felt 'abandoned'.[32] (The thrall was passing and the subsequent scepticism fast arriving; neither Hildegard's family nor she ever joined the
Nazi Party. None the less, this showed how even those without any
particular political leanings – especially children, who had no such
leanings at all – could find themselves being drawn into that
current.)

Satisfaction in pleasing the Führer was also prevalent among the
young; from those who had the chance to perform in the ceremonies
surrounding the 1936 Olympics to the boys and girls sent with the
Hitler Youth and League of German Girls on field trips into the
countryside and the mountains, all harboured the constant idea of
working for the leader. In 1940, eleven-year-old Günther Lothar was
among the Berlin classmates selected for what they thought was a
special school trip into the snowy peaks of Iselsberg, near the town of
Lienz, in Austria. Days of sledging and icy treks, hearty (and to Berlin boys, unusual) meals involving lots of 'pastries' and 'polenta with
raspberry sauce'[33] at their hostel were capped with the treat of listening to broadcasts from the Führer. The postcards they could send
home featured the Führer's image. It was only after some weeks of
this that these children – a cohort of around 700 from inner-city
Berlin – came to understand that they were actually evacuees, and
that this was to be their home indefinitely. Their parents had no say
in the matter. There was an official letter from the Iselsberg youth
leader telling families that 'while in England, the authorities only
care for the children of plutocrats [a strikingly inventive untruth] all
of German youth in areas endangered by bombing has been offered
the opportunity to spend a healthy and untroubled time in other
parts of their beautiful Greater German homeland'.[34] For these boys,
Hitler had become both parent and teacher, his image and speeches
their syllabus.

Earlier than this, Ingeborg Seldte, who had been among the fortunate few chosen for those Olympic displays, revelled at the time in all
the 'hiking and the handicraft evenings'; since she had nothing to
compare the experience with, there seemed a fantastic warmth about
the communion of 'Führer, Volk und Vaterland'.[35] Only as she grew

older – *Kristallnacht* in Berlin was the first moment when she became conscious of unease – could she free herself. By the end of the war, she understood and felt fully the squalor of the regime that she and countless other children had been dazzled by.

None the less, in April 1945, that hold was still there over some of the city's younger inhabitants. On the afternoon of his fifty-sixth birthday there assembled in the garden of the Reich Chancellery a small gathering of Hitler Youth Volkssturm boys, under the eye of the National Youth Leader Artur Axmann. They knew nothing before-hand of their Führer's subterranean existence, or of the disintegration it had wrought. This was a specially prepared ceremony, attended by a film crew. It involved children being awarded Iron Crosses: the val-orization of boy soldiers. One such was Alfred Czech, a twelve-year-old from a farm in Silesia, who, a few weeks previously, had ridden in his father's cart in order to rescue wounded German soldiers facing the advance of the Red Army. On the first foray, young Czech helped retrieve four men from the line of fire; and then, on a second, eight. The boy's bravery had been noted, and news of it had passed up through the hierarchy. He, along with some dozen other boys, was then selected to be honoured.

First, Czech remembered, a general came to the family farmhouse and told him to get ready for a special trip to Berlin. 'My mother was dead against the idea,' Czech said decades later. 'She was afraid I might come to harm on the journey but my father was in favour so I went.'[36] The means of transportation was military aeroplane, and after a short flight he was in a city that was beginning to pulsate under the weight of Soviet guns. He and the other boys who were to be rewarded for their bravery were all given substantial breakfasts. They were also given new, smart Hitler Youth uniforms. By the early afternoon the boys were marshalled in the partially ruined, weed-trailing gardens of the Reich Chancellery. Artur Axmann gave them their instructions for the great honour that was to come. They were lined up in such a way that the attendant newsreel cameramen could find the best angles. This was to be an event that would tell the Ger-man people that final victory would still be theirs; that it would be found in the leonine valour of this young generation.

The distance between this vigorous intention and the appearance of the zombie-like Führer was immense: a useless, twitching left arm, kept clamped to his side; the inability to use the other hand to affix the medals – all his fingers could do was pat and stroke the boys' faces. He reached Alfred Czech, and appeared taken with his tale of courage: 'So you are the youngest of all? Weren't you afraid when you rescued the soldiers?' The boy was suffused with pride but was also shy with nerves and could only reply: 'No, my Führer.'[37] For the benefit of any potential viewers that the newsreel might have, there was a message, said to be from the Führer, concerning the boys and all that they symbolized: the spirit and the valour that would see Germany at last defeating its hated enemies. In the meantime, and with the ceremony over, the boys, proudly wearing their Iron Crosses, were invited into the dilapidated Chancellery for a special tea. The Führer was not present. He had once more vanished beneath the ground.

Six children were about to move into that subterranean twilight too – not war heroes, but the five daughters and son of Goebbels and his wife Magda (she had an elder son from a previous marriage, Harald Quandt, a lieutenant in the Luftwaffe, and at that point a prisoner of war). The other children, their names all beginning with 'H', following a family tradition, were Helga (twelve years old in April 1945), Hildegard (eleven), Helmut (nine), Holdine (eight), Hedwig (six) and Heidrun (four). Mother and children had all been living in the family weekend home of Lanke, on the shores of the Bogensee to the north of Berlin. Even amid that tranquillity, the distant, rolling booms could be heard. Within the next two days, the close passages of the bunker would become both their home and their playground. Hildegard's birthday had fallen just a week beforehand. Why had Frau Goebbels insisted that they all had to stay in Berlin, rather than moving them away to a place of greater safety? Perhaps she shared concerns with countless other Berliners: where could possibly be counted as safe for her young children? Where could they be offered sanctuary, with their enemies now almost within breathing distance? More piercingly, how many other Berliner parents would in the coming days gaze upon their children and make plans to kill them?

The realization that time was finite had now preoccupied all in those bleak tunnels. In the late afternoon of 20 April – the day the Führer would normally be receiving tributes from foreign dignitaries to mark his birthday – Albert Speer was looking on impassively in the Situation Room as Hermann Goering – no longer in his distinctive uniform of silvery grey but instead wearing an olive-green camouflage uniform that seemed, to cynically amused observers, close in design to an American uniform – tried to persuade the Führer that the time had come to leave Berlin; that there was just one last viable north–south route through to Bavaria. But the Führer would not recognize this idea of time; it had no meaning to him. The city was to be defended. In weak, hoarse tones, he told his deputy that he meant to stay. 'How can I call on the troops to undertake this decisive battle for Berlin if at the same moment I withdraw myself to safety?' he said.[38] Goering then announced that he had 'urgent tasks awaiting him in south Germany . . . he would have to leave Berlin that very night'. As Albert Speer observed: 'Hitler gazed at him blankly.'[39] Even if Goering had superficially managed to conceal his anxiety, his fugitive purpose was pitifully obvious. Speer understood that he was witnessing a crucial moment in time; the final sundering of the Nazi regime, confirming its close.

Elsewhere in the complex, Eva Braun was determined that her lover's birthday be marked as it always had been. Refreshments had been ordered to be served in the Reich Chancellery on the surface, and, quite regardless of the jeopardy of potential bombing raids, there was to be a party. The atmosphere of the bunker was already marked by drink; the party's 'golden pheasants' had seemingly unlimited access to liquor, which helped to dissipate their own fearful sense of time sliding away. Now the pheasants themselves were making preparations to take their leave of the city, but there were a few others who were happy to contemplate Frau Braun's idea for an evening of light escapism.

The Führer himself had retired to his living quarters, but Braun, up on the surface, had her old room in the Chancellery made ready with whatever could be procured. Champagne was found, and she was joined by Dr Theodor Morell, the Führer's physician, and by Martin Bormann. The evening needed music; a gramophone player was located. There was only one record: a romantic hit which had first been released in the late 1920s entitled 'Blood Red Roses'; despite the gothic title, this was a sweet and catchy dance melody involving a lover entrancing his intended with the beautiful petals of the rose.[40] As an effort to quell rising dread, it could have had only limited power. Whereas Magda Goebbels at least had the illusion of agency – there had always been the possibility that she might have taken her children from Berlin to Bavaria at least – Eva Braun had none. She had to remain where she was. This had been emphasized by the Führer's hysterical response to the news that another personal physician, Karl Brandt – who had been heavily involved in horrifying euthanasia projects against disabled people across the years – had announced his intention to escape from Berlin. This he had discussed with Eva Braun, and the Führer had regarded it as treachery. Dr Brandt was made to stand in a creaking building before a makeshift court presided over by the National Youth Leader Artur Axmann, who pronounced the only sentence that he could: death. Brandt's life was spared by Himmler and others in the hierarchy (though only briefly; after the war, captured by the British, he was one of the accused in the Nuremberg 'Doctors' Trial' in 1946–7, and was hanged for crimes against humanity). The grim episode had shown Eva Braun quite clearly that she was paralysed by her Führer's side. Yet she had never shown any indication of wanting to be anywhere else.

Some twenty miles to the north, with anxiety gripping its guards, and with time slipping fast away, the gates were opening on one of the regime's darkest secrets. The concentration camp at Sachsenhausen had been used for a variety of purposes: experiments in the most time- and cost-effective ways of murdering large numbers of men and women without inducing panic and resistance in other prisoners; experiments of a medical nature on live subjects; the provision of slave labour to Berlin's factories and industrial complexes. As the evening drew in on 20 April 1945, surviving prisoners who were fit enough to move were being prepared by the camp commandant and SS guards to leave the compound. For many, the prospect of being forced to walk into the uncertain darkness, away from the hope of release by the Allies, must have been heartbreaking. Sachsenhausen – constructed in 1936 and intended as the model concentration camp, in which all the cruelties and the squalor of the system could be refined and then exported to all the other camps – had been used particularly for political prisoners and popular apostates who could not be frightened into silence. In the immediate aftermath of *Kristallnacht*, the camp saw an influx of newly arrested Jews, whose lives were now patterned with excruciating pain and fear. Sachsenhausen had not been intended primarily as an extermination camp, but across those few years the killing rate had none the less been so high that no precise figure could be arrived at: somewhere around 200,000 victims. Some were murdered en masse; others individually by the physical degradation of malnutrition and hypothermia. The site was just far enough from Berlin for its citizens to remain ignorant of what was happening there, although rumours would no doubt have whispered back across those woods and lakes. Since the 1930s, too many Berlin families would have seen relatives arrested and taken there; and only the fortunate ones will have then seen those relatives eventually released – gaunt and silent and hollowed out. There were dissident artists who had been sent there for 'correction' – a fate that George Grosz had foreseen for himself had he stayed. What lay before them went beyond torture: victims had their wrists tied behind their backs, and were raised up high above the floor, dislocating limbs. This was not to elicit intelligence; they were being mutilated simply because that was what this place was for.

At its inception, the camp had also been used for a great many political prisoners, who were brought to a life wholly devoid of any comfort, warmth or kindness: like Auschwitz, the legend 'work will set you free' was wrought above the gates, but their reality was now a prospect of bare, scarcely heated huts, minimal sanitation, decaying food and unending cruelty. As war came, and prisoners were brought there from distant lands, the camp saw a wide array of figures arrive, among them the former French prime minister Paul Reynaud, Austria's former chancellor Kurt Schuschnigg, the Lutheran priest and implacable critic of Nazism Martin Niemöller and even the aristocratic figure of Gottfried Graf von Bismarck-Schönhausen, who had been on the far fringes of the 1944 plot to assassinate Hitler (out of some unusual deference, he was accorded the sort of treatment – no torture, simply imprisonment – that none of his fellow prisoners could expect). This was a training ground for the SS men who would subsequently take their techniques to the death camps in the east: the public infliction of pain, through lash or club, traumatic both for the victims suffering the blows and also for those inmates forced to look on; the brutalities of hard forced labour on intensive industrial or construction work (the camp had an enormous site for the manufacture of bricks and even for testing military footwear, which itself was deployed as a form of torture, keeping prisoners moving for hours in bloodied boots). Sachsenhausen pioneered the use of gas as the most efficient means of extinguishing life in high numbers; this was after other methods – such as telling prisoners they were to be measured, then standing them against walls containing panels that opened behind them to enable delivery of a bullet to the back of the neck – were found wanting.

The brutalizing atmosphere of Sachsenhausen caused the oddest distortions; in its earliest days, artistically inclined prisoners found that one way to maintain some form of communal spirit was through music, and particularly choral work; in this manner the older and the younger prisoners could find a connection either through classical pieces or through folk songs remembered from homelands. Far from stamping out this expression of the spirit, the SS instead took hold of it and made it – and the rendition of Nazi songs – an obligation; as the exhausted prisoners struggled with the heavy loads of hard labour, the harmonies, torn from empty lungs, became a malicious form of mental and physical torture. As one prisoner remembered:

> The SS made singing, like everything else they did, a mockery, a torment for the prisoners . . . those who sang too softly or too loudly were beaten. The SS men always found a reason . . . when in the evening we had to drag our dead and murdered comrades back into the camp, we had to sing. Hour after hour we had to, whether in the burning sun, freezing cold, or in snow or rain storms, on the roll call plaza we had to stand and sing of . . . the girl with the dark brown eyes, the forest or the wood grouse. Meanwhile the dead and dying comrades lay next to us on a ripped up wool blanket or on the frozen or soggy ground.[41]

Now, the Nazi hierarchy was determined that little trace would be left behind of any of these camps, or of their purpose. Earlier in the year, hundreds of children, women and the more elderly male prisoners had been loaded on to the obscene railway wagons, their deaths to be carried out elsewhere. Other vulnerable prisoners were either worked to death or simply shot. In this way, it would be possible for the remaining able-bodied prisoners to be sent on a forced march should it become necessary. With the Red Army now so close – and with so many Soviet prisoners in Sachsenhausen – the nervy SS men were moving swiftly through the barracks and making their selections. There were some 30,000 prisoners in their striped uniforms who – despite varying degrees of illness and malnourishment and deep-in-the-bone exhaustion – were deemed capable of being ordered from their bunks. This included the camp's few remaining women and children. There were a number of other prisoners who were no longer capable of movement; even the threat of extreme violence or execution would not have been enough to impel them' to stand, let alone walk. There was no time left; nothing to be done with them. But as evening turned to night, and then midnight came, the abler-bodied were gathered in groups, the guns of their guards at the ready. No explanations, no details: the camp gates were opened up and their march into the dark began.

With so many thousands of prisoners, in thin clothing, and wearing crude and inadequate footwear, the evacuation was gradual. The column of the march, in cohorts of 500, along the road pointing north-west, grew in length. For a great many of the Nazis' victims, this was to be the final, and unendurable, torture: menaced and threatened by fanatical gun-waving guards, those who stumbled and fell, succumbing to intense fatigue, were simply shot where they lay. Through the grim nights and days to follow, trudging along forest roads, the lights of many spirits began to flicker. 'Incessantly it was said from the right and the left: Faster! Pick it up!' recalled forty-eight-year-old Lithuanian prisoner Mikas Šlaža. 'Tired to death, we sank to where we stood when it was said that we would stay in the forest.'[42] A great many of those prisoners would die on the most nihilistically pointless journey, some murdered, others collapsing with organ failure and exhaustion. After some two weeks, the horrifying futility of all of this finally hit the Nazi guards; most of them broke away and fled, understanding at last that they would be seen as criminals. Their flight was prompted by sightings near Schwerin of US soldiers. It was those same soldiers who found the march survivors; their liberation had finally come. In the meantime, the camp in which they had been imprisoned would, within just a few hours of their departure, be discovered by the Red Army – the latest in a line of horrifying finds. In Sachsenhausen, the Soviet soldiers moved among the comfortless huts, the camp now deserted by the SS, and, within those barracks, they were greeted with the large, haunted eyes of near fleshless bodies. All this just a short distance from what had been the most cultured city on earth.

There was, in the Soviet hierarchy's treatment of the camp liberation, some political sleight of hand, as official emphasis was placed upon the nationalities of the victims as opposed to their religion. The Soviet authorities had their own reasons for downplaying the genocidal persecution of the Jews, one of which was that they strenuously opposed the idea of a unified Jewish identity. There were a great many Jewish people in various divisions of the Red Army – anywhere between 300,000 and 500,000 combatants who fought with all their hearts for this liberation – who had become radicalized by the discovery of the camps. As historian Mordechai Altshuler observed, the Red Army campaign through eastern Europe, surveying the enormity of the crimes committed by the Nazis, began to change the thinking of the Soviet Union's Jewish soldiers.[43] They could see, through Latvia and Ukraine and Poland, how the children had been murdered, and the Judaic culture had been violently erased. These soldiers, who knew only Russian, now began teaching themselves Hebrew, and to give thought to Zionism. But the Soviet authorities sought to crush this. Any suggestion that the Jewish people should have their own homeland was heresy, and any idea that this homeland had an historical basis was in their eyes false. In addition to this, Soviet Jews were expressly taught that even the idea of a Jewish identity ran counter to communism. The socialist Jewish people had no connection in any form to the capitalist Jews who lived in the West. Yet all the rhetoric grated against the horrifying realities. One Jewish officer, who fought all the way through to Berlin, was to recall that one of his first encounters was with a grave-looking German woman dressed all in black. She stared at him from a distance and followed him; over the next few days, he kept on seeing her. Finally, she approached, and handed him a piece of paper upon which she had drawn a Star of David. It was clear that she had been in hiding throughout the war and was at last proclaiming her Jewish identity to the conquering forces. The officer imagined her to be about forty years old. She was sixteen.[44]

It would not be long after the war that the Soviet authorities would give anti-Semitism fresh impetus for their own purposes. And as a bitter afterword to the liberation of Sachsenhausen, even after its horrors were disclosed to the world, it would live on as a Soviet prison camp in the years to come. Those who liberated it, and who were to adapt it for new use, seemed to have no superstitious concerns that such a site might be haunted or cursed. Instead, following the war, fresh waves of inmates were detained there whose political beliefs did not accord with those of the authorities.

Within twenty-four hours of Sachsenhausen's liberation, those civilians in the centre of the city not sheltering recoiled as buildings began to apparently self-combust. The air was heavy with a rolling, ceaseless thunder; shops and apartment blocks near Alexanderplatz collapsed seemingly spontaneously, in clouds of dust and flame, as though under weights too great to bear. This was the result of artillery fire now pouring down upon the city's centre: mighty bombs launched from a distance, aimed wildly and with no warning. The Red Army's bombardment of Berlin lacked the one merciful quality that the Allied air force attacks had always carried: the possibility of warning. Any street, any avenue – and any unfortunate civilian upon them – might now be vaporized in a sudden flash of the most intense white, and at any time of day. There were accounts of old women waiting in queues outside grocery shops, pressed close against walls in the hope that that would bring shelter, some wearing goggles for further protection: that unearthly flare of light, a noise almost too deep to register; and then, in the seconds after, one of those old women on the pavement, bleeding profusely from shrapnel pierced deep into her chest.[45] Even to call for help seemed futile; the frenetic SS men patrolling the streets had no time for hopeless casualties; and even if such victims could be taken to hospital, how could they then be treated without supplies? Now at last the people of Berlin were see-ing what invasion looked like.

The artillery rounds were being fired from Marzahn, a suburb a few miles to the east, where there had been a concentration camp especially intended for Romany people. This was the first area of Berlin to be fully occupied by the Soviets, on 21 April 1945, by the forces of the 5th Shock Army, led by General Nikolai Berzarin, a forty-one-year-old veteran from Leningrad. The artillery fire of his forces was launched from an area of low-rise factories, modest hous-ing and cherry trees; streets that had previously seen only sparse numbers of motor cars were dwarfed by the Soviet tanks that now rolled down them, their vibrations shuddering through foundations. Behind these tanks were swathes of either German prisoners or Ger-man dead. The Red Army was finding ways to make use of some of their captives, especially the younger, more inexperienced ones, deliberately setting a few free so that they might race back to larger units and implore them to surrender rather than simply being shot or crushed or burned. Soon there would be many more sources of Soviet artillery fire, from many more sites and directions, and even those people of Berlin who stayed within the concrete fortresses and shel-ters for most of the hours of the day could not escape the new and constant roar of death from all around. Some 1.8 million shells were to start pulverizing the already maimed city, rendering some districts as unidentifiable as the unfortunate souls caught under this pitiless bombardment. General Berzarin, as the first Soviet commander to enter the city's bounds, was soon to face the extraordinary challenge of taking all those shattered streets and people and somehow piecing them back together. Yet the bloodshed was far from over.

## 13.   Streets of Blood

There were those among the Soviet invaders who had viewed with both wonder and disgust the remaining untouched dignity and wealth still present in some of Berlin's outskirts; the ostentation of all this plenty contrasted with the bare, stark, burned horror of what the Germans had inflicted upon the lands in the east. And many of those Soviet soldiers had also regarded with some bemusement those German citizens who were moving somnambulantly along the pavements in shock. Perhaps if they had known that these people had suffered three months of almost continual bombardment from the skies, night after night, they might have understood how lack of sleep had tortured them. That exhaustion was there to be seen among many German soldiers too: those who were still dodging through the streets, or in the small villages around the city, frequently succumbed to a form of narcolepsy. They broke into houses and cottages in search of beds, like figures from a children's folk tale, and contrived to fall deeply asleep even as the air around them bellowed with tank fire. There was perhaps not just a sense of intense physical tiredness, but also a profound need to escape, to shut out the evil world. By contrast, Soviet soldiers, who now gazed at a prize that would several years back have been difficult to conceive, had adrenaline and exultation pulsing like quicksilver through their veins. The writer Vasily Grossman, who had been with the Red Army throughout its push across eastern Europe, hacking back against the Nazi forces, was now confronted by the prospect of Germany in spring. Of the approach to the city through its surrounding countryside, he wrote: 'The trees along the road – apple and cherry – are all in blossom. The dachas of Berliners. Everything is wallowing in flowers – tulips, lilacs, decorative pink flowers, apple, cherry and apricot blossom.'[1] Though the air snarled with artillery reports and reverberation, nature was heedless: when the guns fell silent, the song of the birds continued as before. 'Nature,' wrote Grossman, 'does not mourn the last days of fascism.'[2]

But on 25 April 1945, the people deep inside the city of Berlin, most of whom were not party members, could not see any of this clearly, or at all. Instead, the limits of their lives – moving from shelters out into the thick, clotted air for food and water – were circumscribed to the barest necessities for survival amid the continuing, howling artillery bombardment that – with random violence – would shatter brick and concrete and stone, the air filled with red-hot knife-sharp fragments, leaving those who escaped to move back into their caverns. There was now also the possibility of pestilence. Not only were the city's electricity supplies now wholly disrupted, so too had water-pumping systems started to fail. All those citizens who had never before questioned how water taps worked were now in no better a position than besieged fourteenth-century town dwellers. And even those who might have considered taking cans or buckets to the river or the canals would then have recoiled; in those days of death, who could have known what toxicity was coursing through those waters? There were standpipes in the streets, more moments of acute vulnerability as mothers and grandfathers filled buckets in the open; but even these supplies could not be trusted, citizens taking the precaution of boiling it, in the absence of gas, on fires fuelled by wood sourced either from local parks or simply from old furniture. In some blocks, the residents were reduced to using foraged twigs. It was in this way that, in the inner city, time was now completely compressed. In the struggle simply to keep children and the elderly fed and watered, it was impossible to think very far beyond the present moment. All that could be focused upon were the immediate emergencies.

Rational decision-making was also difficult because there was no information. Newspapers had ceased printing, and the absence of any reliable facts meant that rumours were now starting to mutate. Few could have known quite how far into the familiarity of their old streets the Soviets had now penetrated. At midday on 25 April, troops of the respective forces of Marshals Konev and Zhukov met at last, just a few miles to the west of the city, near the peaceful area of Potsdam. (Ninety minutes later there was a carefully choreographed moment some sixty-five miles to the south of Berlin as a small delegation from the US Army crossed the Elbe in a boat to meet a party of Soviet soldiers: the symbolic act that confirmed that Germany was now in the hands of the Allies. Yet it would be a while before the Soviets would allow those forces to share Berlin; neither would there ever be peace between them.)

As the remorseless destruction of the city continued, the masonry of public buildings and private dwellings further lacerated amid the rocket-launcher screams that sounded otherworldly, the violence seemed independent of rational calculation. It had its own unstoppable gravity, like a black hole. One of the few who seemed, almost irrationally, as though they might risk everything by standing against this force was fifty-three-year-old General Helmuth Weidling, a lifelong soldier, monocled and belligerent-eyed; unlike the inhabitants of the bunker, his sanity and perspective appear to have held, even though he was acutely aware of what he and the remnants of the Wehrmacht in the city were facing. The tide of the Red Army, the sheer unimaginable numbers – over one and a half million – who were smashing against Berlin's suburban boundaries, was assuredly unstoppable. The defence, which amounted to not quite 50,000 regular soldiers, and another 40,000 or so Volkssturm, plus young boys, was nominally assigned to carefully delineated zones, within the rough outline of the suburban railway loop line. But that fantasy of board-game order was countered by the often frantic anarchic reality; the windows of apartment blocks breathing bright fire, the small bands of men within beaten back, sometimes scorched to death, after targeting Soviet troops in the street with sniper bullets.

The current Berlin Defence Area HQ lay on Hohenzollerndamm, in the south-west of the city; on the morning of the 25th, General Weidling was met by the commander of the SS Charlemagne Division, Gustav Krukenberg (he was born in Bonn, and this command of SS collaborationists from France fell to him by dint of his fluent French). Krukenberg and his men had been summoned back to the city especially; their ferocity and intense belief in their cause were undiminished. Throughout the course of the day, Krukenberg was to make his way across the city to Hermannplatz, close to the monumental Karstadt department store. The type of warfare that he and his men were preparing for was of a looser, more freewheeling, more extemporized variety. It would be about using the urban terrain to launch sudden, savage attacks, but then also to withdraw and regroup invisibly, at speed. It was the type of warfare in which the lives of civilians meant nothing; they were simply bodies who would either help or hinder. This was another of the cold dead ends of Martin Heidegger's exhortations about the Nazi spirit rising; the sole purpose of Krukenberg and his men was to slaughter. In any circumstances they were terrifying, but there were now others closing in who were bringing fresh terrors of their own.

The city's rivers and canals were no longer enough to delay the exuberant onrush of the Red Army; in one of the many inversions of ordinary reality, in the east of the city near Treptower Park, marinas in which some of Berlin's pleasure craft were moored (rather like the smart yacht that Marion Keller had used to sail south of the city) now also contained Soviet military boats as well as a variety of launches commanded by the Red Army. Berlin's waterways could no longer be regarded as part of the city's natural defences.

Moreover, the wide circle around the city that had been intended as the defensive line was now, instead, a noose. Soviet NKVD troops – military security agents previously deployed throughout Red Army lines to deal ruthlessly with desertion and retreat – were posted to strategic points around the city's perimeter, in order to turn it into a vast prison. Although not every road or gap could be plugged, this was none the less a declaration of final intent. The circle was to be held tight until the city within had been purified by bullet and flame. Ivan Serov, deputy to the NKVD's monstrous head, Lavrenty Beria, was in part bemused by the smouldering, smoky urban landscape that lay before him. He had been expecting a series of lethal booby traps, but found nothing he could regard as especially effective. Some sections of autobahn had been mined, and there were the trenches that had been diligently dug out by the Volkssturm, but rather than the frenzied and face-on fighting he had anticipated, it was soon apparent that guerrilla warfare would instead be conducted amid the shadows of burned ruins. This was not the enemy that had been expected. The Soviets had been working on the assumption that their adversaries would be fighting for home, for family, for the generations to come; instead, they were facing cold-eyed sociopaths who would have been happy to see the entire city and its people ablaze as long as that inferno consumed the Bolsheviks too. (The unpleasant and slightly astonishing irony was that, amid the bloodshed that he presided over, Gustav Krukenberg himself would – despite serving a sentence in a Soviet prison – eventually live until 1980.)

There were still Berliners who had managed to retain their own rationality in the face of this onslaught, some of whom were suffused with rage against the government that had betrayed them. The Berlin landmark that Krukenberg was aiming towards – the Karstadt department store in Neukölln, a darkened hulk that had once glowed with modernist elegance against the night – now became the focus of this new anger against the authorities. The store had been the subject of ever more fervid speculation. Its basement and cellars were said to contain lavish supplies not merely of basic foodstuffs, but of alcohol and other luxuries as well. Just a few days beforehand, an American bombing raid hit the street outside the Karstadt store, and many of those who had gathered hopefully outside it were killed instantly. By the morning of 25 April, under skies that threatened lightning death, there were renewed crowds of citizens besieging its locked doors, those in front working to force them open.[3]

At this stage, looting and theft in general were not unusual; hunger had relieved many of any lingering scruples. Even the most conservative of elderly citizens could see that they were now far beyond civic dignity. Railway goods yards to the north of the city had been broken into, by citizens in search of canned food (and even tins of apple sauce were by that stage considered luxurious).[4] Then there were moments of grateful surprise: the wine merchant in the wealthier west of the city who had begun simply to give his entire stock away, partly to deny all the fine bottles of Riesling and Côtes du Rhône and Malbec to the incoming Red Army and partly because there was now a cruel element of futility in keeping a wine shop so well stocked amid the bloodied streets. Meanwhile, the Karstadt store stood as a symbol to Berliners of all that their world had formerly been: a citadel of plenty, from food to furnishings to haute couture, spread up and down nine elegant floors. Even with the privations of the war years, Karstadt and its once delicious-smelling food halls retained a strong place in the popular imagination. Now, locked up and darkened, it had become a furious obsession to ever noisier and more famished citizens. As local house-wife Elfriede Magatter recalled: 'Everyone was pushing and kicking to get through the doors . . . nobody seemed in charge.'[5]

The horde finally got in and found, under the intermittent flicker-ing lighting throughout the dusty building, that there were indeed supplies of condensed milk, and flour, and noodles, as well as bed-ding and towels and footwear. These stocks of both food and clothing had been held in reserve by the city authorities, partly in anticipation of the city enduring a longer siege. 'Women were grabbing coats, dresses and shoes in the clothing department. Bedding, linens and blankets were being dragged away from shelves by others.'[6] Local officials materialized, hoping to prevent the more egregious looting, and at least limit the looters' haul to the foodstuffs they could carry. There were women putting on richly prized boots; in the ash and the rubble outside, proper footwear was itself a pressing necessity.

The store's twin 200-foot towers, with their wide and uninter-rupted view of all the streets below, had given Karstadt a new purpose for the authorities, who manned them with teams of Volkssturm observers. And, while the citizens helped themselves to what they could, the old men with their binoculars high above could see what was coming. There were Soviet soldiers of the 1st and 8th Guards Army gathering close to the edges of the Neukölln suburb, and other platoons drawing close to Treptow and Mariendorf. Although it is still not quite entirely certain who in the end was responsible – most possibly Krukenberg's SS men – the Karstadt department store itself became a target for destruction. When the (frequently elderly and genteel) looters had sated their desires for luxuries such as marma-lade, and warm blankets, the store's doors were once more firmly barred against them. There was a fear that those looming square tow-ers could – if captured by the Red Army – become the most lethal and effective position for teams of snipers to systematically shoot and kill all in the streets below. It is believed by some city chroniclers that others in the Nazi hierarchy had already considered this possibility, and that the store had been threaded with high explosives at key pos-itions well in advance. Whatever the truth, in the building's last few minutes of structural integrity, SS men had raced in to strip out what remained of the food supplies. Demolition came later that day. The first blasts caused the towers to buckle, billowing dust and smoke as they slowly collapsed, raining vast quantities of rubble within the store itself and on to the pavements and the adjacent buildings below. One of the greatest of Berlin's modernist creations, one that had survived Speer's neoclassical fanaticism and years of Allied bombing, was reduced to a prospect of bare, fractured foundations.

Bridges and railway stations across the city were in part transformed by the very presence – wary, preternaturally watchful – of Red Army soldiers. A unit of the 3rd Shock Army managed to establish itself by the grey banks of the Westhafen Canal – a landscape of hollowed, bombed warehouses and shattered gasholders. Like many other ruined industrial landscapes, there was from all angles the continual threat of snipers, of mortars. Yet, to those Red Army soldiers drawn from the vast rural hinterland of the Soviet Union, even this ugly patch of urban life must have seemed arresting, a source of fascination. And the threat they faced was counterbalanced by the distant fat booms and uncanny rocket-launch screams that echoed continuously; the closer the Red Army inched towards Berlin's centre, the more intense the focus of so many millions of tons of explosive, searing and destroying tiles and tarmac, brick and mortar, furniture and heirlooms, brain and bone. The Red Army 220th Tank Brigade was at the Görlitzer Bahnhof in the east of the city, filling the surrounding streets with gouts of fire and foundation-shaking thunder that made it impossible to think. There may have been Muscovites among these men who found themselves making comparisons between the civic architecture of their own home and that of the enemy. But the railway station itself, a once-grand Italianate structure, had long since been punched through by Allied bombing raids; those gathering on its open, weed-sprouting platforms were refugees interspersed with deserters. In among these streets, and others in the east of the city like them, there were men offering themselves for surrender; and there were also increasing numbers of emboldened forced labourers, drawn from France and other European countries, who sought to find ways of signalling to these forces that they were true allies. Elsewhere, one of the Red Army's rifle brigades found itself at Nordhafen, a city harbour and small dock that, like Westhafen, was filled with the clanging ghosts of bombed industry:

buckled rails, damaged gasworks, the sightless windows of brick workshops. And this, like Westhafen, was the landscape of desperate men and boys who genuinely believed that, whatever they now did, death was almost certain. The particular fear, certainly intense among many young German men, was that to be taken prisoner by the Soviets would be akin to being consigned to the undead – a future of slave labour in choking mines, or amid frozen lands, suffering frostbite amputations with no possibility of escape or hope. The city's outer fringes, themselves bleak and now deathly, at least offered alternative possibilities: either sticking close with small bands of increasingly irregular guerrillas, armed with Panzerfausts and rifles, dodging among dusty bombed brickwork and hiding in industrial cellars, or, indeed, scenting the countryside beyond these bounds and evaluating the chances of slipping past ever heavier Soviet patrols to light out for disguise and freedom, or at least capture by the Americans, who would surely behave as humanely as the cowboys in those western films had done.

The Soviets' motivation was fuelled by more than just the conquest and subjugation of the enemy's capital. In a grand house in the southwest of the city, close to the Grunewald, a specialized squad of Soviet soldiers attached to the NKVD made their incursion and laid claim to the scientific grail that they had been seeking. It lay amid streets of dignified villas, flecked and pitted with the wounds of bombing raids, yet still whole. Harnack House, a neoclassical edifice, contained a secret that the Nazi regime had, in its ignorance, blithely overlooked. But it was one of the elements that made Stalin so anxious for the Red Army to reach the city before the Americans. The hidden treasure – the essential building block of atomic weaponry – was uranium oxide, of which the building housed an extraordinary three tons. There was also 250 kilograms of metallic uranium and 'twenty litres of heavy water' (a compound with nuclear properties used in reactors).[7] As previously noted, the overwhelming majority of work in experimental nuclear physics had long been moved out of Berlin, to Hechingen in the south of the country. Also moved out of the city were a great number of the specially formulated uranium cubes devised by Werner Heisenberg, which were being used for atomic experiments as late as March 1945.[8] Yet, owing to an uncharacteristic oversight, fragments of all this material remained in Berlin. And even though the famously great minds – among them, Heisenberg and Otto Hahn – had also been evacuated (soon to be picked up by the US Army) there remained in Berlin some rather brilliant scientists who were preparing for life under their new masters.

The Soviets – and their top theoretical physicists – had been acutely aware of the potential of atomic research for many years. News of fresh discoveries vaulted national borderlines: excitable physicists were always true internationalists. Following Lise Meitner and Otto Hahn's Berlin fission breakthroughs in the late 1930s, Russian scientist Igor Tamm declared to his students: 'Do you know what this new discovery means? It means a bomb can be built that will destroy a city.'[9] Then, with war, came the gnawing anxiety that a rival power might develop that capability, leaving others helpless. Despite the widespread Stalinist purges of the 1930s, which saw the extermination of party officials and members of the intelligentsia, the Soviet Union had continually active physics laboratories not only in Moscow but also in Leningrad and Ukraine. Some were seized with what was termed 'uranium fever'.[10] As in Nazi Germany, there was some initial reluctance among the Soviet authorities to believe what might be achieved; that a sunburst of atomic energy was not merely a fantasy that could only be made real in the far future. Then came the shock of the German invasion of Russia in 1941, and the evacuation of nuclear physics programmes from the larger cities out to the Urals and Kazakhstan. A young scientist who had joined the Soviet Air Force – Georgy Flyorov – noticed that Western scientific journals now had limited information about nuclear progress, and surmised that in the midst of that intelligence dark matter, top-secret work was underway. He wrote directly to Stalin: 'It is essential not to lose any time in building the uranium bomb.'[11] Flyorov was put into contact with senior physicists. At a time when the Nazi armies were brutalizing the country, there was an agonizing dilemma and it was to do with money. The Soviet Union could pursue the dream of building a nuclear bomb, but it might cost more than the entire war effort had so far.

As the German physicists had found, there were seemingly intractable difficulties in effectively manipulating uranium, graphite, heavy water and cyclotrons to produce the theorized effects. As the war

20. With the rise of the Nazis in the 1930s, the streets of Berlin were turned into a grandiloquent backdrop for appropriated holidays such as May Day, the enormous maypole here topped with swastika flags.

21. Horrified foreign correspondents were among those who witnessed the results of *Kristallnacht* in 1938 – from burning synagogues to wrecked family businesses; some gentile Berliners, too, were both profoundly ashamed of and frightened by the violence.

22. The young actress Hildegard Knef had just landed a film contract in 1945 as the Red Army was closing in; her stratagem to escape Soviet soldiers was more extraordinary than any cinematic drama.

23. Goebbels insisted that Berlin's film industry should outdo Hollywood in glossy escapism. Stars such as Marika Rökk, who specialized in romantic comedies, came to be seen as vital for raising morale.

24. Once a striking symbol of Berlin's sleek modernity, by 1945 the Karstadt department store had been stripped by looters. Its towers deemed tempting to Soviet snipers, it was blown up by the Nazis without a second thought.

25. The Volkssturm – too old or too young, and boys, called up to serve – were lionized by many in the Nazi hierarchy, including Heinrich Himmler. By 1945, despite their antique weaponry, they were crucial to the defence of Berlin.

26. The once famously elegant Tiergarten, along with most of the lush parkland of Berlin, had by 1945 been reduced to bombed-out moonscapes, the last of their wood foraged for fuel.

27. Berliners in 1945 had to swiftly adjust to the sight of once salubrious residential streets being turned into defence positions, with barricades and trenches that were intended to hold back Soviet tanks.

28. While Berliners were shocked to see enemy tanks in their residential streets, the soldiers of the Red Army were equally mesmerized by the wealth that they beheld.

29. Just a few miles outside of Berlin lay the stark horror of Sachsenhausen: a concentration camp in which all the murderous cruelties of the death camps had been rehearsed.

30. The vast concrete flak towers of Berlin that doubled as air-raid shelters were akin to medieval fortresses. Some families who sought refuge within their forbidding exteriors were reluctant to leave, even after the bombing had stopped.

31. By 1945, life for many Berliners had become subterranean: endless alarms, and endless nights and days spent entombed within dank brickwork listening to the thumps and booms above.

32. The Red Army's triumphant exploration of the Führerbunker in May 1945 exposed a dripping labyrinth of gothic contrasts: paintings and coat-stands, blast doors and bloodstains.

33. Parts of the centre of Berlin were, by the end of the war, skeletal ghosts of the streets that once were. Unburied bodies made the warming air nauseatingly cloying.

34. Amid the devastation, the occupying Soviet forces quickly identified Berlin's civic leaders and engineers: water, electricity and even the U-Bahn were restored at startling speed.

35. The 'rubble women', conscripted into clearing Berlin's ruins so that the materials could be used for rebuilding, became internationally recognized icons of a defeated and shamed nation.

36. Through the jagged urban landscape, small children played games that surprised the occupying US forces: many were innocently pretending to be Wild West cowboys.

37. With so many homes now derelict, some families were forced to share accommodation with strangers in blocks that were half-demolished while others returned to their old ravaged homes.

started to turn, and the Soviets began to drive the Nazis back across those ravaged lands, the Russian physicists made an approach to the Danish atomic pioneer Niels Bohr, now based in Sweden. He considered the offer to go to Russia, and declined. At around this time, the Soviets were also starting to receive a steady stream of intelligence from America, provided stealthily by the communist-sympathizing atomic scientist Klaus Fuchs, who had been recruited to Los Alamos for the Manhattan Project. From him, they learned with certainty that the Americans were summoning the dream of an atomic bomb into corporeal life. But Niels Bohr was not the only physicist that the Soviets were thinking about. Also on their list of scientists that they wished to co-opt were the quartet of Berlin physicists who had made the pact discussed in Chapter 7. Even in April 1945, with the end of the Nazi regime very obviously in sight, the next moves had to be most delicate; if their plans had been discovered, there was nothing to stop any of these men being pulled to one side by the SS and shot for treachery.

The members of the pact – Professors von Ardenne, Thiessen, Volmer and Hertz – wanted guarantees from the Soviets. One was that they would all be able to continue their work without any great interruption. Another, crucially, was an amnesty or pre-emptive pardon: freedom from any possible future prosecution over actions committed under the Nazi regime. Of the four, it seemed that Professor Thiessen, the head of the Kaiser Wilhelm Institute, had the closest links with the National Socialists (he shared a flat near the institute on elegant Faradayweg with the eminent professor of chemistry Rudolf Mentzel, who had joined the NSDAP as early as 1925 and specialized in research for chemical warfare). But all scientists, even non-party members, were theoretically vulnerable and those in the pact – who knew how valuable their atomic knowledge was – were particularly anxious. Gustav Hertz later told colleagues that he had inclined towards the Soviet Union because America already had an extraordinary quantity of experts in the field that had been picked up; working in such a crowd might be stifling, whereas his Soviet peers might create more room for fresh discoveries.[12]

And it was at the same institute that first contact was made between the Soviets and Professor Thiessen, who outlined the conditions the of the pact to the victorious invaders as they marched through the doors. It is possible to imagine some bemusement among the NKVD, but one reason that the Soviets so urgently needed to win the race to Berlin, outflanking the Americans, was so they could swoop on the institute before that part of the conquered city fell into the zone to be occupied by the Americans. The NKVD men supervised the immediate removal of the valuable elements, again under instruction from their own physicists. There was also a matter of the specialized equipment; although much had already been removed to southern Germany by the Nazis, the remaining instrumentation had great value. If Professors Thiessen and Volmer had had any noble aims to somehow keep this technology close by, they were dashed in a matter of hours. And very shortly after the Soviets had consolidated their hold on the institute, Professor Thiessen was taken in an armoured car just a few streets further south to another grand house, in the neighbourhood of Lichterfelde. This was the location of the private laboratories of Manfred von Ardenne. As with Professor Thiessen, the Soviet NKVD agents and the physicists who had advised them were keenly aware that von Ardenne would be a most valuable recruit. His laboratories were a source of wonder in themselves: they boasted, among other sights, the heavy metallic wheel-shaped core of a particle-accelerating cyclotron and the strange elegance of electron microscopes[13] (in the 1940s these resembled periscopes in cupboards). The young aristocrat seemed perfectly willing to help the communist invaders. But their demands would come to revolutionize the lives of both him and his young family.

Perhaps von Ardenne, amid the implosion of the Nazi regime, saw a future only of dead ends. Now that his private institute was placed under NKVD 'protection',[14] he too was inextricably in the power of the Soviets. Might he – like fellow aristocrat Wernher von Braun – have welcomed instead a transplantation to the United States? Unlike von Braun, who dwelled in the shadows of grim atrocities, von Ardenne had no such burden. Did he simply regard the Soviets as the new face of Europe? He certainly did not hesitate long to accept the Soviet offer for his regenerated career: he was asked to set up – and to direct – a brand-new physics institute. His Russian peers knew of his expertise in magnetic isotope separation and mass spectrometry (esoteric-sounding fields with intensely practical nuclear applications), among other matters. Where was this new institute to be? Certainly not within Berlin. Instead, he and his laboratory would be moved wholesale to deep within the Soviet Union: the small Abkhazian seaside city of Sokhumi, on the east coast of the Black Sea.[15] Certainly here, amid the remnants of grand nineteenth-century architecture and distant, wild, rugged hills, he would find an intense focus: a deeper contrast to the lurid modernity of Berlin could hardly be found. Nor would he be alone: as well as by his family, he would be joined by Professor Hertz, who was to work in an adjoining institute, along with thirty or so other German scientists. Elsewhere, Professors Thiessen and Volmer would find themselves in Moscow; Volmer immersed in work with heavy water at Institute 9.[16] Thiessen, meanwhile, was cautious with his new Soviet paymasters. They wanted his expertise used directly on formulating atomic weaponry, but Professor Thiessen argued that he would be more effective in his own slightly removed field of porous barriers for isotope separation (which, when mastered, held a range of possibilities for the benevolent aim of atomic energy). His reasoning: if he were to get pulled into a gravitational whirlpool of military nuclear weaponry, he might never have a chance to leave Russia again. His aim – one shared by his fellows – was eventually to return to Germany. For Thiessen and Professor Hertz, this would happen just a few years later. In the mid 1950s, Hertz was relocated to the East German city of Leipzig. Thiessen, whose nuclear research work in Moscow had earned him great favour – and the Stalin Prize – returned to East Berlin.[17] Meanwhile, Manfred von Ardenne was also granted his desire to resume life in Germany. He selected the beautiful (though hideously bomb-damaged) Dresden, and it was here that his career would find a new lease of prodigious inventiveness. From 1955, and with his facilities established in an elegant villa, his creativity embraced everything from nuclear physics to cancer therapy.[18]

Berlin was paralysed. The U-Bahn had stopped running by 21 April 1945 (it was extraordinary that any form of service had continued at all in the past few days), and not even in the most desperate circumstances was walking a possibility. Too many of the bridges across the maze of the city's waterways were blocked, and those that were not were liable to be crowded with Red Army invaders. In the south-west and east of the city, Berliners in basements could hear above them the growl of tank engines and the repetitive squeaks of their slow-moving caterpillar tracks. They could feel them too: a vibration that juddered through the air, making lights and furniture tremble, a resonance that quivered through the body. The dread was no less jagged in the areas a little further out. Fifteen-year-old Christa Ronke was with her mother in Dahlem. Her life was now largely confined to the basement of the building they shared with a couple of other households. In total, there were five other women and a fourteen-year-old boy called Hans-Jörg. The youngsters knew there was danger to them both, but could not yet formulate precisely what it might entail. The occupants of the basement were studying a leaflet that had been left some days before. Christa remembered that the wording was lurid, and along the lines of: 'Order from Reich Defence Minister Dr Goebbels – the city of Berlin is defended to the last! Fight with fanatical doggedness for your wife, your children, your mother!'[19]

'We've been sleeping on mattresses in the basement,' she told her diary, though proper rest was elusive; part of the torment of the time was the sleep deprivation. 'I couldn't sleep because the artillery and the flak were shooting so loudly outside.'[20] And barely had the sun started to materialize amid the smouldering stones than the next day's exhausting quest to find food began. 'At six o'clock in the morning, we all arose and returned to the queues,' she wrote. 'That is now the most important thing because soon there will be nothing more.'[21] Like huge numbers of their fellow citizens, Christa and her basement neighbours were hoping to secure enough non-perishable food to sustain them when all other supplies inevitably dwindled to nothing. Even if these city-dwellers felt safe enough to venture into the city's woods – which were seething with soldiers and gunfire – the foraging possibilities were sparse. By that stage, shooting in the streets seemed wholly immaterial to both her and her housemates: there was, in those queues, a beguiling new rumour whispering down the line. 'The people say that we made peace with America and England,' wrote Christa, 'and that we are fighting together against the Russians.'[22] This was a cruelly accurate echo of the fantasy that had lately pervaded some corners of the Reich Chancellery: that capitulation to the Western Allies might lead to the conflict being reset, and the Americans and British at last realizing who the true enemy was. There were few signs that the fantasy was being accepted by many in Christa's queue. In the last few days, the suburbs of Berlin had seen not only bombing from Soviet planes but also vast explosions, seemingly from nowhere, as the Red Army's artillery sliced through. All around the city, the Soviets – anticipating a psychopathic defence from the SS – were deploying over a million projectiles from positions on river banks or on the main trunk roads. Submission was not enough; the Nazi enemy had to be dismembered and crushed. Berliners were that enemy. Within a few hours, the cruel delusion of wishful thinking among citizens hoping for salvation would become even clearer.

A little further out still, some were formulating their own ways of squaring up to the Russians. For the film and sound technician Marion Keller, living aboard her yacht in Werder and working with her team in the ad hoc laboratory they had established in the town's hilltop brewery, there were practical steps that could be taken. She suspected – judging by the ever more proximate echoes of explosion – that the Red Army was now moving through the woods and round the lakes. 'So we are preparing in our own way for the invasion of the Red Army,' she wrote. 'The laboratory team is learning Russian.'[23] Presumably they were acquiring the basic conversational staples at an intense speed. The aim, as Marion Keller said, was to see if there could be 'a transition to peace' without any further 'wounds'.[24] Such sentiments, if uttered aloud in the centre of the city, were still sufficient to spark the crazed rage of SS officers and 'Werewolves'. Out near the rippling lakes, under the warming spring sky, and with fewer people about, there were more opportunities for frankness. That didn't mean that the district was free of fear. Indeed, it was as susceptible to frightened rumour as any inner-city flak tower. There were bargemen on the River Havel who had thought they had seen or heard the approach of murderous soldiers on the banks; the bargemen had stripped out what they could of their cargoes – focusing on food – and become fugitives in the woods. There were farmhouses dotted around where the occupants were working hard to find ways of concealing themselves. And, closer to Marion Keller's work, there were dramatic scenes involving

the jam factory next door, mostly staffed by French and Polish prisoners of war and forced labourers. What was left of its produce was now
at the centre of a frenzy resembling a human insect swarm, to which
she was not immune. She descended upon the factory with a wicker
basket and was able to find a small supply of caster sugar (which, of
course, flowed through the wicker).[25]

The almost slapstick activity helped to dispel the heart-hammering
unease; in addition, there was that strange sense of solidarity (which
was apparent in other factories too) between the foreign forced
labourers and civilian Berliners. And there were some Berliners who
were beginning to feel the full moral weight of what the regime had
done; that ordinary people had contributed to this. Ingeborg Seldte,
whose only serious and unknowing transgression was to have performed as a girl in a dance at the opening of the 1936 Olympics, had
been aware of the ever-more pressing weight as the war ground on.
She also recalled how her childhood Christian faith had been sup-
planted by the nature worship of the League of German Girls; she
had come to believe in the late 1930s, 'as the swastika fluttered ahead'
on their hikes in the wild woods, that she and her comrades belonged
to the only truly civilized race.[26] But that belief began to waver in the
years of conflict. Frau Seldte saw how her 'childhood friends lost
their lives one after the other', and she saw how 'Hitler had cheated
these young people out of their lives'.[27] It was, amid the ruins of the
city, still too dangerous to give open voice to such thoughts, but, she
recalled, 'a part of me stopped living. I ran out of ideals.'[28] Even the
remnants of her religion had been razed. 'I could no longer talk to
a God who allowed this horror,' she wrote. The Fatherland had
become 'synonymous with guilt' and this guilt, she believed, was
something 'we all had on us'.[29]

The uncomfortable obverse of that argument was that this collective
guilt deserved retribution. And, when it came to the mass rapes, this
was the opposite of a moral position; this was the collapse into the
darkest atavism. Even before the Red Army had encircled and
embraced the city, some of its soldiers had been seen moving through
the streets, hunting out snipers and SS guerrillas; they were – with
some courage – moving through a shattered labyrinth in which their

enemies could at any stage have been awaiting the chance to slaughter them. The numbers might not have been vast, but the danger was, and there were many Soviet casualties as the hidden defenders struck from the recesses of darkened ruins. But as the street fighting intensified, and as Berlin's women now sought to withdraw from sight, another sort of terrible instinct seemed to communicate its way back to those men who were still approaching the outskirts of the city. In some senses, there had been the appearance of a steely element of discipline in the Red Army; unlike the Nazis, who had seen to it that their soldiers had access to brothels – state-sanctioned rape of forced sex workers, many kidnapped from eastern Europe – the Red Army prized suborning such desires into a renewed focus on vanquishing the enemy. Yet that could not begin to explain what was to follow when they knew that victory was theirs. The phenomenon of mass sexual attack was so terrifying that, for decades afterwards, many women could not articulate the full trauma of what had been done to them.

Some women in the outermost districts, living with families and neighbours in crowded basements, tried to formulate means of escaping the coming threat. In long streets of broken terraced apartment buildings, a rumour would spread that Soviet soldiers had been seen moving through the district. Women sitting silently in rooms coated with the dust of nearby bombings feared the sudden draught of cold air as a door from the outside was opened by one of the invaders. The first priority of most Berlin women was to ensure that there were no German men in uniform in their building; not only would such men be killed, but the retaliations could gather pace. The next step was either concealment or disguise. There were young women who rubbed ash into their hair, padded out their clothing and partially covered their faces to give the impression of being old and unattractive. Others sought hiding places within those residential blocks: secret covered corners of cellars or easily overlooked angles in attics. Yet such stratagems also had the quality of a nightmare: these were the very hiding places that edgy, frightened Soviet soldiers would check when hunting out hidden German snipers. And, of course, there were men who would not be so easily discouraged.

In half-lit cellars, dusted with crumbling brick, women young and old anticipated the arrival of the Russians; they were expecting drunken barbarians. The rapists, when they came, in fact took a wide variety of forms. There were indeed men suffused with alcohol, who wanted to participate in violent gang rapes. There were also younger soldiers, remembered by their victims as seeming somewhat nervous. And still others who seemed unthreatening and instead apparently dazed that they were in the German capital at all.

The Jewish fugitive Marie Jalowicz-Simon, living under an assumed identity in the outer eastern suburb of Kaulsdorf in a small house with a gentile household who had bravely taken her in, was at first relieved at what seemed to be the end of the war. The days and nights of unending barrage – and the agonies of taking shelter in a zig-zag slit trench open to the sky – seemed to be drawing to a close. When the first men from the Red Army appeared amid the gardens and small houses of the modest suburb, there seemed initially a form of mutual surprise and silence. 'Someone said, "It's over. The Russians are here. We'd better come out",' she wrote in her memoir.[30] The people around her were climbing out of the slit trench and raising their arms. She remembered her first impression of the man she considered her liberator. 'The Russian who faced me first was a picture-book example, a pock-marked Mongolian. I embraced him and thanked him . . . This simple soldier looked rather shocked.'[31] And, in what should have been the most intense moment for a young Jewish woman who had survived the Nazi war while staying in the regime's heart, she recalled that instead she felt 'no emotion at all'.[32]

But the mood surrounding the Red Army soldiers swiftly changed. More arrived in Kaulsdorf. 'The Soviet soldiers came into the houses,' wrote Frau Simon; there was now something immediately menacing in their attitude.[33] At first, the soldiers demanded wristwatches and jewellery, then odd items of food, including hoarded jars of home-made preserves in the cellars. The frightening unpredictability intensified from that point. 'A gigantically tall and corpulent man' incongruously tried on a little hat belonging to the woman who had given Frau Simon shelter; he then also tried on 'a plush jacket that she had made for herself'.[34] The attacks started soon after:

The Soviet soldiers . . . rampaged through the houses raping women. Naturally I was among them. I slept in the attic, where I was visited that night by a sturdy, friendly character called Ivan Dedoborez. I didn't mind too much. Afterwards he wrote a note in pencil and left it on my door. This was his fiancée in here, it said, and everyone else was to leave her alone. In fact after that no one else did pester me.[35]

If Frau Simon appeared to take this attack with extraordinary calm, she also acknowledged the suffering of the woman who had given her shelter, Frau Koch; there was 'hysterical screaming and screeching' from her room. 'Looking out of the window a little later,' she wrote, 'I saw a tall, slender and dazzlingly handsome man of Mediterranean appearance leaving the house. This Soviet soldier was clearly high-ranking, probably even an officer.'[36]

That matter-of-factness about these violations – chilling in the suggestion of unspoken trauma – was also to be heard in accounts from women all over the city. Others recalled the urban rumours that had spread about how one might be spared. 'She insists that the Russians don't touch girls who wear glasses,' wrote one diarist of a conversation with another woman in a cellar.[37] A young Jewish woman called Inge Deutschkron was initially elated when she heard the approaching weight of a Soviet tank in her Berlin suburban neighbourhood. She went out to approach the soldiers; one of them began grabbing at her clothes, while murmuring, 'Komm, Fräulein, komm.' The young woman tore herself away and ran back indoors; her mother sighed, 'So it is true after all.'[38] They imagined for a short while that if they were to show their (carefully hidden) Jewish identity cards, the soldiers would understand and spare them. The soldiers understood nothing. And now the women were forced to escape into terrified hiding, living every moment in fear of discovery and rape. 'I could no longer really be happy,' said Frau Deutschkron of life in the city afterwards.[39] In other harrowing cases, women in cellars bargained with soldiers in an effort to spare younger siblings; some victims were thrown into rooms where groups of men awaited them; others were very simply murdered – sometimes butchered – after the rape had taken place. Yet there seemed to be little surprise in the voices of those who recounted the violence. In some terrible way, the Red Army were fulfilling the hysterical predictions of Joseph Goebbels, who had issued warnings for months about how the Soviets would mark their victory. In all of this, there were other accounts that illuminated the sometimes perplexing shades of human nature. There were recollections of Red Army soldiers who committed the rapes, and then returned to those apartment blocks the following day, bearing random gifts that they had looted from else-where in the city, in the hope of kindling affection and kindness from their victims. Sometimes they also brought food and alcohol. There were also the rapists who appeared to have formed romantic attach-ments to their victims; men who would not only return with gifts but also evince a desire to form a relationship with the women they had assaulted.

There were also stories that were touched with a bleak ambiguity; the women who had attracted the attentions of Red Army officers who, with their authority over other men and cultured manners, brought with them a measure of protection from less refined brutality. In the famous memoir *A Woman in Berlin*, published anonymously in 1954 but decades later presumed to be the work of journalist Marta Hillers, the diarist recalled her own ghastly practicality when it came to sex and survival. Having been raped in her apartment block, she had to find a way of trying to prevent it happening again. 'I need a wolf who will keep the wolves away from me,' she wrote. 'An officer, as high as possible, Kommandant, General, whatever I can get. For what do I have my spirit and my little knowledge of foreign languages?'[40] She found such a man and, via the terrible connection made in the darkness as they lay within the half-ruined house, she achieved her goal. He certainly did provide protection, for both her and the whole household, and also brought bounty such as wax candles and alcohol. Rape had become part of the economic structure of the hollow city; a means of procuring consumer goods.

An additional element of emotional ambiguity came with the Soviet soldiers' treatment of small children: there were a great many stories of kindness. Infants seemed to bring out a latent and powerful sentimentality in the fighting men; there were stories of grand-mothers tentatively approaching makeshift Soviet HQs and tents in the outer suburbs, holding the hands of their tiny grandchildren; language, it seemed, was not necessary. There were large smiles, expostulations and then gifts of rations – meat, bread, substantial portions of butter – intended for the infants. There were other startling instances; Soviet soldiers who had discovered the storerooms of shops and had come away with an almost comical variety of goods were generous with them. One small boy – as his older self recalled decades later – caught the attention of a Soviet soldier who had plundered a department store. The soldier could see that the boy was in some distress; and he made him a gift of a pair of roller skates.

In his recollections of those days, Marshal Zhukov relayed a curious scene he witnessed 'on the outskirts of Berlin'.[41] There was a crowd: Berlin women, some Red Army soldiers. One of those soldiers was holding a small boy in his arms, and telling the boy's aunt that his own wife and two little children had been killed by the Nazis. The soldier had discovered that this boy's parents had been shot by the SS. He was pleading with the child's aunt to let him adopt the orphan. The aunt told the soldier: 'No, I can't give him up to you.' And it was at this point that Zhukov himself intervened, telling the soldier that he would 'find himself' a son when he returned home; that the Soviet Union now had 'many orphans'. The soldier 'kissed the boy and sighed sadly'. Then the scene started to break up, with the soldiers handing out 'bread, sugar, tinned meat and biscuits' to the gathered women and children.[42]

For some Red Army soldiers, girls in their early teens were sexual prey rather than children. As far as was humanly possible, they had to be hidden. Sometimes the hiding places – beneath kitchen tables, for instance – were pitifully inadequate. The noise of Red Army boots on stairs had the quality of the most terrifying nightmare. Women sometimes went to remarkable lengths to stay safe from attack.

A few had, with some ingenuity, escaped the outer suburbs, over the ring road and through the forests or across the lakes into the countryside. Office worker Mechtild Evers, whom we met earlier, had made her mind up a few days beforehand when she, her boss and several of her colleagues had availed themselves of the office safe to take three months' salary.[43] Frau Evers had a very specific destination in mind, one she was sure would be free of both Russians and Americans: Hiddensee – an island just off the north German port of Stralsund that she and her husband (who was fighting with the

Wehrmacht) had come to regard as a form of paradise. The island barely had electricity. What it did have, though, was a small fishing community and snug stone cottages. For Mechtild, after months of continual bombing and sleep-fractured nights, the idea of the place alone was a balm. In addition to this, her husband was sometimes stationed in the barracks at Stralsund. The chances were that they might be reunited there.

Eventually, after a frightening journey during which she was strafed by Allied fighter planes, she arrived at Stralsund unhurt and found that her husband had indeed been returned to the barracks. They enjoyed a short moment of connubial bliss when a Stralsund resident, for whom the husband had dug a defensive slit trench in the garden, lent the young couple his bed for the night. Frau Evers's husband was confined to the area – at this moment of extremity, there was no possibility of leave for any man of fighting age – so Mechtild sailed alone to Hiddensee, where she imagined she might find some solitude. In fact, the island was teeming with terrified refugees,[44] and it was not long before the Red Army sailed in. Initially, Frau Evers was a little relieved: 'The Soviet occupying power had not yet become conspicuous, except for the loud boozing at the victory celebration,' she recalled. 'Neither the boyish sub lieutenant nor the Siberian team resembled the image of the "Bolshevik subhuman" that the Nazi propaganda had brought before our eyes for years.'[45]

As the days passed, however, the atmosphere was to change. Even for a female Berliner who had broken free of the bounds of the city, there was apparently no escape or refuge to be found. Swiftly her life became like a suffocating bad dream. Her husband was taken to a Soviet prisoner-of-war camp and she herself was put to work on the mainland, first in a railway goods depot and then on a secluded farm with a party of other women. Some had children from whom they had been separated; others were elderly. With each new set of guards the air of hostility and threat increased. Now Frau Evers saw to her horror that among the guards were liberated forced labourers – men who had been kidnapped by the Germans from Poland. Out on those flat, featureless fields, the assaults began. One young woman was grabbed and taken to a nearby ditch, where she screamed and fought violently. A gunshot was heard; she was last seen covered in blood.[46]

Mechtild and the other women – traumatized and terrified – were forced to continue digging the beets. When evening fell, they were all taken to a barn and locked in, despite the pleas of mothers desperate to be reunited with their small children. Now the terror was palpable, though, 'at some point, we all fell asleep on the hay in exhaustion'.[47] In the middle of the night, the barn door creaked open; the men rushed in, and all the women in the barn were raped – some several times.[48] Frau Evers recalled a time back in Berlin in 1942, when she and her grandmother had been watching a party of forced labourers carrying out exhausting work at a rail depot. There had been a moment when one woman straightened up to ease her back: the Nazi guard shot at her, then clubbed her with his rifle butt as everyone else looked on. The grandmother had murmured quietly: 'If this should ever come the other way around . . .'[49]

In the south-west of Berlin, Hildegard Knef – holed up within various bomb-fractured residential buildings near the industrial grey of the Schmargendorf marshalling yard with her fiancé – was still disguised as a soldier to avoid this horror. Yet the charade was not without consequence; as the Red Army closed in, she was caught up in artillery raids. The explosions were one thing; the psychological extremity of the screaming noise made by the rocket launchers (nicknamed 'Stalin's Organs') was another. The noise had been calculated to make rational thought impossible: piercing cries that reached into the more primitive corners of the brain. 'The trembling starts in the feet, the shivering, the shaking, creeps up my body, takes hold of my teeth until they chatter, till my face bangs on the stones,' she wrote.[50] The men around her in the damp, dripping apartment that was the Schmargendorf HQ were understanding; having been through it quite a few times, they knew of that initial physical reaction. But the Red Army artillery was ineluctable; and, even though there was something oddly quotidian about the fact that it was being fired from 'a local allotment', it was horribly effective. The apartment building was hit directly and the makeshift defences were no more use than wet cardboard. 'The iron door is lifted from its frame, pushes two old men across the room, and squashes them against the wall,' wrote Frau Knef. 'We run out, fall into smoking holes, scramble across to the ruins, stumble over rubble, trip over the machine gun – the hand grenades, dear God, don't let them explode.'[51]

Yet the extemporized defences of the city were not wholly ineffective; small platoons such as these, sometimes led by regular soldiers, others commanded by branches of the SS, and many containing teenaged boys, were creating many Soviet casualties. Some 300 men of the SS Charlemagne Division – those French collaborationists who had joined the German forces months earlier – were, in tiny bands and briefly, holding up the progress of Soviet vehicles with machine guns, destroying Soviet tanks with Panzerfausts. Large apartment blocks in outlying districts had been transformed into warrens, with an abundance of rooms and attics and cellars from which to launch surprise attacks; into these labyrinths, the Soviets deployed flamethrowers. The street battles chronicled by Hildegard Knef were at once utterly futile and yet also infused with their own unique logic: a game of survival played at the most basic level. She recalled the moments of silence around the railway lines where she, her fiancé and the random men who ebbed and flowed from their unit were hiding behind embankments or vast oil drums. In stark contrast, nearby remained a world where there were tennis courts and garden sheds, 'watering cans and rakes',[52] the tokens of affluent domesticity. She made her way into the railway shed. 'The rain drums on the roof, seeping through, making puddles.'[53] A lieutenant had caught a rabbit and was skinning it; there were some cigarettes, spotted brown by the raindrops. The fusion of total war and close-up normality was disorientating. A little later, under the shades of evening, Frau Knef could hear, in the distance, 'dreadful heart-rending screams, high, thin, shrill'.[54] She knew what it was: Russians had entered a house and had 'started on the women'.

All parties knew that, even in the darkest depths of war, rape was criminal, but there seemed to be no serious sanctions. The attitude towards the women of Berlin was in part articulated sardonically by Soviet novelist and journalist Leonid Leonov, who observed: 'Our patrols now stride through Berlin and German ladies gaze in their eyes invitingly, ready to begin payment of "reparations" at once.'[55] The curdling image reduced rape to a form of justice in itself, the women of Berlin there to offer redress for all the manifold crimes of the Nazi forces in the east. This perhaps was why some Soviet soldiers had no conscience about the sadistic cruelty of public rape; in one instance, a young woman working in a grocery shop was violated on the shop counter, in full view of the street outside. Just as the Red Army was helping itself to all the material goods that it could find, so Berlin's women became another form of commodity. Conversely, and strikingly, those women understood bitterly that the dissolving Nazi patriarchy – a society built on images of Aryan husbands protecting their families – had always been an illusion. For the last few years of the war, Berlin's women had been central to the functioning of the city, from the factories to transport, as well as shouldering the responsibilities of family care. In the end, the absolute failure of the regime to protect these women from the most harrowing trauma seemed to evoke no surprise. The fact that in none of these accounts was rape unexpected speaks of Berliners who had been completely abandoned to the forces of degradation.

In April 1945, there were an estimated 1.4 million women in Berlin; the numbers who were raped is unknowable, but there have been estimates of around half a million. Certainly the figures for the city's abortion rates in the weeks that followed ran into many thousands; the laws forbidding the procedure had been suspended. In the guttered hollows of the city, these were operations that had to be carried out without anaesthetic – supplies in Berlin hospitals and surgeries were pitiably low – and, since it was an extremity that many of these women would not have been willing to contemplate in normal times, this was a grim metonym of citywide trauma and desperation. In the Neukölln district, in the weeks following the end of the war, the health authorities were receiving large numbers of abortion permits, together with statements from victims on why the proposed termination was an absolute necessity.[56] Curiously, as historian Atina Grossmann pointed out, the reasons concerned not so much the violence and the terror that had surrounded the conception as the straitened economic circumstances of the women involved; great numbers asserted that, given the ruinous circumstances of the city, and the need to work combined with constant hunger, it would simply not be desirable in any way to bring a child into such a world. There was another reason for abortions being agreed to as a sad necessity – one that had the sharp sting of racism: pregnant women testifying to doctors that their rapists had been of 'Mongol/Asiatic type'.[57]

In addition to the terminations, there were huge case-numbers of sexually transmitted diseases, which, again, occupied overworked clinics in the days and weeks that followed the trauma. It has been observed, though, that in Berlin – if not, perhaps, in smaller towns and villages – the phenomenon of mass rape was clearly understood among women as a collective experience. Unlike the aftermath of individual cases, frequently resulting in silent trauma and a sense of taintedness, a striking number of the city's women were quite straightforward and articulate in diaries and letters and conversations with one another about what was happening to them, even if they could not guess at the long-term psychological repercussions. But there were also grim Berliner jokes. One was about how American GIs would at least take the woman to dinner and ply her with gifts before sleeping with her; with the Red Army, it was the other way round.

For younger victims, the jokes were not so funny. They were simply left in a void of pure shock. The diarist Christa Ronke was in a half-basement with her mother when, through the pavement-level window, they saw the approaching boots. The first Soviet soldiers to enter the cellar were friendly in manner; they asked if the women and girls had seen any German soldiers or weaponry, to which they answered, truthfully, in the negative. The soldiers left, but, not long afterwards, another Red Army soldier – a man with an eye injury – burst in, looked around and grabbed Christa. Her mother cried out in protest but the soldier pointed his gun at her. He then took Christa out of the basement into an adjoining cellar and raped her. Years later, she was extraordinarily sanguine about the attack, simply recalling that she 'staggered a little with disgust but was glad to be alive'.[58]

The modernity of Berlin – the wealth and culture and sophistication – had been gradually eroded by the Nazis, and, across the years, they had also dissolved the guarantee of safety for numbers of its citizens. Political dissidents, disabled people, Jewish people and gay people had seen their rights peeled away until finally the state had decided that their lives could be ended without consequence. The women of Berlin knew that they too no longer had any form of protection. Like so many of their fellow citizens, they were now merely bodies; devoid of rights. Their homes and their streets had also been bleached of their meaning. The Red Army soldiers who now commandeered those pavements, who marched in dirt-stiffened uniforms and stank of alcohol, made Berlin itself hostile territory for the millions who had once lived and worked ordinary lives. Huge numbers of those citizens would decide that there was now no future; and that the only possible course was self-extermination.

## 14.  Oblivion

Glass capsules containing potassium cyanide were carried around by some Berliners like amulets or talismanic charms, worn on string around the neck and kept next to the heart, beneath jackets and sweaters and coats. Any woman seen picking her way carefully across the loose stones and bricks of ashen streets might conceivably have been carrying a dose. Lethal poison had been abundantly available in Berlin for much of the last year. The authorities, far from imposing fierce controls on local pharmacists, had seemed instead to be encouraging the trade.[1] It was never exactly open, but anxious women and men – some of them parents with small children, some of them in the foothills of old age – made their discreet inquiries in quiet shops, and with equal discretion those pharmacists had handed over packages containing small glass phials secured with corks.[2] Some women confided to their diaries that they had secured their doses and in doing so had somehow found a plateau of relief. In this, they were unconsciously following the example of some seven thousand Jewish Berliners who – between 1942 and 1943 – also managed to procure poisons, choosing despairing suicide over deportation. Each capsule contained just a small amount of coarse, sharp, white crystals. These were to be swallowed; though a few who had obtained their cyanide were unclear how best to take it. Some thought a simple inhalation would be enough.[3] What was most striking was the fact that the subject of self-destruction was so widespread. Berlin – which now smelled powerfully of decomposition – was a city in which suicide seemed both desirable and natural. In this, the Nazis had provided their own inspiration.

When Goebbels had made his regular radio addresses in the weeks and months before the siege, there were frequent references to self-sacrifice. He talked of Frederick the Great, and of the noble ideal: victory or death. He also made references to Roman figures such as Cato of Utica, who chose death over submission to Caesar. Goebbels declared publicly that he would 'cheerfully throw away his life'.[4] The implication was that others should follow his example. In total war, this principle extended from leaders and warriors and out to all civilians. There could be no honour in surrender. And all civilians were bound to the martial virtue of honour. By combining this with horrifying (and frequently accurate) scare stories of the Red Army's rampages through the smaller towns and villages of the east, Goebbels had summoned a vision of Armageddon, a lurid sunset on a civilized world and a world to follow that was a prospect too terrible to endure. In this way, suicide was made to seem natural, washed free of the stigma of mental instability. It was also, in a terrible way, an echo – possibly deliberate – of a German Romantic leitmotif of suicide and self-sacrifice. In the late eighteenth century, Johann Wolfgang von Goethe's novel *The Sorrows of Young Werther* – the tragedy of a tortured young man, helplessly in love with a married woman, who finally decides that his suffering can be ended only by taking his own life – was said to have inspired a large number of its readers to follow the same course. Whereas the Church taught the inherent and grave sinfulness of self-destruction, Goethe depicted it as the heart-rending result of acute sensitivity and sensibility; exquisite passions tormented beyond reason. This was the dawn of German romanticism. The novel was embraced warmly within the approved canon of Nazi culture. In addition to this was another echo of dark romanticism: that of the operas of Wagner, which had been fixtures of Berlin's artistic life, and their recurring themes of women sacrificing themselves and their lives in order to find a form of redemption: Senta in *The Flying Dutchman*, Brünnhilde in *Götterdämmerung*, Elisabeth in *Tannhäuser*. It had also been a leitmotif in Berlin popular culture: the unfortunate woman throwing herself off a bridge in the documentary-style film *Berlin: Symphony of a Great City* (1927); and the anti-hero of Erich Kästner's popular 1931 Berlin novel *Going to the Dogs* similarly drowning himself.

The urban rumours and conversations suggested that cyanide was a painless path to oblivion – a method derived from antiquity, and from the ancient discovery of the lethal potential of bitter almonds. It was believed by some to be a calm and non-violent death. The opposite was true. As soon as the crystals were ingested, and as they reacted to the chemicals in the stomach lining, the sensation was one of violent suffocation and asphyxia, as the cyanide acted upon the organs and the nervous system to smother the circulation of oxygen. Very shortly afterwards, the involuntary jerks and convulsions would begin as the subject – still wholly conscious – began struggling for air. The face and the flesh would turn a deep, mottled red as hot blood, coursing with rejected oxygen, settled thickly in the veins. Consciousness persisted as the cyanide took hold of the lungs and of the heart and squeezed tight, producing agonizing cardiac failure. There was no possibility of even gasping in pain. The mortal struggle, as the torment rose, could continue for anything between two and five minutes: an eternity.[5] Even those who affected to believe the stories of easy, pain-free passing, and who kept the ampoules on them at all times, must have daily been struck by the cold fear of uncertainty.

On 30 April 1945 the Nazi regime was to reach its climax of nihilism with the suicide of its leader. It had been preceded – and would be followed – by many thousands of suicides among ordinary Berliners. 'The danger of a suicide epidemic exists,' declared Pastor Gerhard Jacobi of the Kaiser Wilhelm Memorial Church to a Swedish journalist in 1944. 'I am sought out by members of my parish who confide in me that they have secured cyanide . . . the person chiefly responsible . . . is Dr Goebbels.'[6] By 30 April 1945 the responsibility was still his, but the triggers for thousands of cases of self-destruction were many. As historian Christian Goeschel noted, one such was rape. He cited the journalist Margret Boveri, who knew of several young women who had attempted to kill themselves in the wake of violent assault. 'They were totally shattered, would happily have poisoned themselves, but had no poison: they found razor blades and wanted to slit their wrists, but for whatever reasons, put it off.'[7] Another trigger was the terror of being captured and condemned to an unending life of slavery and torture under the Red Army. There were large numbers of people in Berlin who had observed the gaunt misery of the foreign forced labourers in the factories, and who had witnessed the sadistic blows inflicted by the Nazi guards. If the future consisted of symmetrical retribution – of being transported, like the Jewish people, to the forests of the east – then death seemed to hold a quality of mercy.

Then there were those whose final despair will have been cumulative: to have walked through once-familiar streets, now composed of loose bricks and body parts; to have sat in dark shelters with no radio and no information from the outside world, surrounded by crying children and silent grandparents; to have been rendered almost delirious through lack of meaningful sleep, and a constant hunger, and an even more pressing constant thirst, exhausted many to the point where hope was invisible. In the Tempelhof district, the wife of an academic calmly found another way to destroy herself: a stash of saved sleeping pills.[8] In other suburbs, where once-smart terraces of apartment blocks had been torn open by Soviet shells, some residents took what remained of the tatters of sheets, wound them to door and window frames and hanged themselves, sometimes with their bodies dangling out of the windows over the streets below. Then there were occasions when height itself presented too great a temptation, such as for the woman in Pankow on the top floor of a bombed apartment building who threw herself down its now hollowed stairwell.

As time became dislocated, so too among many came a sense that it had come to an end. On the residential streets where villas and apartment blocks were still standing, there were tokens of time having spooled violently backwards: the Red Army supply chains were sometimes made up of animal-drawn carts; small encampments circled around fires were set up in the middle of salubrious avenues, suggestive of medieval warfare. For the Berliners who were accustomed to the clean, sleek modernity of their architecturally pioneering city, and who had once taken the inviolability of their property for granted, this was confirmation of a civilizational collapse beyond which there lay nothing. This was now a place without adequate and secure shelter, without work (beyond the prospect of slave labour), with no guarantees of sufficient food or untainted water or schools for the children or anywhere for them to play. Total war had brought total destruction. Many simply could not see beyond the dust; others, deranged by lack of sleep, could hear only the banshee cries of the Katyusha rockets. One civilian in late middle age had summoned his family for a special lunch in their damaged apartment. He and his wife and those of their children who were still in Berlin sat down around the kitchen table. Moments later, they were all ripped apart. He had managed to secure hand grenades, two of which he had tied to the legs of the table.[9]

These final moments, at least, were private. Some people chose to end their lives in public. On the Gitschiner Strasse, near to the centre of the city, close to the river, there lay on the pavement a woman of indeterminate age, wearing a hat. Next to her was a bench, upon which was an old-fashioned handbag, and several items of clothing were strewn around. The woman's own clothing, also old-fashioned, was dark. She lay on her side, eyes open, one hand frozen into a claw shape. She presumably had sat down to take the poison, and, as its convulsive effects gripped harder, had fallen helplessly from the bench, and remained in the dust as her lungs filled and her heart was tightened until it stopped. Was she alone in life? Had she left family behind? Hers was only one of something approaching 100,000 civilian corpses that lay in the city, buried and unburied, victims of months of bombing as well as the Red Army onslaughts. There were no curious crowds gathered round her; no one in authority either to help, or even simply to show pity. There was none left.

Because of the intense dangers and difficulties of moving beyond one's own area or district, Berliners were also isolated from one another: friends in different neighbourhoods who might otherwise have helped to provide some succour or relief could not meet or communicate in any way. The once easy availability of telephones had disappeared. There was, naturally, no postal service. Civilians had no way of knowing if their friends were even still alive. This awful blankness helped to distort perspectives further. Those who lived and sheltered in areas where the houses and flats had crumpled could only assume that the same was true across the whole city. The working-class residents who lived close to the vast Siemensstadt industrial complex – now a prospect of dripping, skeletal ruins, buildings reduced to stark steel frames, a few tall chimneys and towers still standing, seemingly in defiance of natural laws – could only assume that all Berlin's factories and electrical works and power stations had been brought to similar ruin. Great numbers of civilians were conducting most of their lives beneath the streets in the tunnels of the now wholly inoperative U-Bahn. Perhaps some thought to use tunnels and elevated sections (the system swoops and climbs below and above the ground) to traverse the city unseen, but even this idea was weighted with the dread of what was approaching: stories of Red Army tanks making it into the tunnels, crushing and shooting civilians as they went. Uncertainty was now the only constant. In those final days it is estimated that 3,996 women and 3,091 men took their own lives,[10] but those were simply the cases that were counted. In that vortex of destruction, the true figures were almost certainly higher.

In contrast to these silent endings, there were also fevered outbreaks of emotion across the city; the relentlessness thunder of the bombardment's percussion, combined with the hallucinatory strangeness of seeing allotments and tennis courts punctuated with detached and bloodied limbs, induced unexpected psychological effects. One anonymous diarist wrote that the spectacle of so much death somehow only greatly sharpened her appetite for life, no matter what was to come next.[11] In their Schmargendorf goods-depot hideout, Hildegard Knef and Ewald von Demandowsky were suffering symptoms of post-traumatic stress, having almost been buried in the wet, sandy soil by the Soviet mortars. It was at this point that von Demandowsky had turned to Knef and asked her to marry him. She pointed out sharply that he was already married. His response was 'nobody knows that here'. The impulse had been triggered by the idea that 'it might already be too late'.[12]

The couple had picked their way through an alien terrain of overturned rail carriages and streets filled with slow-moving tanks, their eyes reflecting the molten glare of explosions as men and boys fired projectiles. In the semi-darkness of unlit streets, rain had fallen, hissing, on smashed paving. Knef and Demandowsky kept to the shadows and found some steps leading down to a cellar filled with people. 'They're sitting there in rows, stiff, silent, around a candle stub amid bundles, buckets, crates, sitting there reverently on garden chairs, kitchen chairs. Go away, they shout, we don't want any military here, they'll murder us if they find you here, clear out.'[13] But could they at least spare any water? A 'toothless old woman' produced a single bottle, and Frau Knef's thought as she turned to leave that darkness was of insanity: 'waiting for the end like sheep in a slaughter house'.[14] But, for many of the elderly, there were no other possibilities. To go outside was to run the high risk of being sliced down by gunfire and bomb blasts. And there was no prospect – even if one were willing to take that risk – of finding refuge anywhere else. Where else was there?

By contrast, just a handful of miles away were some corners where life – if still jagged, the deep, distant thunder a constant pressure upon the nerves – had moments of surprising peace. The underground Jewish refugee Marie Jalowicz-Simon, still living in the small home of Frau Koch, was fascinated by visits from foreign forced labourers who were cautiously and mistrustfully testing out new, strange freedoms. These women and men had been treated with savage cruelty, but in those dying days of the war the Kochs had quietly performed acts of kindness. There were many Ukrainian men in the nearby camp; by bribing a camp guard with cigarettes over a period of weeks, the Kochs had persuaded him to send some of these men over, ostensibly to chop wood for them. Instead, the Kochs had allowed the Ukrainians to rest in their small house, and bathed the lash weals on their backs. Such tenderness had been forbidden; under the Nazis, there was a strict ban on any form of contact or communication between indigenous Berliners and the forced labourers from right the way across Europe. Now, the camp appeared open.[15] Two Polish women who had been befriended by the Kochs paid a hesitant visit to the house. One, called Krystyna, was looking at Frau Koch's piano. Frau Koch asked her 'in the way one addresses foreigners' if she knew the tune 'Chopsticks'. Krystyna indicated that she did not. In place of this, Krystyna sat down at the piano and gave an impromptu recital of Mozart's A Major piano sonata. It emerged that she had studied music at a conservatory in Krakow.[16] This brief moment of escape must have seemed – at a time when radios were silent – transcendent. For, as Simon wrote, 'the approaching sound of battle had become our constant background music'.[17]

Something similar had been unfolding amid the watery landscape of Werder, a few miles south-west of Berlin. By 30 April, Marion Keller in her film technicians' laboratory was also seeing new relationships blossom between forced labourers and the Germans who were forbidden to speak to them. The withdrawal of senior Nazi official-dom from the area – all that remained were the unstable remnants of the Volkssturm, amounting to shouting boys – had brought the forced labourers out into 'broad daylight'. In this sense, Berlin's former spirit of pan-European cosmopolitanism was being unconsciously rekindled. There was a practical reason for the spirit of conciliation too, though: a shared fear of the Red Army. This was not so much an anti-Soviet sentiment as simply one of the oldest terrors of war. Frau Keller and her new friend Fo Bloom, a forced labourer from Amsterdam, hoped to offer 'the besiegers' something more than merely peaceful surrender. Bloom, who had a little Russian, 'agreed to deliver' a message to the closest Red Army camp.[18] This sounded simple: in fact the entire idea was barbed with hazard.

Bloom would have to negotiate a forest that might still have contained terrified, trigger-finger-twitching Volkssturm and Wehrmacht deserters and a wide expanse of water in which anyone sailing was an acutely vulnerable target in a sniper's crosshairs. Despite the risks, he and a companion undertook the mission with enthusiasm at dawn the next day; they would return some hours later. The response was to trigger the most extraordinary and baroque plan of action from Marion Keller and her team.

Meanwhile, in the heart of the city, Red Army tanks were finally crossing the Moltke Bridge, just a little to the north of the Reichstag. They had almost been thwarted by the most intense resistance, and even now they still faced fire. It was here and in the streets behind the bridge that, over the space of the last couple of days, the Soviets had seen the full frenzied force of those last-ditch SS and other units: bullets issuing from broken windows and from darkened, smouldering rooms; the sudden materialization (and equally swift disappearance) in the streets of uniformed boys and men with Panzerfausts, which frequently proved lethally effective against the Soviet tanks, resulting in explosions and dreadful burning wounds and death. The Moltke Bridge, spanning the Spree, was a nineteenth-century confection redolent of twilit lovers' walks, soft lamps and the city's light glittering on turbid waters. It remains so today, but at the end of April 1945 it was defended by an extraordinary convocation of some 5,000 SS men, together with older Volkssturm men, who had set up elaborate barricades at both the north and south ends of the bridge. And they had gone further yet, rigging the underside of the structure with explosives to be detonated should any tank get close enough to cross. The units of the Soviet 3rd Shock Army who moved in to fight were repulsed by the sheer number of defenders, many of whom exhibited martyrs' instincts, being perfectly willing to die to protect the Reichstag (ironically, a building the Nazis had only ever shown a lazy contempt for). The sheer firepower of the Red Army meant that finally they would inevitably prevail, but not before the explosives under the bridge were set off by the SS. Not all of them detonated, and, although a substantial chunk of the structure disappeared into the Spree, it remained crossable. The entry of Red Army tanks would have seemed to any onlooker one of the starkest symbols of a new power crushing the old. Yet that old power was not ready to relinquish its place in the light.

On the other side of the Reichstag, approaching from the southwest, were further Red Army rifle divisions. This advance, too, was stoutly resisted. The mighty fortress of the zoo flak tower had proved an invaluable and lethal vantage point from which to defend. Soviet casualties were heavy. Another deadly position was held by German units at the once magnificent Kroll Opera House, closer to the Reichstag; bombed by the Allies into open ruins, there was still enough of it left from which to pierce the surrounding air with white-hot bullets and explosives. The urgency with which units of the Red Army pushed towards their symbolic goal of the Reichstag – upon which the red banner would be unfurled – was countered by the suicidal fixation of men who must have understood in their hearts that all possible windows of escape had long been shut tight.

It is possible that many of the German fighters were motivated by another factor contributing to what might have seemed like psychosis: a chronic and continuing lack of sleep. There were reports of some men beginning to hallucinate; even in the parts of the city where the Red Army had yet to be seen, soldiers and SS men were seen screeching with distress and anger, pointing at people in the street who weren't there. Somehow, like automatons, their bodies continued to move, but their minds had now drifted to some other realm of living, screaming dreams. It is conceivable that many of them were in that state as they were eventually cut down by the real Red Army fire that they had seen in those visions.

Others took refuge in looted alcohol, members of the SS who realized now that they required the oblivion of spirits in order to face what was coming for them. There were still a few bars containing bottles ready for pilfering, especially in the west of the city, which had seen the least artillery damage. They were reaching for the liquor that had fortified previous Berliners: not just schnapps but the flavoured spirits and brandies too. Some SS men had made their way into the once elegant and exclusive glass-and-velvet surrounds of the Hotel Adlon bar; the hotel itself, blockaded against possible bomb blasts, had long been converted in part into a military hospital, its old glamour a ghostly memory, but its cellars were still well stocked. Had these SS men always yearned, like Goering, for such plutocratic luxuries? Or was there some instinct, some knowledge, that this was the last that they would see of such things? And, as ever, it was as though they – and the ordinary Berlin civilians who would be facing the oncoming vengeance without any form of defence – were somehow, at that point, two different, bifurcated species. To what extent would the Red Army view the civilians as a different species as well?

Elsewhere, enough alternative crossings across Berlin's waterways had been repaired that Soviet troops could push towards the centre along multiple arteries. 'The enemy, though agonized, continued to fight,' wrote Marshal Georgy Zhukov years later, 'clinging to every house and every cellar, and every floor and roof.'[19] And so it was that those terraces of apartments were methodically hit by Soviet explosives, one by one removing all those floors and roofs and cellars so that there was nowhere left for any desperate men to hide. And amid the continual keening of shells, there were senior Soviets who – as well as sharply surveying the cityscape for any and all desirable machinery, technology and works of art that might be procured for the USSR – were already planning for when conquest was fully achieved. Not all Berliners had responded with fear to the Soviet incursion; some older civilians, rooting through damaged homes, searched for old cards that they had carefully hidden years back lest any Nazis saw them; emblems of a previous life when the city was free: membership of the Communist Party. These civilians were seeking out Red Army officers to approach and commissars to whom they might declare their true fealty. One of Zhukov's senior commanders, forty-one-year-old Nikolai Berzarin, had been designated the new Commandant of Berlin, a tribute to the fact that, the 5th Shock Army, which he had led, had been the first to penetrate the city. Berzarin had a genuine, serious zeal. While one objective certainly was to methodically strip Berlin of its industrial and cultural wealth – desperately needed reparations, as the conquerors understood it – those victorious forces also had to find ways to capture the hearts of those whose city they had overrun, to bring their war to an end, to turn them to productivity once more and to use that productivity to restore the Soviet Union; and, even if the presumption had to be that Berliners were unshakeable fascists, they still had to be fed. More than this: the infrastructure of the city had to be repaired and replenished. The Soviet Union was owed, and the industrial powerhouse of the German capital would be helping to pay that debt.

Lieutenant Colonel F. U. Galkin led the assault force that moved in upon the mighty edifice of the Klingenberg electricity-generating station. The Nazis, noted Zhukov in his memoirs, had been preparing to blow it up. 'When Galkin's detachment broke into the power station it was still working full blast. The station was promptly de-mined. Complete contact was established with the remaining workers who undertook the technical maintenance of the power station.'[20] These had been forced labourers; now their labour was no longer forced.

There was one native Berliner among all the Soviets who had been planning for this moment a very long time, and whose shadow would soon be cast across Berlin and what would become East Germany for years hence. He was someone with a special genius for organization and administration, the better to entrench total power. The communist apparatchik Walter Ulbricht – a balding man in his early fifties with a high voice and almost complete, waxwork-like absence of any form of charisma – had not seen Berlin since 1933; he was among the last of the city politicians to deliver anti-Nazi speeches in the

Reichstag before the never-to-be-forgotten night when it was devoured by flames. As an unyielding Stalinist – Ulbricht's years in Berlin had been an unceasing diorama of factory infiltration, fiery propaganda sheets and ugly political fights in industrial streets – his philosophy was always that a communist Germany should bow before Russia, the progenitor of the world revolution. Since 1933 he had been in exile; by 1937 he had been stripped of his German citizenship. At first moving across Europe, Ulbricht had ended up in Moscow with a number of other communist German expatriates. Stalin's Terror – the purges at all levels of society of those perceived to oppose the purity of the leader's purpose; a litany of echoing foot-steps in night-time corridors, arrests by the secret police, brutality in deep cells, death by either bloody torture or execution – had come to many of them. By some miracle, Ulbricht had survived this period. He had visited German prisoners of war – former Hitler Youth members – and had attempted, in his curious high tones, to enthuse them with dialectics, Bolshevist self-criticism and the intricacies of Marxist–Leninist theory. The response, broadly, was satirical and vulgar. Ulbricht's view of the German people darkened even further. The nearing of the end of the war saw Ulbricht positioned to return to them, this time to secure power, and to hold it on behalf of his Moscow superiors. And now, via plane from Moscow, he and what was termed the 'Ulbricht Group' had landed at an airfield a few miles east of Berlin.[21]

Like Berzarin, he was fixated on the need to restore food and fuel and water supplies to Berlin's people, not through compassion, but from an understanding that, like machines, these citizens had to be recalibrated to serve new masters. Unlike Berzarin, Ulbricht was also cynically cunning about the methods by which the city could be ruled from that point onwards. The city (and not just the zone desig-nated for Soviet occupation) would need a new mayor, and new borough councillors; it would need engineers and civil servants. And he was insistent: they should not all be drawn from the Communist Party; that would look like a coup. There had to be Social Democrats too. In the early 1930s, he and the communists had regarded Social Democrats as simply enablers of fascism. Now they were to be used ruthlessly:

In the middle-class sections – Zehlendorf, Wilmersdorf, Charlottenburg – we must appoint someone from the middle class – a former member of the Centre, Democratic or German People's Party. It would be best if he were an intellectual, but in any event he must be an anti-fascist, someone with whom we can cooperate . . . As for deputy mayors in charge of food supplies, the economy, social welfare and transport, let's pick Social Democrats who know something about municipal affairs.

He made his aim quite clear: 'It must look democratic. But we must have complete control.'[22]

Meanwhile, Berzarin, having established himself in headquarters just a little to the east of the city centre, was planning his own martial methods to restore order, and for the Soviets to assert control over the slaughterhouse. Unlike Ulbricht and his group, many of whom saw Berlin civilians as Nazi subjects who had an equal share in guilt for Nazi crimes, and who had to be deprogrammed and reconfigured to place their faith in Stalin, Berzarin was slightly more concerned on the human level too: perhaps a simpler way to bring peace to Berliners would be to re-erect the pillars of culture and civilization. Berzarin was swift to issue 'Order Number One': the reconnection of gas and water and electricity supplies.[23] This was the bare minimum. He was already thinking ahead to the speedy reopening of theatres and concert halls. There had once been great art in this city; Berzarin determined that it should return under the grace of Soviet guidance. Among the theatrical actor/directors summoned to meet Berzarin was Paul Wegener, who had remained in his home in the south-west of the city; his Golem, that creature of avenging clay, though first seen twenty-five years beforehand, was still fresh in Soviet memory.

The writer Vasily Grossman was on hand to witness Berzarin's wider fashioning of the peace:

A day in Berzarin's office. The Creation of the World. Germans, Germans, Germans – Burgermeisters, directors of Berlin's electricity supply, Berlin water, sewerage, underground, trams . . . factory owners . . . They obtain new positions in this office. Vice-directors become directors, chiefs of regional enterprises become chiefs on a national scale . . . An old man, a house painter, produces his [Communist] Party identity card. He has been a member since 1920. This does not make a strong impression . . .

Oh, how weak human nature is! All these big officials brought up by Hitler, successful and sleek, how quickly and passionately they have forsaken and cursed their regime, their leaders, their Party.[24]

Yet it was also only natural for each such renunciation to be treated with intense caution and scepticism; a regime that had turned young boys into grenade-holding sacrificial bombers had presumably exerted a form of mass brainwashing that surely could not have dissipated so quickly.

There were still – amid all the devastation of the centre of Berlin – corners of the city that were extraordinarily untouched. In the east, for example, there was a small eighteenth-century palace, Friedrichsfelde, set in the heart of partially stripped parkland; a gentle symphony of neoclassicism, partly clothed in ivy. The park itself had been created in the style of an English landscaped garden, complete with lake. This was the Berlin home of the aristocratic and very elderly Sigismund von Treskow (he had a castle elsewhere in the country too). It had been his Wilhelmine involvement in politics that had brought modern transport and new housing to that area of Berlin, and even throughout the earthquakes of the German Revolution, the Weimar Republic, the rise of Nazism and thence the war, Friedrichsfelde had seemed to exist within its own fold of time. The eighty-year-old von Treskow, who was alone, might have imagined that he would die there, but the incoming Soviet forces robbed the end of his life of peace. They forced him out of the house, and off the estate, and he began wandering east along the road out of Berlin. At some length, still on foot, he managed to reach the outer suburb of Dahlwitz, where his cousin Heinrich lived, but von Treskow, a diabetic deprived of insulin, collapsed and died on a pavement there.[25] By contrast to this grim end, von Treskow's palace and its grounds, somehow, despite the military takeover, retained its serene tranquillity. Again, Vasily Grossman was there to inspect the former world of the German aristocracy; with no idea about who the palace's owner had been, he settled in one of the drawing rooms and began to write:

Schloss Treskow. Evening. Park. Half-dark rooms. A clock is
chiming . . . Fireplace. Through the windows can be heard artillery
fire and the howling of Katyushas. Suddenly, there is thunder from
the skies. The sky is yellow and cloudy. It is warm, rainy, there is an
odour of lilac. There's an old pond in the park. The silhouettes of the
statues are indistinct. I am sitting in an armchair by the fireplace. The
clock is chiming, infinitely sad and melodic, like poetry itself.

I am holding an old book in my hands. Fine pages. Written in a
trembling, apparently old man's hand is 'von Treskow'. He must have
been the owner.[26]

This was how the power of the old regime ebbed suddenly, like a
fast tide. Yet some of its waves and currents continued to crash and
swirl furiously. The initial unfurling of the red banner on the Reichstag on 30 April should have been a moment of triumph, but it was
startlingly snatched away. There was still a viper-strength to the German fighters who were managing to hold on, despite drink and sleep
deprivation. Major General Sayanov of the Red Army's 150th Rifle
Division had, with his men, succeeded in fighting his way in through a
back entrance of the Reichstag as darkness enveloped the city. A red
banner was secured, flying from the roof, but in those shadows lurked
determined German defenders – and before long they had removed
it. They would not allow symbolism, even though all around them
the reality must have been clear.

A few miles across the city, to the south-west, the grand structure
of the Cecilienhof – like von Treskow's palace, its English half-
timbered styling and its large gardens similarly untouched by the
onslaught – had also been seized by the Soviets. Former Crown Prince
Wilhelm had vacated his home several months beforehand; his wife,
the Duchess Cecilie, some weeks beforehand. She had made her way
south, to Bavaria, and the private sanatorium of the late Kaiser's physician, Paul Sotier. From there, in the weeks that followed, the duchess
was reunited with her convalescent husband, who was in a modest
property in the Swabian town of Hechingen, the skyline of which was
dominated by the extraordinary turrets and spires of Hohenzollern
Castle – a constant reminder of the elevated realm that their family
had once occupied. They were there in time to see the US Army

move through; just as the Soviets had sought out uranium in Berlin, so the specialized US team was focused upon the relocated Institute for Physics in Hechingen, in particular its nuclear reactor and the physicists who were working there. This too was a world that existed in a separate dimension to the dispossessed and dislocated Hohenzollerns.

The couple would never see Cecilienhof again. They had taken all the valued possessions that they could from the palace, but their furnished private apartments within it had been left almost as they were. The Soviets were swift to alight upon all the ornaments and art that had been left behind, but with unusual carelessness lost them to a fire that tore through the dairy outbuilding where they were being stored. Cecilienhof had been purged of its old identity. Within a matter of weeks, the palace was to take on a wholly regenerated life and meaning, and acquire a place in the history books.

And so it was in Berlin that those contemplating death, and those thinking of the life to come, ran on two almost parallel tracks, mutually uncomprehending. Some of those civilians intent upon taking their own lives had been wholly immersed in their belief in the Nazis. They had taken to heart the sentiment once declared by the philosopher Martin Heidegger back in 1933: 'Let not theories or "ideas" be the rule of your being. The Führer himself and he alone is German reality and its law, today and for the future.'[27] For some Berliners, that future without the framework that had been constructed by the Nazis was too difficult to imagine; the propaganda about 'Asiatic hordes' too grimly effective. There were civilian members of the Nazi Party, among them civil servants, who would have understood with a terrible clarity that the oncoming Soviet forces would either simply execute them or devise for them life-long punishments. Death by their own hand was not merely about honour, but also about dignity, and about the demonstration of contempt for, as they saw it, barbarism.

One civil servant who had worked in the Ministry of Propaganda shot himself. Not far from that building, in the warren beneath the streets, his Führer – a pale, raving, shaking spectre who could no longer summon even imaginary armies – was preparing for his own end. He might well have been hearing Wagner's score for the opera *Lohengrin* in his head, but here was simply squalor and bathos. His beloved dog, Blondi, was killed. The Führer withdrew with his new bride and closed the door of his private room. Eva Braun, her feet tucked up behind her on the sofa, broke open the ampoule of poison; Hitler aimed the gun at his head. Death was as empty as life.

Under this regime, death had become akin to a contagion, enveloping even the youngest. There were mothers who killed their children before taking their own lives: a combination, as Christian Goeschel noted, of fear and unarticulated anger at their abandonment by the men whom the Nazis had portrayed as their protectors; soldiers now either lost in battle or prisoners of the Soviets.[28] Yet the most famous of these mothers, Magda Goebbels, was on 30 April, in the wake of her Führer, planning her own death and that of her six children for different reasons.

# 15. 'The shadows on our souls'

The air was warm, and cloyingly chemical: burned rubber, wood, flesh. On the slopes of the boulder-like slabs of rubble that lined the ruined streets lay a variety of bodies in a variety of positions and shapes, uniformed and civilian. It was May Day, and the stunning obscenity of this spectacle in the centre of Berlin was the inversion of all the triumphal choreographed Nazi parades that had taken place just a few years beforehand throughout the 1930s. Moving through those streets now were the Soviet soldiers who themselves most felt the resonance of May Day – the one truly secular holiday, as Eric Hobsbawm averred, that had managed to establish itself in an otherwise religious calendar, a day devoted to celebrating the workers, and which in previous years had seen awe-inspiring numbers of people, civilians and military alike, march through Moscow. Like those rival religions, communism was itself a faith, in the perfectibility of human nature. On 1 May 1945, those Red Army soldiers who had fought their way through to the centre of Berlin continued – in places like Niederwallstrasse, a little to the south-east of the Brandenburg Gate – to encounter among those tall buildings armoured vehicles with missile launchers. Soviet firepower was greater; these SS men, with assorted fighters from other units, were soon forced to pull back, and in time their retreat led this particular small band of Nazi cultists to the empty and near-ruined State Opera House. After six years, this was how their war would end; in the darkness of a dusty auditorium, pulling out knives, even picking up hammers and shovels as finally their Red Army enemies closed in to overwhelm them. There was grotesque comedy in this: men who imagined they were battling for an eternal regime in the end fighting like drunken hoodlums on a stage.

To the west of the centre, near Kurfürstendamm, there was more carnage around the zoo, and around the vast zoo flak tower. The surviving animals in their compounds, pacing and turning circles in their intense distress, were joined by pockets of German soldiers, using the artificial landscapes and terrains as cover. The Red Army soldiers who moved through the grounds of the zoo were themselves unnerved by the keening and the howling of the penned animals. A monkey was shot out of a tree, collapsing at the feet of one soldier; out of the corner of someone's eye, the shape had looked like a sniper. There were still one or two elderly keepers who were desperately trying to look after all the helpless creatures – a rare glint of selfless compassion in a city where tenderness no longer seemed possible.

The forced capitulation of the zoo flak tower itself required on the part of the Red Army soldiers at least some human understanding. There were some several thousand civilians within its concrete passages, terrified of retribution. In addition to this, there were also many hundreds of casualties in its makeshift field hospital, many writhing in pain that – in the absence of analgesics – could not be relieved. But there could also – from the point of view of the Soviet soldiers – have been heavily armed SS units. Their apprehension was partly correct; there were still active soldiers inside. How to seize the fortress safely and persuade those wary civilians to leave? Some of the Red Army's German prisoners were sent in with guarantees of safe passage. A time limit was set and the commander in the tower, Colonel Haller, promised that his men would capitulate by midnight. Instead, under cover of the blackout, a number of soldiers made their escape an hour beforehand, undetected by the Soviets, leaving the civilians and wounded behind them. An hour later, out poured a stream of pale humanity driven to the extremities of fear.

A little distance to the east, the Führer's bunker had also been steadily emptying, not at Soviet gunpoint but as senior and secondary figures such as Martin Bormann and Artur Axmann attempted to flee the city. Bormann was killed by a Red Army patrol on some railway lines. Axmann somehow summoned the guile to move beyond the city's bounds (and indeed would remain under the radar of the authorities until December 1945, when US agents infiltrated a Nazi revival movement in Lübeck that he was a part of).

Staying within that grim, fast-emptying concrete maze were Joseph

Goebbels, his wife and young children. Goebbels was now the Chancellor, named as such in the Führer's will, and for this one day he ruled over the broken, bleeding realm that he had helped to create and shape. His wife Magda gazed into an imagined future and could see only merciless degradation. 'The world that will come after the Führer and National Socialism will not be worth living in, and therefore I have taken my children away,' she wrote in what was to be her final testimony. 'They are too dear to endure what is coming next and a merciful God will understand my intentions in delivering them from it. We have now only one aim: loyalty unto death to the Führer. That we can end our lives with him is a mercy of fate that we never dared hope for.'[1] She also believed that 'merciful God' was observing all of this; perhaps it was some image of the Old Testament God that she owed faith to.[2] She had chosen cyanide for her children. There was a plan to ameliorate their terminal suffering, and that terrible plan was set into motion on the afternoon of 1 May. One of their favourite treats in the bunker was hot chocolate, which the late Führer had sometimes shared with them. Now the treat was infused with drugs that induced unconsciousness. Then (although this can only be presumed, as the murders were not witnessed), the cyanide was dropped into their sleeping mouths, so that, when it took hold, the infants would not know. There have been suggestions that the plan did not work so smoothly with the eldest daughter; that, when her body was discovered with the others, there had been signs of a struggle. She had, finally, wanted to live. Her own mother could not allow it. Here was all the horror and futility and nihilism of the last twelve years encapsulated. As with the Führer and Eva Braun, orders had been given for the bodies to be burned in the garden of the Reich Chancellery; this was to avoid their violation by the incoming armies. The Führer's body was deemed insufficiently destroyed by the first blaze, and had to be set alight again in order to achieve a more thorough destruction. The same care was not taken with Dr Goebbels and his wife. The flames left their charred bodies still recognizable. These corpses – the remains of Goebbels identifiable partly by his deformed foot – would become the stuff of sideshow macabre curiosity for the Soviets.

★

The fight, Berliners sensed, was ending; but the fear would not abate. They had heard, via the osmosis of street whispers and cellar talk, the news of Hitler's death; it had been delicately adjusted by the torn remnants of the Nazi regime to frame his suicide as an act of 'self-sacrifice', suggestive of a final heroic stand against his Soviet enemies.[3] But even as Berliners began to understand that the war was at an end, they also knew that there was no prospect of peace. There was no assurance or comfort or certainty to be found anywhere. Not one citizen knew that the immediate future of the city, and its division between the Allied powers, had already been planned some months beforehand. In the wet, grey dawn of 2 May 1945, as flames continued to flower from sullen ruins, and the rain coursed down on the butchered bodies of horses and brown-shirted men in the streets, it might have been inconceivable that Berlin had a recognizable future. In addition to this, the Soviet invaders were working to Moscow time. Over the last twelve years, the Nazis had sought to inculcate the belief that the German people were eternal and unchanging – 'in almost every place where their boots struck the ground', wrote historian Karl Alexander von Müller, 'old memories rang like echoes of the past'[4] – and that the pure Teutonic soul, enduring across centuries, and grievously attacked during and after the Great War by the sinister forces of Western capitalism, Bolshevism and Judaism, had been resurrected most perfectly in Hitler. His death, for those German citizens who had displaced any conventional religious feeling in favour of the pagan exhilaration offered by the symbols of Nazism, meant the sharp fracture of meaning. The triumph of the Red Army was also the brutal confirmation that the world conjured by the Nazis – the spectacle, the implacable cruelty apparently intended for the good of all – was a chimera. In the case of a great many Berliners – only one in eight had ever been members of the Nazi Party – that faith had never been quite as pervasive as elsewhere in smaller German towns and cities. None the less, even the most cynical of women and men had no familiar voices in authority to listen to. They were in freefall.

In the early hours of 2 May 1945, surrender was being offered to the Red Army by General Weidling. Only days before, he had been placed in charge of defending the city against some half a million Soviet soldiers (and 13,000 artillery pieces and 1,500 tanks) with a force of some 100,000 exhausted, terrified men and children. They had been exhorted to fight for the city 'to the last man and the last shell'.[5] On 30 April, after the Führer had shot himself, Weidling had been summoned to face Dr Goebbels, Martin Bormann and General Hans Krebs (a monocle-favouring career soldier whose pathological anti-Semitism had developed quite independently of Nazi influence). Krebs had sworn Weidling to secrecy about the Führer's suicide; only Stalin was to know. And it was Krebs that night who approached the Soviets under the delusion – fostered by Goebbels – that a truce was possible. The Soviets made it coldly clear that only unconditional surrender would be accepted. Krebs returned, shattered, and the contagion of suicide took hold of him. After Goebbels and his wife murdered their children and killed themselves, Krebs, together with General Wilhelm Burgdorf, found the bunker's supply of brandy and consumed a great deal of it. Thus anaesthetized, they then took their revolvers and succeeded in shooting themselves in the head. This left General Weidling to shoulder the immediate destiny of Berlin's citizens.

Crossing a makeshift bridge over the Landwehr Canal under the steely, scudding sky in the early morning of 2 May, Berlin's chief defender was to meet the commander of the 8th Guards Army, General Vasily Chuikov, when he was to sign a declaration of surrender that Weidling himself had written:

> On 30 April, the Führer committed suicide, and thus abandoned those who had sworn loyalty by him. According to the Führer's order, German soldiers would have had to go on fighting for Berlin despite the fact that our ammunition has run out and despite the general situation which makes our further resistance meaningless.[6]

That life-denying meaninglessness had lain at the heart of Nazism from the start.

Still there could be no relief for any of Berlin's citizens. The Soviets, even as they removed everything, from furnishings to gold bars, 'Champagne and dresses',[7] from the city's apartments and vaults, could only look at the people emerging fearfully from cellars and wonder if they too were devoted Nazis, prepared to blow their brains out in the name of ideology.

The Allied world looked on at the twitching death throes of the Nazi regime, which was soon to result in Admiral Doenitz's vanishingly brief assumption of power. Doenitz was the Supreme Commander of the Navy whose lethal U-boat campaign had come close to severing Britain's supply lines. Now, he had the quixotic idea that it might be possible to offer Germany's unconditional surrender to the Americans only, excluding the Soviets. Ridiculous, naturally, but the snapping of the final threads of government was not the most pressing concern for many Berliners. Instead they were entering their ceiling-buckled, window-shattered flats in search of white sheets and white items of clothing. The Nazi Werewolves were retreating into the forests, and with the threatening shadow of the SS lifting (some small units were holding out in isolated apartment-block eyries) these Berliners were suddenly anxious to use the forbidden sign – the white flag – to show their Soviet conquerors that their homes did not harbour any soldiers. According to the terms of the surrender, the guns and the battles were to cease by 1 p.m., but there was a dual absurdity in the orderliness of the idea. The Soviets already had complete control of the streets – the muddy tanks jarringly juxtaposed with some of the swisher undamaged villas in the city's more salubrious districts – and were poised for the extraordinary symbolic gesture of (finally) securing the Red Flag to the roof of the gutted Reichstag. Nor would the guns die down until the more adamant of the city's remaining SS men were either captured or killed. For the men of the Volkssturm as well as the city's police and the fire services, this was paradoxically a moment of acute danger. Red Army soldiers – who were moving through basements and shelters and the now wholly unlit fortresses of the Humboldthain and zoo flak towers, forcing the last few soldiers caught in torchlight in that foul, clammy darkness to give up their arms – were also rounding up any man in any uniform. Unarmed firemen were taken prisoner alongside bedraggled Wehrmacht soldiers, and marched, hands held high, along fractured roads.

And sometimes the new tumult appeared to be random, or at least beyond explicable rationale. On the morning of 2 May 1945, the north–south S-Bahn railway tunnel beneath the Landwehr Canal shuddered as a large blast rippled through it. The reinforced concrete ceiling of the tunnel was shattered; and millions of gallons of the water from above rushed through, inundating the line, swiftly reaching the stations at Potsdamer Platz and Unter den Linden and gushing down into large sections of the adjoining tunnels. In amid those fast currents were some 150 corpses, borne along. The tunnel, completed in the earliest days of Nazism as a means of underlining the city's new fascist modernity, had provided shelter for uncountable numbers of people a few months previously at the climax of the Allied bombing raids. Now, on this morning of 2 May, it was unclear whether yet more bodies of those who had sought refuge were still down there.

A little to the west, in the smart district of Charlottenburg, there was a once elegant square – Savignyplatz – which was now an expressionist prospect of buildings bisected, blind windows staring over a central space of dust, framed at one end by the fragile-looking structure of an S-Bahn railway bridge across which trains no longer rumbled. It was in this once grassy arena that a significant meeting took place that morning as Soviet tanks driven by units from the 1st Belorussian and the 1st Ukrainian armies met for the first time, signifying the complete envelopment of the city. For some of the invading troops there was an exhilaration that was not about greed (the opulent possessions that could be theirs) or lust (the Berlin women who could be seized); rather, it was the fact that the strength and the audacity of the Soviet system had carried them deep into the heart of one of the world's centres of capitalism, and that this city was now theirs, its destiny to be shaped and moulded by socialism.[8] Like the citizens of Berlin, these soldiers were not privy to the geopolitical strategies of the Allied leaders. In Savignyplatz that morning, it is more than likely that curious local children were looking on at the spectacle of the tanks greeting one another. Meanwhile, the former easy opulence of that square also told its own story of the destruction of the city's conventional wealth and economic power. Trade, from the handful of grocers that could still open their shutters, was primitive. The citizens still had money – many had withdrawn cash from banks in a panic before the Soviet invasion, stashing it in hiding places in their homes – but that money now apparently meant nothing. All the old certainties of Berlin – and in the violent rush of revolution, fascism and war, these had been few enough in the last thirty years – were now swirling as though in a kaleidoscope.

The most senior Nazis had either killed themselves or fled igno-
miniously. Yet one of the most familiar – all Berlin citizens, and
Germans throughout the country knew his voice – suddenly stepped
forward to make his own offer of surrender to the Soviets, on behalf
of all his fellow citizens. Dr Hans Fritzsche had been Germany's leading professional broadcaster (leaving the theatrical hysteria to his
immediate superior, Dr Goebbels). His regular show, *Hans Fritzsche
Speaks*, had been listened to by large numbers of Germans.[9] Born in
1900, Fritzsche was among those who had been at the centre of
Berlin's most turbulent historic lurches. He fought in the Great War
from 1917 onwards; in the Weimar years, he had made a strong career
in journalism and his impatience and exasperation with von Papen
and other figures in the dying Weimar days brought him tight within
the embrace of the Nazis. He had not required much encouragement.
His anti-Semitism lacked the mad rhetorical fire of the hierarchy, but
had an equally chilling quality of quietness. Indeed, it was subtly
more menacing, because he was not aiming to stir up thuggish
crowds, but rather to talk conversationally, in a friendly tone, in people's living rooms. When he gave these radio broadcasts he argued, in
a tone that suggested the illusion of calm rationality, that Judaism
was by its nature a menace to German society. In 1941 he had declared:
'The fate of Jewry in Europe has turned out to be as unpleasant as the
Führer predicted it would be in the event of a European war.'[10] Dr
Fritzsche would later assert, as he argued for his life at the Nuremberg Trials, that he had known nothing about the murder of the
Jews and was simply elaborating on a metaphorical prophecy made
by the Führer. This was certainly not true of subsequent broadcasts:
in 1942 he had been sent to fight in Ukraine, and he was all too fully
aware of the mass slaughters carried out. Yet, returning to his radio
fireside chats, his tone remained one of implacable justification. In
1944 he had declared that it was not 'a system of government, not a
young nationalism, not a new and well-applied socialism that brought
about this war'.[11] 'The guilty ones,' he said, 'are exclusively the Jews
and the Plutocrats . . . This clique of Jews and Plutocrats have invested
their money in armaments and they had to see to it that they would
get their interest and sinking funds. Hence they unleashed this war.'[12]
He also went on to say that he welcomed future discussions on this

subject. With the suicide of his boss and protector Dr Goebbels, Fritzsche – who had been in the Reich bunker throughout those dying days – finally understood that there were to be no further discussions.

There had been a drunken fight with a deranged general who had tried to stop Dr Fritzsche sending a message of capitulation to the Soviet hierarchy by threatening him at gunpoint. The bullet had bounced off the concrete. By 2 May, Fritzsche was in Soviet custody, and was soon to face physical torture of a distinctly medieval nature – not just the bloody removal of teeth but also confinement within a cell so small that it was impossible to stand upright or lie down. But he had one use: it was his familiar voice that was heard broadcasting from the city's remaining loudspeakers (and those attached to vans) proclaiming the superiority of the Soviet forces, and the urgent need for all citizens to submit instantly. Dr Fritzsche's voice, once associated with calm authority, was the means by which a number of Berliners learned of the official end of Nazism.

By the mid morning of 2 May, the overcast city seemed composed of 'smoke, smoke, smoke'.[13] Through the bitter haze, there were countless uniformed prisoners, some emerging from the darkness of U-Bahn stations, climbing the steps with wary, weary eyes as their Soviet captors bade them to throw their arms on to ever-growing piles. Their faces were tired, 'scared', philosophical; daubed with mud, drawn with tension.[14] Among them were old men with white beards, wearing caps and wrapped in scarves. A few of them might even have been too old to have fought in the front lines of the Great War. They looked wizened and small. Other, younger men, swaddled in green greatcoats, were made to form lines against vast shell-gouged walls. Many German soldiers in the days and weeks beforehand had deserted and tried to make their way westward in the hope of falling into the custody of the British or the Americans. It was understood with a terrible clarity that the Soviets would not extend the conventional protections to any prisoners that they took. Yet, from the point of view of the Red Army, they were seeing the human vulnerability of the forces that had committed such unspeakable atrocities from Riga to Romania. Since the Battle of Stalingrad in 1942–3, and following the great push west, the Soviets had amassed some two and a half million German prisoners of war, held in camps across the east and used as forced labour in reconstruction projects. The uniformed men of Berlin were to be sent east to swell these numbers, and their weakness was observed. It did not arouse pity; rather, it appeared to inspire in some cases a fresh vengefulness, and many German soldiers would recount how their lives became punctuated with regular beatings, as well as other, more refined cruelties from food deprivation to the theft of sentimental keepsakes. Some of the Berlin captives were almost paralysed with dread at the prospect of the ordeals to come: one soldier simply fell down crying, and had to be helped along by his comrades. Others, including some from the SS Charlemagne Division, who had fought with such manic intensity, surrendered with sullen meekness. In other instances, young wives walked alongside their prisoner husbands as they were marched into detention, imploring them to remain hopeful. 'Long columns of German prisoners cast shadows on our souls,' wrote the anonymous diarist later published as *A Woman in Berlin*.[15]

Any form of hope, for many captured young German soldiers, was to be tested sorely over the coming weeks, months and years. The fact that Soviet prisoners of war had previously been murderously ill treated and starved to death by the Nazis had meant nothing to many regular German soldiers who had been fighting in various other theatres of war and had never seen the conditions of the prison camps. For some, like Dieter Pfeiffer, twenty years old when he was captured by the Red Army, the ordeal that was to follow was exhausting and excruciating, yet it also taught him something about the extremities of human nature. He and his fellow captives were at first treated with civility by their Red Army guards, as the long march into eastern Europe began; there were prison camps where food was scarce, and often came in the form of soup that was barely more than warm water, but the guards were assiduous about protecting Pfeiffer and those around him from more vengefully minded soldiers whose home regions had suffered the foulest Nazi atrocities.[16] At this stage, the men were able to hold on to small personal belongings such as watches, but then they were transferred, via goods wagons, to new labour camps in Romania, where all such items were seized and the beatings began.[17] He and those around him were slaves, and regarded as eminently expendable. As he was subsequently moved hundreds more miles, to camps beyond the Urals, engaged in tasks such as peat digging, he watched as those around him grew thinner, weaker, and succumbed to disease and starvation. Food was a shallow ladle of soup and a fragment of bread weighed on scales. Corpses were stacked in wash-houses, and buried in pits by night.[18] He and thousands of other former German soldiers were working in quarries, in mines and then on urban building sites within the Soviet Union, their labour intended as direct reparation for Nazi destruction. (For Pfeiffer, and many thousands of others, weeks were to become years; they had no way of knowing about the complex negotiations that the Western Allies conducted with the Soviets about their return, and Stalin had no intention of giving up the slave labour that not only built stadiums and housing but went down the mines.) On one occasion, Pfeiffer got into conversation with one of his guards, who asked what would happen if there was to be another war between Germany and Russia; and what would happen if Pfeiffer found himself standing in Russia as an armed soldier, aiming his gun at the man now guarding him.[19] The point of the conversation – a rare moment of peace – was that both men knew that they were not killers, but ordinary men.

As Stalin's Russia began reconstruction, Berlin's ruins looked frozen in time. On that same 2 May, a number of Soviet soldiers were gazing upon seething, cracking brick, upon curious children, and upon women of all ages, exhausted and afraid, but still making every effort to maintain a respectable appearance. In the outer suburb of Kaulsdorf, this fastidiousness was not confined to the women. Marie Jalowicz-Simon, the 'underground' Jewish refugee who had been given sanctuary in a family home, and who had been raped, along with others in the household, by a Red Army soldier, now found that some of these soldiers wanted their uniform white scarves, worn inside the collars of their tunics, washed and ironed so they might look a little smarter. Frau Simon recalled of her new skivvying role: 'I had not expected liberation to take exactly that form', adding that 'some of the men were very helpful, touchingly kind to children and showed respect for the old.'[20]

In the centre of the city, near the gaunt ruins of the Reichstag and the Reich Chancellery, and in the vast space of the Tiergarten, largely denuded of its trees, victory was signalled with waves of pure noise: machine guns fired off into the air, chants, shouting, singing. 'Everybody is dancing, laughing, singing,' observed Vasily Grossman. 'Hundreds of coloured rockets are fired into the air.'[21] In the mild air, there was news of emergent spring; wildflowers materializing from the deathly grey dust. There were also flashes and slabs of red to be seen on every avenue and path: the Soviet flag, waved and raised. Down the central roads of the Tiergarten rumbled Soviet tanks, themselves now bedecked with flowers gathered from elsewhere. Before this, parties of Soviet soldiers had descended into the dripping concrete passages of the Führer bunker. The few who were left down there, after the hierarchy had either destroyed themselves or escaped out into the country, were in no position to take any last heroic stand. Also down there were nurses and medics. The bunker now more resembled a catacomb; a source of almost necrophilic fascination for those who explored its maze of rooms. There had been a premium placed upon the prize of Hitler's body; General Berzarin had promised that there would be a Gold Star Hero of the Soviet Union reward.

The quest for the Führer's corpse was of intense significance, much more than simple symbolism. It had to be established beyond doubt that he had perished, lest the simple idea of his survival inspired the Nazi Werewolves and the general population to hold fast to their ideological beliefs. It was also essential to Stalin's presentation of the conflict ending in total Soviet victory. His propagandists had a short-term interest in creating confusion to the disadvantage of his allies: in that immediate aftermath of the conquest of Berlin, Soviet media suggested that perhaps the Führer had indeed managed to escape, and that he had fled west. This had the effect of making the Americans and the British look clumsy and complicit, and also suggesting that the flames of Nazism might yet spring up in the future. *The Times'* diplomatic correspondent wrote: 'Those who have followed German events closely are not disposed to credit the theory that the story of Hitler's death is all a fake. It would be more satisfactory if the body could be produced, and the Russians, having completed the conquest of Berlin, may yet be able to do it.'[22] The

Soviet authorities then followed this with a statement encompassed within their declaration of triumph in Berlin that the prisoner Dr Hans Fritzsche had 'deposed' that Hitler, Goebbels and General Krebs had indeed committed suicide.[23] (Dr Fritzsche's immediate usefulness was now at an end; what faced him was a journey to Moscow, an extended period of intense and terrible questioning in the Lubyanka, then a return under guard to Germany for the Nuremberg Trials in 1946, at which he was acquitted since the court could not accept that he had incited the people to commit atrocities.) In the days to come, the search for the body would be turned into a pressing mission for Soviet SMERSH agents. Soviet ambiguity about the death of the Führer was to continue, Red Army guards patrolling the environs of the bunker flatly declaring to British officers that the Führer had escaped at the last minute by plane. However, there was no corresponding ambiguity or curiosity apparent among the citizens of Berlin. The nation as a whole had yet to surrender – Field Marshal Wilhelm Keitel finally signing the capitulation on 8 May – but Berliners were already adapting to yet one more revolution.

The overwhelming concern, and obsession, was hunger, and the availability of food. The stomach pangs were universal, and could not be assuaged either by the grim and soft potatoes, decayed blue at their centre, that in any case could scarcely be cooked by sputtering tiny gas flames, or indeed by the occasional gifts of herring and black bread brought by the more gallant Red Army soldiers in part recompense for sexual violation. Berlin's courtyards – the inner residential districts, with their apartment blocks, were frequently arranged around these enclosed patches of green – had already been thoroughly stripped of their nettles, even as that wet spring brought forth more weeds and wildflowers. Those same courtyards had sometimes been used as impromptu burial grounds: frantically hurried ceremonies, cheap rudimentary coffins, shallow graves. It was noted that some of the women seen at these extemporized rituals looked almost Neolithic: unkempt, unwashed (and undyed) hair, stiff tangles of grey framing aged faces and hunched postures.[24] This owed much to circumstance, but in broader terms it was also an illustration of profound exhaustion: the weakness of being famished, combined with the heavy continual weight of anxiety and, on top of all else, the endlessly shattered sleep that left some almost numb with weariness. One observer recalled trying to relax by sitting down with a novel, only to become fixated upon a passage where the heroine, in pique and distress, rises from the lavishly appointed table and leaves her food untouched. The very idea of such a thing now seemed both fascinating and horrific.

The Soviet authorities were acutely aware of all these privations, and from 2 May onwards were working fast towards the introduction of a new ration scheme that would be a shade more generous than that administered in the final days of Nazi power. In many older civilians, the deprivation had resulted in apathy, but the distress of mothers with babies and young children was more apparent, not least the intense and daily fear that emergency milk supplies – already dwindling – would simply run out. In terms of other foodstuffs, Berliners were experiencing a form of subsistence living, managing on whatever they could find or had hoarded. Some still had supplies of split peas, barley and flour, though there was often no way of making the raw ingredients edible. Canned food was an exquisite luxury; fatty canned meat an unlikely object of desire. Electric light had long ceased to illuminate much of the city. Mixed households shared a single candle; anyone using the bathroom would take it with them, leaving the rest of the household in muffled darkness until their return. With some 600,000 apartments damaged or destroyed in bombing, domestic arrangements had taken on an ad hoc quality that reflected the complete dissolution of the old class system. Households that once would never have crossed paths now found themselves living with strangers, social distinctions (if not annoying personal idiosyncrasies) temporarily forgotten. Some still aimed for refinement as they gathered around tea chests or stools for inadequate meals of thin soup with carrots or turnips, the unappetizing fare served on delicate plates and eaten using antique cutlery. There were also attempts to repair damaged homes by at least restoring secure front doors, blown in by shelling; usable wood was scarce but, when it was found, women and men alike set to work. In the small hours of the night, these barriers were tried and kicked by frustrated Soviet soldiers.

The primal needs of so many civilians also highlighted the way that the sudden disappearance of the Nazi regime had left a gaping vacuum in Berlin's society, for there was not a professional body, nor a union, nor even a local residents' association that had not been wholly taken over by the party. Added to this was an overall absence of the young men who would once have constituted the main workforce. In terms of immediate day-to-day civic life, from keeping the water supplies flowing to restoring a functioning civil service, the Soviets knew that many of those Germans responsible for running the city were probably Nazis, simply because the Nazis had made it a necessity. However, unlike the Americans and the British, who were concerned about the urgent need to denazify all Germans, the Soviets calculated that the ideology could be excised without coercion. It was not, they reasoned, a natural German trait, an instinct that lay deep in Prussian military bones. Nazism had instead been a very modern symptom of monopoly capitalism and its excesses. Moreover, they had long planned for the day when at last communism would be brought to the heart of Germany. German communists in long years of exile in Russia had been tutored in the many roles they would take throughout society when they were returned.

By 2 May, hundreds of thousands of Berlin's women were already very well versed in self-reliance. The frightening contrasts of the Red Army – soldiers as ruthless, violent rapists who took possession of the night yet also handed out food and treats to children – somehow quickly became an accepted feature of the Berlin landscape. The sheer numbers of the invaders, and the extraordinary range of their backgrounds, were staggering: here were men who had been drawn from the sands of Kazakhstan, from the mosquito forests of Siberia, but there were also men from close to the Baltic Sea whose backgrounds were almost Germanic. There were men who were unpredictably violent, inveigling their way into houses and apartments, stubbornly sitting amid the wrecked domesticity of Berlin kitchens after months of marching across blasted plains of death, their rage suddenly blasting out like an explosion. There were junior officers, keen to impress upon the young ladies of Berlin the genius of Alexander Pushkin and the cadences of Russian poetry. There

were outbreaks of intense sentimentality – soldiers from the Cauca-
sus asking women not merely to wrap parcels to be sent to loved ones
back home (containing stolen household items such as table linen and
cutlery) but to sew them decoratively in packages of cloth, as old
tradition demanded.[25] In the eyes of the Red Army forces who continued pouring into this hollowed yet still unfathomably rich city,
the people were clearly frightened but also often surprisingly fast to
adapt to the new reality. To those soldiers happily wandering the
streets with stolen trappings of government office, symbolism mattered; to the women of Berlin, nothing could have mattered less, and
had ceased doing so a very long time ago.

In the echoing emptiness of the Reichstag – the Nazis never had
any use for the chambers of debate, and the last few years of Allied
raids had left it skeletal – Red Army soldiers moved around in
some wonder, having finally picked off the last of the desperate
Volkssturm snipers. The Soviet hierarchy was fixated on the idea that
the building symbolized the Nazi state, and were as alive as the Germans to the universal language of photography. One of the most
compelling images of the war – the hammer and sickle flying giddyingly high above the wet, sooty streets – was as artfully arranged as
any modern advertising photoshoot. Yevgeny Khaldei, using a Leica
camera, ascended to the roof with the flag (apparently stitched by a
relative) and a couple of young soldiers.[26] He found the angle
he needed: a few feet above the position of the flag-bearers, so that
he might also capture the striking silhouettes of statues further
along the roof, looking themselves for all the world like triumphant Russians, and also to place in frame the buildings below, with
their shattered roofs, and a sense of the city's skyline. The soldier
holding the flag, and the flagpole, balancing atop an ornamented
column on the roof edge, was clearly easy with heights; there was
something in his stance that recalled the cliff-hanging American
silent-film star Harold Lloyd. And once the image was captured, it
was subjected to further work before publication, to heighten and
edit reality. More smoke was added to the background of the image,
giving the impression of distant buildings smouldering, and the
flag bearer's comrade at the foot of the column, who had appeared
to be wearing two watches (many of his comrades proudly wore

more of these recent acquisitions), had one of them carefully excised from the photograph.

Berliners now had no access to imagery of any sort, manipulated or otherwise. No newspaper had been published for days, and the city's radio stations broadcast just a blank hiss. Rumours passed on in the queues for the standpipes seemed to be the main source of information. There was a disconcerting absence that was noted by all: the echoing silence in the wake of the surrender, and of the cessation of the mighty guns and the screaming rockets. This did not mean the immediate return of birdsong; the city's birds had long flown. Nor was there the solace of at last filling that silence with much-loved and much-missed music: whether it was younger women with prized (and probably illicit) jazz records, or older people with treasured recordings of classical concerts and operas, there was either too much damage to record players or little enough certainty about flickering electricity supplies, or simply too much fear of attracting drunken Red Army soldiers, inviting violence and theft, for people even to think of allowing themselves this rich comfort. Yet art and artifice, music and drama, the sheer pleasure that they could bring, and the urgency of their restoration to the lives of Berliners, were also much on the minds of General Berzarin's team. Part of this was a wish to exorcize Nazism from the city by reminding it of its older, true soul, but there was also a genuine aesthetic conviction that nourishment could be found in art: a secular faith in secular transcendence. So, amid the bodies crushed by tanks, and the dust of concrete stained red, and with the humanitarian crises of hunger and thirst and illness in the city's elderly and very young, there was also a weird and nervous exuberance among Berlin's artists and theatre directors and actors, painters and musicians. Suffocated for twelve years by National Socialism – and frequently forced either into hideous compromises to please the regime, or otherwise disappear underground – the innovative and creative souls of the city gazed upon the incoming Soviets and saw redemption.

Members of the art world were beginning to congregate at a grand house on Schlüterstrasse, in the smart western area of Charlottenburg.[27] This house had been, under the Nazis, the new premises for the Chamber for Arts and Culture. In the days and weeks to come it would be the centre for an extraordinary aesthetic efflorescence, this time firmly under the iron guidance of Stalin's socialism. Among those soon to be welcomed there was the seventy-one-year-old screen actor Paul Wegener. His own apartment was on Binger Strasse in the district of Friedenau; remarkably, it had been untouched either by Allied bombing or by Soviet shelling. He had been recognized in the street by Red Army soldiers, his films clearly having some longevity and popularity in the Soviet Union, and, even though Wegener had appeared in films made under the Nazis until near the end, there had still been no expression of support. (A little later, it would be said of Wegener by an American cultural officer that 'he is an uncompromising German of the kind you seldom come across . . . His hatred of everything in any way connected with National Socialism is credible.')[28] Within days he had been noted by Marshal Zhukov as being one of the key figures the Soviet forces should work with in the matter of 'opening the theatres'.[29] The same was emphatically not true of his fellow screen stars Werner Krauss and Emil Jannings, who were to find this new landscape rather more difficult to negotiate. For Wegener, though, there was an additional bonus to his recognition by the victors. A sign was placed upon the fence outside his home, written in Russian, which proclaimed: 'This is the house of the great artist Paul Wegener, loved and honoured throughout the world.'[30] At a point when Red Army soldiers were eyeing all properties in the city, and thinking it natural to break in and take everything, such a sign was akin to a magical force field.

That force field also appeared to have been thrown over the nearby town of Werder, where Marion Keller and her team had prepared their stratagems by which they and the forced labourers from local factories might survive the influx of the Red Army. Dutch prisoner Fo Bloom had succeeded in his mission to cross the lake and make contact with Soviet forces, and had secured from whomever he met a promise that, as long as the people of Werder surrendered without resistance, no one would come to harm. It was at this point that Frau Keller suddenly felt the absence of authority most vividly – there was no mayor to tell, no council to inform – but the civilians of Werder, as though by osmosis, began organizing for themselves: houses and workplaces were swiftly draped with white cloths and linens. She and her team were fundamentally scientists: did that mean that the Red Army would instantly turn them into specialized forced labour? And amid the queasy apprehension, there was a note of comedy too: Werder's brewery and vineyard – occupied by the technicians – still had vast stores of a popular local wine. It suddenly seemed imperative to prevent the Soviet soldiers from discovering this, not out of truculence but for fear that the alcohol would make them murderous. The effort to tip it all away – plus the beverages of other local producers – became, as she recalled, a farce that came to look like a Brueghel painting. The agony of seeing such delicious wine poured down drains was too much for Werder's population, who also began frantically drinking it. By the end of the day, great numbers of the town's otherwise sedate population were helplessly groggy.[31] Yet there was also a deadly seriousness here: self-preservation, and the focus on ensuring that the occupiers did not simply set out to destroy.

Those tanks drew closer. Frau Keller had had the presence of mind to paint a makeshift sign in Russian on the outside of her workplace, which read: 'Scientific Chemical Laboratory'.[32] She wore her bright white laboratory coat; removed her nail polish; tied her hair up in a severe bun. Since any escape plans would involve her boat and a voyage west to Brandenburg and to the Elbe beyond into another realm of dangerous uncertainties, she calculated that her chances were better if she presented herself as a very modern technocrat amid a backdrop of glass phials and test tubes. The first tanks rolled in and contact was made: a Soviet soldier walking into the laboratory with 'a piece of paper in his hand'. It was a request for medicine, but the linguistic barrier was too great for detail. 'We're not a pharmacy,' Keller protested in fragmented Russian,[33] but the soldier would not leave. There were more attempts on both sides to understand, and Frau Keller reached up to the shelf for a handbook of chemical compounds. The soldier looked over her shoulder as she leafed through it and found what seemed approximate to his request: and, as she presented him with a 'white powder', he withdrew, seemingly satisfied.[34]

And all the while, outside, the Soviet tanks were being greeted with a kind of joyous pagan welcome: 'The foreign workers at the jam factory' ran down the town's picturesque steps 'with branches of lilac and cherry blossom', and they and the Soviet soldiers commingled in a form of rapture.[35] What seemed to Berliners a thunderously oppressive and frightening invasion equally seemed to the forced labourers who had coexisted with them the sweetest and most exquisite liberation. This exhilaration was shared by those soldiers: after years of harrowing grief and horror and hardship, here was the giddy simplicity of laughter. As the forced labourers embraced the soldiers, there were still pockets of anxious apprehension. Some of the townspeople of Werder 'were frozen behind their windows in the face of this spectacle'.[36]

In the new, disconcerting stillness, increasing numbers of inner-city Berliners began to emerge not just for water or for food but now to satisfy an overwhelming human curiosity, tentatively walking further from home in the hope of finding friends and relatives. Were there even any bridges left, or had they all been blown up in a last desperate attempt to hold back the tanks? In those first few hours of the ceasefire, the air still tasted of smoke and the streets were muffled, thick with silencing dust. Some walkers soon became disorientated; apartment and tenement blocks had either vanished or been so violently disassembled that familiar districts were now alien. Long-established shops had disappeared. And that silence carried an almost supernatural charge of unease for women who walked through canyons of ruined terraces, their steps wet with mud, the buildings seemingly empty and the darkened window frames glassless and shadowed. Was there anyone there? Or were these buildings simply full of sightless dead bodies? In the more industrial landscapes, the silence was somehow even more marked; a railway goods yard, some of the rails still intact, others twisted into fantastical shapes by shell hits, and rolling stock, motionless and dark. In the warming air, the sticky perfume of death was rising; amid the rubble and the foundations were the half-buried dead, who by now were attracting dense black clouds of plump flies.

Even in the relatively less-scarred suburbs, there was social disorientation. A small boy called Peter Lorenz looked on with widened eyes as a Russian tank 'demolished' the back garden fence of his family home.[37] That home had already been damaged enough: he and his mother sleeping amid 'mortar, rubble, and the smell of rubbish'.[38] The soldiers were full of 'energy and alcohol',[39] and he recalled how his mother took to disguising herself as a man. Similarly, the actress Hildegard Knef, who had not thrown off her male soldier guise, was at this point running like a fugitive with her partner, and the city that they moved through had taken on an hallucinatory quality, punctuated with the 'blue faces' of dead children in military uniform.[40] At one point they found temporary sanctuary in the smart home of an elderly family friend, an old lady who herself seemed not entirely moored to reality. Here, just off the Kurfürstendamm, was an apartment that still had 'Regency chairs' but also a 'cabinet full of broken glasses';[41] this could not remain a hideout for long. The old lady told the young actress that if she and her partner were found, then the entire house would be demolished around them. Their escape into the streets – briefly hampered when they became entangled in barbed wire on those roads – was fired with the instinct to make for the forests that lay outside the city. Elsewhere, other women, surveying the dead landscape, went exploring what had been the central business districts where only weeks beforehand they had been working. Many buildings were either creaking after bombardment, trickles of dust ominously falling from ceilings, or reeked of excrement, having been occupied by desperate bands of Volkssturm and SS men who had used them as encampments. Here too were purpled or blackened body parts. Berlin's banks, meanwhile, were wide open and ruined, having been explored and raided by the incoming armies. In broader terms, the Soviet authorities had simply acquired Deutsche Bank. For ordinary Berliners, there would have been scarcely any solace to be drawn from these institutions. Money had been drained of meaning. As with the hyperinflation of the early 1920s, they had to adjust to a world in which cash offered no assurance.

Closer to the centre, the zoo was both a mausoleum and a madhouse; the helpless animals that had survived weeks of bombing and shelling, and that had endured the cacophony as the city around them turned into a vast battlefield, were bloating with starvation, their raw and bleeding injuries untended. 'Hungry tigers and lions . . . were

trying to hunt sparrows and mice that scurried in their cages,'
observed Vasily Grossman. There were 'corpses of marmosets, trop-
ical birds, bears'.[42] He came across an old keeper, who may have been
in a form of trance, as he explained very carefully that he had been
looking after the zoo's apes for thirty-seven years. He appeared to be
keeping vigil over the body of a gorilla; the animal, he told Grossman, had only seemed fierce because it had roared loudly. Human
beings, he said, were fiercer.

If there had been any surviving domestic pets, any cats or dogs as
close to the edge of starvation as their human companions, all would
have fled by instinct from the bellowing, thunderous streets and into
the heaths and woodlands. And so the city's older ladies and gentlemen had had their lives stripped away layer by layer; sons and
grandsons, either dead or the prisoners of a regime that they regarded
as terrifyingly barbaric; daughters and granddaughters grotesquely
violated; old friends and associates killed instantly and meaning-
lessly, either in shelling or in crossfire or by their own hands via
cyanide; their once elegant and neat homes jagged with broken glass,
much-loved keepsakes and heirlooms that formed the core of memory and identity lost for ever. In addition, the city outside their doors
was deformed and unrecognizable. Some recalled a pervasive 'yellow
smoke',[43] and daylight skies that had taken on that same sickly hue.
These were citizens who had become accustomed during the last
twenty-five years or so to having stability suddenly snatched away;
even so, there were some who now wondered whether the great city
could ever be revived.

This, then, was the obverse of Berlin's rise into the light of modernity; it had been caught and pulled sharply back through the centuries.
Many contemporary accounts now seem either startlingly blank or
blindly accepting of these obscene spectacles, which will have caused
years of nauseating trauma, torn nights of crying dreams. Writing
after the discovery of the Nazis' concentration camps, few gentile
Berliners wanted to portray themselves as victims when their fellow
Jewish citizens had suffered so much worse.

One of those citizens was Lothar Orbach, the young man who had
contrived to stay underground for so long. He had been betrayed in

1944 and sent to Auschwitz, where he 'breathed the air of hell'.[44] He was marched to Buchenwald and then, as the end of the war drew close, was freed when the camp was liberated by American GIs. They gave him a new jacket and handsome rations. Orbach had swiftly returned to Berlin by train, now deliberately sporting a yellow star with angry ostentation; his fellow Germans felt obliged to look away, or to glance at him 'with fear'. One young mother begged him directly for some of his rations for her toddler son; Orbach's humanity was underlined to all their fellow passengers as he leaned over and fed the child some of his Spam. Orbach was initially disorientated by the remnants of his old city, but on learning that his mother had moved to a modernist housing estate relatively unscathed, he sped there and they enjoyed an exultant reunion. In the weeks and months to come, other Jewish Berliners who had survived those nightmare ordeals in the camps would also make the return to the city, but, as one of the first, Orbach did find one aspect of life rather striking: the ubiquity of Soviet authority. His future lay emphatically not with the communists but with his American liberators; he had already been earmarked for a post-war intelligence unit. By 1946 he was sailing for America, and for a regenerated life in New Jersey.

Although the Russian language was considered by some to sound curiously melodious in comparison with their harsher native German, it was still alien. Makeshift street signs had been materializing, together with posters and other notices, all in Cyrillic script. The fear inspired by Red Army soldiers clumping down the steps of damp basements, talking and shouting, was heightened by the fact that the vanquished citizens could not understand what was being demanded of them. Young soldiers in kitchens might be talking to each other in reasonable, measured tones and then suddenly become furiously angry when an old man entered, their torrent of bellowed words incomprehensible, save for the terrified assumption that these were accusations: sometimes angry monologues would be punctuated by the young soldiers proffering photographs of Russian towns and villages. Meanwhile, for the women picking their way to the nearest standpipe, the indecipherable lettering everywhere spoke of a permanence about the city's conquest. They had been expecting the Americans to step in and stop the violence, to reimpose civic values, yet there was no sign anywhere around Berlin that this would materialize. Berliners had no contact with the world beyond. They knew that the Führer was dead, and they knew that they had been defeated, but they had no way of knowing what their conquerors had planned for them. The language barrier intensified that sense of impenetrability (and, indeed, even for high-ranking Allied officials outside Berlin, it was never fully possible to divine what was passing through the mind of Stalin).

'The Germans had no knowledge of Russian,' wrote historian Katherina Filips. 'Russian had not been taught in German schools.'[45] Yet in a city as polyglot as Berlin, there had always been exceptions. There were, as Filips acknowledged, the intellectuals, some of whom had studied Russian literature. There were also in the city a few Baltic Germans, from regions closer to, and more familiar with, Russian speakers. Then there was the city's formerly substantial Russian population, refugees and émigrés from the Bolshevik Revolution who had brought their language to various streets and shops and delicatessens and poetry journals in the 1920s. And, of course, the thousands of Russian-speaking prisoners who had been slave labourers in the factories.

It was never the Soviet intention to alienate Berliners by forcing a new language upon them; in political terms, there were already words in use that were recognizable across the spectrum, including 'Revanchist', 'Imperialismus' and 'Reaktion'.[46] Marxism had not originated in Moscow, and even terms such as 'dialectic' were known across the continent. In this sense, the urban committees that the Soviet conquerors were now assembling throughout the city were finding some common ground. They had no desire to stoke resistance to communism; instead, Berliners were to be lured towards it.

Nor were Berliners new to the fissile politics of language; they had been living under a regime that, since 1933, had been policing public discourse every bit as ruthlessly as the communists. The makeshift Russian signs that were erected to rename streets and squares were in some cases themselves replacements for Nazi impositions. Hermann-Goering-Strasse was clearly not going to remain so; the Soviets reverted to its old Weimar name, Ebertstrasse.[47] Similarly, the square in working-class Friedrichshain that until May 1945 was Horst-Wessel-Platz (the Nazis had changed it from Bülowplatz in honour of the murdered thug in the mid 1930s) was also swiftly revised. Its new name spoke of a Soviet effort to rekindle old social-ist fervour: Liebknechtplatz.[48]

Yet these were days in which horror still suffused the streets, the mild air above sickly with decay. 'Berlin is a city of the dead,' wrote Harold King, a British newspaper correspondent, who had – a rare privilege – been allowed to tour the territory with General Berzarin. 'As a metropolis, it has simply ceased to exist. Every house within miles of the centre seems to have had its own bomb.'[49] For those whose bodies had remained whole, every backyard was a graveyard. The monumental concrete flak towers in the Humboldthain and out-side the zoo were themselves now hecatombs, their dark concrete passages punctuated with the bodies of military personnel and others who had taken their own lives. The remaining life of the city belonged in large part to its women, and it was they who kept the civic pulse flickering. From the first day of the Soviet occupation, the women who worked in the huge industrial concerns, from AEG to Osram, could see what the conquerors intended even if they did not under-stand their words. They were being compelled to dismantle entire production lines, and painstakingly to remove every mechanical part from every item of apparatus, and pass them along hand to hand until finally those parts were in railway loading bays to be transported east. They also believed that these vast industrial concerns they were deconstructing would never be restored.

This strange twilight life seemed to some as though it might continue indefinitely. In Britain, 8 May 1945 brought the jubilant floodlit celebrations of VE Day. The territories that had been liber-ated by the Allies were, if only for a short, fizzing period before the exhaustion and the privations and the traumatic losses of the war resumed their ache, similarly buoyant. In Berlin, the women and the old men and the young children knew nothing of any of this. Among those legitimate citizens were a great many others, constantly dodg-ing out of sight, continuing to hide in basements and attics: young men in patchworks of civilian clothes who had deserted the Wehr-macht and were now seeking to evade capture by the Red Army; refugees from the countryside east of the city who seemed in a state of confusion and distress.

Just outside the city, and struggling to return, were women such as the office worker Mechtild Evers, who had been raped several times during her rural forced labour and now was on foot, surviving upon the kindness of, as she wrote, 'those in striped concentration camp clothes or in Russian soldiers' uniform, whose souls the war had not been able to kill, who shared their only piece of bread with me'.[50] The skies above the flat countryside were a painterly blue, but the homeland was a wilderness. Also trekking back to the city along dusty country roads was Hildegard Knef. She had been briefly captured by the Soviets and held in a camp, where she persuaded the jailers of her true identity and negotiated her freedom. She had not bathed 'for three months'.[51] Her clothes were rigid, and seething with lice. All that sustained her was an address in Berlin given to her by her lover Demandowsky, now captive and later to be executed. She knew that the city could not offer reliable sanctuary, and yet the urge to return to it was like the twitch upon the thread. On her journey she learned of women who not only had been raped but also had been shot, and heard stories almost too baroque to believe, including one about some young rural Red Army troops who took some unwashed potatoes into an apartment and deposited them in the lavatory – presumably, so the tenants thought, to wash them. In fact, they simply did not know what a flushing toilet was. And, when the pulled chain made the potatoes disappear, the soldiers became crazed with rage and accused the tenants at gunpoint of 'sabotage'.[52]

If anyone had told these Berliners that within a fortnight of 8 May the authorities would reopen some of the city's cinemas and theatres and concert halls, or that, just days later, the conductor Wilhelm Furt-wängler would be in Berlin once more, standing before an assembled orchestra performing Mendelssohn – they would have been dismissed as a fantasist. Yet it was the case; even as Berliners grew hungrier, and more disorientated by this landscape of death and suicide, Soviet cultural committees were importing Russian films for the edification of German citizens, in preparation for the swift reopening of Berlin's viable cinemas: stout, earnest documentaries about the purity of life on Soviet collective farms, but also light entertainment in the form of visual comedies that did not require much in the way of translation. There would also be shown a 1938 drama that was intended as the first suggestion of re-education and admonition: *Professor Mamlock* was the story of a Jewish surgeon cruelly persecuted by the Nazis, even though they needed his skill. The tragedy ends with the doctor's violent death. It had been a hit – the first film drama to focus unflinchingly on Nazi anti-Semitism – though the Soviets had earlier been forced to withdraw the film quickly in the wake of the Molotov–Ribbentrop Pact of 1939. Several years later, the film was once more a staple on the Soviet cinema circuit. (It had been successful in the US too, where the poster proclaimed 'A crushing indictment of Nazi terror!')[53] For Berliners starved of their favourite art form, this was to be one of the first productions they would be faced with, just days after the Soviet conquest; many more severe films were to follow.

In addition to this, when they were not being pressed into labour, or being sexually appraised by ruthless eyes, Berliners found that even in their own streets and districts, they were viewed by their conquerors with a moral curiosity, as though they too had been the monsters. For these citizens, 8 May 1945 meant very little; the dust-choked days were all the same. Yet those last few weeks of epochal destruction, which had swallowed many thousands of civilian lives and left countless more without the semblance of a civilized home, were also going to cast their shadow far into the future. Like the rest of the world, they yearned for peace. In the days and years to follow, the people of Berlin would find, instead, that the eyes of the world would never leave them, and that those eyes were gazing with some fear into a crucible out of which a new and even more terrible conflict could come.

# PART THREE

# Possession

# 16.   Complicity

The older Berliners remembered what it was like to be hated. The previous defeat in 1918 had brought with it a chilly recoil of disgust from the victorious nations, as though the German people themselves had been uniquely culpable for the conflict. Now, in that early summer of 1945, Berliners knew that those waves of anger would come crashing in again. In America, the revered German novelist and author of *Buddenbrooks*, Thomas Mann, who had spent the Nazi years in exile, broadcasting vehement anti-Hitler speeches in a Californian émigré community that included Bertolt Brecht, gave a talk at the US Library of Congress. It concerned Nazi crimes and the roots of German evil; these roots reached back to Martin Luther, and the dark possibilities of German romanticism had been perceived by Goethe. 'It is all within me,' Mann said. 'I have been through it all.'[1] He declared, 'There are not two Germanys, an evil and a good, but only one, which through devil's cunning, transformed its best into evil.'[2] The suggestion was that evil had coursed through the entire German people; they felt it, even if they themselves had not committed the crimes. On reading the speech, Bertolt Brecht was horrified that Berliners and others might stand accused of wickedness committed by tyrants, and not by the people. No Berliners had the opportunity to hear this address, but they none the less understood that they would stand accused. Many of them had – throughout the last few years – heard the rumours of where the city's Jews had been deported to, and of what had awaited them in those terrible camps. And so Berliners knew that the cycle of opprobrium was to begin again. They had been complicit, even if they personally felt no guilt. They might not have seen the camps, or the railway trucks, but they had known about them. And what they certainly *had* seen was the violence of *Kristallnacht* in 1938; the howling, shouting groups of civilians. That was the night upon which no Berliner could claim to be in ignorance of the depth of malevolence directed towards the Jewish people. The philosopher Hannah Arendt was later to make

the distinction between 'collective guilt' and 'collective responsibility' – the former meaning that, in essence, no single individual was
guilty, the latter obliging German society as a whole to acknowledge
what had been done in its name.[3] For the hungry and sexually violated Berliners in 1945 such distinctions will at the time have felt
abstract. But defeat and chaos and helplessness had concrete qualities.
The older Berliners remembered the dusty flavour of capitulation following the Great War, and the roller-coaster of political instability
that followed. But unlike 1918, there was now an occupying power,
one that was at once frightening and reassuring. It was a power that
was trying to pretend that this new revolution – a new totalitarianism –
was no such thing; that the task of restoring life to Berlin was a
common endeavour willed by the German people.

In the early days of summer 1945 there were still no American or
British or French forces to be seen in the capital; the Soviets had, for
the moment, full control. The removal of the city's riches had been
voracious: from the Old Masters retrieved from their ignominious
storage in the Friedrichshain flak tower to the scientists, senior and
junior, attached to AEG, Osram and Siemens who had potential use
in the Soviet nuclear programme, Berlin was picked apart like a chicken
carcass. Now the city's radios came alive once more, breaking at least
that part of the silence; at the start of June 1945 the voice issuing a proclamation was that of the city's newly installed Burgermeister, Dr Arthur
Werner. He was broadcasting a warning to his fellow citizens:

> Anyone who wants to impede our administration is an enemy of the
> people, and an irresponsible criminal who harms our country . . .
> such criminals and deluded persons are still to be found who by acts
> of madness are preventing the return of law and order . . . particularly
> the members of the former Hitler Youth.[4]

Dr Werner then went on to issue a threat that had ironically precise echoes of the regime that had gone before. For every single
attempt upon the life of a Red Army soldier or Soviet official, he
pronounced, fifty former members of the Nazi Party would be shot.[5]
Explicit in this was the idea that all such Nazis – at even the lowliest
levels of the party – had been identified. More broadly, the Soviet
rhetoric was calculated to convey a sense that many such functionaries

would be deradicalized via education. The city's anti-fascists were said to be helping the Soviet authorities by 'guiding them through the maze . . . of civilian life'.[6] But the friendliness – the idea of leading by moral example, proving that Soviet civilization was superior – could only ever be a veneer; there were illimitable outbreaks of vengefulness that continued: industrialists held at gunpoint while their wives were raped by Red Army soldiers. There were said to have been instances of deliberate arson: on one occasion, the accused, two teenage boys denounced as 'Hitler Youth', were themselves murdered by being thrown into the flames.[7] The occupiers were not kind; nor, given the obscenities perpetrated by the Nazis in their homelands, could anyone expect them to be.

Despite the continued violence, Berliners found that their city was not wholly dead, and for those who managed to avoid the cold gaze of the new authorities, away from the pulverized centre, there were startling sparks of renewal. As Burgermeister, Werner was emblematic of this regeneration. He was an architect and a civil engineer who had run a technical college in Berlin until the Nazis closed it in 1942. Now the Soviets needed someone who was both an expert at the physical challenges of reconstruction and someone who did not appear simply to have been imposed by Moscow. Walter Ulbricht – who was now living and working in a building on Prinzenallee in the northern suburb of Gesundbrunnen, and occasionally using local cinemas as venues to deliver lectures to gathered officials – took the greatest care that the communist takeover should not be seen as such. 'We believe it would be wrong to force the Soviet system on Germany,' he had written in a party manifesto. 'We believe the over-riding interests of the German people at present prescribe a different road – the establishment of an anti-fascist, democratic regime . . . with all democratic rights and liberties for the people.'[8] Democracy was one of those terms with a suitably elastic definition. In the weeks before the Red Army permitted their American and British counterparts into Berlin, the Ulbricht Group was determinedly building a new framework of power; it had to be strong enough to withstand resistance.

Placing German communists – and a careful selection of non-party officials, to give the impression of a coalition of political interests – at the heart of the city's day-to-day administration, made it implicit that the duty of those leaders was to prevent the immediate catastrophe of starvation. The death of General Berzarin – killed in a motorbike accident in the east of the city on 16 June 1945, aged forty-one – did not help; he had striven hard, as had officials within the Soviet Military Administration HQ in the green eastern suburb of Karlshorst, to restart civic engines.[9] Yet there was still frighteningly little food in the city; supplies seized from the defeated Wehrmacht were funnelled through. Rationing – in strict tiers, with some groups, like builders and (for some reason) actors, receiving a little more – was continuing. The aim was for each citizen to receive 1,100 calories a day: pitifully little, but just enough to function. The daily allowance was 200g of bread, 400g of potatoes and 40g of meat. Frequently the aim seemed idealistic, but the Soviets were efficient at ensuring that the bread and potato supply was reasonably constant. The grocery shops that had not been seriously damaged in the previous weeks and months were extremely busy. There were rumours of coffee – often dashed, but a measure too of how, for Berliners, even the most quotidian comforts now carried an enchanted quality.

And more of those placards were put up around the streets of the inner suburbs, declaring that surviving 'restaurants . . . cinemas and music halls' should reopen.[10] In some districts, this was fanciful, especially the notion of restaurants; but there were concerted efforts to restart the whirr of film projectors in the few undamaged auditoriums. Other signs of renewal in those early summer days will have seemed like a miraculous illusion: the fresh roar from beneath the ground of restored U-Bahn trains running along cleared lines; the sight of the overhead S-Bahn trains gliding across urban viaducts. With remarkable speed, tram lines were reconstructed and rethreaded. Wood-burning buses started moving again on limited routes. Then there were the domestic necessities: about 200,000 citizens of the inner suburb of Moabit, for instance, had been drawing their water from standpipes for months. By the early days of June 1945, the water supplies were restored.[11] This was one less anxiety for the women who had been corralled by local officials into the arduous labour gangs removing the boulders and bricks from bomb sites and roads: the 'rubble women', whose images – standing in lines on mounds of debris, buckets in hand – became famous around the world. The work was low-paid and frequently excruciating; just a few degrees away from the forced labour that so many of those same women had witnessed in the city's factories and industrial plants. Reluctant workers were told that a refusal would mean the curtailing of their ration cards, so in the rising temperature of an early Berlin summer, they found themselves negotiating mounds of dust and heaving great lumps of masonry down a line from early light to late afternoon. Although unspoken, there was clearly an element of collective punishment: the work was obviously necessary, but it also afforded a form of public spectacle. Because many Berlin women had taken their best clothes to the bomb shelters, and the rest had been destroyed in the vast battle and bombardment, many were on these unforgiving work parties wearing fine, frequently delicate dresses. Spare clothes or material to adapt to work clothes were at a premium; one woman had taken a vast scarlet-and-black swastika flag, carefully removed the emblem and used the remaining cloth to fashion for herself a makeshift dress. The rubble women were piercingly aware of the authorities and their press departments taking their photographs; sometimes they met the lenses with scowls or defiant drags on cigarettes. It was a form of humiliation, following a period of the most intense trauma. But even this grim conscription was, they knew, not the worst; there had been rumours concerning those men who had been sent deep into the Soviet east, and of the kind of physical work down mines and in the hearts of mountains that many could not survive.

The rubble women also had the consolation of seeing the practical effects of their work as terraces and avenues were once more opened to traffic and the bricks and stones were stored for repurposing. Any remaining builders or joiners in the city were similarly drafted into compulsory labour; their task was to move among the broken buildings, appraise them and repair those that could be patched up sufficiently to become habitable once more. More posters and placards were erected for propaganda purposes, adjacent to some of the city's more extensive bomb sites. They bore messages such as: 'This you owe to Hitler' and 'Shame on Hitler and his work: rubble, rubble, rubble'.[12] The premise of these declarations appeared to be about wrenching Berliners away from their former faith. But they were also shrewd, in the sense of avoiding the accusation that Berliners had brought death upon themselves. In this strange, silent period before the other Allies were allowed to take up their own intended sectors of occupation, there was no great emphasis on blaming Berliners for the crimes their country had committed. Even though conscription to the rubble gangs felt to some like a form of humiliation, it could at least be rationalized by humanitarian necessity: a great many of the 600,000 homes that had been ruined during the battle for Berlin might be salvaged using materials from those that had been pulverized completely.

There was another housing possibility in the city, one that existed in a borderland of civic acceptability. Since the turn of the century, as Berlin's new, fiery industrial heart roared, some Berliners had taken to living on their garden allotments in the suburbs. Sheds were transformed into small homes, sometimes with two storeys. In one sense these were simply miniature shanty towns, yet in another they reflected Berlin's contrariness. These 'allotment colonies', as they had come to be known, now took on a fresh lease of life.[13] They were primitive – sewage flowed into cesspits, they had no electricity and life within could be a constant battle with ants – but, set as they were among fruit trees and vegetable patches, they also represented a kind of Edenic escape. Some 50,000 families in those weeks after the city's fall made their way to their quiet allotment sanctuaries. The new communist authorities were not wholly comfortable with the idea of these separate communities and their private smallholdings that somehow lay beyond their control, yet neither could they quite find reason enough to stop them.

That the Nazis had not demolished such structures in the years beforehand was in itself quite remarkable. They could never have had any conceivable part in Albert Speer's monumental civic visions. Even before that, in the era of the Kaiser, the allotment colonies (there were about 120,000 such houses at the time of the Great War) were a source of intense frustration to the city authorities. Yet in times of economic calamity, these green homesteads were an invaluable valve for the afflicted city: one answer to homelessness. Even the Nazis could see that there was another element to these improvised communities, one that could appeal to even their ideological purity: that Berliners, in choosing this simple life, were also shaking off the sickly degeneracy of the city. 'The Green city dweller connects with the soil,' ran one Nazi editorial.[14] This was ever more the case throughout the war, and the start of the deadly bombing campaign against Berlin. The city authorities had attempted to discourage these communities but, by 1944, anyone who had been bombed out of their apartment was legally entitled to find an allotment, and to build their own new home. Moreover, they were allowed to keep a few animals – chickens or pigs. By 1945, the Soviets, who had widened their eyes at the wealth and the opulence of Berlin's unharmed villas, were also facing the challenge of bringing allotment colonists into line with party thinking.

During their brief period of sole control the Soviets also addressed the question of how the city's young people might be deprogrammed from their 'Hitler Youth' training. The orders had come from Marshal Zhukov, who had called for 'the final extermination of the remnants of fascism' to be achieved in part through 'anti-fascist organizations'.[15]

The Berliner selected to re-educate the city's young was a man who, like Walter Ulbricht, had been in exile in Russia since the ascension of the Nazis. Johannes R. Becher was a poet and novelist as well as a politician. His brief was not merely to remove the infection of Nazism from young minds but to redirect them towards the self-evident high morality of communism. He immediately called for the 'moral regeneration of our nation', founding the Kulturbund zur demokratischen Erneuerung Deutschlands (Cultural League for the Democratic Renewal of Germany).[16] Born in 1891, Becher was a creative figure of quite formidable intensity, prone to suicidal impulses and morphine addiction. But the communism of Karl Liebknecht shot through his poetry and prose like a lightning bolt, and he had been very active in the party throughout the Weimar years. His poetry was termed expressionist, and it was the sort of literature that the rising fascists would denounce as degenerate. There was never any possibility of an accommodation with the Nazi regime; he had no choice but to flee into exile. Yet there was little ease or comfort to be found in Stalin's Soviet Union at the time of the purges and beyond. To have survived that wilderness of paranoia and betrayal was remarkable. To have maintained a steadfast moral view of how Germany and Berlin were to be reshaped into an ideal society was even more so. 'If we do not clear away the rubble,' Becher declared, 'if we do not achieve a renewal in the spiritual realm and a moral rebirth of our people, then material reconstruction would be . . . doomed to failure.'[17]

And, in common with his party colleagues, he did not view Nazism as a movement that had reflected an innate corruption in the German character; rather, it was the fearful result of a certain kind of rapacious capitalism. Becher believed that there was an essential creative German continuity through the centuries which was only now on the point of finding its true incandescence through socialism. 'In the moral and political attitude of our people we must now give clear, strong, convincing expression to this rich heritage of humanism, of classicism, to the rich heritage of the workers' movement,' he declared in a speech.[18] For children and adults alike, this meant that under the guidance of the Soviets, pre-Nazi culture would still be central to life in Germany's Soviet zone: Schiller and Goethe would still be revered. Indeed, Goethe was raised to the status of a hero, the 'symbol of our unified national culture', as Berlin's Communist Party leader Otto Grotewohl declared, who had, though his poetry, fiction and drama, transformed 'our nation from the twilight of historical emptiness to the rank of a world nation'.[19] This wasn't merely a calculated nationalist appeal: it was also reassurance to educated Berliners who feared that Bolshevism would raze the old culture and seek to replace it with something entirely new.

The Ulbricht Group, instead, presented itself as a most natural form of continuity; Walter Ulbricht had been a Spartacist in 1919, inspired by Rosa Luxemburg and Karl Liebknecht, and he knew Berlin intimately. The same was true of Johannes Becher, and the others in the group. The image they sought to portray was that of true Germans, returned from cruel exile, who were there to guide the city and the country back on to a truer path. However, both Ulbricht and Becher understood very well that there had been profound abuses in Russia too; that the terror woven through the framework of the Stalinist system would soon jolt through Berlin. This mattered nothing to them. The eyes of faith can adjust easily to darkness; and they had become adept at seeing a distant light that all must move towards to find salvation. While Ulbricht and Becher wanted to offer Berliners the assurance of cultural tradition, they were also icily clear that compromise would not be tolerated.

The purity of artistic expression in this new society should not be allowed to help create 'a sort of second Weimar Republic', as Becher proclaimed.[20] As a communist, he believed that would have invited regression to a form of decadence (and liberal thought) that made fascism possible. Instead, throughout theatres and opera houses, concert halls and cinemas, and even in popular fiction, there had to be an unyielding framework of political rectitude. It was noted that among Berlin's young, one constant had existed alongside both Weimar liberalism and Nazi totalitarianism: pulp fiction, and its cinematic equivalent. The violent Wild West adventures of Old Shatterhand had remained required reading for adolescent boys, and under those blue skies of early summer their younger brothers, unable to attend non-existent lessons in bombed-out schools, had reverted to the games that children were playing across continental Europe, Britain and, of course, America: illimitable variations of cowboys and Indians.

Others adopted a more modern slant. Years later, one Berliner recalled with a sort of baffled but affectionate nostalgia how the ruins of the Ackerstrasse provided the most exhilarating backdrop for his boyhood 'International Detective Agency'; he and his friends contrived to fashion make-believe business cards, and they conducted make-believe investigations and pursuits of villains amid the collapsed buildings.[21] And there were also constant echoes of the war: boys imitating guns and grenades in rough games. Johannes R. Becher was among those German communists who had a Jesuitical belief that the children born in the shadow of Hitler needed comprehensive re-education, that their souls might be realigned; conversely, it might also have been the case that many of those Berlin children had quite happily and unconsciously found their own inspirations far from fascism.

Certainly, the childhood appetite for Soviet improving literature – austere books and journals detailing the lives of great heroes of society, who had fought fascism in a variety of ways, and who embodied the virtues of Soviet equality – was scanty. As time moved along, the Soviet authorities would, with slightly set jaws, adjust their approach, recalibrating dry parables as stirring adventure stories – high up in the mountains, deep beneath the sea – packed with hazard and mortal peril. There was another consideration: the education system had been traumatically splintered. The schools had closed several months beforehand and, even then, many children had been living under the permanent chill of missing relatives and killed parents. Their trauma was almost too great to contemplate. Those children continued their games on desolate, ruined sites that were – ironically – even more dangerous than mountain tops and ocean depths.

Nor was there solace to be found in what had once been the city's vast and elegant pleasure gardens. The Tiergarten was now an apocalyptic landscape of stripped and skeletal trees, vast sandy craters and abandoned hardware, from burned-out tanks to discarded Panzerfausts. Children roamed amid these jagged abstract sculptures, the ground beneath their feet crunching with bullet casings. Many of them at least still had the security of a grown-up to take care of them. What did these young minds, then, make of their more ragged contemporaries: the orphan refugees who were beginning to enter the city, with makeshift guardians? This was the first intimation of a vast human calamity that would unfold over the next few years: the forced expulsion of millions of German families from former Nazi-occupied territories across Europe that would lead to hundreds of thousands of deaths.

The forests that surrounded the city had for years provided a valuable imaginative escape for Berlin's children: the silent paths through mazes of trees and the wide, inviting lakes. Yet even these were now, in the warming days of summer, deathly reminders of the recent carnage. A great many Wehrmacht and SS men had attempted and failed to find refuge in the deep woods, in the hope that they might strike back against the approaching foe. But the bombs and the flamethrowers had made a nonsense of this sanctuary; and there were still body parts scattered under ferns or being worried over by birds and animals in sandy clearings. For Berlin's children, the war had not really ended. True innocence was impossible, no matter how much the eerie bomb sites and battlegrounds were transfigured as backdrops for boisterous games learned from adventure stories.

It had only been a matter of weeks since the Grand Duchess Cecilie, wife of the former Hohenzollern crown prince, had finally vacated the vast Tudor-style palace outside the city that had been built in her name. By the summer, the Soviet Military Administration had – with careful choreography from Moscow – finally admitted the US and British forces into the city, after weeks of jittery and ill-tempered misunderstandings and provocations. Now, in mid July 1945, it was time for the three Allied leaders to meet once more, and for the final time, and their meeting place for the Potsdam Conference was to be the grand duchess's home. The Cecilienhof, which had remained unscathed even under the rough enthusiasm of Soviet occupation, presented a curious spectacle so close to the torn, haunted city: the house and its landscaped gardens still suggestive of ordered tranquillity. The property belonged to a different world. Yet the Soviets had been careful in their preparation for this major summit. A flowerbed in one of the central courtyards had been re-dug and replanted; it blazed scarlet, a lake of red roses, fashioned in the shape of the red Soviet star.[22]

There was now a new US president following the death of Roosevelt: Harry S. Truman; and there was to be an outgoing British prime minister too. As the Potsdam Conference got underway, the results of the UK general election (slightly delayed by the fact of servicemen's votes being sent from around the world) came through. The electorate had decided that Winston Churchill had fulfilled his wartime purpose, and that the immediate future should instead be represented by his Labour deputy, Clement Attlee. So while Churchill had led the British delegation at Potsdam in its first few days, he was thereafter replaced and it was Attlee who took his seat beside the US and Soviet leaders for the conference's conclusion. In this sense, Stalin was the emblem of continuity; the one wartime leader to remain in power by the end of the conflict. At Cecilienhof there was security and paranoia in abundance; around Stalin stood an unbroken wall of soldiers and agents. The food for the conference was entirely ordered and shipped from Moscow and the food tasters were Russian. Delegations from the British and American teams were allocated apartments for their offices within the sprawling palace, and all was arranged so that not even Churchill could have approached Stalin without a vast close-protection team intervening. The traffic around the Cecilienhof estate, meanwhile, was directed by Soviet women waving yellow and red flags.

The agenda that was agreed to in these halls was to have the most terrifying consequences for millions of families. The intentions of Potsdam were not overtly malign, yet what Truman, Churchill, Attlee and Stalin agreed to was to prove a death sentence for countless civilians. Those Germans who had moved into the territories and lands that had been annexed by the Nazis were to be expelled: this was a decree that would stretch from Poland, through Czechoslovakia and Hungary. There might have been a naïve assumption on the part of Churchill that such a process could be orderly, and that families might be able to escape without encountering violence or hardship. But much of the continent comprised starving people in burned ruins, and there was little forgiveness to be found anywhere.

None the less, those leaders and foreign secretaries and diplomats at the Potsdam Conference were determined to bring judgement upon Nazi wickedness; it was at Cecilienhof that the framework for postwar prosecution was erected. The criterion at first glance was one that could be defined with ease: the difference between actions taken during the normal course of war and 'war crimes'.[23] The magnitude of the Holocaust – its sheer incomprehensible scale – had brought the reality of unalloyed evil before the world. The senior Nazis who had not committed suicide would face trial at Nuremberg. So too would figures lower down the Nazi hierarchy, who had taken on active and zealously homicidal roles. For the population to be denazified, all of the regime's institutions would have to be torn down and rebuilt.[24] For this to happen without a feared resurgence of the cult of Hitler, it would be necessary for the entire population to be re-educated and evaluated. The morality of ordinary people was to be measured. How else might any German thence be recruited to a position of power and influence? The more satirical citizens of Berlin – occasionally greeting each other with exaggerated and mocking 'Heil Hitler!'s – would very soon find that they would have to moderate their tones.

In terms of the absolutes of morality, there were other undercurrents at Cecilienhof in those two weeks of summer: President Truman – informed by the team in the New Mexico desert at Los Alamos that the atomic bomb was ready – issued a proclamation to the Japanese government demanding instant capitulation. If not, then America would have the power to visit terrible and unspecified destruction upon that country. Stalin was notified at Cecilienhof of the new secret super-weapon and appeared, according to Secretary of State James F. Byrnes, to be only mildly interested. But the Americans at that stage did not know that Stalin had also been briefed by his intelligence service, or that his agents had already scoured Berlin for uranium and scientists who would help advance his own bomb. It was also the case at Cecilienhof that there seemed little discomfort among any of the delegates about the morality of an atomic attack. While the German people were about to face judgement en masse, the very notion that killing thousands of civilians through an atomic blast and radiation poisoning might itself be seen as a crime did not appear to occur to the Allied leaders and their deputies. The war had to be ended, and in the exhaustion of the world's bloodiest conflict the means were no longer important. Four days after the Allies had concluded their discussions at Potsdam, an atomic bomb was detonated over Hiroshima, and then, three days after that, a second over Nagasaki. The consequences were to ripple back to Berlin in the years to come.

By this stage, Berliners had been permitted to move a little out of the obscurity of isolation; under the Soviets, new newspapers had been established. Schools had begun to function as well, despite the difficulties of roofless classrooms and perpetually hungry children. The communists had been swift to establish one advantage for themselves: Berlin's pupils were now being taught Russian as their second language. Schoolgirl Christa Ronke was pleased to be back; but there were certain areas of silence. There were thirteen girls in her class, she recalled, and almost all of them had suffered sexual attacks. Aside from a brief acknowledgement that it had happened, no one spoke about it thereafter. By that summer, the Soviets had also succeeded in restoring some of the city's aesthetic comforts. Christa recalled the excitement of going to hear the soprano Erna Berger at a Berlin Philharmonic concert. Her own musically inclined family had lost their radio, gramophone and piano; it was indescribably sweet to her and others, as she recalled, simply to hear music again.[25]

Meanwhile, Stalin's Soviet Union consolidated its tight hold on central and eastern Europe; all those lands conquered and razed by the Nazis were subsumed under a new form of unrelenting totalitarianism. As the first of the American, British and French occupying forces arrived to take jurisdiction of their agreed sectors there was an awareness that the Soviets would retain control not only of the east of the city, but of all the countryside around it. The forests and the lands beyond were in the Soviet zone. Berlin was to become a city of anomalies; a grim carnival of black marketeering and smuggling, from meat to household electrical appliances, as the chrome sleekness of American wealth chafed against the virtuous poverty of the communists. It was also to become a site of macabre tourism among military and diplomatic visitors from Britain and America, staring at the gaunt civilians and wondering if the flame of Nazism had been extinguished within them. The British historian and wartime code-breaker Hugh Trevor-Roper was among those picking their way through the eerie ruins as part of the investigation into the authenticity of Hitler's death and the fate of his corpse. The *unheimlich* (uncanny) atmosphere of the bunker and the near-demolished Chancellery radiated out, touching the city's other ruins and making the shuffling elderly citizens with carts who were simply foraging for fuel seem equally unsettling.[26] Yet even amid the confusion and the terrible hardships to come, there were threads of continuity; eight-year-old Margot Sharma, who lived with her parents in the southern suburb of Neukölln, recalled the music in her home – folk songs that had originated in the Ore mountains and been passed through the family, which they had never stopped singing and which they continued to sing.[27] There were small but crucial traditions that some families could hold fast to; traditions that had already survived the violent revolutions of 1919 and 1933, and would survive the new revolution that was unfolding. Such family comforts could not buttress against grief or fear, but they could help establish some small point of stability in a city that seemed very far away from knowing any kind of peace.

In all the stages of their degradation – the intense hunger, the inescapable cold, the gastric illnesses, the lice – they were being observed as though they were laboratory specimens. The people of Berlin were objects of terrible gothic curiosity to those who now were supervising their lives. The Americans, the British and the French had claimed their sectors of occupation. To those who had lived in these streets all their lives, the borders were arbitrary – marked by occasional sentry points, severe officials demanding paperwork on suburban trains, white lines on the roads – and involved moments of bewildering cultural adjustment. The American sector, under a succession of generals and an energetic deputy called Frank Howley, encompassed the south-western quarter of the city, including the physics laboratories that had been so carefully emptied by the Soviets; one young Berlin civilian recalled how her friends had rehearsed their first words in English: 'Can I have some chewing gum?'[1] There had been moments of astonishment when Berliners switching their radios on heard swing music blaring, broadcast by the American Forces Network. But these new rulers were implacable in different ways; homes that had suffered relatively little damage were requisitioned unannounced for US staff, the rightful occupants forced to pack meagre bags and find rooms elsewhere. Bars began to reopen in the US sector, although Germans were not permitted to drink in them. Instead, they could work as bar staff, watching officers consume the sorts of delicious cocktails that they themselves had enjoyed an impossibly long time ago.

'I had to drop out of school after the war,' wrote Christa Ronke. 'My mother could no longer pay the fees. By chance I was offered a job as a waitress in an American Officers' Mess in Berlin-Dahlem. There I had good food, found warmth in winter, and was even able secretly to carry small bundles of food home.'[2] Yet the initial attitude of the officers towards her and her colleagues was disturbing; the waitresses were known collectively as the 'Nazi Gretchens'. Smiles disappeared as they approached. They were among the presumed guilty.

In broader terms, some of the American soldiers were Jewish, and Berliners found themselves being stared at hard, most especially when they were reporting to the new authorities and declaring that they had never been members of the Nazi Party. Sometimes, in those offices, civilians would suddenly double up with pain, or simply faint, not because of the questioning but because they were suffering from dysentery. The city's doctors had endured as much in the bombing and the battles as everyone else; operating from makeshift surgeries, there was frequently little they could do for patients who were struggling to survive on 800 calories a day.

The British sector covered many of the western suburbs, which had once been enclaves of middle-class elegance. The British officials too were looking at Berlin women who were ill with dysentery, and sometimes diphtheria. They, like the Americans, were implacable about requisitioning the finer houses for administrative or residential use; some Berliners who thought they had had at least the luxury of re-established homes now found themselves, bewildered, back in the cellars that they had occupied throughout the bombing. Resentment was contained; the British and the Americans were, as many reasoned among themselves, the liberators. Like the Americans, the British were sifting through the civilians with the aim of isolating the Nazis. The most senior party members and anyone who had joined before 1933, as verified by the Nazi Party's own surviving records, were whisked before tribunals, facing imprisonment before lengthier trials. A huge number of Berliners occupied more ambiguous territory, and the authorities imagined that they might be able to identify them with the emerging technology of punch-card computing. The means by which they did so – starting with German administrators and civil servants – was the *Fragebogen*. This was a six-page questionnaire intended as a confessional. As well as all of one's personal information – from distinguishing marks to educational attainments – there were many questions about membership of or participation in the various Nazi organizations that had reached deep into every corner of German life. The idea was that the data might be processed

38. During the 1945 Potsdam conference, female Red Army personnel were deployed to direct traffic. Across the city, temporary Russian signs were erected: striking visual reminders to Berliners of their new rulers.

39. The Hotel Adlon, once the luxurious haunt of Berlin's aristocracy was now a gaunt, burned shell. From 1945 the hotel lay just within the Soviet sector, overseen by Stalin's stern gaze.

40. In the Soviet sector of divided Berlin, leader Walter Ulbricht – as well as overseeing brutal repression – was sincere about building clean, modernist dwellings, though not in the 'Americanized' style.

41. The director Billy Wilder had begun his career in Berlin; his 1947 black comedy *A Foreign Affair*, set amid the city's devastation and starring another ex-Berliner, Marlene Dietrich, was both funny and harrowing.

42. The Berlin Blockade of 1948–9, imposed by the Soviets on the west of the city, led to an heroic airlift of vital supplies. The Soviets, meanwhile, tried to seduce West Berliners with offers of delicacies and fuel.

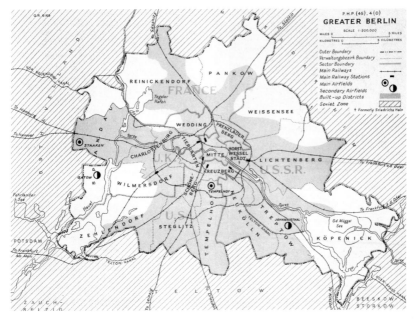

43. At the time of the Blockade, politicians in the West studied maps of divided Berlin – a Western-occupied island in a communist ocean – with mounting anxiety.

44. Bertolt Brecht (seen here with wife Helene Weigel, staging the 1949 Berliner Ensemble production of *Mother Courage and Her Children*) gave the communists a huge cultural boost during the blockade.

45. The extraordinary 1956 revelation of a Berlin UK/US spy tunnel tapping East Berlin telephone lines exposed how the city had become Europe's centre of espionage during the Cold War.

46. The elaborate tunnel, with its sophisticated technology, had been revealed to the Soviets months before by MI6 double agent George Blake. Its discovery sharpened Cold War paranoia on both sides.

47. Parents in East and West Berlin alike were alarmed by what they saw as gaudy, sexualized and delinquent 1950s US youth culture, embraced in the city's dance halls, and by the new magazine *Bravo*.

48. The 1953 Berlin uprising – a revolt against Ulbricht's hardline and often brutal government – started as a workers' protest and radiated out across the German Democratic Republic.

49. East Berlin protestors in their thousands were considered enough of a threat to the stability of the communist regime to bring Soviet tanks back to the streets of the city. The communists claimed the demonstrations were a covert US plot.

50. The grimly featureless East Berlin apartment blocks decreed by Ulbricht were – in aesthetic terms – not hugely different from many similar developments in cities such as London (though the hot water was unreliable).

51. In West Berlin there were efforts to turn brutalist apartment blocks in the decorative direction of Le Corbusier's style of architecture – the same principles as East Berlin, but with more money.

52. East and West Berlin had different television shows. The communists had one international success with an animated children's show called *Unser Sandmännchen*, which was calculated to lull little ones into feeling sleepy at bedtime.

53. On 12–13 August 1961 a recurring fear of all Berliners was at last realized as Ulbricht ordered the complete split of the city and the construction of a wall that would sunder families, friends and lovers.

54. The starkness of the Berlin Wall made it part of the landscape of the world: a concrete symbol of oppression. Hundreds were to die trying to cross it. For decades, it seemed permanent and immovable; its fall, on 9 November 1989, seemed miraculous.

55. The breaching of the Wall continues to have such resonance because it became a universal symbol of freedom and more: it captured the yearning for reconciliation. Divided Berlin was healed.

by the kind of new machinery that had been used elsewhere for decryption purposes. The reality was very different; the sheer number of questionnaires to be processed defeated both calculating machines and the human equivalent. In the early stages, there was some openness and honesty, even when answering questions involving the theft of Jewish goods and property. Yet many Berliners were too hungry and too ill to exercise the expected German punctiliousness, and it soon became common knowledge what sorts of answers made for a smoother existence. After some months the system became almost paralysed with data, by which stage the Americans – as the Soviets had already realized – understood that, for civil society to be rebuilt swiftly, the public message had to be one of rehabilitation as opposed to revenge.

The French, meanwhile, had the rather less salubrious north-west corner of the city; the rusted ruins of bombed, looted industry and the ghosts of old tenement blocks, marked only by fragments of foundations and pipes. The sight of French military uniforms in these streets was disagreeably hypnotic to older residents – this was more than an echo of the humiliations of 1918, rather the definitive emblem of defeat in all senses. The Allies in turn were looking at Berliners through a darker glass of historical morality: how could it be discerned which among these people were the 'good' Germans and which the 'bad'? The author of *Berlin Alexanderplatz*, Alfred Döblin, at the end of his long years of exile, had become attached to French military intelligence, and, when he returned to the city that he had once depicted as frenetic with life and crime, he was dazed. The city was 'dead and not dead'; an 'eerie silence' reigned; there was a 'broad street with no traffic, few people, and no noise'.[3]

Nor was it merely military eyes that were trained upon the pinched populace. From the summer of 1945 there were cameras – film and still – near busy street corners, or mounted on aeroplanes flying overhead. They were recording and cataloguing ruins under pale blue skies. By 1947, Berlin had spawned a new genre of cinematic art. The city that had contributed so much to the creation of Hollywood became itself a macabre backdrop not just for newsreels and documentaries, but for fictional murder mysteries and even black farce. The cold reality of Berlin's high mortality rate (especially, and most distressingly, among infants), and the unending struggle for food and proper shelter, and the humiliation of once-proud families having to scurry and barter in black-market goods – everything from cigarettes to cuts of meat to cooking utensils to record players – was being reflected on celluloid; even fiction had a dimension of voyeurism. But these films were also being made because the victorious powers were trying to fathom the depths of human nature. The film-makers and photographers were opening up this question – what manner of people were these? – to audiences in darkened auditoriums thousands of miles away.

Ironically, Berlin had been the first city in the wake of the Great War to explore and analyse itself on film. Now its people, undergoing denazification, were entering those cinemas in the American zone in order to watch the reality of the Nazi atrocities that had been directed from the capital. The feature itself – *Death Mills* – was short, running at twenty-two minutes, having been cut from an original ninety. This was an American-made documentary that carried horrific footage from Buchenwald. But the director who stepped in to cut it down did so with an unusually intimate knowledge of Berlin audiences. He was now Colonel Billy Wilder of the US Army Psychological Warfare Division. His burgeoning and successful Hollywood career was paused as he returned to the city in which his talent had been nurtured.

Just fifteen years previously, young Jewish screenwriter Billie Wilder, fresh from Vienna, had devised the scenario for the fantastically successful 1930 comedy docudrama *People on Sunday*. Now, the Romanisches Café, in which he had sat in raptures of observation, was dust. And there was a dreadful darkness in his own life: when he had quit Germany for the US in the early 1930s, he had left his mother and grandmother behind. He had had no word from them in years. It was inevitable that they were among the victims who had been dispatched to the death camps. Yet at the same time there was no way of knowing absolutely; no one could find any records. This was a piercingly cruel kind of uncertainty in which only the most anguished form of speculation could be possible, and which offered only the hope that the suffering of loved ones had been brief. Yet somehow, with all that within his breast, Wilder looked at the people of Berlin and considered how best they might have their humanity restored. As a former Berliner, he was genuinely torn about whether he should return there. 'None of us – I mean the émigrés – really knew where we stood,' he later said. 'Should we go home? Where was home?'[4]

The US Army Psychological Warfare Division was faced with the prospect of making Berliners and all other Germans within the American sphere of influence see the truth of what the Nazis had done; the evidence of film would burn away the whispers and the rumours that such stories were not and could not be true. There were to be what were termed 'education films'. And *Death Mills*, made with footage taken at the nightmare discovery of the camps, was directed by Hanuš Burger. The narrating voice, provided by Oskar Seidlin, was openly accusatory of ordinary people, as the film juxtaposed images from Leni Riefenstahl's *Triumph of the Will* and from the death camps. 'Yesterday, while millions were dying in German concentration camps, Germans jammed into Nuremberg to cheer the Nazi Party and sing hymns of hate,' ran the narration. 'Today, those same Germans who cheered the destruction of humanity in their own land, who cheered attacks on helpless neighbours, who cheered the enslavement of Europe, beg for your sympathy. They are the same Germans who heiled Hitler.'[5]

This was quite different from the subtler Soviet approach, which sought to erase Nazism by reaching further back and appealing to a sense of a deeper historical continuity, against which Hitler was an aberration. The thesis of *Death Mills* – combined with distributed photographs of Nazi obscenities – was that all Germans had contributed to this. Billy Wilder was among those who saw that, even if it was so, the idea of immersing those Germans in those atrocities would be psychologically counter-productive. So he edited it down to just over twenty minutes. His instinct, having worked in the Berlin film industry, was that the seduction techniques of cinema were universal. 'Get rid of the schmaltzy stuff,' he declared. 'Nobody cares about that anyway. And as for the horror stories, only what is necessary. I don't want to see it any more . . . you know how it works: first shock, then tears, then another shock, and then comes the tranquillizer – that this kind of thing can never happen again.'[6]

The shorter film certainly shocked; Berliners were reportedly deeply shaken by their first sight of the camps. But Wilder's sense that a longer film might cause some of the audience simply to close themselves off from the horror – because it was too much, and because they did not feel themselves to be personally guilty – was acute. Throughout the first few years of occupation, many Berliners who had not joined or actively supported the Nazi Party did begin to record a sense of accusation that they could simply do nothing about.

In this, Wilder was in accord with higher US authorities, but for different reasons. Those higher powers were concerned about alienating Berliners and other Germans. 'They are our logical allies of tomorrow,' stated one pre-Cold War memo. 'And as such, we simply cannot antagonize them.'[7] General Eisenhower said elsewhere: 'We are not here to degrade the German people, but to make it impossible to wage war.'[8]

It was one of the curious echoes of Berlin continuity that the city came to understand the weight of Nazi crimes, and the measure of the loss, and the depth of the trauma, through the medium of cinema. So much so that an entirely new genre, the *Trümmerfilm* (rubble film), came into being. The careful aesthetics of black-and-white cinematography made what was intolerable in reality somehow bearable to watch when projected through silvery darkness on to large screens. And it was the Soviet Military Administration that first encouraged the regeneration of the Berlin film industry after a meeting in what remained of the Hotel Adlon in the autumn of 1945. The first production to go before the cameras in Babelsberg was a noirish psychological drama: *The Murderers are Among Us*. Revolving around a military surgeon who can no longer bear to treat patients owing to flashbacks; a young woman, Susanne Wallner, who is a concentration-camp survivor; and a former Wehrmacht captain who has evaded detection for an atrocity carried out in a Polish village, the film used the ravaged city as an extension of the broken mental states of the protagonists.

The film – which had a visual style that echoed some of the great expressionist Fritz Lang thrillers of the early 1930s – opened in 1946 in the Soviet sector, and played in the theatre where the Berlin Opera had made its temporary home. Soon it was distributed throughout

Soviet-occupied Germany, where millions queued to see it. More than this: the fascination of the theme of guilt, and of where that guilt truly lay, brought the film international attention. It was nominated for a prize at the Venice Film Festival. In America, the highbrow *New Yorker* magazine reviewed it enthusiastically. Here, it seemed, Berliners had found the way to navigate a dark moral labyrinth via the medium that they understood best, and the shadows and the ruins so starkly depicted in monochrome could be understood as metaphors for the shadows of their own natures. There was one glaring criticism, however, from Berlin audiences: that Susanne, the young concentration-camp survivor, looked too immaculate and beautiful in make-up and in clothes that were not worn out.

All this was certainly the case; it was acknowledged elsewhere, and in rubble films to follow, that fashion and beauty were frequently counterpoised against jagged, ugly ruins. But the actress who played Susanne in *The Murderers are Among Us* knew very well the reality of wartime filth, for it was none other than Hildegard Knef, who only months earlier had been trudging, bleeding, at the point of a gun, and in the clothes of a man in order to avoid rape by Red Army soldiers. It was remarkable that she had been restored to her former glamour. Her immediate post-war experience, having escaped the Soviets, was dominated cruelly by hunger; there were days when even a plate of thick soup was an unattainable luxury. On other days, there could be gifts of food from US officials and soldiers. Frau Knef had been reunited with some of her theatrical friends, and in the American sector a theatre was swiftly restored and she was invited to join the troupe, acting in everything from light musical revues to Shakespeare, while all the time suffering violent gastric pains from having devoured a sandwich or a hamburger at speed. At one point the director demanded to know if she was pregnant; she was not. Her stomach was distended by the irregularity of her eating patterns.[9]

The filming of *The Murderers are Among Us* was often at night, on location, in shattered streets in the Soviet sector. The success of the film was to help Knef's future acting career greatly. No one seemed to question, however, the gruesomely bad taste of having her character – a concentration-camp survivor – portrayed by a glamorously styled gentile. (Certainly not a Jewish US Army officer called Kurt Hirsch, who had fallen head over heels for her, and who would in time marry her.) Frau Knef was to cultivate a talent for innocent provocation; several years later, in a film entitled *The Sinner*, she re-established one of the city's older traditions by performing a scene in the nude. That which had once been welcomed in certain forests and lakes was, however, regarded as an outrage upon the big screen. An international career was to follow. What appeared to matter more about *The Murderers are Among Us* was that a tone was being set for conversations about rehabilitation. The Soviets were the first occupiers to understand that cinema to Berliners was not a trivial matter. The audiences were leaving their gutted, leaking homes and troubled, traumatized family and neighbours in order to find undisturbed respite in these auditoriums. Escapism does not always mean fantasy. Berliners who understood that the world was looking at them with disgust were responding to dramas that faced these matters unflinchingly.

Billy Wilder, meanwhile, returned once more, to make another rubble film that had the distinction of horrifying the US authorities. *A Foreign Affair* (1948) was an extraordinarily cynical comedy – another story involving Berlin black marketeering, with the twists of intense fraternization and morality that could shift like quicksilver. It starred Marlene Dietrich, herself returning from a long exile from the city; she portrayed a nightclub vamp inhabiting the skeletal ruin of an apartment while exploring the city's new opportunities for sexual trading with its US Army occupiers. And even though the location filming was carefully staged (locals became background extras, acting out pantomimes of their own real lives) there was still something ruthless about it; the spectacle of once affluent and sophisticated Berliners now reduced to haggling and bartering pathetic items near the Brandenburg Gate in the hope of some invaluable tinned food. Wilder's glittering script was constructed as farce, but was also as black as night. The film was loathed by the US establishment. And it was not shown on West German television until the early 1970s.[10]

And there was one real-life scene that did not feature in the film, but which lodged with mischief in Wilder's imagination. While he was out surveying possible locations, in a US jeep with American

soldiers, a rather vague pedestrian was almost hit on the Kurfürstendamm. Shocked by the near miss, the pedestrian shouted out a strong
German obscenity. Wilder, whose own colloquial German had remained
crisp, ordered the car to stop. He approached the by now intimidated
pedestrian and ordered him to wait exactly where he was: the military police would be along to arrest him. A few hours later, at the
day's end, Wilder was driving back along the same stretch. The
pedestrian was still there, in exactly the same position, still waiting.
Had German civilians been guilty through all those years of the crime
of excessive obedience?[11]

The contrasts between disease and distress and the city's efforts to
restore some of its old spirit were striking. The beleaguered doctors
had to begin giving typhus injections; even with the streets cleared
and some of the infrastructure repaired, there were medieval outbreaks of illness. Tuberculosis was rife. Yet, even in the midst of that,
the vast shopping strip of the Kurfürstendamm was beginning
to stir. The stores that had not been demolished, and which had
been able to obtain glass for their windows, attempted sparse displays of goods. 'One can see the windows in Kurfürstendamm again,
small and clean and tastefully decorated, a delight for the eye,' wrote
playwright Max Frisch in September 1945. 'There is the understandable desire to see something that is whole again, new and
beautiful.'[12]

But where was the money for anyone to buy such goods coming
from? Many Berliners were still at subsistence levels. It was common,
months after the end of the war, to see women and old men on foraging expeditions not in the country, but in suburban woodlands, and
the liminal spaces where vegetation was growing through ruins: trees
were stripped of nuts and berries; nettles were pulled up. Yet, in all the
occupied sectors, the traditional municipal roles, from police to fire
service, were being restored; and in the offices and the banks that had
not been either gutted or simply ransacked and expropriated by the
Soviets, a form of office life was also returning. Cadaverous-looking
middle managers were commuting through the wrecked centre in
shirts and ties. In the western sectors, with the Nazis apparently
weeded out (the reality of the *Fragebogen* was that very few were – and,
when there were prosecutions, there was some resentment among

Berliners that minor functionaries were being punished when so many other, more active Nazi Party members had escaped by simply reinventing their pasts), other services and industries were being gradually repopulated at all levels. The resurrection of one of the city's mightiest industrial complexes – that of Siemensstadt, in the north – was among the most extraordinary. Over half of the factory space had been simply flattened by bombing. The Soviets had removed every last working component and also the firm's accounts and much of its financing. Only months later, workers and young apprentices were once more walking through those gates, or arriving by restored light railway, and clocking on. The paternalistic management structure brought with it a sense of security that had long been fugitive. It was still some months before production on many electrical goods could be properly resumed, but by focusing on simple necessities, such as frying pans, these and other factories were signalling their intent.

Running side by side with this apparent return to a form of normality was a black market throughout the city that was wholly visible; the daily desperate, shaming trade in stolen goods, in family valuables, in watches and cameras (especially coveted by Russian soldiers), in alcohol, chocolate and cigarettes that took place in huddles near collapsed houses, or near the thoroughfares of the partly restored railway stations. It was not long before the markets attained greater exposure, on concourses like Alexanderplatz and Brandenburg Tor. In this sense, everyone, including children dodging through streets with purloined items, was engaged in strategies for making a living, legitimate or otherwise. For many women, sex was now part of this survivalist economy. Allied troops stationed in the city had been instructed that 'fraternization' was forbidden, yet the flouting of this rule was in one way a gruesome continuation of sexual coercion (and there was something faintly obscene about the sheer glowing health of the US soldiers when compared to exhausted Berliners – Hildegard Knef described 'soldiers with swelling rumps and glittering rifles').[13] Meanwhile, with Berliners now also jostling with multitudes of refugees, who were not permitted to stay in the city, and also had nowhere to go, the distribution of food remained the most perplexing difficulty for the authorities, even as the lights in Berlin's cabarets came on once more.

There was juvenile crime, too; a citywide phenomenon, but one that still had an element of an east–west divide. There were teenagers who were too disturbed to tolerate school but who could not find any work amid the disordered streets, brought up in fractured, traumatized households, their fathers having returned from wartime captivity with broken, jagged minds, their mothers exhausted, overworked and fighting an unending battle to obtain enough food to live on. The ubiquity of the black market meant that the older generation was frequently in no position to offer any moral or social example. The busy hub of Alexanderplatz became a magnet for juvenile street gangs, stealing and selling goods sourced from affluent areas in the west.[14] In 1946 the Soviet Military Administration inaugurated Freie Deutsche Jugend (Free German Youth), an organization for anyone aged fourteen to twenty-five. As well as seeking to inculcate elastic young minds into the hermetic intricacies of Marxism–Leninism, the movement offered hiking trips, concerts and dances. This was the intended anti-fascist counter to the Hitler Youth, and in the decades to come its membership would stretch into the millions. But the authorities would have other uses for these young people too; in time, cohorts of Free German Youth could be relied upon to appear at demonstrations, or on marches into the west of the city. Meanwhile, the more dedicated young delinquents who decided to move full-time to the more enticing west of Berlin were quietly relinquished by Ulbricht's government. (By the 1950s, West Berlin would see its first generation of biker gangs.)[15]

In addition to all this, there were the first distant growls of a new approaching storm. What drove the earliest friction in the fast-developing Cold War was the fundamental misapprehension that existed between the Americans and the Soviets, and the assumptions and second-guessing about what either side intended. Berlin was an island in a deep ocean of Soviet red. It was Stalin's presumption that the Western Allies would soon forsake their occupied sectors so that the city, and then the country, might be united under his rule. Some had assumed that Stalin's intentions were not predatory, and that the Soviets would not need to be contained or countered. Soviet efforts to mould the political landscape of Berlin to Stalinism, however, began causing alarm even before there was border friction between the occupied sectors. As much as it was skilled in deploying soft power to win Germans over to the Soviet vision of society, the Stalinist regime was also chillingly and implacably ruthless with anyone perceived to be hindering this effort; hence why Sachsenhausen concentration camp was not closed after the war: the Soviets now needed it for a fresh generation of political prisoners. Communist rubber truncheons replaced Nazi whips; the ethos of unceasing brutality remained the same.[16] At first, the men and sometimes women being removed from the streets by Soviet agents were said to be fugitive Nazis, but, in the months that followed, the political manoeuvrings focusing on the Soviet plan to merge the popular Social Democratic Party with the less popular Communist Party – creating the Socialist Unity Party, which could then take over government – yielded up fresh numbers of victims being detained for 'interrogations' that could last for weeks. An estimated 5,000 SDP members and politicians who objected to the merger with the communists were simply kidnapped, a great number of them from Western-occupied sectors. The Soviets had little fear of retaliation from the Americans and the British, and they also imagined that Berliners – as well as the east of Germany as a whole – might not be too concerned that the Communist Party was positioned to dominate every aspect of their lives.

They were wrong. The contrariness of Berlin politicians – and their subsequent demands for a secret, citywide ballot on the issue – startled the Soviets. In concrete terms, they could exercise little influence over how the Western-occupied sectors were governed, and even kidnapping and other methods of intimidation could not help to sway the views of large numbers of Berliners. This was a city that had not known anything of democracy since 1933; the appetite in many corners for an extension of totalitarian rule was low. To the anger of the Soviets, this was also true in the city's more working-class districts, such as Wedding, which fell within the French sector. Older Berliners had no difficulty recalling the broken teeth and bloodied pavements that had come in the wake of communist vs Nazi street fights. In addition to this – important for the younger people – the Western occupiers had brought with them a hugely refreshing tide of new, bright and addictive popular culture; exciting films, faster music.

The Soviets shrewdly countered such vulgarity by restoring to Berliners some of their older, more serious and dignified cultural pursuits. The 1920s journal *Die Weltbühne*, the beating heart of the intellectual left presided over by Kurt Tucholsky, was resurrected in 1946, once more to carry passionate, closely observed essays about reordering the evils of society and of the world. It was intended, as one article put it, 'for the democratic education of the people of Germany'.[17] In terms of music, the Soviet authorities were also careful to ensure that the Germans once more came to celebrate and exult in their rich heritage – from Beethoven to Brahms – without having to consider the shadow of the regime that had been. There were nights, recalled one Berliner, when it was 'standing room only' for concerts.[18] Like cinema, music afforded sweet release from cold, threadbare, darkened homes. Then there was a deliberate effort to recolour the entire feeling of *Heimat*, that sense that the land was home; it was the communist Berliners who once more began rhapsodizing on the importance of walking expeditions, drinking in the beauty of the countryside and the forests around the city. (Such walks could be suddenly halted in nauseated fright: throughout the grim process of merging the communists and the Social Democrats, murderous purges had resulted, and outside the city the corpses of recently killed dissidents might be stumbled across on woodland trails, rigid hands emerging from snow or leaf-fall. The authorities explained each instance of this by claiming they were corpses of war, but many of these bodies were fresh, and the obvious lie had an element of impatience about it.[19])

In the theatre, too, there were artists who felt that the Soviet vision for Berlin had a purity that neither the British nor the Americans could ever really understand. Bertolt Brecht had been an exile from the city since the advent of Hitler; he had careened from Europe to America. But, in the wake of the war, the American political establishment turned upon Brecht – as well as many others – with a fresh suspicion of his politics. He was blacklisted by Hollywood studios for perceived communist sympathies and summoned to testify before the House Un-American Activities Committee; the summons alone was enough to cast cold shadows on artistic careers. So, in the earliest post-war years, this figurehead of Weimar culture returned to Berlin to form yet one more bridgehead to the past. Brecht was a prestigious addition to the communist landscape: a playwright with a gift that could entertain all, with a political philosophy that would help secure the cultural foundations of the new regime. Brecht believed that theatre had the power to change society. He had obviously taken the liveliest interest in the ongoing Soviet revolution; nor was he blind to the darker cruelties and purges of Stalinism. Yet, when balanced against the horrors inflicted by the Third Reich, he was equally certain that Germany's future now had to be navigated under the influence of Soviet gravity. He and his wife moved back to East Berlin in 1948 and formed a new theatre company called the Berliner Ensemble.[20] Brecht was also able to draw on European bank accounts (unlike his fellow citizens), into which his theatre royalties had been paid across the years.

In terms of courage, that demonstrated by the numbers of Jewish concentration-camp survivors who returned to the city in those immediate post-war years is almost unfathomable. In reality, many had no choice but to come back; nowhere else had been home. In some exceptional cases, it had never stopped being so; Marie Jalowicz-Simon had gone 'underground' and had survived through the kindness of near-strangers. In the dazed aftermath of the conflict, she walked from the suburb of Kaulsdorf back into the city; within a few weeks she was established in a flat in Pankow, in the north-east of the city. A little time after that, she was enrolling at Berlin University. She wrote a remarkable letter to a friend, Aaron Kleinberger, explaining her decision to remain in the city rather than leave for a new life. 'Please don't be surprised if I tell you I that feel I've emigrated already,' she wrote. 'I have emigrated from Hitler's Germany to the Germany of Goethe and Johann Sebastian Bach and I feel very comfortable there.'[21] Yet it was while studying that the repercussive waves of all those years of terror finally hit her; in 1946, she had a breakdown. Over time, she recovered, and decided – after a short period of doubt about her fellow citizens – to stay in Berlin for good, rising through the university as an academic, becoming a professor in philosophy and philology. She married Heinrich Simon in 1948, and the university, in the Soviet sector, was to remain at the core of her intellectual life for decades afterwards.

Others were equally clear that Berlin could not be home again. Instead, it was to be a transit point. These survivors were quite different from the Russian Jewish men and women in the Red Army who had been among those who conquered Berlin. These soldiers were in strict terms secular, but becoming more and more sharply aware of their Jewish identity as the extent of the Nazi nightmare was revealed. As the vanquishers, they had little to fear from the defeated and subdued Germans. But for those who had suffered in the camps the fear was ineradicable. This fear was justified, too. In those post-war months, the US Army quietly conducted a survey in its sector of the city concerning civilian attitudes towards the Jewish people. They found that at least 39 per cent were openly anti-Semitic – 18 per cent of the total radically so.[22] Well over a third of respondents voiced the belief that it would be preferable if the Jewish people remained away from the city.

The US authorities were swift to ensure that everything possible be done to help people who had lived through unimaginable horror, even as their wider families had been murdered. There was a policy of *Wiedergutmachung* – or reparation – that sought to restore stolen property and businesses to those few Jewish people still alive to claim them. The policy was also quickly adopted in the British and the French zones of occupation. The Jewish people were to be afforded as much assistance as possible in recovering these fragments of their lost lives. Even with this avowed intent, few Jewish people could imagine staying. Among those who could not face returning at all was Rabbi Leo Baeck, who had been imprisoned in Theresienstadt and later found a home in Britain. He declared: 'The history of Jews in Germany has found its end. It is impossible for it to come back. The chasm is too great.'[23] This was to be echoed in an official proclamation from the World Jewish Congress a couple of years later when it asserted 'the determination of the Jewish people never again to settle on the blood-stained soil of Germany'.[24] The truth was that hatred of Jewish people was hardly unique to Berliners, or to Germans; it also manifested in Britain and America, and was shortly to be deployed as a weapon by Stalin's Russia. But Berlin was seen as the crucible of this hatred. In the months to follow, for some 250,000 displaced Jewish survivors – a few of whom were initially reluctant to leave newly liberated camps in Poland, for understandable fear of the people who lay beyond those gates – Berlin would be the necessary and brief staging post on a longer journey. Some would emigrate to America (despite some in the US administration being reluctant to accept Jewish immigrants); others were fixed upon Palestine. Amid the ashes of Berlin, there was little that could be done immediately to restore synagogues and old cemeteries to their former dignified beauty. But the Western Allies were at least alive to their humanitarian duties, and the need to offer succour.

In some ways, the communist authorities in the east of Berlin were also sensitive; it had been their armies that had uncovered the vilest of the Nazi atrocities. 'Awareness and shame must burn in every German person,' those authorities declared.[25] And there were Jewish people coming to Berlin who were secular in outlook, and who wished to be part of the reconstruction of a society. 'Nobody came to live as a Jew in East Germany,' said sociologist and writer Irene Runge. 'They wanted to live as Communists. They repressed everything Jewish.'[26] Yet when it came to reparation, Walter Ulbricht and the Soviets were implacable. Property could not be restored to individuals and their families. Nor could businesses be returned. The reason: all property and business rights – regardless of origin – now belonged to the state. Every house and flat, every shop and bank that had been stolen from Jewish owners by the Nazis in the 1930s would now be held by the city's authorities. What they would offer the returning Jewish people was instead a system of marginally advanced healthcare and housing and employment opportunities. In other words, Jewish people would benefit from the new state welfare system, in which housing and work were allocated. There could be no exemptions in a new universal system of equality.

An exception was made in the cases of communal property: old surviving synagogues and cemeteries and Jewish community halls would be returned to the Jewish people. The exquisite golden dome of the Neue Synagoge had been destroyed under blazing skies; but the buildings on either side that had also belonged to the Jewish community survived. As a result, by 1946, these and the remains of the synagogue became one of the focuses for the Jüdische Gemeinde zu Berlin. This body was run by one of the remarkable Jewish figures who had survived the Nazis and the war by going 'underground' in the city. Erich Nehlhans had worked swiftly in the wake of the war to have the less damaged Rykestrasse synagogue in the district of Pankow reopened. This turn-of-the-century structure, with suggestions of modernism in its brick facade, had survived the war in part by being used for military storage. After the war, enough of the synagogue was swiftly restored to hold services there once more; on one occasion, General Berzarin attended as an honoured guest.[27] This synagogue also became an intense draw for camp survivors entering the city; the rooms and offices around the building offered both comfort and sanctuary. There was a brief time when Ulbricht's authorities were helpful about the practicalities of starting to rebuild and reconstruct this and other Jewish centres. And there were Jewish socialists who put their trust in Ulbricht's vision. But, under the Stalinists, this period of safety for Jews throughout Soviet Europe would not last long; under the guise of anti-Zionism, a ghastly new tide of anti-Semitism was to rise. Even by 1947 it was being reported that there were numbers of Polish Jewish people seeking to avoid the east of Germany, and the east of Berlin, by crossing Europe via Czechoslovakia in order to reach the American-occupied zone of Germany more easily.[28] There were also refugees passing through the British and French zones equally determined to reach the US zone. The American authorities could not and would not hold them back.

There was a striking cultural effort in the city to assure the Jewish people that the persecution was over. In the autumn of 1945 there was what might be termed a command performance of an eighteenth-century play called *Nathan the Wise* by Gotthold Ephraim Lessing, which had been banned throughout the Nazi years. The play was set in twelfth-century Jerusalem, at the time of the Third Crusade, and was the story of how a Jewish merchant – his adopted daughter saved from a house fire by a Christian Knight Templar, who falls in love with her – is set a test by the ruler, Saladin, who asks him as part of it: 'Which religion is true?' The challenge – to name which of the Abrahamic faiths is supreme – is shrewd, but it remarkably ends in an affectionate friendship between them. Nathan is then targeted by the Christian Patriarch of Jerusalem, who wants to see him burned at the stake for apostasy. Through various extraordinary turns of events, it turns out that Nathan's adopted daughter was born a Christian, but has blood ties to another Islamic family branch. The play in essence was a heady plea for understanding that all three Abrahamic faiths were equal, and that those who followed them should have no barriers to their love. The figure of Nathan was said to have been based in part upon the eighteenth-century philosopher Moses Mendelssohn, and the part was essayed by the actor so beloved of the Red Army, Paul Wegener. Twenty-five years beforehand, Wegener had mesmerized the world with a magical Jewish folk tale. Now, after the unbearable foulness of the Holocaust, he was once more upon a Berlin stage, a gentile playing a Jew, in an effort to help restore some humanity to the city. Unfortunately, according to historian Atina Grossmann, the audiences were not composed of ordinary Berliners, but rather mostly military officers from both the US and the Soviet sides: Jewish personnel who could speak German.[29] Yet Wegener was still making a powerful symbolic statement with his performance. It came to form the epilogue for his life; when the play was revived once more – this time for audiences of Berliner civilians in 1948 – Wegener collapsed on the first night. He died a short time later.

Elsewhere there were outbreaks of extraordinary insensitivity. Bearing in mind the apocryphal dictum from one Hollywood producer that 'he who controls cinema controls Germany'[30] (itself paraphrasing Lenin's 'He who controls Berlin controls Germany; and he who controls Germany controls Europe'), the British sector had in 1949 called upon studio owner J. Arthur Rank to export a range of British films to western Germany, and to Berlin cinemas. Adaptations of Charles Dickens novels were felt to have suitable universality; recent versions of *Great Expectations* (1946) and *Nicholas Nickleby* (1947) were shipped out, as was David Lean's 1948 production of *Oliver Twist*. This was scheduled to play at the Kurbel in February 1949. As soon as it was exhibited, the outcry began. By the second screening there were protestors in the cinema. After a week or so there were an estimated 200 demonstrators outside the building, chanting and throwing stones at police. The police responded with truncheon blows and fire hoses. At one stage, gunshots were fired into the cold night air.[31] The reason for the fury was the portrayal of Fagin by Alec Guinness, who had been fitted with a prosthetic hook nose and a matted fright wig, and who gave the character an exaggerated accent and droning tone. Lit luridly, and shot from disconcerting angles, Lean and Guinness between them had created an almost medieval Jewish stereotype. From the perspective of those protesting, there was little difference between this and the notorious Nazi Werner Krauss vehicle *Jud Süss*. The reaction came as no surprise in the US sector; the film had been withheld from American cinemas because of these very concerns. 'Between Dickens and director Lean,' declared *Life* magazine, history had 'interposed the ghosts of six million murdered Jews and the spectre of genocide'. It was 'hard to guess' why the British authorities had not only passed the film, but also then persisted in screening it even as the protests grew.[32] The film was withdrawn days later.

And, at around the same time, the director of *Jud Süss* was facing trial on a charge that his 1940 film had encouraged crimes against humanity. Veit Harlan, having seen the controversy around Lean's *Twist*, pleaded to the members of the court that if his film had whipped up poisonous hatred, then exactly the same charge should be levelled against David Lean and J. Arthur Rank.[33] This might have been one reason why, eventually, Harlan was acquitted. But the star of *Jud Süss* was treated more severely. Werner Krauss, who had once terrified world audiences as Dr Caligari, was initially banned from acting in German films or on the German stage. He underwent a denazification programme and the ban was gradually lifted, but his return to the West Berlin stage in Ibsen's *John Gabriel Borkmann* in 1950 (to the delight of many theatre-going fans) also sparked fiercely anguished protests outside the Kurfürstendamm theatre and his swift withdrawal. There were clearly those in Berlin who were eager to forget, and many younger people who would not let them.

How might hearts be won? In the British sector in the summer of 1947 there was a curiously gauche entertainment given at the vast Olympic stadium, which for this one performance attracted large numbers of curious Berliners. The show was a gala military tattoo staged by the British army. Even the idea of it had caused flutters of bewilderment back in London. There were questions asked in the House of Commons about its purpose. The response: to raise money for needy Berliner children.[34] As such, the cause was unanswerable. Yet the spectacle presented to those Berliner children, and many thousands of adults, was at best a naïve attempt to project the benevolence of the occupying British soldiers. The show began with marching bands; there was a recreation of an eighteenth-century cavalry charge, horses and flags flowing elegantly. There were synchronized displays of physical training exercises with weights and movement; Highland dancing was accompanied lustily on bagpipes as the men from five Scottish regiments executed their moves arm-in-arm around crossed swords. Perhaps the most curious aspect of this entire show came as the sun set, and as the British soldiers began marching around the stadium with flaming torches, their figures picked out with intense searchlights. The aesthetic echo of Albert Speer, and of the Nazis' dramatic contrast of fire and darkness, was both odd and misjudged. As would be expected, the military governor of the British Zone of Occupation, Marshal of the Royal Air Force William Sholto Douglas, was there; his guest for the evening was General Lucius Clay, military governor of the US zone. While it is difficult to know what many of the spectators made of the show, word did not take long to reach the authorities in the Soviet sector. A few weeks later there was British outrage at a short documentary film – part of the *Der Augenzeuge* (The Eyewitness) series made by the Soviets – being shown in cinemas across the city. It took footage from the grand British tattoo and footage of the British soldiers talking to Berliner children, and spliced these images with horrific shots of the war dead, mutilated and decaying, and with shots of makeshift wooden crosses half buried in snow. The message of the film was that the British were glorifying military violence, and that the Olympic stadium show was one step along an imperialist road that could only ever lead to death.[35]

But it was an Italian director who – fresh from cataloguing the aftermath of fascism in his own land – was intent upon exploring Berlin's most gaping psychic wounds. Roberto Rossellini had in mind a story that would lay bare the city's crushing weight of grief and nihilistic hopelessness. His scenario was *Germany Year Zero* (the idea of 'Year Zero' was used among the Allies to describe the need to reset the German consciousness in the wake of the Nazis); it remains nauseatingly powerful and bleak today. The story involved a twelve-year-old boy living with his ill father and an older sister under pressure to prostitute herself. The boy tries to learn the dodges of black marketeering, falls in with a group of delinquent adolescents and then encounters a former schoolteacher who has lost none of his Nazi beliefs, and who now also seems to be a child molester. The boy's sick father declares that he wants to die, and that he wishes he had the courage to commit suicide. The boy, taking this outpouring seriously, procures poison, puts it in his father's tea and kills him. Now in despair, the boy climbs the ruins of a church and throws himself from the top.

The actors were not professionals; Rossellini preferred using amateurs. There were multiple layers of terrible sadness; the leading boy was cast because he strongly resembled Rossellini's late son. The starkness of the locations, combined with the gruelling vision of Berliners on the edge of a moral abyss and the final horror of a child committing suicide, meant that there was no appetite to see the film in Berlin itself. Even internationally there was a sense of critical dismay. Some were anxious that the rest of the world should not become accustomed to looking at Berlin and Berliners like this; what hope for the future could there be if they did? (This horrible realism was markedly different from the stylized noir of *The Murderers are Among Us*.)

Yet, in 1948, the power and reach of newsreel film – documentary images rather than dramatic ones – were going to help convey to the world a different kind of desperation, and this time a narrative of American heroes flying in to help Berlin's children. The post-war ambiguity of Berlin disguised the fact that the city had become of crucial importance to both the Soviets and the Americans. The power share was messy, and frayed at the edges, the Soviets aggressively policing council meetings, the Americans suffusing the city with the seduction of their RIAS (Radio in the American Sector) broadcasts, rich with jazz and swing. Quite without either of the new super-powers consciously realizing it, the city had moved beyond illustrating their respective victories to symbolizing the most acutely sensitive Cold War nerve ending; a potential nuclear flashpoint.

## 18.   The Islanders

Even before the Wall was built, its shadow could be discerned. It had been prophesied in a Berlin satirical magazine called *Ulenspiegel*, which in 1946 published a cartoon featuring the city bisected by bricks, with a figure holding an American flag on one side, and, on the other side, a man with the Soviet flag.[1] By 1948, Berlin was a city in a quantum state, with different realities being lived within its borders simultaneously. On Ackerstrasse, to the north of the city centre, and close to the decaying concrete hulk of the Humboldthain flak tower, the chasm that was growing between West and East developed in part close to the line of this street's course as it met with Bernauer Strasse, at first in occasional bushes of barbed wire amid the semi-ruined tenement blocks. In 1948, and from there onwards, a section of this street – and the borderline upon which it stood – would become one of the most visibly sensitive sites in the accelerating mistrust and fear on both sides. It was Berlin areas such as this that would soon draw the eyes of the world: not now for reasons of queasy moral fascination about the dissolution of Nazism but because of icy tension about the explosive possibilities of new conflict that could spread from here across the continent. Ackerstrasse had always been one of Berlin's rawest areas; earlier in the century, Meyerhof, a mighty near-slum tenement complex, rising high into the sky and fretted through with nine inner courtyards so enclosed by vertiginous walls that daylight could barely reach the bottom, was regarded with a terrible kind of wonder. Artists had long been drawn to Ackerstrasse; ever unhelpfully, the skittish and hard-eyed George Grosz drew a hideous picture of a decapitated corpse lying on a bed within one of the tenements and called the sketch 'Lustmord in der Ackerstrasse'.[2] No less ominously, Gustav Wunderwald painted an epic canvas called 'Brücke über die Ackerstrasse' in 1927 – a powerfully lowering composition of a mighty iron railway bridge bisecting the street with its high-rise tenements, under a thick and muddy sky.[3] Ackerstrasse had also been renowned for its

Weimar violence; the regular blade and bullet confrontations between young Nazis and communists. This was, as one resident who was later to become a policeman in the post-war city put it, an area of crime and prostitution, punctuated with bars filled with 'easy girls and big men'.[4] Yet it had its moments of solidarity too; it was in Ackerstrasse in the war years that some residents offered help and support to cruelly treated forced labourers. Now, working-class women and their families were being pulled in two directions. The Soviets, who had inspired such fear, and had inflicted such mass sexual trauma, were seeking to reassure Berliners that theirs was the true civilization; that through grand concerts of German classical composers, and performances of classic German plays, and with uplifting radio broadcasts, they were the power that would restore Berlin's greatness. Nothing was said of the all-enveloping new East German security service, with its penchant for clandestine violence against those held arbitrarily, and which stood comparison with the Gestapo and SS, nor of the continued existence of Berlin's concentration camp, nor of the countless still-missing Berlin soldiers who had been captured by the Red Army at the end of the war. At the same time, the civilians living on that intersection between Ackerstrasse and Bernauer Strasse looked towards the Western-occupied sectors, and their brighter seductions: the joyous return to cinema screens of rich Technicolor and, for the younger people in the dance halls, ever more addictive swing music.

In those first post-war months, the internal borders of Berlin were perfectly porous; women and men could move from east to west and vice versa for work, for leisure, for family and friends, as long as they had identity papers to hand. But the tensions had been building ever since the Western Allies in the lands outside Berlin had pulled back, leaving the east of Germany to be subsumed wholly within the Soviet system. Even though the country had yet to be formally split into two nations, there was an Inner German Border that ran down the length of the divided nation; Dr Alfred Wege recalled how outside the city at Marienborn, a railway station on the border, 'interzone passes' had to be shown, and Red Army soldiers would pursue civilians who were dodging across rails to clamber on to departing trains without showing their papers.[5] Matters were more complex in Berlin itself; lying deep within Soviet territory, the city became in some

ways a Schrödinger-like anomaly; simultaneously communist and capitalist, simultaneously speaking Russian and English, simultaneously
listening to Soviet radio talks concerning industrial reconstruction
and the sweet blue notes of American jazz. Some things were still
universal: the winter of 1947 was exceptionally torturous, and all
households, east and west, suffered atrociously in frozen homes with
scanty food and coal supplies. Berlin's winters were already renowned
for their harshness; after the hunger and depletions of conflict and
bombing, the snow found fresh opportunities to swirl and infiltrate
into all corners of life. And then, emerging from this cruelty, Berliners were to find in 1948 that a new rigidity was coming to the lines
that divided their city into sectors of occupation.

The city's internal borders were mostly invisible; they ran through
courtyards and cemeteries alike, across roads, through lush patches
of woodland. Yet on either side of this internal line – which also
at some points bisected apartment buildings, meaning that one could
leave a flat, walk along a corridor, find a fire exit and enter another
sector – there were different laws and ideologies a universe apart.
Those who were paid to enforce these laws frequently lived on the
other side of this divide: many policemen in the American sector
of Berlin had their homes in the Soviet sector, for example.[6] Occasionally, at busy traffic junctions, the border was marked out with painted
white lines; signage warned which sector lay ahead in German, Russian, English and French. But anomalies were also causing friction
along these divisions: not merely the tides of Coca-Cola that flowed
through the US sector, and then east, to which Berliner children
became instantly addicted; not merely curious spectacles like the return
of pony-and-trap races out at the racecourse, with the city's more affluent women dressed as elegantly in the New Look as any Parisian
socialite;[7] but also other matters, such as the abundance of meat to be
(shadily) obtained in the western sectors when supplies of the better
cuts in the east were sparser. The result was expeditions in which even
vast shoulders of meat were concealed beneath coats and taken back
east on U-Bahn trains that were filled with sharp-eyed Soviet-sector
policemen there to catch anyone seeking to violate rationing and
restrictions on food movement. Then there was the disparity in currency. In the west of the city, old Reichsmarks were being used. New

Reichsmarks were printed by the Soviets, but, because they printed so many, their value diminished by the day.

The crackling growls of thunder that followed war, and which seemed to herald fresh conflict, continued to be heard throughout the city. This was partly in the form of occasional nocturnal bursts of gunfire, as drunken Soviet and US servicemen threatened one another emptily; but mostly they found shape in hard economics. Following the devastation that had swallowed millions of lives, and hollowed out the world's finances, the Americans looked upon their western zone of Germany, and determined that its banking and trade had to be rebuilt and made better than before. Its industries had to be fully restored, and the profitable benefits then be seen to be rippling out across Europe and (by extension) back to America. This confuted the Soviet claim to long-term reparations from the German nation. The US plan equally applied to Allied-occupied Berlin, since it too contained vast and innovative industry, including Siemens and AEG Turbinen. In addition to this was the idea of propping up regeneration with US aid money: the Marshall Plan. And here could be seen the first magnesium flashes of anger as the Soviets wholly rejected the principle of capitalist funding. It was a bald extension of power. Not only would such money be rejected from Soviet Europe, but it would also – they determined – play no part in Berlin.

It had been the assumption of the Soviets that, in a short time, the British and the Americans would withdraw both from Berlin and from western Germany; their planning was for a wholly unified country that would be subsumed into communism and answerable only to Moscow. President Truman had not suggested that an American presence was to be permanent. However, the sparks of irritation and intransigence in Berlin between the US and Soviet sectors were building. The Americans and the British in the meantime halted the movement of some technological and industrial equipment from west to east. There was more. The Americans were determined that, in western Germany as a whole, there had to be a fresh, regenerated currency, guarding against the conflagration of inflation and giving economic stability and legitimacy to businesses of all sizes. This currency – the Deutschmark – would be introduced in the west of Berlin too. It became legal tender in the late spring of 1948.

The Soviet authorities refused to countenance the new currency; there were proclamations that only Reichsmarks were permissible. Yet what in their eyes was an infection had already taken hold. Using the transport corridors across rural Soviet eastern Germany into the west of Berlin – air, rail, road – the Americans had imported some 250 million fresh new Deutschmarks into their sector of the city, which was to be merged with the British and French districts to create a 'tri-zone' in August 1948. Very swiftly, despite the fact that they were not legal tender in the Soviet zone, they spread across the border like a virus. All of this was intolerable to the communists; it corroded the foundations of the society that they were trying to lay down. In addition to this was their frustration that Berlin had a city-wide municipal authority that resisted the communist grip, despite agitators at meetings. The Soviets withdrew from this layer of administration. All of this was akin to a maddening itch on Stalinist skin. That snarling roar of post-war thunder grew louder and closer. Now the Soviets were certain – for the sake of their own system – that the Americans had to be pressurized out. The entirety of Berlin had to be theirs. This meant that the combined troops and officials of the Americans, British and French sectors would have to be forced out.

And it was here that the decisive geopolitical realignment of an entire continent was frozen in place. US diplomat George Kennan had outlined in his 'long telegram' (an 8,000-word essay sent via telegram to Secretary of State James Byrnes) the need for the Soviets – and for Stalin's tendency towards conspiracy – to be contained.[8] Berlin was the border at which the flashpoint of a new world war was possible. And for those Berliners living in the American, British and French zones, there was arising a new source of uncertain dread: reports of Soviet tanks barring key roads, and of railway lines being blocked, and even of some of the city's waterways being jammed by Soviet vessels. There had been a minor form of blockade a few weeks earlier: trains to and from the west of Germany had been held for hours and even days at checkpoints by Soviet officials. This tactic highlighted the acute vulnerability of those routes out of West Berlin. These transport corridors, crossing a hundred miles of Soviet territory before reaching the West, were slender: delicate veins upon which pressure could easily be exerted. They were there on trust, an agreement between the Soviets and the US, a Potsdam afterthought. Now the Soviets were severing them. On 24 June 1948, rail traffic was halted between east and west, and by both sides; the US was stopping industrial resources being sent into the Soviet zone.

In West Berlin there arose immediate and profound fear that this would be a hunger blockade; a siege intended to starve them. Since the end of the war, urban famine had been a constant – and perfectly rational – fear. Now it sharpened. West Berlin had thirty-six days' supply of food, it was reported, and a little over six weeks' worth of fuel. People began stockpiling in dizzy flurries of distress. Moreover, the Soviets had control of most of the city's electricity-generating stations, so as well as the prospect of precariously dwindling supplies of bread, potatoes, milk and other necessities, West Berliners were also facing the idea of evenings in darkness. Overall, the Allied sectors of the city were portrayed as being in sudden, terrible, isolation, at the mercy of the monstrous tyranny of Stalin. Yet, over the next few months, both superpowers were to magnify their own propaganda as the Berlin Blockade got underway, for as the Americans denounced the cold cruelty, so the Soviets declared that they were imagining it. Soviet Military Governor Marshal Sokolovsky proclaimed: 'There was and is no blockade of Berlin.'[9] In a sly way, there was an atom of truth in this. The city, this quantum realm, continued to hold within itself multiple realities. At the start of the crisis, the Western authorities were genuinely alarmed: US figures foresaw 'an almost total breakdown' of West Berlin;[10] as well as hunger and cold, they envisaged the factories and offices closing, and unemployment – that old Berlin spectre – returning; they foresaw a reversion to the primitive survivalism of 1945, and of mass civil unrest on the streets. Yet, although the world's newsreel cameras were to be trained upon the soon-to-unfold spectacular heroism of the Allied response, there was ambiguity on the streets that lay close to the as-yet undivided Berlin interior border zones. Those in West Berlin were apprised of the fact that they were under siege; those in the eastern sector, many of whom had families and friends in the west, were told that the Americans and the British were behaving hysterically; that if needs be, the Soviets could always provide.

The Berlin Airlift was an operation that few thought possible. The one route into the west of the city that had not been jammed by the Soviets was the air corridor that had been permitted from the west of Germany. At first, the Americans did not consider that sending aeroplanes into West Berlin with essential supplies could even begin to touch the crisis; the sheer number of aeroplanes needed, combined with the super-fast turnaround required to get the cargo unloaded and each plane back in the air before another following close behind arrived seemed too daunting. It was the British sector, however, that had pointed the way; during earlier mini-blockades several months previously, the RAF had been used to bring in supplies. Britain's pugnacious Labour foreign secretary Ernest Bevin was now enthusiastically supporting the idea of unfurling this on a grander scale. The unconfirmed Mayor of Berlin (unconfirmed because the Soviets vetoed his appointment) was Ernst Reuter. US General Lucius Clay told him:

> Look, I am ready to try an airlift. I can't guarantee it will work. I am sure that even at its best, people are going to be cold and people are going to be hungry. And if the people of Berlin won't stand that, it will fail. And I don't want to go into this unless I have your assurance that the people will be heavily in approval.[11]

Reuter – who had been in exile throughout the Nazi years, and who had no intention of tolerating the totalitarianism of Stalin – would prove adept at galvanizing the spirits of West Berliners. For, even at the start, the idea of the 'people of Berlin' excluded the communist supporters of East Berlin.

The superpowers were a universe apart, but those who lived under them in Berlin were not doing so for ideological reasons. These were streets in which ideologies were a matter of chance; they just happened to be where their homes were. Their futures had been determined by improvised lines drawn on maps elsewhere. There were a great many in the west of the city who counted themselves exceedingly fortunate that their lives lay under that American umbrella, but there were also people in the east who approved of the socialist path; a number of young women, especially, appreciated the gestures to workplace equality that the Soviet system offered.[12] The people of East Berlin were themselves informed via Soviet media that what the US called a blockade was simply the Soviet Union taking over 'supply of the population of all Berlin'.[13]

The crisis that developed found a visually arresting locus at Tempelhof airport, in the south of the city, one of the more elegant Nazi legacies to Berlin. As the daily airlift – Operation Vittles – got underway, the weird beauty of it captured the imaginations of younger Berliners: those who had only the haziest memories of the Allied bombing campaign. From July 1948 the skies above the city glinted with silver at ever more frequent intervals as, with mere seconds between them, a variety of aircraft approached, circled, landed, refuelled and took off once more. The logistics were mesmeric: even discounting the occasions when the planes were harried by Soviet fighters, or dazzled by Soviet floodlights (it was reckoned that there were several hundred such incidents) there was an astounding geometric precision to the patterns of the flights, and the careful spacing between them. There were accidents; planes overshooting the runway, flames and crew deaths. Tragic though these were, the overwhelming majority of the flights reached the tarmac in safety. West Berliners soon became accustomed to the regularity of the droning. Children gathered by the landing strips at Tempelhof and Wiesbaden; the spectacle of the silver Dakotas, the idea of all the fine food being hauled out from within, the crews served coffee from vans, the planes taxiing out on to the runways, the exquisite rhythm and roar of the take-off as they soared upwards into the clouds. These planes were not just providing civilian supplies and civilian household fuel, but also imported food, drink and textiles for the occupying US forces and their wives and families. Thus for the West, the story of Berlin was simple and stark: Stalin was starving civilians and it was the duty of America and Britain to stand by the Berliners and help them through this hour of mortal desperation. The Berlin Blockade was both a frightening moment of revelation – the unveiling of the true animosity and bottomless distrust between the US and the Soviets as the world's only superpowers – but also an opportunity for the US to display the virtue of its principles to the wider world. There were a great number of newsreels made for consumption not only in US and British cinemas but also in the cinemas of West Berlin. The unceasing aerial procession of glittering aeroplanes, the succour of those large sacks of vegetables, of tinned fish and meat, being lowered down the ramps, and the footage of young Berlin women, elegantly attired in the Kurfürstendamm, pausing by shops that had been forced to shutter by shortages, powerfully conveyed the impression of a total siege.

There were days of electrical drama. In September, after repeated disturbances created by communist supporters at the Neues Stadthaus who leaned towards what they saw as the purity of the Soviet vision, the city council reconvened in the British sector. At a vast mass counter-demonstration held on 9 September, the mayor, Ernst Reuter, took to the steps of the ruined Reichstag, looking out over a prospect of 300,000 Berliners. When at last he spoke, the roar from the vast crowd was like a tidal wave. 'Today, no diplomat or general will speak or negotiate,' he declared. 'Today the people of Berlin make their voice heard. People of America, England, France, Italy – look at this city. You cannot abandon this city and its people. You should not abandon it.'[14]

The tensions were stretched by the curious unreadability of the Soviet reasons for the blockade. It was understood that they wanted to eject the US, British and French authorities, and their soldiers, and their families; it was understood they wanted complete political dominion over this symbolically strategic capital. What was not understood was how far they were willing to risk armed conflict to do so. Was this a declaration of a new war? Or were they acting upon the assumption that the Americans would soon give up maintaining a presence in Germany and Europe generally, and that pressure was required to hasten the process?

Nor it seemed would the Soviets relent. As the year rolled on and the days darkened, one of the sharpest deprivations was that of the comfort of light. Each district of the city was allocated a rationed period of electricity – two hours in the morning, another two in the late afternoon/early evening. But the hours became distended; sometimes the electricity allocation for a street or area would not come on until 11 p.m. And even though local news information kept citizens abreast of when they might have a chance to do some cooking, or even simply read by lamplight, the erratic rationed hours in turn affected the circadian rhythms of the working population. The effect was tiredness and tension. That tension was magnified for those reliant upon a reliable supply of electricity: for instance, dentists who did not want their drills to cut out halfway through excavating a patient's tooth.[15] There was also a period in which household candles were in very short supply. Yet as people continued to go to their jobs, and children continued to go to school, and as the supplies of vegetables and tinned goods in the grocery shops appeared to remain stable (though there was dismay about the quantities of dried potato powder, which could be used to make mash), it might also have become clearer that the Berlin Blockade was not simply about naked Stalinist aggression, but also comprised a curious struggle for hearts and souls. In those lightless autumn blockade evenings, West Berliners who were near to the Reichstag could look through the Brandenburg Gate to the Soviet sector beyond, where it was possible to see 'brightly lit streets and neon signs'.[16]

Yet it was also possible for West Berliners with identity papers and inter-zone passes to do more than see: they could pass into the Soviet sector and walk around those brightly lit streets themselves. Those interior borders were still porous to a limited extent. Public transportation was fragmented; 'underground trains run from the east to the Soviet boundary but they stop there and go back'.[17] Tram routes were similarly bisected in places. But, for those on foot, there were fewer hindrances to crossing over those sectors. As the blockade continued, the Soviets encouraged such movement, like figures from a fairy tale laying a trail of sweets. Most strikingly, they offered West Berliners special rations of food and fuel from the Soviet-controlled east of the country. The Soviets were portraying themselves as paternalistic providers, unifying Berliners where the Americans and the British sought only to divide them. 'Soviet help for Berliners!' declared the headline in one eastern sector newspaper.[18] Another shouted: 'West Berliners! Food and fuel lies stacked up in the Eastern sector for Western sector populace!'[19] Nor was this a complete Stalinist lie; extra supplies had indeed been shipped in and there state-run shops that were offering not only food but also cigarettes and 'textiles'.[20] So many perishable groceries had been brought into East Berlin that the surplus began to spoil. By the autumn of 1948, some 5 per cent of West Berliners agreed to receiving supplies from the east. The other 95 per cent declined.

Part of the reason for this – resistance to totalitarianism aside – was that the airlift itself was so successful; it was estimated that, in terms of daily calorie intake, West Berliners were actually marginally better off than they had been before the blockade started. In addition to this, they had risen with enthusiasm to practical challenges, such as repairing the Tempelhof runway and constructing an additional one before the deep ice of winter. There was no need of either Soviet food or Soviet cigarettes. In addition to this, the US Air Force, in conjunction with the government, was shrewdly adept with propaganda. The heart-warming story of Gail Halvorsen, the pilot who brought sweets, chocolates and chewing gum over with West Berlin's deprived children in mind, captured imaginations effortlessly. After one food drop, Halvorsen – waiting on the Tempelhof field – was haunted by the gaunt gathered children. He offered them what chewing gum he had; the intense care with which they broke the sticks for sharing, and even sniffed the wrappers, touched him.[21] Halvorsen let it be known, via newspaper and newsreel interviews, that when he flew over he would give the wings of the plane a 'wiggle' so that they would know that it was him. And from this plane he would drop – in handkerchief parachutes – everything from boiled sweets to spearmint gum. He was now 'Uncle Wiggly Wings' and he dropped somewhere in the region of twenty-three tons of confectionery.[22] Just three years previously, pilots like Halvorsen had been dropping incendiaries and setting the city ablaze. Now the world could see their benevolence. British foreign secretary Ernest Bevin – a socialist, and also a dedicated anti-communist – had declared in a speech that the Berlin Airlift would show the Soviets 'what air power could do'.[23] But this was a new kind of power extended to an ingenious degree. Where the Soviets moved with cruelty – the prison camps, the disorientating trials and speedy executions – the Americans were seen to be bringing joy to the children of their former enemies. Christmas of 1948 saw the daily arrival of American planes laden with brightly wrapped presents: children were taken to Tempelhof airfield, and were mute with delight as aeroplane doors opened to reveal Santa Claus. Gift packages were handed out; the children were filmed poring over toys and games, and sharing sweets.[24] The airlift meant too that the West Berlin shops dazzled at Christmas; the trees, the toy cars, the toy dolls. In community halls, children were filmed enjoying mass Christmas lunches. The implication was that, in the Soviet sector, such joy and abundance were prohibited. Yet, even with all this, there were Berliners who felt ambivalent: these were still foreign powers that had ultimate control over their lives and, it seemed, their prosperity.

'They felt like the children of an unhappy home,' ran one report at the end of 1948, concerning the way Berliners viewed all the occupying forces. 'When the grown-ups came to blows, the children felt it best to look the other way and get on with their own games. Further, they felt nothing can be much worse than what they had passed through in the war and in the peace; and he who knows the worst has little to fear . . . They are,' the correspondent concluded, 'the worst targets in the world for propaganda.'[25] Perhaps so; but the propaganda was not entirely intended for Berliner consumption. It was there to explain to Western readers why this was a way of life worth defending.

But nor did the wider world hear much of the surprising flexibility that existed in this period between west and east when it came to industrial power supplies, nor of Berliners making day trips out to the surrounding (communist) woods, and the moments when Berliners from both sides would greet each other on those rich forest paths, all quietly foraging for fruits and nuts, regardless of political affiliation or belief. In the British sector, the factories were still working, obtaining about a quarter of their fuel from the Soviet sector via labyrinthine yet open-eyed deals. The British deputy commander disclosed that, 'despite the blockade, far more raw materials come from the Soviet area of control than from the western zones'.[26]

From the point of view of West Berliner families, that quantum state of seeing and moving through different realities became ever more layered. In the east of the city, a new kind of 'free shop' began opening up, offering 'luxury goods' as well as food;[27] West Berliners were most welcome to cross the city, identity papers and ration coupons permitting, and explore these intriguing retail opportunities. Nor would there be any trouble with the Soviet-sector police checking for contraband, for each purchase would come with specially approved coupons. As the autumn air gave way to the knife-sharpness of Berlin winter, those West Berliners who had not been able to obtain sufficient coal from their own suppliers via the airlifts were instead invited to board S-Bahn suburban trains for the short journey across the zonal border to the wooded town of Potsdam; there, the

Soviet authorities had ensured that there were large quantities of brown coal, which could be carried back with relative ease on the return trains. On some streets there were checkpoints; on some tram routes police officers made random searches of bags and briefcases. Such checks were not made in the postal system, though: sundered families, with relatives dotted in both sectors, still received mail, and people in the Soviet sector who found that they had a little food to spare – from bratwurst to macaroni to small jars of jam – were free to post them to West Berlin. There were mentions made in the US and British press of black marketeering, but each situation with each individual family was rather more nebulous than that.

And, while the spirit of resistance to monolithic Soviet control was strong in the west of the city, the bald fact was that these Berliners were by themselves almost wholly powerless. Throughout the blockade, the calculations of calories, and the precise levels of rations required, were decided by the US and the British authorities, not by those they were feeding. Near the start of the airlift, there had been abrasive encounters between the Americans and the British about increasing the rations, and also about the provision of coal; it was the Americans who decreed that the West Berliners could tolerate more austerity, and that, even in the paralysing cold of the Berlin winter, too much household coal might paradoxically encourage illness, by constantly changing the temperatures of homes (a not uncommon belief at a time before central heating). The Americans possibly had the deeper psychological understanding of the people they were both governing and looking after; older Berliners indeed had great experience of both hunger and cold. They understood that chaos could become perfectly routine. It was noted a little after the blockade by a US health journal that 'austerity was no new thing to them', and that, while 2,000 calories a day was a precarious subsistence, it was still better than the 1,800 calories a day they had been living on beforehand.[28] There were cases of 'under-nutrition', with appearances of 'pallor' and gauntness; these were to be found chiefly among 'boys, adolescents, and men of large physique'.[29] There was an appetite, above all, for fat and for sugar. Throughout the blockade, there had been plentiful dried meat, but it was 'far from popular'.[30] While 'Uncle Wiggly Wings' made the hearts of the children soar, their parents dreamed of cheese. But West Berliners, in the main, were perfectly able to endure the privations. They wanted the Americans to stay. And, as the terms of the world's new geopolitical conflict resolved and became clearer, President Truman was adamant that they would stay too. Throughout the blockade, a bitterly realistic term had gained currency: 'Wir sind bloss Objekte' ('We are just objects').[31] The citizens understood that, although Berlin held the world's gaze as the tectonic fault line between two mighty powers, they had very little agency themselves.

Food was not the only battleground; so too was art. It was in the middle of the Berlin Blockade that the city's greatest playwright, Bertolt Brecht, had elected to return, and to offer his services to the Soviets. In January 1949 the Soviet zone claimed a cultural victory with the staging of Brecht's *Mother Courage and Her Children*, set during the seventeenth-century Thirty Years' War, when blood flowed in rivers across Europe.[32] Brecht's modernism seemed on the one hand to be on a happy continuum from the creative vortex of Weimar; on the other, it signified dignity. It would take several years before Brecht began to see a little more of the truth behind the regime of Walter Ulbricht.

But, while the Soviet sector could boast of nutritious theatre and exquisite opera, the British sector authorities offered – again at the height of the blockade – a quite different form of culture for the citizens who lived under their jurisdiction. Late summer 1948 brought the Festival of Elizabethan England.[33] In one way, this seemed as quirky an idea for entertaining the masses as the earlier military tattoos. Yet here was the Cambridge Christopher Marlowe Society performing *Measure for Measure*. There was music in beautiful surroundings too. 'Saturday's concert of motets, madrigals and English folk songs took place in the spacious garden of a Berlin mansion in the Grunewald district,' wrote *The Times* correspondent.[34] Above the singers, lending a note of unintended kitsch, were 'British soldiers dressed in the scarlet and black costumes of Beefeaters'.[35]

The blockade also brought forth comedy, which might have proved the most potent cultural force of all. The American services radio channel RIAS commissioned a new regular Berlin satire/cabaret show called *Die Insulaner* (The Islanders). Here again was an echo of Weimar, but this time sponsored by the Americans, and avowedly anti-Soviet. Led by Günter Neumann, kicking off with a stirring theme song proclaiming that 'the islanders will never lose their calm'[36] (those 'islanders' being blockaded West Berliners) and with a band of actors who played recurring Berlin stereotypes to be found in both west and east, the show delighted a gleeful audience in all sectors. There were two female characters who met in the Kurfürstendamm to gossip scandalously about their neighbours; there were sketches involving confused telephone calls between ordinary Berliners and municipal Socialist Unity Party (SED) functionaries; and there was a quirky Soviet scientist called Professor Quatschnie. The initial aim of the show was to bolster – through sheer high spirits – the resolve of West Berliners in standing up to the oppressive weight of the Soviets. But laughter at its purest is ungovernable, and cannot be kept within arbitrary borders.

The Soviets revoked the blockade on 12 May 1949, some eleven months after they had begun it. A little over a week later, in the west of the country, the advent of the Federal Republic of Germany was announced. Nazism was deemed to be exorcized; many (though by no means all) of the guilty had hanged at Nuremberg. West Germany would have its own constitution, its own reconfigured electoral processes, its own democratic multiparty system. It would also continue to have American and British troops, and their bases; West Germans had no army of their own now, and it was deemed that they needed defending. The North Atlantic Treaty Organization – NATO – was summoned into being. Crucially, even though West Berlin was adrift like a ship far from shore, and even though it was not wholly folded into the West German constitution, it none the less retained the protection and the currency and the same political will; and there too the soldiers would remain. It also benefited from the extraordinary rising tide of trade and prosperity of the new federal West Germany. There was one psychic blow in all of this, however; West Germany needed its own capital – and the modest city of Bonn was selected. Yet the pledges to the people of West Berlin that they would remain a part of this new world were firm. In addition, the accidentally redemptive effect of the Berlin Blockade had been to make the wider world start to see Berliners as something other than Nazis.

If the Soviet calculation over the blockade had been to harass and menace the Western Allies into leaving the city, it had been based on flawed psychology and ideological misunderstanding. Months later, in October 1949, Soviet-controlled eastern Germany itself became the German Democratic Republic, sealing it, and the rest of Berlin, close within the web of communist rule. But, even with the gravitational forces of two opposed superpowers pulling on one city, the borders within Berlin remained frequently invisible and the anomalies became ever more bewildering. The radio stations – American and communist – broadcast their competing programmes, and citizens continued to visit friends and family, and travel to workplaces in other sectors. With two different currencies, two very different legal systems and two diametrically opposed approaches to dealing with dissidents, the impossible contradictions made life increasingly hazardous for many civilians. It would soon be those in the east who paid the most terrible price. For the watching world, the neurosis started by the Berlin Blockade was now to become a continual, gnawing anxiety.

# 19. 'The crowd started howling'

Under skies of grave pale blue, people from either side of the fractured city simply sought to live in a way that much of the world took for granted: working, falling in love, raising families. There was even a resurfacing of the enthusiasm for nudity around certain lakes and woods – more difficult for East Berliners because the post-war communists associated naturism with fascism (though that did not stop a small number of defiant practitioners). The divided city was filled with incongruities. Even the most unremarkable of daily commuter freedoms – a few beers after work before taking the S-Bahn train home – had become jagged with potential hazard. There were instances of inebriated western passengers falling asleep and ending up in the Soviet sector and finding themselves detained in an East Berlin cell if their identity papers were deemed unsatisfactory. Even those who were perfectly sober could be caught out; in the early 1950s the show-business agent of the British musical-film star Gracie Fields was himself held in the Soviet sector for several days on the thinnest of pretexts.[1] The red-and-cream liveried S-Bahn carriages that grumbled across the proud Berlin viaducts were under the sole control of the Soviet authorities, and it was the East Berlin communists who trained the drivers and kept the system supplied with electricity. The stations, even in the western sectors, were avatars for the communist regime. The only newspapers for sale in the kiosks were communist and the guards who patrolled the system were likewise all East Berliners. For West Berlin commuters, and for those travelling to see friends and family, this oddness – following the years of hunger and all of the death that came before that – was simply one more thing to be observed with a cynical eye. This untidy arrangement, whereby Berliners could slip from one ideological universe to another and back again without even especially acknowledging it, was inevitably not to last. On the main rail system, the Soviets had already begun to lay new loop-lines, so that trains from the east had no need to pass through the American and British zones before exiting the city. Transportation by road became akin to the city's nervous system, sparks of tension causing painful shocks. Johann Burianek, a lorry driver, was arrested by the communist authorities and accused of using his border-straddling job for espionage. An East Berlin court found him guilty of terrorist activities. He was guillotined.[2]

In the summer of 1952 more and more 'rifle and machine-gun posts'[3] were springing up in Berlin's more liminal areas: bomb sites, public parks, woodland copses. In the suburbs, on the wider avenues and on suburban heathland, there were 'trenches dug, barricades built'.[4] Walter Ulbricht's communist authorities increasingly sought to make movement in and out of their sector difficult and intimidating. The air occasionally chattered with gunfire; isolated incidents with Russian military threatening to take aim at US military vehicles deemed to be too close to their perimeter. The anger was continual; both sides' newspapers simmered with official denunciations and boiled with rhetoric. In the meantime, the city's lush woodlands were alive with military activity. Trees were felled in lines, creating bare, straight clearings which corresponded to the map-drawn borders; this was not only to monitor walkers through the woods, but also to create clear lines of sight for Soviet border guards to aim and fire – there had to be very good reasons for any walker to be crossing those lines. In 1952, Ulbricht's officials introduced an intensified system of identification for eastern-zone residents; those from the outside required a new permit that could frequently be frustrating to obtain. The blockade had not really ended, merely abated. Now there was a subtler effort from the Soviets to create tighter seals for their territory without sparking armed confrontation with the Americans and the British. In that same summer of 1952 the Soviet authorities severed telephone connections between east and west; this applied to businesses and households alike. Telephone calls, they announced, had been used expressly to communicate 'anti-democratic information' to an extent that had fired 'righteous indignation' in the citizens of the east.[5] The broader intention appeared to be to heighten West Berliners' sense of isolation and vulnerability; how did life on their island seem when they could no longer even make telephone calls to family and friends across the city? But it also made West

Berliners even less trusting of the Soviets; this heavy-handed use
of power was the kind of totalitarianism that they had seen before.
There were retaliatory moves from the US and the British authorities in the city, acting with the mayor, Ernst Reuter. The first involved
radio: another of the anomalies of the Potsdam settlement was that
the large broadcasting station that lay within the British sector was
operated and programmed by the Soviets. For a few days in the
summer of 1952 a minor siege developed; British troops and West Berlin
officials and police surrounded the building to ensure that no one
could enter. Those within were free to leave, but many chose not to.

This performative siege had its moments of bathos. Food and drink
were allowed into the building, the water and electricity supplies
were maintained (despite the claims of the communist authorities
to the contrary) and the heavyweight radio programming – including
lectures on progressive agricultural methods, and upon the future
of industry – continued. But there were more escapist programmes
too, including live performances of light classical German music. A
rumour circulated in West Berlin that the trombonists had been
seen leaving the radio building. This was countered by enthusiastic
broadcasts of trombone playing to prove that they had not.[6]

There were other curious moments when that precarious Berlin
peace was threatened: one came with a small community on the very
north-western outskirts called Eiskeller (ice cellar – so named because,
in the profound Berlin winters, this tiny area somehow contrived to
be ten degrees colder even than the rest of the city). Although semi-
rural, its thin trees shivering in freezing winds, it lay within the
British sector, part of a zone described as a 'frying pan', with Eiskeller
being the pan and the route joining it to the city the handle.[7] It also
lay close to Spandau prison, where Albert Speer and other prominent
Nazis were serving their sentences. There was intense dismay among
the few citizens of Eiskeller when – at around the same time as the
minor radio-station siege – the Soviet military authorities began digging trenches directly across the path that gave them access to the city.
As the Soviets saw it, this was an area that lay within the East German
countryside; the residents saw themselves as staunch West Berliners.
There was little the British forces and West Berlin police could do other
than take up positions on that bleak and less-travelled roadway

themselves. Eiskeller residents were harassed by Soviet military and East German police on every journey. As the radio crisis began to ease – the British authorities once more allowed the communists into the building, albeit now with special passes – so too did the pressure on Eiskeller, with the guards at the trenches visibly relaxing.

There had been a similar moment of crisis over another village, this one at the edge of Zehlendorf in the south-western extremity of the city. The hamlet of Steinstücken had barely 150 inhabitants, and, by some quirk that had occurred when these borders were drawn on maps, it too became part of West Berlin, joined only by the most slender of land corridors. It was seized once by East German police in 1951, again to the intense distress of the inhabitants. The communists had then withdrawn but, like Eiskeller, there was continual surveillance of the one route into West Berlin. For the US authorities, the tiny village was a synecdoche; it even commanded the attention of US Secretary of State Dean Acheson as he paid an official visit to West Berlin that summer. Any attack on Berlin, he declared, would be viewed as an attack upon the Western powers generally. The Americans were in Berlin 'as a matter of right and duty' and would 'remain there until its freedom was secure'.[8]

But Walter Ulbricht's German Democratic Republic continued turning the screw on the West, sometimes subtly, sometimes crudely. In the French sector, an old cemetery through which the borderline between east and west was deemed to run was violated by East Berlin guards. They had no thought or care of family distress as graves were dug into. Elsewhere, a fresh edict was issued: any West Berliners who had either property or business in the east of the city would no longer be issued with permits allowing them to travel and work there unless they agreed to move there permanently and live under communist rule. There was no suggestion of compensation if this choice was not made. Ordinary workers were similarly pressured: twenty-five West Berliners in peripheral roles on the S-Bahn were summarily sacked, then told that they could have their jobs back if they and their families moved east. There was still no physical barrier at that stage, but the communists were creating something akin to an invisible force field. On Berlin's roads, drivers and pedestrians in the west found new routes to avoid the eastern sector; the border zones were becoming troublesome even to approach. The pressure exerted by Ulbricht was intended to counter the threat of 'western imperialism'.[9] Yet for Berlin's residents, life was rather more layered than the barbed binary rhetoric.

The communist authorities in East Berlin were sincere in their desire to provide new homes. Even before the city was so devastated by the Allies, housing for the labouring classes had frequently been in shocking condition. The 'rental barracks' – those grim tenement blocks with their mazes of receding and darkening courtyards – sometimes barely had running water even before the war.[10] There could be no return to that. In planning a new East Berlin, Walter Ulbricht was criticized (later, even by architects within the German Democratic Republic) for rejecting the dazzling modernism for which Berlin had become famous only a generation before. He refused all ideas of reconstruction that involved 'the Bauhaus style'.[11] The end result of that, he said, was 'American boxes' and 'Hitleresque barracks'.[12] He wanted something with more of an element of *Heimat*; a sense of German home and heritage. The early results – oddly formal blocks in a style known as 'Soviet classicism' – were aesthetically flattening,[13] and even cheaper apartment blocks a little further out seemed simply to be grey right angles, devoid of features. Despite this, they also represented bright new life; many of the Berliners who were to move into them had never before known such comfort. There were kitchens with appliances that worked, water that flowed (albeit not always hot), clean, modern rooms with fresh carpets and simple furniture. And here too was a promise of equality: apartments allocated according to need. Perhaps there were those in the west of the city who would have regarded these new builds with an artistic shudder; and the GDR's chronic lack of money and manpower meant that these homes had to be constructed as cheaply as possible, sometimes even prefabricated; but after the years of war and violence, and the era of intense poverty that had come before it, these homes were for many older Berliners a taste of a future that could never have before seemed possible. Ulbricht instituted a 'Five Year Plan for Peaceful Reconstruction'[14] long before such pronouncements and phrasing came to seem comic.

The use of precast concrete panels in East Berlin was an idea that transcended the borders of grey communist ideology, for at the same time parts of London's East End were being similarly reconstructed. This was a new era of technocratic city planning. The new style of high-rise housing may have looked stark, but there was a curious aesthetic symmetry between the different ideologies of communism and social democracy; and very similar ideas to do with the use of green spaces and amenities and children's playgrounds. Brutalism was universal, and, as restored 1950s and 60s housing blocks and civic halls around the city demonstrate, there is still quite an appetite for it today.

There were forms of spiritual sustenance that also remained in equilibrium across the whole of the city at this time. For ordinary Berliners, this was to prove a golden period for opera, for classical music and for ballet. As well as the native talents of the city, the authorities on both sides went out of their way to invite the world's finest performers to their theatres. Horst Koegler was a young opera and ballet producer in towns across the fledgling German Democratic Republic. Although he had enjoyed a remarkable amount of artistic freedom in the late 1940s and early 1950s (including an opera performance with a topless prima donna),[15] there was none the less a large amount of political weight placed upon him and his companies, with the authorities demanding carefully written 'declarations of loyalty'.[16] His colleagues begged him for help, frightened that their statements might somehow be deliberately misinterpreted and used against them later. Koegler acted on impulse. He travelled to Berlin, caught an S-Bahn train to the west of the city and handed himself over to officials as 'an East German refugee'.[17] This was in the early 1950s; he was among the first few to defect. Vast numbers would follow in the years to come. Koegler was immediately assigned work on the U-Bahn railway system, at Zoo station. His antennae also guided him swiftly to West Berlin's ballet and opera companies, where he soon made valued friends and began writing as a ballet critic for art magazines (one of which, *Monat*, was funded by the Americans). Art made free movement between zones possible; he got 'review tickets everywhere, even in East Berlin, where I saw premieres by Brecht'.[18] Throughout the early 1950s, West Berlin received visits from the New York City Ballet as well as writers and poets such as W. H. Auden and Truman Capote. But there was a sense of rivalry too; the

East Berlin authorities were able to call upon the greatest of the Russian ballet companies as well as dancers and musicians from throughout central and eastern Europe. The desire for rich culture was intense. As Koegler observed, it was now 'possible to get in touch again with what had happened outside during the years of our isolation'.[19] He would later become friends with Lotte Lenya, who had launched her extraordinary career in the Weimar period with *Die Dreigroschenoper*, the music written by her former husband Kurt Weill, and who returned to West Berlin in 1955 to record new versions of Weill songs. In the east of the city, Lenya's former collaborator Bertolt Brecht, with wife Helene Weigel, was coolly assessing the ever more sharply Stalinist government of Ulbricht and his puppet prime minister Otto Grotewohl. Little of this impinged on the work of his Berliner Ensemble theatre company. Brecht's undeviating aim was, as he said, to 'make a lively use of all means, old and new . . . in order to put living reality in the hands of living people so it could be mastered'.[20] Yet the dialectics of theatre were rickety constructs compared with the living reality of East Berlin's manual workers.

Throughout the early 1950s, Walter Ulbricht's leadership had been hardening; private businesses were persecuted, landowners harassed from their holdings. Ever larger numbers of farmers and businessmen decided that they could survive only in the west of Germany. This left gaping voids in East Berlin's economy and, beyond the city, made for a poor 1952 harvest on collectivized farms. By 1953, East Berlin's workers were facing fast-rising prices, combined with shop shelves that were ever more bare. There were even difficulties with electricity supplies, which started to stutter. It felt as though all progress was slowing, and moving into reverse. Those same East Berliners knew that, across the city in the American sector, there were no shortages; that those who worked in the factories there were getting fairer wages and decent overtime (Ulbricht's government could not afford to pay this). So the tensions were not merely about want but also about inequality, and with the death of Stalin in March 1953 came jolting repercussions of political uncertainty. The rising magma of public anger was first seen on East Berlin's Stalinallee in June 1953. This was a grand boulevard, one and a half miles long, the centrepiece of communist reconstruction, its buildings in the Soviet classical style – a wide prospect of 'palaces for the workers', intended to demonstrate to the West that socialism provided luxury living for its citizens.[21] The Weberwiese tower block, an elegant oblong structure, boasted not only a modish exterior of pale stone and tiling but also interiors that included parquet floors and central heating. That it was those who worked for the party who tended to be allocated homes on Stalinallee did not detract from their essential function as crowing advertisements for the moral superiority of communism. 'High as the sky, bright as the beautiful sun/ We'll keep on building as long as the tower cranes run!' ran 'The Reconstruction Waltz', a tune that was played frequently on East Berlin radio.[22] The boulevard also made key attractions of shops and restaurants. But all this could be achieved at speed only by increasing labour targets on the building sites, and it was construction workers on Stalinallee who on 16 June 1953 sparked into rebellion. It began when builders working on Block 40 on the boulevard threw down their tools and walked out. They were joined by others, and very soon a crowd of 2,000 became 10,000. There was an echo here of Weimar era discontent, and of the propensity of Berliners to take quickly to the streets to proclaim their rage.

The protests would swiftly radiate out through the GDR; demonstrations broke out in Dresden and Leipzig, among other cities. East Berlin was an especially sensitive nerve for the Soviet authorities in Moscow. As the Berlin crowds marched upon the government buildings, Walter Ulbricht seemed to have become transfixed, or paralysed, by what was unfolding, even as his secret police – the freshly formed Stasi – insinuated themselves among the demonstrators, noting the prime movers. It is more than possible that he believed the lawless demonstrations to have been catalysed by 'fascist agents' from the city's American sector – right-wing saboteurs who wished not only to bring socialism crashing down but also to completely destroy the Soviet aspiration towards a united Germany.[23] The American radio station, for instance, was reporting on the ever-swelling crowds, and this in turn was believed to have encouraged ever more East Berliners to join them. There were sporadic cries calling for free elections. Yet even Ulbricht's Soviet controllers were unhappy about the extremity of his transformation of East German society. By the evening of 16 June 1953, it appeared that Ulbricht had relented on the issue of the increased work quotas, but the anger was not so easily dampened and by the next day the entire German Democratic Republic was in tumult. On 17 June there was genuine fear among the Soviet forces that their sector of the city might be lost; in the first rays of dawn that day, the protestors moved fast and the security services and police seemed helpless before them. Just before 10 a.m., at the House of Ministries, a group of demonstrators managed to get past security. Posters and Communist Party literature were set alight. The gusty air fluttered with small tornadoes of flaming leaflets. As officials in front of municipal buildings vainly pleaded with the crowds to disperse, the breakaway group had illuminated an unexpected fragility; Ulbricht had already been spirited away to the outskirts of the city. The humiliation of the regime's police and secret security was intense. And the Soviets could not allow it to stand. The city's military forces were mobilized. Martial law was declared.

Red Army tanks were once again on the streets, and in intimidating numbers; Stalinallee was conveniently wide. The roar of gunfire was heard once more. 'The Russians were coming,' recalled Horst Kreeter, then a young petrol-pump attendant. 'The crowd started howling . . . We threw stones at the tanks.'[24] Some protestors were crushed. Herr Kreeter remembered hearing that 'someone had died on Marx-Engels Square'.[25] In the end, the tanks were too much for the crowds to face, and the re-energized Stasi and their helpers now moved with zeal among ringleaders and onlookers alike. There were some 15,000 arrests and hundreds of bleeding wounds and broken limbs. About forty people were shot dead, a few of whom were the state's own security officials who had refused to turn against the demonstrators. In the aftermath came instantaneous executions after feverishly fast trials. Berliners, long accustomed to violent repression, would have seen nothing new in all this; there was a sense of state-sponsored vengefulness that recalled the German Revolution of only a little over thirty years previously. In Berlin, and across the GDR, state control was reasserted (and was to be steadily strengthened; the era of letter-opening machines and mass surveillance was dawning).

For all this, the protests had not been ineffective. Amid the ruthlessness there were concessions, first on the disputed work quotas and second upon temporarily easing the tight controls on movement between east and west. The Soviet authorities were placing Walter Ulbricht under pressure; whereas he had moved towards communist totalitarianism with speed, the post-Stalin approach was to be more subtle and less openly confrontational. None the less, days later, Ulbricht and his colleagues set about analysing the roots of the crisis, eventually reporting:

> The enemy . . . hurled his gangster columns, armed with guns and oil-filled bottles, across the sector border. Their job was to get the construction workers to lay down their tools and to mislead them with inflammatory slogans into a demonstration against the government. Arson, looting and shooting were to give the demonstration the appearance of an uprising . . . The fascist scum who had sneaked over from West Berlin and who were directed from there, organized attacks on food warehouses, school dormitories, clubhouses and shops . . . that is how a Fascist regime was to be established [in the GDR].[26]

For Bertolt Brecht, who for all of his Leninist thought, was ever alive to the flawed reality of communism, the uprising inspired a satirical poem that is widely quoted in good humour even today. Yet it was also possible to see a genuine grimace of anguish behind it. Starting with the bitter and only slightly absurd premise that a Writers' Union functionary had issued a leaflet saying that the workers had lost 'the confidence of the government' by refusing their work quotas, Brecht wrote: 'Would it not in that case be simpler/ for the government/ To dissolve the people/ And elect another?'[27]

Yet this renewed Berliner obstinacy had significance far beyond the city; in a sense, Ulbricht was correct in his paranoia. Although the Americans had not sparked the crisis, it was certainly true that events were being watched with raptor focus all the way to the White House. The Soviets were pushing towards a programme of 'moderation' in East Berlin and the GDR – even to the extent of allowing 'bourgeois' elements to continue – and this was because of their continued desire to see Germany unified.[28] Conversely, the Americans – and Konrad Adenauer, the first Chancellor of the new Federal Republic of Germany – wanted no such thing. Central and eastern European nations were now Soviet satellites, and it was perfectly possible that they might win hearts and souls further west too. So it was better to maintain not only division but also a very visible demarcation of ideology. For the US, and the economically booming West Germany, a unified nation could be postponed indefinitely. As it was, a geopolitical balance – precarious, fraught – had been accidentally found down the line of the Inner German Border. That border was already tightening by the week, chiefly from the Soviet side. But Berlin – despite the mighty canyon of lives and beliefs that had yawned open – still remained one city. And the Americans – in a neat reversal of the blockade five years previously – settled upon an idea to keep discontent with Walter Ulbricht and the SED seething. They would start distributing food parcels.

Berlin's tram system was by this stage bisected; the trolleys stopped at the border and came back again. But East Berliners were still free to travel to the west of the city on the S-Bahn. The offer of food gifts was made known via the American radio service. All the East Berliners had to do was to come to collect them. Given the shortages induced by a bad harvest, and by Ulbricht's overenthusiastic collectivization programmes, the sense of want was sharp. None the less, the numbers who claimed this aid were extraordinary. Many travelled from the countryside into East Berlin in order to catch those trains and collect their parcels. It was calculated that some 75 per cent of East Berliners had also taken up the offer.[29]

Ulbricht's politburo sent special agitators – young people of the Free Youth Movement who brought passionate fervour to their own socialist beliefs – into the west of the city to 'incite unrest' near distribution centres, but with little effect.[30] The East Berlin newspapers were molten; the US programme was termed *Bettelpakete*, or 'beggar's packages', and those who sought them were figures of contempt.[31] But Brecht's public was not listening. The American delicacies were too rich a prospect for self-denial. There was at this time in the US a 'Psychological Strategy Board' that was engaged in further ideas to aim at East Berlin without bringing the Soviets to the point of armed confrontation. East Berliners should receive 'sympathy and asylum' but 'no arms'.[32] There was discussion of a Day of Mourning to commemorate the East Berliners who were killed in their uprising; and although the Americans continued to insist that they had no part in fomenting that rebellion, their aim, via radio and other mediums, was to 'nourish resistance to communist oppression'.[33] More than this was the sheer power of money: at around this time, $50 million (which would be worth about $500 million now) was pledged by the US to be spent directly upon the reconstruction of West Berlin. The prosperity that this would bring in terms of full, well-paid employment (that money went further then, owing to lower labour and material costs) would be starkly obvious to all citizens. In the east, meanwhile, local party operatives were reporting back to their politburo what they had monitored the workers saying. According to some free-talking labourers, 'the Soviet Army' was 'under pressure from the Western powers' and 'the American and British occupation forces would soon victoriously enter the area'.[34] One East Berliner was reported to have said: 'Soon we can start learning English.'[35]

There were those who were making the crossing from east to west as refugees; others with the economic wherewithal who were moving to be with old friends or business associates. Academics were making the journey across the city to make a completely new life in what was in effect the next-door district. Throughout the rest of the country, the East German border that ran through the countryside was now punctuated with sentry posts, gun towers and barbed wire. These spoke of a fear of infection, as well as a fear of escape. That fear would soon become pathological, and engulf the city.

## 20. The Widening Chasm

Sometimes, as they gazed at the screens, ghostly figures would flicker into view, faintly talking. In the earliest days of television in the German Democratic Republic (the spread of sets there was almost as rapid as in the West), programmes in East Berlin would be distorted by traces of forbidden images from across the city – different dramas and documentaries bleeding through: parallel lives, familiar and yet increasingly distant. East Berliners were becoming accustomed to the unease of knowing that there was news they were not hearing, truths that they were not being told. The Cold War had, by 1956, brought fresh turbulence and bloodshed (there was a statue-toppling uprising in Hungary, vast and spirited, which saw Marshal Zhukov – now Soviet defence minister – order Soviet tanks to take key strategic points across Budapest amid a grim and violent campaign to suppress the revolt and install a new government) and it brought another sort of atmosphere to Berlin: that of an uncanny hall of mirrors. There was illusion and conspiracy. It had become a thriving, lively centre for espionage, a vast chessboard for the superpowers; here, where the border was still more of a soft membrane than a barrier, agents circulated on either side, engaged frequently in missions of deep complexity. The CIA and the KGB both had offices and operatives, and the territory was bountiful. 'Berlin was the central circuit of east European communications,' stated the author of a confidential National Security Agency report in America.[1] In the mid 1950s, this network was the prize sought by the CIA and MI6, and, in the mid 1950s, a top-secret and ingeniously constructed 1,500ft tunnel, filled with specialized eavesdropping equipment and secret listeners, ran alongside the old bones of a cemetery in the south of the city and, probing from west to east, gave access to communist telephone exchanges. The mirror world reached even there: one of the senior British agents involved in the planning of the tunnel was George Blake, a Soviet double agent who had faithfully fed the intelligence to his handlers even as it was excavated. The Soviets let the operation continue, chiefly to protect their valuable asset; if they were to 'discover' the tunnel too soon, Blake might have been exposed as the mole. In early 1956, by which time Blake had been transferred by MI6 to the Middle East, the Soviets felt free to 'accidentally' happen across Operation Gold. They dug through from its eastern side. Press were invited into the cavern, to gaze upon typical US perfidy, which the Americans did not deny. The extraordinary story beguiled the world's newspapers: a metonym for a cold war that was being fought beneath the surface of everyday life in Berlin, not with guns and bombs but with cunning and treachery, and all for the prize of capturing the souls of the people on the surface.

To the Soviets' chagrin, increasing numbers of those souls were wrestling free. There were weekly headlines in the Western press about East Berliners, sometimes several thousand a day, streaming across the city to claim asylum. Among them were prominent East German government officials, scientists and skilled engineers. In an attempt to stem the flow and make the case for this new communist society, shrewd direct appeals were made that invoked the city's radical past, a pre-Nazi era when the working men and women stood together to create their new socialist world. In West Berlin, by contrast, it was commerce and trade, the brightness of youth and the startling innovations of post-war material comfort that were deployed as weapons of persuasion. As well as being at the centre of a secret intelligence war, Berlin was a hinterland in which wider cultural struggles broke out too.

The statues had long vanished; Frederick the Great had been removed from his prominent plinth on Unter den Linden in the early days of the East Berlin regime (though he was not destroyed entirely). For Walter Ulbricht, there were monuments and buildings that cast too many dark shadows of the past. This was not just about extinguishing all traces and fragments of the Nazi regime. Other landmarks were deemed oppressive. The grand Berliner Schloss, once the palace of the Hohenzollern dynasty, mostly ruined after the bombing and the battle of 1945, had been initially rehabilitated by the communists as a temporary gallery for exhibitions of Soviet realist art. By 1950

Ulbricht found it intolerable; he had it demolished. The city had to be stripped of its 'militaristic past'.[2] (The structure that took its place many years later, in 1976 – the Palace of the Republic – was a glass-and-concrete venue with debating chambers, concert facilities and a theatre. When the tide of history turned once more, and its turn came for destruction, there was genuine ill will among many former East Berliners who had the fondest affection for it.)

But there were other totems worthy of celebration. In early 1956, some 100,000 East Berliners gathered (or were cajoled and pressurized into gathering) for a day of parades and marches to mark the thirty-seventh anniversary of the killings of Karl Liebknecht and Rosa Luxemburg, Berlin's Spartacus revolutionaries. Events were centred around the easterly Friedrichsfelde cemetery, where Liebknecht and Luxemburg were buried (Ludwig Mies van der Rohe had created a modernist memorial there of rectilinear brickwork surmounted with a vast Soviet star and hammer and sickle; the Nazis had very swiftly destroyed it, and now there was a further restoration). Although the East Germans were seeking to extinguish 'the superstition of religion', they were still happy to invoke the spirits of dead socialists to suggest that Berlin's communist present was rooted firmly in its radical past.[3] Among the thousands of people who marched were Factory Fighting Groups (paramilitary outfits) and the Organization for Sport and Technics (a paramilitary youth outfit for teenagers).[4] One of the themes of the day was 'Against militarism and aggressive NATO policies'.[5] There were also calls for the formation of an East German army; it would be there to 'protect socialist achievement'.[6] The paranoia was sharpening.

Partly this was to do with the contagion of the new youth culture. Berlin's teenagers had been born into a city that was enveloped in the darkness of war. By 1956 the young had a craving for the life that they could see in magazines and could hear thrumming from their radios. If once there had been a fear among parents, and among the occupying powers, that the new, rising generation would contain the seeds of a regenerated Nazism, it receded slightly in the face of a rather more uniform Western anxiety. In West and East Berlin alike, the music of Elvis Presley – who briefly served in Germany with the US Army – was a galvanic thunderbolt. His songs were played in the

West Berlin nightclub Hothouse; young women were observed drinking Coca-Cola and dancing, even with one another. In them, and in the young men who hoped to partner them, there were observed 'vulgar and erotically expressive movements'.[7] Bill Haley's 'Rock Around the Clock', meanwhile, was also the catalyst for 'public displays of sexual drives' and for outbreaks of delinquency too.[8] In this, the older people who formed the authorities of both East and West Berlin seemed to find agreement. This new phenomenon was to them in many ways abhorrent. It was worse than the underground wartime craze of 'Swing Heinis' in which youths had dressed up in transgressively dandyish fashion to listen to jazz. The advent of rock 'n' roll was seen as a racialized threat, even in the most progressive circles. The West German youth magazine *Bravo* – focusing on all the newest films and television programmes and which made its debut in 1956 with a cover featuring Marilyn Monroe – noted the shock caused by 'sultry negro songs'.[9] *Der Spiegel* declared of Elvis that he was the cause and 'symptom of collective erotic eruptions'.[10] Other publications discussed his appearance and his stage movements in racialized terms. Just as anti-Semitism could never have been erased from Germany in an instant, so other racial prejudices proved stubborn. An entire population had been taught – assured – that theirs was the superior race, intellectually and aesthetically. The assumption had been passed on, quite unconsciously, and had remained (as similar assumptions also had, it should be recalled, in many parts of the United States, and in many other countries across Europe). There were youth magazines in East Germany too; these objected to young women making themselves more overtly sexual in nightclubs. Socialism was supposed to bring equality of the sexes, but not the spectacle of girls wearing mannish clothing – 'tight pants and short jackets'.[11] Rock 'n' roll was fundamentally alien, and it roared across the city, unstoppable, ineluctable. To the East Berlin authorities, this was *Unkultur*.[12] Nor could they stop their own young people crossing the city to spend evenings in 'Boogie clubs',[13] or to spend their Saturdays gazing at the sumptuous window displays of West Berlin boutiques, wherein lay all the newest fashions aimed at the young. (Even the very young of East Berlin were not immune to American culture: Elke Rosin, ten years old at the time, recalled how she 'learned to be a smuggler early in life', chiefly by bringing 'Mickey Mouse magazines' back to the family home on that borderline of Bernauer Strasse.)[14]

But the West Berlin authorities themselves were conscious of an additional charge of menace; the way that this popular culture seemed to spark unthinking aggression in the *Halbstarke* – or semi-strong – teenage working-class male delinquents.[15] There were fights in cinemas and outside clubs. Berlin was not the only city experiencing a violently rebellious teenage subculture. It had been there before the onset of rock 'n' roll, but the new music seemed to have an extra degree of sensitivity here: a nauseating, frivolous vulgarity that contrasted horribly with the shadow of national guilt, and which also appeared to threaten German cultural heritage. There were serious jazz critics in Berlin who sought at that time to distance its more distinguished, subtle performers from the young women and men who would go to concerts and dance in a frenzied anarchic style that led East Berlin commentators to suggest that they had been possessed. The city had seen sexualized subcultures before; what might have made this new outbreak unsettling to all its citizens was the fact that it was being sought – or imposed – from outside. It was not German, or European, but American. This was the culture of an occupying force.

Unbearably for the East German authorities, it was precisely towards the luridly Americanized world that so many of its own citizens were fleeing. Even communist newspapers admitted that 'leading scientists and skilled workers' had been seduced by 'American monopoly capitalists and their German agents'.[16] There were high-profile flights from east to west: the actor Horst Rienitz, who had become better known to his East Berlin audience as a popular radio presenter, was to cross into West Berlin to claim asylum (and, it must be presumed, greater artistic freedom). Such figures were regarded as traitors. A leaflet issued by the Socialist Unity Party stated that 'both from the moral standpoint as well as in terms of the interests of the whole German nation, leaving the GDR is an act of political and moral backwardness and depravity'.[17] They were 'leaving a land of progress' for a realm that was 'out-dated, backward'[18] and prone to the old sins: there was mention of 'Junkers' and militarism.[19] More than this: the consequences for those left behind could be hideous. A chemical engineer called Max Held was sentenced to death by an East Berlin court for helping a friend in his flight to the West.[20] Eva Helm, a typist with the same firm, was accused of having been in on the scheme: she received a life sentence of hard labour.[21] Heinz Griese, a government finance official, was another who crossed the border. As the humiliating departures continued, the authorities grew more vengeful. In 1955 Elli Barczatis, secretary to the erstwhile East German leader Otto Grotewohl, was arrested and sentenced to death for 'Spying for the west'.[22] She had been under investigation by the Stasi for several years. Her lover, Karl Laurenz, was a journalist and translator with US contacts, and she was suspected of passing documents. In the end, and even after the rigours of intense Stasi interrogation, there was nothing definitive that could point to guilt, but her case – and that of her lover – was held in a closed court, and she was given no legal representation. She was sent to the guillotine. It was only in 2006 that her name was rehabilitated by the authorities.

Nor could there ever be the certainty of safety in West Berlin. A communist 'People's Police' inspector called Robert Bialek who had fled there was invited to a house party some months later. He was seen in the small hours by the building concierge 'unconscious and delirious [*sic*]'.[23] Before the concierge could raise the alarm, Bialek was scooped up by a former colleague from the People's Police 'and an unidentified woman'.[24] They placed him in their car and drove off, back across the border.

There were a few who fled in the opposite direction; a few years previously, the British journalist John Peet, a Berlin correspondent for Reuters, held a press conference in the Soviet sector and announced that he was moving there permanently, citing the re-armament of West Germany as well as his belief in a socialist future.[25] Another high-profile arrival was the atomic physicist Klaus Fuchs; while working on the Manhattan Project to develop the atom bomb during the war, Fuchs secretly relayed intelligence to Russia. He was later uncovered and jailed in the north of England. Upon release, after serving nine years, he immediately left the country and made for East Berlin. Then there was the curious episode of the German Grand Prix champion Manfred von Brauchitsch. He had come from a prominent military family (his uncle was the German army's wartime commander-in-chief General Walther von Brauchitsch) but his chief successes were on the track, between the wars. After 1945, his association with the National Socialist Motor Corps did not augur well for his future career, and he stumbled in business. There seems to have been a brush with espionage; he was held for a time by the West German authorities in 1955, and when released on bail he immediately ran for the East. The communists made good use of this defector: he was appointed head of a new national motor sport organization.[26] Here was velocity combined with technological prowess: this was precisely the sort of modernism that the East Berliners wished to show the world. There was also an echo of the city's old fascination with speed and the adrenaline it brought.

But even these valuable moments of affirmation for the regime did nothing to quell the ever-rising numbers of people from across the GDR making the journey to Berlin and across the line. One reason was fear of rearmament, and of conscription into a new army; the trauma of war lay too deep in too many bones.[27] Even by the late 1950s, some teenagers were only meeting their gaunt, broken fathers for the first time after their long-delayed release from Soviet labour camps, where they had been working in mines or engaged in rebuilding shattered Russian towns and cities. In addition to this was perhaps an increasing sense of suffocation under surveillance. Under the Nazis, Berliners had become accustomed to keeping their true views and feelings in check; no one knew who might be an informer. Similarly, tenants in apartment blocks had been careful to keep on the right side of concierges or block wardens, as they too were possibly agents of the regime (as they were with increasing frequency). Now, in the east of the city, it was becoming clearer that the Soviet system was taking this monitoring further. The secret state apparatus, the Stasi, which had been formed in 1950, found a new lease of independence in 1955 when it was made a ministry in its own right, giving it even greater powers of control and oppression.

Its agents – 'politically reliable', carefully trained, frequently plucked from Socialist Unity Party youth organizations and moulded ruthlessly – were sent out invisibly into the industrial landscape of East Germany and East Berlin.[28] They took up jobs in every factory, became guards on trains, teachers in schools, doctors and nurses. Not everyone was a Stasi agent or informer, but anyone might have been (across the years, there were some 275,000 full-time Stasi employees in East Germany, and an unknowable number of informants). And it was that possibility that had the effect of freezing free conversations and free thought. Even late-evening bar-room jokes had to be related in whispers outdoors, away from unfamiliar drinkers. Stasi tenants in large housing estates would cast cold eyes on new faces paying visits to neighbours, keeping careful track of every detail. This was once more a world in which Berliners could be arrested, imprisoned, subjected to violence, on no more say-so than the whim of an official; in this sense, the suffocating oppression and fear were little different from those inaugurated in 1933.

Yet, even then, there were other reasons why, by 1960, over 200,000 East Berliners had made their way to that narrow gap in the Iron Curtain to begin new lives. There was, it was reported, 'anxiety' felt by parents 'about their children' and 'education'.[29] There was the ever-widening economic imbalance; East Berliners who had jobs in West Berlin generally received higher wages than their peers who remained in the Soviet sector. With this additional money, those East Berliners had the chance to shop in the more abundantly stocked department stores in the western sector; they brought back a range of new consumer goods, from clothes to record players to television sets. This in turn led to very visible outbreaks of inequality in otherwise identical blocks of East Berlin housing, which in turn were noted by Stasi informants. Yet it also had the effect of hardening hearts against what was described as the 'drab and aggravating' way of life in the Soviet sector.[30] (By now, East and West Berlin each had its own ever-increasingly distinctive rival television broadcasting service; the West featured more in the way of light entertainment, but the East had a popular crime drama called *Blue Light*: in this, the People's Police were the heroes, fighting subversives and capitalists, such as fine-art thieves. And the GDR had one genuine international TV success: an animated children's puppet show called *Unser Sand-männchen*. The chief character, brought to life with stop-motion techniques, got into a range of gentle adventures that took him flying across the world. From the point of view of parents, the value was soporific; at the end of each episode there would be songs exhorting little children to get ready for sleep. The other attraction of the series was that – almost uniquely for the GDR – it did not appear to be freighted with ideological significance.)

Walter Ulbricht's government also faced stubborn resistance from the many East Berliners who retained the religious traditions and beliefs they had learned as children and were now passing on to their own offspring. Protestant and evangelical parents found that their children were being targeted at school, teachers and party officials seeking to erase their nascent faith, and by doing so erase that of the parents as well. Margot Schorr was a teacher in her early twenties when she found herself 'clashing' with the GDR 'education officials';[31] they demanded total adherence to Marxism–Leninism but she was a 'Christian'.[32] This was a pungently strong echo of the previous regime, which had also sought to stamp out religious feeling; communism, like fascism, could admit of no god other than the party and its leadership. In 1960, an unbiddable West Berliner – Bishop Friedrich Karl Otto Dibelius, of the German Evangelical Church – was crossing the city's internal borders to keep hope and faith alive. In earlier decades, he had been a furious anti-Semite, supporting the conspiratorial belief in the overweening power of the Jewish people, and thus their persecution. In the aftermath of the war, both Soviet and Western authorities allowed him to start piecing together the fragments of the shattered German Church establishment. But the Soviets had failed to identify his other abiding hatred: communism. His preaching visits to East Berlin were a source of increasing anger as Bishop Dibelius in turn inflamed his congregants. He was eventually declared persona non grata, but more families in the meantime had seen that they could only find the freedom they wanted in the West.

Most damaging economically to East Berlin and the GDR was the ever-increasing number of highly skilled professionals and 'intellectuals' who were abandoning the vision of socialist unity. 'Doctors, teachers, engineers, journalists and artists' were fleeing the regime;[33] by early 1961 it was reckoned that the last year alone had seen an increase in this flight of around 32 per cent. Ulbricht's regime had already conceded that living standards in the East did not match those of the West. Perhaps the ever-growing defection of the intelligentsia would have had only a marginal effect on the GDR's industrial output – they were not the innovators on the factory floors – but it was the tacit declaration of lack of belief in socialism that caused pain. Ulbricht tried to address the problem of the divided city from another angle. 'It is time the espionage centres and diversion bases of West German militarism and the foreign military organs disappear from West Berlin,' he announced. 'It is time . . . West Berlin establishes normal contractual relations with its surrounding world.'[34] That surrounding world was Soviet; this was a final, futile, empty call for the Americans and the British to allow West Berlin to be subsumed into communism.

The gulf grew sharper by the day. Now, those in East Berlin who commuted to the West every day for work were termed – by their own government – *Grenzgaenger*, or 'border-crossers'.[35] What had once been natural was now deemed abnormal. But the daily border-crossers were not the reason for the sense of crisis and instability that hung over the East. There was a new pan-continental gravitational force: the establishment in recent years of the new Common Market in western Europe; and, among the states that had originally joined, West Germany was the most passionate and heartfelt partner. This development was viewed coldly in Moscow, which had never lost sight of the hope that West Germany, after Konrad Adenauer's term came to an end, might be persuaded to orientate itself more towards Russia. In the meantime, the numbers of East German citizens who had been travelling to the city and then making permanent moves across the border had been growing fast – so much so that a special camp for refugees had been instituted in West Berlin to process these new arrivals. Some high-profile defectors caused acute embarrassment to the Ulbricht regime: one such, who made the journey in his car with a family of nine packed in, was an East German Supreme Court judge called Horst Hetzar. Just days before that, Dr Hans Günther Pfeiffer-Bothner – the chief physician of the dedicated People's Police hospital – also slid across the border and took his place in that refugee camp. It was estimated that since 1949, when Germany had been cleft, some three million people had left to join the 'economic miracle' of the West. Now, in that airless Berlin August, the rhetoric on both sides was becoming increasingly hostile.

The Young Pioneers – the East German youth organization – was demanding in early August that Ulbricht's government should be taking action against those East Berlin parents who persisted in sending their children to schools across the border every day; this was one of those curious anomalies that had survived, with communist pupils immersed in capitalist syllabi. It had also been the case in the city's higher education that students could decide which system they preferred to learn from: and some from the West continued to enrol in the communist-run Humboldt University. For the Young Pioneers, the idea of young children being exposed to American imperialist dogma was intolerable, and they wanted the errant parents punished. It was around this time, in early August, that the People's Police established an even more intense presence on trains heading into the city; in some instances, passengers were made to disembark at Potsdam, a few miles out, while the officers questioned families and checked their identities and interrogated their intentions once they reached Berlin: were they, too, thinking of leaving? Pressure was brought to bear to turn them back.

And, for the everyday *Grenzgaenger* themselves, the East Berlin authorities also exerted new intimidatory measures. In early August, many male workers found themselves detained in their own homes by the People's Police, forbidden to go to work that day. Instead, their wives were ordered to cross over the border to their workplaces and collect their employment cards. The men would never be returning; instead, they were to find similar work in East Germany. This sort of oppressive innovation was noted elsewhere. In Britain, a junior Conservative minister called Edward Heath (by 1970 he would be prime minister) wondered aloud in the House of Commons about the root of this ever more totalitarian behaviour. Was it, he said, because West Berlin was 'the shop window of the West' in the 'middle of the arid zone' of Soviet Germany?[36] Elsewhere, a report smuggled out of East Berlin revealed that one district's local party had calculated that if another 200,000 skilled workers were lost, then East Germany as a whole would be economically stricken. In a speech, Walter Ulbricht sounded almost hysterical. The borders of

East Germany, he declared, had to be defended. And refugees 'would soon call themselves idiots' for 'running away from social- ism', which would, in any case, 'catch up with them'.[37] There was discussion of a complete ban on travel into and out of East Berlin. This was on 10 August 1961. Several days later, with the weighty paraphernalia of police and soldiers patrolling the lines between the zones, the Brandenburg Gate was identified as one of the last places where refugees might cross over. More citizens did so, either in cars or on foot, and in the meantime crowds of young West Berliners had gathered on their side of the Gate to demonstrate, shouting slogans and abuse at the East Berlin officials. 'Germany remains Germany!' 'Hang Ulbricht!' 'Open the Gate!' 'Freedom!' 'Ivan go home!'[38] On East German radio, meanwhile, the ultimatum hardened: that, until West Berlin became a 'demilitarized free city', the East would have to take all measures to protect itself. A wall that had existed only as a hor- rible theoretical possibility was now about to take on stark corporeal form; a literally concrete expression of fear and paranoiac aggression. By 2.30 a.m. on 13 August, the two halves of the city were sealed up against one another. Under the ground, the U-Bahn trains that had glided over the border simply stopped before they reached it. On the north–south lines, they continued through, but the trains did not stop at stations in the western sector. On the surface, the line of the wall at last became visible, first with barbed wire and extra patrols, but very swiftly with the construction workers.

There were only hours left in which to probe and exploit the remaining anomalous gaps in this spiritual and physical barrier. Under the shades of humid amethyst summer nights, East Berliners found mazy routes through 'ruins' and 'gardens' and 'backyards'.[39] Others slipped into the black, oily waters of the Spree, possessions tied to them, and swam across the divide. And, as they did so, numbers of Berlin's young on both sides made their passionate feelings known through furious demonstrations. Stones and other projectiles were thrown; the People's Police had tear gas and water cannon at the ready, although they did not deploy them. Nor were there any Rus- sian officials or soldiers to be seen in public places. Their calculation perhaps was that the youth protests would evaporate of their own accord.

The world beyond took a short while to comprehend the enormity of what was unfolding here, save for a minor outbreak of what were termed 'Wall Street jitters', or reactive market fluctuations.[40] This was an act that looked hostile – ripping up whatever remained of the Four Powers Agreement over Berlin – and yet one that could hardly be met with any sort of military response. The East was asserting its border; the West could not stop it doing so. In those first few hours after the borders were sealed with barbed wire, barriers and new guard posts, few seemed to imagine that the arrangement would literally be set in concrete; there were still strong memories of the capriciousness of the Berlin Blockade some thirteen years beforehand. Even when it became apparent that the concrete was being delivered, there were few who could seriously imagine what would follow – that parents would be cut off from children, families ripped apart, lovers permanently sundered. No Berliners could envisage how their lives were about to become amputated. There were some – even among the soldiers and labourers constructing it – who were certain that it would be 'temporary'.[41] 'We got special treatment,' recalled Dieter Weber, who was then delivering the concrete. 'Tea with rum. Or rum with tea – we were pretty sloshed.'[42] The workers were also given a great deal of chocolate, 'for energy'.[43]

Work went on: twenty-seven miles of concrete wall and chain-link fencing gradually materializing within the snaking line of the city's internal east–west border; ninety-one miles of it stretching around the perimeter of West Berlin, closing off all access to the East German countryside around. The walls in many places near the city centre would rise to thirteen feet, enough to discourage bifurcated families from gathering on either side. Soviet premier Nikita Khrushchev had asked Walter Ulbricht how this impermeable barrier could ever work in those grey anomalous areas where the border did not follow roads. 'We have a specific plan,' Ulbricht told him. 'In the houses with exits to West Berlin, they will be walled up.'[44] This extremity aside – underlining the domestic character of the tragedy to come for so many dislocated families – walls along borders are by themselves not wholly remarkable, though the modernist brutalism of the concrete Berlin variety was new. It – or to be more precise, they, since in some central sections pairs of walls were built in parallel, two lines of rough concrete in tandem across the city — seemed to reflect back on the stark, fast, clumsiness of some of the eastern housing estates. But, in those sections of double walling, it was not so much the walls themselves that were uncanny, but the naked space that lay between them. The land between the walls came to be known as the 'death strip'. It was a void; an empty area to be floodlit, and sprayed with gunfire in the event of anyone setting foot upon it in order to cross to the other side. The concept was new and yet familiar; as soon as any man or woman, intent upon escape, ventured on to the death strip, they were immediately an un-person, nothing more than a moving target. Yet the terrible echoes were there: the watchtowers, updated versions of the sentinel posts that presided over the death camps; and, for those who sought to cross over, the immediate deprivation of all rights, and the sluicing away of identity that made violent death easily dispensed. The space between those parallel walls was itself an un-space, in which nothing but violence was possible.

## 21. There is a World Elsewhere

There were those in the earliest days of the Berlin Wall who reached out to touch its cold, rough surface; palms on pitted concrete. Some paced beneath it with agitation and distress. It was largely extemporized, yet the concrete carried a terrible suggestion of permanence. Others were bolder: children standing upon each other's shoulders; young women and men finding footing on nearby window ledges, stretching their necks so that they might look over it. Theirs was little more than avid curiosity; the chances of glimpsing, over that divide, the faces of friends or loved ones were remote. These gestures were futile; they could achieve nothing. None the less, people could not help themselves. They were now both prisoners and at the same time free. These were the people of West Berlin, whose lives were now circumscribed by an impenetrable wall, fringed in places with barbed wire, that completely surrounded their part of the city. The narrow transport corridors – road, rail and air – were still open, but the people were now wholly shut off from the east of the city, and from the wider countryside that lay beyond. West Berliners had the guaranteed protection still of US and UK military personnel; and they had the jobs and the abundant shops and giddy entertainment, the sheer velocity of early 1960s popular culture. In that sense, time was moving at slightly different speeds on either side of the Wall. But these West Berlin citizens were anomalies dwelling in an island fortress surrounded by a regime that was grave and lethally serious about its own ideals. Families were severed. Relatives wondered if they might ever see each other again. The oldest friendships were now dislocated. The division was absolute. Walls are sometimes understood by artists and writers as symbolic of death because one cannot see what lies beyond. The stark implacability of the Berlin Wall gave it an immediate global significance, as the borderline of the neurotic Cold War, which made it part of the landscape of the world. From the start, there were Berliners who could never accept the new boundaries of their lives; but these were not the islanders: they were East Berliners who in theory had the freedom of the continent stretching to the east.

Western governments voiced their horror about the Wall; President Kennedy visited West Berlin in 1963 and, in front of a vast crowd, said: 'There are some who say in Europe and elsewhere we can work with the communists. Let them come to Berlin.'[1] But it was also clear that the Americans would never move to demolish the Wall. Why risk war when this structure brought a paradoxical stasis? The quantum instabilities of the city were now strictly compartmentalized. Walter Ulbricht's government – which might have sincerely believed what it told its citizens – insisted that the Wall was there as protection, a defence, against the rapacious, fascist-adjacent forces of America.[2] That East Berliners were being shielded from the predations and exploitation of ruthless capitalists.

One of its first victims – one of the first people to refuse to acknowledge the limits that the Wall would set upon her life – was an eighty-year-old woman called Olga Segler. She lived in an apartment on Bernauer Strasse, one of the streets that lay directly on the border; the front entrance of the block lay within the Soviet zone, but the street that she looked down upon from her back window belonged to the Western Allies. The line between two worlds ran through her apartment. Her daughter lived just several minutes' walk away, in the western sector of the city, and elderly, lonely Frau Segler was reliant upon her. When the Wall began to rise, on 13 August 1961, Frau Segler and everyone else in her block were suddenly subjected to a form of house arrest: guards patrolled the building day and night, boarding up ground-floor windows and doors for fear of the residents staging defections to that street at the back. Ironically, the very idea then began to spread like a contagion. And with the help of West Berlin fire crews, residents were making the decision to flee, and jumping from several floors up into tightly held nets and sheets below. A fifty-eight-year-old resident called Ida Siekmann – a nurse – was the first to die in the effort to simply cross over that line; having thrown an eiderdown and some possessions from her third-floor window into that West Berlin street below, she then jumped fractionally before the firemen were ready with that net.[3]

Frau Segler was galvanized several weeks later when the East Berlin security services announced that all residents would simply be evicted from the block and given accommodation elsewhere. (Among her neighbours was the now teenaged Elke Rosin, who had recently 'smuggled nylon stockings' home from the western sector; she and her parents, on the first floor, also knew that they could not stay, and prepared simply to lower themselves down with a few belongings.)[4] The familiar threads of Frau Segler's life were being cut, and, up there on the second floor, there was only one direction she could go. With her daughter gazing up at her from that street some thirty feet below, the eighty-year-old woman looked down at the firemen from her window, preparing to let herself fall. With some courage, she did so, and was caught, but the landing was awkward, and her back was damaged. She died a day later; it was said that the ordeal had been too great for her elderly heart.[5]

That, at least, was an accident (one of many, including people injured trying to use clothes lines for abseiling). The deliberate killings started quickly. Günter Litfin was a twenty-four-year-old young man, a gifted tailor who had lived in the east of the city but worked in the west; he had aspirations towards becoming a costume designer for the theatre. In the summer of 1961, Litfin had been planning upon moving into a flat in the western district of Charlottenburg – but also intent on hiding this information from the East Berlin authorities as he did not wish to be labelled a 'republic fugitive'.[6] The day before the Wall went up, he was in the west of the city with his mother and sister for a day out. They all travelled back across into the communist zone, and the next day Litfin found that his future had been blockaded. He had no intention of accepting this; immediately he began devising potential means of crossing this terrible border. On 24 August 1961 – just days after the imposition of the Wall – Litfin set out. In the heat of the afternoon, he was dodging among the rails near Friedrichstrasse station; then, pursued by transport police, running through the grounds of the Charité hospital; and from there, clambering over a wall that adjoined the River Spree. He was in the water, intent on reaching the other side, when police on a railway bridge above ordered him to stop. Litfin would not; and the police opened fire. A bullet pierced the back of his skull. He was the first to be shot trying to cross. Though his corpse drifted close to the western shore, the entire river was in the communist domain and Litfin's body was recovered three hours later by the East Berlin authorities. There was outrage in West Berlin; in the East, Litfin's family learned of their loss only when the People's Police pulled them in for all-night interrogations.[7]

There were those who had pressing political reasons for trying to flee. Twenty-five-year-old Udo Düllick, a railway engineer, intelligent and impulsive, found it impossible to resist criticizing the state. One night in October 1961 he got into a fight with his boss at a works party, and tore the man's uniform. Düllick then fled, via taxi, to Warschauer Strasse in the south-east, and the Oberbaum Bridge (an extraordinary nineteenth-century double-decked confection with mock-medieval towers). From here, close to midnight, away from the pools of street light, he stripped down to his underwear and slid into the turbid water. Düllick was seen almost instantly. The darkness was lit with flares followed by warning shots and then, as he persisted, targeted fire. Düllick was a fine swimmer, and he showed enormous courage in diving deep below the surface to avoid the bullets. A boat was launched to head him off; Düllick surfaced and dived again. He was close to the western shore when he disappeared into the river's swirl for the final time. West Berliners retrieved his lifeless body. The initial assumption was that he had been shot; instead, it seemed, his unmarked body had probably succumbed to a heart attack after the frenzied stress of the chase.[8]

Yet there were others – young people who had been born in the darkness of Berlin's wartime fall – who seized hold of the GDR ideology and held it close to their hearts. In East Berlin there was housing for all (even if the hot water remained sporadic and even if vast numbers of homes were bugged by a hostile Stasi) and allocated according to need and situation; and there was work for all too (albeit the precise jobs and forms of work were dictated by the needs of the state). One woman identified only as Siegrid M felt this regime offered her more opportunities than the sexist west ever would; here, in East Berlin, men 'took her political opinions and career hopes seriously'.[9] It was possible to have a professional career – in her case journalism – while also having children; in West Germany, the social obstacles to women breaking out from traditional housewife roles were still intense.

In both sides of the city there was throughout the 1950s and 1960s an echo of Berlin's earlier pioneering approach to sexual orientation. The prosecution of homosexuality under the historic Paragraph 175 – suspended in the Weimar era, and reactivated so terribly and murderously under the Nazis, with gay people sent to the concentration camps – was once more quietly dispensed with. In theory, it was still a criminal offence, but one the 'People's Police' had little interest in pursuing. In East Berlin, this was the case from 1957 onwards. The Ulbricht regime had its limits of tolerance: there was still fierce censorship of any literature or journalism involving the gay community, and there were also implacably enforced bans on official gatherings of gay people. Beyond this, though, the monolithic GDR found a means of silently accommodating the fact of gay men and women. By 1968 it had completely decriminalized homosexuality (a year ahead of West Berlin and West Germany, which both proved more rigidly conservative on the issue). By the 1970s gay men and women were openly cohabiting. The case of a man identified only as 'Jörg B' showed that households could be remarkably fluid: in the late 1960s, as a student, he moved into a one-room flat with 'a male lover'; by the 1970s, he met his wife-to-be, and, soon after their marriage, they moved to a two-roomed flat; they divorced, but continued living together, now with the addition of Jörg's new boyfriend, who apparently hailed from Cuba.[10] Some of the unshockable spirit of the old city had been transfused to these new estates of high-rise towers.

Yet one of the dark elements of the Nazi past remained integral to the lives of these children of the war: that of mass domestic surveillance by a security apparatus hungry to hear of ideological transgressions. By the 1960s and 1970s, the Stasi was woven deep into the fabric of every single household in East Berlin and East Germany. Telephones were tapped, conversations routinely monitored; a great many of those one- and two-bedroomed flats on those modern concrete estates were implanted with hidden listening devices. The Stasi by this stage had brought new technology to the opening of letters, with even faster machines that could open and then reseal them on an industrial scale. As long as one lived within the parameters rigidly set out in party meetings, then one might live peacefully. But if friends or family members were perceived to have criticized any element of the regime, then social networks and relatives could expect to feel the grim repercussions: hours of hostile questioning, the threat of imprisonment, the cold withdrawal of employment opportunities. Lives could be ruined by neighbourly rumour, or by the ill will of a housing block warden. For many East Berliners, it required the most intense discipline to keep one's public identity firmly in line with party thought, while simultaneously privately dissenting. In this sense, the older generation had more experience of keeping their true feelings shielded; they had learned to hide their inner selves from Nazi surveillance and perhaps transmitted this skill to their offspring. Not even the Nazis had thought to install mass listening devices, though; this was a fresh domestic hazard. In the still darkness of the night, anyone's dreams – and muttered sleep-talking – might potentially betray them.

But even the most unsmiling totalitarianism relies to a degree on consent, and in the 1960s the regime did what it could to respond to a world in which Beatlemania and other forms of pop culture were bewitching that post-war generation. In East Berlin, the gritted determination of those young people to listen to forbidden music – their parents having immersed themselves in censored jazz and swing throughout the Nazi years – continued strongly. Walter Ulbricht was heard to complain of the Beatles that all their 'yeah yeah yeahs' were deadening and monotonous (bold words from one of the least scintillating orators of the century). But the Wall was not so impermeable that their music broadcast from West Berlin's radio stations could not be picked up furtively on East German transistors. As a result, throughout the 1960s, East Berlin's television and radio stations were filled with the competing distractions of pleasing, catchy *Schlager* (sunny, simple tunes); this was politically approved pop. Pretty young singers such as Ina Martell, Chris Doerk and Ruth Brandin performed bouncy compositions, in bright but demure dresses, sometimes on location against the backdrop of East Berlin's modernist architecture. There was a professionalism here that matched the West; these performances in many cases were indistinguishable from their light-entertainment counterparts – Cilla Black, Sandie Shaw – performing on kitschy television shows in Britain. Yet still the young of East Berlin knew and understood what they were missing. At the end of the decade, in 1969, a rumour swept Berlin that the Rolling Stones would be performing a concert on the roof of the newly constructed high-rise headquarters of media mogul Axel Springer in West Berlin. The whisper itself, and its spread from west to east, was a further insight into the impossibility of completely dividing a city. The rumour solidified; a date, a particular afternoon seemed confirmed. And since the Axel Springer building was so close to the Wall, huge numbers of young East Berliners began to gather, determined that they would not miss this momentous gig. This was too much for the Stasi – not merely the unlawful mass gathering, but also the sullying of ideological purity. There were beatings, arrests and in many cases imprisonment. To the GDR authorities, even the desire to listen to such music was evidence of deranged delinquency that would have to be corrected. As it transpired, the rumour was just that; the Stones never materialized.

In the popular spy thrillers that made up so much of western Europe's 1960s film entertainment, East Berlin was always portrayed as ruined and leached of colour other than brown and dark grey. Alfred Hitchcock's *Torn Curtain* (1966) suggested vistas of ashy ruins, uncannily empty streets, grimly dark, monumental state hotels and weirdly deserted museums. Yet it was never so simple; the reconstructed plaza of Alexanderplatz was by the mid 1960s a lively and busy open prospect of bright modernist concrete, glinting glass and metal: a vast paved concourse with fountains, an artfully sculpted 'world clock' (part rotunda, with steel hoops and spheres representing the solar system) and (thinly stocked) shopping parades and cafes; in West Berlin, the luxurious Kurfürstendamm, with its expensive boutiques and stores (and the fragrant KaDeWe department store on Tauentzienstrasse), differed largely by degrees of gaudiness (as well as wealth), with greater numbers of neon signs and candy-coloured awnings. The reality of East Berlin was, even at that point, sparse shelves and queues for food staples. But in architectural terms there was a curious ideological parity between the two; a recourse to concrete and height, but also to the more moulded sculpted possibilities of that concrete: in West Berlin, an old church was renovated with new angular concrete shapes; in the East, an animal-research laboratory lay within an elegantly curved grey construction, looking from some angles a little like an elephant in repose. In housing too (surveillance aside) there was little apart from money that divided the hyper-rectilinear high-rise flats of West Berlin's version of Le Corbusier's Unité d'Habitation and East Berlin's early 1970s Leninplatz housing estate, itself a mass of modish curving and sharp angles (albeit arranged around a vast statue of Lenin).

Throughout the centre of it all, like a concrete scar, ran the Wall. But even by the late 1960s this construction too became part of Berlin's endlessly restless architectural nature. Like so many of the buildings and streets that it divided, it was a palimpsest, with new layers and rearrangements. The original 1961 construction – which, had another decision been arrived at, would have been composed mainly of barbed and linked wire rather than concrete, an impregnable fence rather than a wall – had been fast and impulsive, with little thought of how long it might last. Parts of it – weathered and crumbling – now needed replacing. The Wall, averred one observer, showed 'an amazing tendency towards mutation'.[11] And so those sections that ran through the city's heart were carefully refined. More tall sentry posts were added, further echoes of the old concentration camps. And with the strengthened concrete came – in some sections – the introduction of rounded concrete piping running along the top; should anyone succeed in clambering up the wall, the newly curved surface would make it impossible to get a purchase to haul themselves over.

Certainly, the Wall's grim pattern of life-shattering injuries and death was unchanged; in 1968, when in Paris and other western cities the student movement was parading the streets pushing for revolution, there were East Berliners seeking to escape revolution's nightmare results. Some with engineering expertise planned and constructed ingenious tunnels leading from apartment-block basements under the border (though these were frequently detected by the omnipresent Stasi). Others fixed on more impulsive, desperate methods. Twenty-five-year-old furniture upholsterer Dieter Weckeiser and his twenty-two-year-old wife Elke (he had been married

once before, and had three young children) became fixated upon
returning to the West, where he and his mother had once lived. It
was an icy February night in 1968 when the young couple agreed on
an ambitious route that involved pressing through barbed wire and
guard dogs near the Reichstag, climbing a ten-foot-high mesh fence,
swimming the near-frozen Spree and then somehow hauling themselves over the vast concrete border wall that lay on the other side.
They barely made it past the first of those obstacles. Guards in the
watchtower at around 11 p.m. saw them trying to get through the
barbed wire. The gesture of warning shots was dispensed with and
the air was filled with molten bullets. Dieter's skull was shattered and
Elke was hit in the legs and chest. She was the first to die; he succumbed the following day.[12] Those who fired the shots received
commendations and were promoted.

And so, to West Berliners, those who were slaughtered, either in
the water or in the 'death strips', were exemplars of the true defiant
spirit of a city that had been divided with abominable cruelty. Citizens spoke periodically of hearing shots ringing out along those
death strips, and they were not mistaken. It is reckoned that some 243
people died in the course of trying to get across the Wall between 1961
and 1989 (although the casualties were less frequent in later years, the
horror remained). And yet the Cold War was not immutable, and the
two halves of Berlin were always changing. The skyline of the entire
city was pierced in 1969 by the opening of the GDR Berlin Television Tower – 1,200 feet in height, a futuristic slender line,
surmounted by a vast ball designed to look like a Soviet satellite.
Although the cost of the construction of the Berlin Wall had led to
austerity in the east of the city, money was found for this elegant
monument to socialist futurism.

The diplomatic atmosphere was changing too: the advent of West
German Chancellor Willy Brandt, with an enthusiasm for what was
termed *Ostpolitik* (an optimistic determination to engage and 'nor-
malize relations' with this mirror Germany), plus a new approach
between America and Russia of détente (with Leonid Brezhnev leading the Soviet Union), led to slight though significant relaxations. By
the early 1970s, it was at last possible once more for families on either
side of the Wall to talk on the telephone. The GDR authorities also

relented when it came to the elderly; they had made it possible for pensioners to cross over from East Berlin to West Berlin and West Germany beyond, if they wished to go to live with families over the border. For the older generations, it was sometimes too late, in the sense that other elderly relatives and long-lost friends across the divide were now dead. But the slight thaw meant a lot to the young. The long reign of Walter Ulbricht gave way (after a forced resignation) in 1971 to that of his successor, Erich Honecker – a fifty-eight-year-old lifelong party apparatchik, a portrait of whom, bespectacled and beige-suited, was placed in every classroom – who was eager for the legitimacy of East Germany as a state in its own right to be recognized. It was now permissible for West Berliners to visit the east of the city for short periods, with the proviso that they exchanged a certain quantity of western Deutschmarks for eastern Ostmarks. This aside, the possibility of day visits was for families still a joyous concession that seemed miraculous to some. Honecker was no less rigid than Ulbricht, and, under his rule, the Stasi grew ever larger and more influential, its tendrils reaching into the most intimate corners of all East German lives, but he was alive to the eyes of the wider world, and shrewd about deploying terms such as 'consumer socialism'; by 1972 he had succeeded in having East Germany recognized as a full member of the United Nations. In a decade when western Europe would suffer the economic aftershocks of the OPEC oil crisis, with accompanying inflation and recession, the austere streets of East Berlin were not all that distinguishable from other European city centres – the concrete brutalist landscapes to be found from Cologne to Birmingham.

Honecker was also alive to a new culture of human rights; at the 1975 Helsinki Conference on Security and Cooperation in Europe, the 'Helsinki Accords' were signed by nations west and east alike: they entailed pledges to respect fundamental freedoms, including thought, while also guaranteeing the territorial integrity of the signatory states. The golden idea was to promote lasting peace via more cooperation – not just political, but industrial, intellectual, scientific and artistic. By suggesting that Western democracies and Eastern Bloc communist states essentially had a moral parity, the Accords further burnished the legitimacy of the GDR. But, even though it was now the case that many East German dissidents, rather than being imprisoned, were instead being expelled to West Berlin, and the wider West beyond (the GDR sending them into an exile many must have yearned for), Honecker also viewed the two mighty ideologies of the superpowers as too antithetical to survive porous borders. 'How can a lasting peace be secured?' he declared in the late 1970s. 'Some claim that all we need are more travel and human contact. Life has proven this stance to be not only naïve but a conscious deception. It puts people on the wrong track and diverts attention from the roots of the war danger . . . which is perpetuated by the most aggressive circles of monopoly capital.'[13] Berlin had once been one of the world's most open cities; now half of it was shrinking back in fear. But, in some senses, to Honecker's generation, such fear was understandable; they had witnessed the rise of the Nazis, and had no difficulty imagining them arising in some new form once more.

In the 1970s, the Berlin Wall was the keystone to the entire geopolitical structure of Europe. Any attempt to remove it, or even parts of it, would – it was thought on both sides – create a lethal instability that would then cause fractures and fissures across the continent. The Soviets, with the East Germans, contrived a series of hypothetical scenarios for war games: what would happen if the GDR were to demolish the Berlin Wall? What would then prevent the onrush of that predatory 'monopoly capital'? How would the GDR respond? How much force would be required to secure the whole of Berlin, thus properly and finally subsuming it into the GDR? How much more European territory would they then have to expand into to protect these gains? But the end result of these games was nuclear war; and the Cold War was entering a new era of intercontinental missiles: the sort of mass death by remote control that, in an earlier era, Nazi rocket scientist Wernher von Braun might have dreamed of. It was as though East and West Berlin were matter and antimatter; force them together and the result would be a fearful chain reaction, resulting in a vast and unstoppable atomic disaster.

The Wall itself was further refined in the mid to late 1970s, fashioned to resemble 'a national border like any other',[14] though there were few if any such borders elsewhere in the world. On the replaced sections, the concrete was now 'seamlessly smooth'.[15] The prefabricated blocks had been tested elsewhere beforehand – not for strength, but for their ability to withstand the efforts of those trying to climb over or blast their way through. 'Athletic persons'[16] were selected to take runs at it to see if they could successfully climb it; 'small trucks' laden with explosives were driven at it. Tests successfully completed, the city-centre Wall was, section by section, installed and reworked; on its western side, the new smooth surface became a gift to graffiti artists, who slathered it with satirical portraits and slogans. Thus, ironically, a great symbol of oppression also came to illustrate Berlin's other spirit, that of a certain obdurate and colourful ungovernability.

On the GDR side, there was a border guard who had watched the new sections of the Wall being installed in the mid 1970s, and who – after hour upon hour of staring and thinking – suddenly found himself struck by a terrible insight that turned all the assumptions of his life inside out. He had been taught that, above all, this Wall was to keep people out. 'They always said it was an anti-fascist protection rampart,' the unnamed guard later said. 'But the whole thing was built back to front . . . It was built so no one from our side could go over. But from the other side they could have rolled right over it . . . That is where it started to dawn on me. Before that, I had never seen The Wall.'[17] (One faint but consistent embarrassment for the GDR regime was the number of border guards across the years who had seized lightning opportunities from their privileged positions to escape to the West.)

As with any totalitarian regime, many appointed to guard it exulted in their power to shoot, but many others did not. A particularly tragic incident in 1981 illustrated the painful positions in which these border guards could be placed. A young doctor from Bavaria, Johannes Muschol, was visiting friends in West Berlin, having driven there on the transit highway that crossed the East German countryside. He was suffering from schizophrenia, and was at that stage in poor mental health. He disappeared from the streets for a while, and somehow later materialized in an East Berlin nursing home. It was unclear how he had crossed over and ended up there. Dr Muschol was returned by the authorities across the border, but later was seen

at the section of Wall that lay near Alt-Reinickendorf in a northern
suburb. He climbed 'a viewing platform' next to the Wall, thence on
to the Wall itself, and then he dropped into the death strip.[18] There
was one guard in particular who could see that Dr Muschol was
clearly not well. He approached him, and told him to halt. The
guard followed as the doctor, distracted and distressed, refused to
listen and ran towards the interior, nine-foot-high wall. The guard
told the doctor that he had no wish to shoot, but to his horror,
before he could issue any further reassurance, the doctor convulsed
and fell; another guard on the watchtower had opened fire. The
Stasi cover-up began at once. Dr Muschol's body was taken for cre-
mation, and money found in his wallet was used to pay for it. On the
western side, all that could be initially confirmed was that someone had been shot dead. The East German government refused to
confirm his identity. This added a layer of needless anguish to the
grief of Dr Muschol's family, who had to wait years before they
received official confirmation of their loss.[19] But this was also the
action of a government and security service which had ossified as
the world around them changed; and as the Soviet Union ushered in
the rule of Mikhail Gorbachev in 1985, and his realistic assessments
of a rigid, buckling, ever more bankrupt system, so the regime in East
Berlin became an oppressive authoritarian anachronism, outside the
general flow of time. Erich Honecker was an unyielding hardliner
increasingly at odds with the liberalizing reforms – including the
*glasnost* (openness, or a certain freedom of expression) being promoted in Russia by Gorbachev. East Berliners were acutely aware,
through (still forbidden) West Berlin television and radio, of the vast
icebergs of communism creaking and calving.

By this time, punk rock had finally established itself in certain
corners of East Berlin; brave young men with extravagant Mohicans
playing loud music who – startlingly – found firm allies within the
Lutheran Church. The music and style were very strictly forbidden
by the GDR authorities, the Stasi even ordering one of its agents to
dress in the punk manner and infiltrate an East Berlin grouping. The
community halls of certain churches afforded the punks a measure of
sanctuary, for as much as the communists loathed organized religion,
it was considered unwise to press down too hard upon it by raiding

churches. On the face of it, perhaps the alliance between punk rockers and Lutherans was not so unlikely: like the punks, the clergy had a resilience and a measure of defiance when it came to living under authorities that were suspicious and hostile; and, in the face of an aggressive and oppressive regime, both the Church and the young punks valued the honest expression of the inner heart.

Yet even in the late 1980s, as the tides of the world changed once more, the lives of East Berliners were still forfeit if they tried to leave. The last person to die trying to cross the Berlin Wall was a thirty-two-year-old electrical engineer called Winfried Freudenberg. He and his wife Sabine had decided by the end of 1988 that it was intolerable to be held within the borders of the East, when so many opportunities lay in the West. Both scientifically trained, their plan was both courageous and practical; he took a job in the gas supply department of an East Berlin state energy concern. Then, over the course of months, the couple bought quantities of polythene sheeting and heavy-duty adhesive tape.

By the spring of 1989 they were ready. On the evening of 7 March they drove to the northern wooded suburb of Blankenburg, where there was a gas storage station to which Freudenberg had access. And it was here, in a yard by the otherwise darkened facility, that the Freudenbergs began to fill with natural gas the vast balloon that they had painstakingly constructed. But, as the balloon inflated, there was a terrible setback; a worker in another part of the plant saw the balloon and telephoned the authorities. By the time they arrived, the balloon was almost ready to fly, but the Freudenbergs were frantically worried that it was not quite full enough to carry two. On the spur of the moment, the couple decided that Winfried should make the escape alone. The ropes were cut and the balloon rose into the night, almost immediately colliding with a power cable as it did so.

Freudenberg survived that, but their panicked calculations had been wrong. The balloon *should* have taken two, and now it was too lightly ballasted, and rising uncontrollably fast. The direction was right – it was heading towards West Berlin – but there had been some damage and Freudenberg seemed unable to control its altitude. And so it was that, instead of an hour's flight, he floated, helpless, in the ever-colder night air, with no protection or help. And the balloon's altitude was such that, in the cross-current of winds, it became impossible to handle. What then followed could only be speculated upon by the authorities in the horrible aftermath: one theory was that Freudenberg had tried to climb the rope netting to cut the balloon fabric, thus facilitating descent, but instead, in that ice-cold air, lost his grip. His hands may simply have been too frozen to be able to hang on. Whatever the cause, he fell hundreds of feet, crashing to the ground in a back garden near Grunewald in West Berlin, his body broken beyond measure and his death instantaneous.[20] His widow Sabine was arrested, charged with 'attempting to breach the border' and sentenced to – by Stasi standards – a lenient three years' probation.[21]

She received her amnesty on 27 October 1989. The East German government was dissolving around her. The Cold War thaw had become a crystalline flood. By 9 November, thanks in part to a bungled East Berlin government press conference, where it was suggested by officials in confusion that all borders would be open with immediate effect, the latest Berlin Revolution was underway, some seventy years after the Great War. But, in this revolution, the stony guards laid their weapons aside. And the vast crowds who gathered on either side of the Wall were both active participants and observers, the breach in the Wall both real and symbolic. There was exultant disbelief: that the one consistent force that had held much of the continent in its grip for decades – that of totalitarianism – had vanished like a ghost. That night of 9 November 1989 saw illimitable tears as East and West Berliners conjoined fully and freely for the first time since 1961; for those in the East, the first true freedom that they had known since 1933, and the advent of the Nazis. This final Berlin Revolution of the twentieth century was the truly definitive one; the oppressive wall was danced upon before being hacked at by countless euphoric souvenir hunters. This was not, to use the overworn phrase of historian Francis Fukuyama, the End of History (and nor did he ever mean it quite like that); but for Berlin, it was a resolution.

# Afterword

The Wall is still there; the death strip and the watchtowers too. They persist as a fragment of that stark insanity; this is a short stretch preserved as an official museum on Bernauer Strasse, solemn in atmosphere, almost a shrine. Why memorialize when the reality can serve as the memorial? In this sense, Berlin seems allergic to metaphor. Undemolished sections of the wall can also be found at St Hedwig's cemetery; an almost mile-long section along the banks of the Spree (where the Wall's concrete was painted over by 118 contributing artists, forming the East Side Gallery); sentinel-like segments at the station at Potsdamer Platz; and, of course, a section at Checkpoint Charlie, the crossing point immortalized in the Western imagination in a hundred procedural spy films.

But the modern city is also a palimpsest; and having seen so much erased in 1945, and again in the wake of the fall of communism in 1989, there seems to be an instinct to preserve what remains, with echoes of history to be seen within the brick and stone. There is a very famous nightclub called Berghain (one of a great many famous nightclubs to be found in the city) in the Friedrichshain district: it is situated within one of the city's former mighty power stations, which was built by the East German government in 1953 in the Stalinist neoclassical style and which was decommissioned in the 1980s. This gaunt monument stands just by the old border. Any other European city might have looked at this industrial hulk and decreed a luxury apartment or museum development (rather like the old Bankside power station in London). Instead, the building was dedicated to that other great Berliner tradition of pulse-quickening music and carefully curated hedonism. Other sites close by once occupied by heavy industry now pound out industrial music, and clubs such as Cassiopeia, based in a former factory in Friedrichshain, are at night bathed in the richest yellow and purple lights; Kurt Tucholsky might time-travel from the 1920s Luna Park and understand that thread of nocturnal pleasure-seeking. Similarly the sexual-research pioneer Magnus Hirschfeld might have been amused by the modern iteration of the KitKatClub, which features an array of spaces and alcoves where some of the more specialized tastes are practised and celebrated. Last and not least, the philosopher Walter Benjamin might also have understood the spirit of these venues perfectly: in the wake of the Great War, he found himself in a Berlin nightclub where, as he wrote, there was a female prostitute 'in a very tight-fitting white sailor's suit', who 'determined my erotic fantasies for years to come'.[1]

Yet there are other threads of continuity – some surprising – running through the city. The sometimes controversial rebuilding and resurrection of the grand (and once royal) eighteenth-century Berliner Schloss, in the form of the Humboldt Forum (itself a pleasing tribute to Alexander von Humboldt), has also brought to public attention a continuing campaign by some members of the aristocratic Hohenzollern family to reclaim art and property that was seized by the incoming Soviets in 1945; does the silent hope still burn in some breasts that they might one day be restored to a position of influence?

It is always best to understand a city by walking it; a day of golden September sunshine, warm but with the promise of the autumn to come, bathes the streets and buildings and monuments in a luxurious light that makes it possible to see why so many have been irresistibly drawn here across the years. There are the terraces of tall white apartment blocks in Moabit (Kurt Tucholsky territory) that still carry a little of the dignity of the last Wilhelmine days; the lovely leafy streets near Kurfürstendamm that were comprehensively destroyed in the war (such as the tiny and very pretty Prager Platz) and which have been rebuilt so sensitively that the previous trauma is impossible to discern; and even the vulgarized tourist attraction of Checkpoint Charlie none the less has a certain crackling vigour about it. The artists, musicians and assorted bohemians, in their repurposed realms of cavernous factory halls and disused rail depots, have the same transgressive instincts as George Grosz and the Bauhaus students. Has Berlin always favoured the young? The image of the youthful stone-washed-denimed women and men scrambling over the Wall that night in 1989 helped to cement a sense that the city had carried for a long time; that, even in the face of fascism, and of stony communist authoritarianism, there was always an element of the population that was fundamentally resistant to totalitarianism. That the acidic, cynical humour for which the city's population had always been famous could never be entirely quelled. In essence, Berlin was never really Hitler's city. Nor was it ever Stalin's. However hard they sought to impress their version of history on its people and streets, either with garlands of swastikas or with the grim ideology of uniformity, the city remained stubbornly immutable at its heart.

History never ends; who might guess what form the next revolution to sweep Berlin will take? But we might draw faith from the essential elements that survived the dreadful firestorm of the twentieth century, and flourished once more, like the colourful wildflowers around the concrete Humboldthain. If a city can ever be said to have a spirit, then Berlin — youthful, open, contrary — might be assured that its own will survive.

# Acknowledgements

Throughout what has been a rather intense couple of years for everyone, my gratitude and thanks, to so many, are – if anything – deeper than usual. To begin with, I want to pay tribute to Gertrud Achinger and Dr Eva Geffers, who have done such outstanding work with the Zeitzeugenbörse in Berlin, and who, as well as kindly sparing the time to see me, provided me with a wonderful array of material. This wonderful organization has given voice to huge numbers of older Berliners who in previous years were not encouraged to tell their extraordinary stories: layers of collective post-war guilt settled upon and muffled vivid and illuminating memories. The Zeitzeugenbörse not only records and films its contributors, so that their voices may last beyond their own lifetimes, but also arranges brilliant educational sessions where young people meet with old and experiences are related and shared. There is also a monthly newsletter, frequently packed with short, wonderfully detailed entries from contemporary witnesses – memories ranging from post-war playground games to the grim division of the Wall. For further information, see https://zeitzeugenboerse.de/. In addition to all this, and in wider terms, the Bundesarchiv – the federal archive – holds everything concerning Berlin life from correspondence to audio recordings and films. For more information, see www.bundesarchiv.de/EN/Navigation/Home/home.html.

Also invaluable in so many ways is the city's extraordinary Jewish Museum; I was set upon many paths of exploration by its powerful and moving exhibitions of Jewish life in the city. The museum also has the most extraordinary archives (www.jmberlin.de/en/archive). Among them are diaries, documentation, letters and keepsakes, stretching from the nineteenth century, through the gathering dark of the twentieth and beyond into the post-war years. This archive also has strong links with the Wiener Library in London, focusing upon the years of Nazi atrocity and terror (wienerholocaustlibrary.org).

Gratitude is due, as ever, to the London Library, its limitless stacks holding hundreds of unsuspected historic treasures (and also for working to keep those treasures broadly available through a time of restrictions); also to the British Library and its invaluable newspaper archive, which is itself now an historiographical phenomenon, and to the National Archives.

My deepest thanks as ever to Daniel Crewe, my publisher at Viking – the idea for the book was (once more) his. And he oversaw it with wise patience, guiding it safely into harbour. I also owe a serious debt to commissioning editor Connor Brown, whose brilliant notes and advice helped me through some dense mists along the way. Meanwhile Trevor Horwood, as always, has proven an ambassador for both clarity and poetry through his crystalline and fantastic copy-editing. Thanks too to the brilliantly creative and lateral Olivia Mead, and her energetic drive for publicity; to Annie Moore for her marketing; to Emma Brown (editorial management) and Annie Underwood (production). A deep bow as ever to Anna Power, my extraordinary agent, who arranged all of this in the first place, and to Helene Butler, for such a wide range of international deals (and Claire Morris, also brilliant on the international side). A quick word of thanks as well (and he might not even remember this) to Berlin-based television broadcaster Dennis Wagner, with whom I spent a day filming last year; his insouciant good humour, plus tales of growing up in the GDR, first set me on the trail of a range of themes to explore. As we all emerge from the global cocoon, do have a think about visiting Berlin if you haven't already. There is still so much this extraordinary and open-hearted city can teach us.

# Selected Bibliography

Anonymous, *A Woman in Berlin*, trans. Philip Boehm (Virago Modern Classics, 2011)

Hannah Arendt, *The Origins of Totalitarianism* (Penguin Classics, 2017)

Antony Beevor, *Berlin: The Downfall, 1945* (Viking, 2002)

Walter Benjamin, *One-Way Street and Other Writings*, trans. J. A. Underwood (Penguin Classics, 2009)

———, *Reflections: Essays, Aphorisms, Autobiographical Writings*, trans. Edmund Jephcott (Mariner, 2019)

John Borneman, *Belonging in the Two Berlins: Kin, State, Nation* (Cambridge University Press, 1992)

Denis Brian, *Einstein: A Life* (John Wiley 1996)

Alfred Döblin, *Berlin Alexanderplatz*, trans. Michael Hofmann (Penguin, 2018)

Magdalena Droste, *Bauhaus, 1919–1933* (Taschen, 2015)

Joseph Goebbels, *The Goebbels Diaries* (Hamish Hamilton, 1948)

Vasily Grossman, *A Writer at War: Vasily Grossman with the Red Army, 1941–1945*, ed. and trans. Antony Beevor and Luba Vinogradova (Pimlico, 2006)

George Grosz, *A Small Yes and a Big No: The Autobiography of George Grosz*, trans. Arnold J. Pomerans (Allison & Busby, 1982)

W. L. Guttsman, *Workers' Culture in Weimar Germany: Between Tradition and Commitment* (Berg, 1990)

Franz Hessel, *Walking in Berlin: A Flaneur in the Capital*, trans. Amanda DeMarco (Scribe, 2016)

Eric Hobsbawm, *Interesting Times: A Twentieth-Century Life* (Allen Lane, 2002)

Florian Huber, *Promise Me You'll Shoot Yourself: The Downfall of Ordinary Germans, 1945*, trans. Imogen Taylor (Allen Lane, 2019)

Christopher Isherwood, *Christopher and His Kind* (Vintage Classics, 2012)

Harald Jähner, *Aftermath: Life in the Fallout of the Third Reich, 1945–1955*, trans. Shaun Whiteside (WH Allen, 2021)

Marie Jalowicz-Simon, *Underground in Berlin: A Young Woman's Extraordinary Tale of Survival in the Heart of Nazi Germany* (Back Bay Books, 2014)

Tony Judt, *Postwar: A History of Europe Since 1945* (William Heinemann, 2005)

Jennifer M. Kapczynski and Michael D. Richardson (eds.), *A New History of German Cinema* (Camden House, 2012)

Ursula von Kardorff, *Diary of a Nightmare: Berlin, 1942–1945* (Rupert Hart-Davis, 1965)

Erich Kästner, *Going to the Dogs: The Story of a Moralist*, trans. Cyrus Brooks (NYRB Classics, 2013)

Ian Kershaw, *The End: Germany, 1944–45* (Allen Lane, 2011)

Count Harry Kessler, *The Diaries of a Cosmopolitan: Count Harry Kessler, 1918–1937* (Weidenfeld and Nicolson, 1971)

Victor Klemperer, *The Language of the Third Reich (A Philologist's Notebook)*, trans. Martin Brady (Athlone Press, 2000)

Hildegard Knef, *The Gift Horse* (André Deutsch, 1971)

Rory MacLean, *Berlin: Imagine a City* (Weidenfeld and Nicolson, 2014)

Roger Moorhouse, *Berlin at War: Life and Death in Hitler's Capital, 1939–45* (The Bodley Head, 2010)

Vladimir Nabokov, *The Gift* (Penguin Modern Classics, 2017)

Michael J. Neufeld, *Von Braun: Dreamer of Space, Engineer of War* (Knopf, 2007)

Larry Orbach and Vivien Orbach-Smith, *Young Lothar: An Underground Fugitive in Nazi Berlin* (I. B. Tauris, 2017)

Richard Overy, *The Bombing War: Europe 1939–45* (Allen Lane, 2013)

Jan Palmowski, *Inventing a Socialist Nation: Heimat and the Politics of Everyday Life in the GDR 1945–90* (Cambridge University Press, 2009)

Heinz Rein, *Berlin Finale*, trans. Shaun Whiteside (Penguin Modern Classics, 2017)

Alexandra Richie, *Faust's Metropolis: A History of Berlin* (Harper Press, 1998)

Joseph Roth, *What I Saw: Reports from Berlin, 1920–1933*, trans Michael Hofmann (Granta, 2003)

Wolfgang Schivelbusch, *In a Cold Crater: Cultural and Intellectual Life in Berlin 1945–1948* (University of California Press, 1998)

Gitta Sereny, *Albert Speer: His Battle with Truth* (Macmillan, 1995)

Sam H. Shirakawa, *The Devil's Music Master: The Controversial Life and Career of Wilhelm Furtwängler* (Oxford University Press, 1992)

William L. Shirer, *Berlin Diary: The Journal of a Foreign Correspondent, 1934–1941* (Hamish Hamilton, 1942)

Albert Speer, *Inside the Third Reich*, trans. Richard and Clara Winston (Weidenfeld and Nicolson, 1970)

Paul Stangl, *Risen from Ruins: The Cultural Politics of Rebuilding East Berlin* (Stanford University Press, 2018)

Carola Stern, *Ulbricht: A Political Biography* (Pall Mall Press, 1965)

Hans-Georg von Studnitz, *While Berlin Burns: The Diary of Hans-Georg von Studnitz, 1943–1945*, trans. R. H. Stevens (Weidenfeld and Nicolson, 1964)

Adam Tooze, *The Deluge: The Great War and the Remaking of the Global Order, 1916–1931* (Allen Lane, 2014)

Kurt Tucholsky, *Germany? Germany! Satirical Writings: The Kurt Tucholsky Reader*, trans. Harry Zohn (Berlinica, 2017)

Marie 'Missie' Vassiltchikov, *The Berlin Diaries 1940–1945 of Marie 'Missie' Vassiltchikov* (Chatto & Windus, 1985)

Charlotte Wolff, *Magnus Hirschfeld: A Portrait of a Pioneer in Sexology* (Quartet, 1986)

Marshal G. K. Zhukov, *The Memoirs of Marshal Zhukov* (Jonathan Cape, 1971)

# Notes

## Preface: 'Every city has history, but Berlin has too much!'

1 This from a sharply observed September 1968 essay by Stephen Spender for the *New York Review of Books*, 'The Young in Berlin', focusing on student politics but noticing a certain continuity in the faces seen on the streets of West Berlin.

2 From a 1930 essay by Joseph Roth, 'Stone Berlin', which can now be found, among his other collected monographs, in *What I Saw: Reports from Berlin, 1920–1933*, trans. Michael Hofmann (Granta, 2003).

3 As quoted in 'Hello to Berlin', an essay by Anthony Grafton for the *New York Review of Books*, August 1997.

4 As quoted in 'Berlin in Pictures: Weimar City and the Loss of Landscape' by An Paenhuysen, *New German Critique*, no. 109, Winter 2010 – a fascinating monograph about the way the electrical revolution transformed the aesthetic face of the city, and about the tensions created by this new-forged urban landscape.

5 From Harold Nicolson, then a diplomat, in his essay 'The Charm of Berlin', published in *Der Querschnitt* magazine in 1929. Like many Berlin memories of the period, it also echoes with the thunder of 'elevated trains'.

6 Cited by Eric Hobsbawm in 'Memories of Weimar', an essay for the *London Review of Books*, January 2008. Hobsbawm's own memoirs, which will be referenced later, are a fantastically evocative account of the period.

7 *A Small Yes and a Big No: The Autobiography of George Grosz*, trans. Arnold J. Pomerans (Allison & Busby, 1982), first published in 1955; a mesmerizingly well-written – and often howlingly funny – account of the author's colourful life.

8 Quoted in the *Financial Times*, 13 September 2019.

## 1. The Dwellers in the Dark

1 As quoted in *A Woman in Berlin* (1954), whose author is anonymous, though widely thought to be the journalist Marta Hillers; trans. Philip Boehm (Virago Modern Classics, 2011). As referenced later, it is the most extraordinarily affecting – and richly observed – account of the terror of those days for the city's female population.

2 Mentioned in several diaries of the period, including *A Woman in Berlin*.

3 As quoted in a monograph by Jeremy Hicks for the *Russian Review* (April 2013) on Simonov's piece 'The Extermination Camp' as well as the slightly later descriptions of death camps relayed by writer Vasily Grossman.

4 Brigitte Lempke's haunting memoirs are among those that have been collected by the Zeitzeugenbörse (Centre for Witnesses to Contemporary History) and feature in a short monograph issued in 2003 titled *Jugend Unter Brauner Diktatur*. The organization's monthly newsletter carries a range of fascinating accounts not just of Berlin's war, but also about life in the city before and afterwards; see https://zeitzeugenboerse.de.

5 Philip E. Mosely, 'The German Occupation: New Light on How the Zones Were Drawn', *Foreign Affairs*, July 1950.

6 *Daily Telegraph*, 2 April 1945.

7 As quoted in Nicholas Stargardt, *The German War* (2015).

8 Gerda's story was recovered and relayed in absorbing detail by Elinor Florence in a blog post that can be found at www.elinorflorence.com/blog/berlin-bombing/.

9 As quoted in *The Language of the Third Reich (A Philologist's Notebook)* by Victor Klemperer (Athlone Press, 2000), first published in Germany in 1957. A Jewish academic based in Dresden who survived both the Holocaust and the firebombing of his home city, Professor Klemperer was a compelling diarist and thinker; this book is hugely illuminating on the various means by which the Nazis sought to appropriate the German language itself, and mould it to their will.

10 Ibid.

11 Ibid.

12 As quoted in *Submerged on the Surface: The Not-So-Hidden Jews of Nazi Berlin, 1941–1945* by Richard N. Lutjens Jr (Berghahn Books, 2019).

13 Ibid.

14 From *Underground in Berlin: A Young Woman's Extraordinary Tale of Survival in the Heart of Nazi Germany* by Marie Jalowicz-Simon, trans. Anthea Bell (Back Bay Books, 2014).

15 Ibid.

16 As quoted in *Seeking Peace in the Wake of War* (Amsterdam University Press, 2015), ed. Stefan Ludwig-Hoffmann, Sandrine Kott et al.

17 Ibid.

18 Ibid.

19 Quoted in 'Germans into Allies: Writing a Diary in 1945' by Stefan Ludwig-Hoffmann, in *Seeking Peace in the Wake of War*.

## 2. The Sacrificial Children

1 Czech (or Zech) was interviewed for many years after the war, featuring in documentaries and articles; one such piece ran in the *Independent* newspaper as recently as 16 November 2005.

2 Ley's beliefs were cited sardonically by Hitler's Minister of Armaments and War Production Albert Speer, of all people, in his autobiography *Inside the Third Reich* (Weidenfeld and Nicolson, 1970), and have been quoted by academics exploring the Nazi weakness for fantasy science bordering on the occultist. Speer regarded himself as a balanced rationalist; this makes his un-self-aware memoirs all the more chilling.

3 Horst Basemann's memoirs, collected by the Zeitzeugenbörse.

4 Ibid.

5 Ibid.

6 Ibid.

7 Ibid.

8 Ibid.

9 There is a brilliant and rather moving passage in Grosz's memoir *A Small Yes and a Big No* when the young artist decides to visit his hero Karl May in Dresden; it is a stormy autumnal day, and the venerable author's home – filled with cosy nineteenth-century clutter – is as far away from the wide-open prairies and their attendant perils as could be imagined.

10  Quoted in *Inside the Third Reich*. Speer observed that, in his Berchtes-
    gaden retreat, Hitler had an entire alcove shelf devoted to the novels of
    Karl May.

11  A rich description from Grosz, *A Small Yes and a Big No*.

12  Quoted in a chilling but gripping monograph outlining not only the
    way the murder was seized upon, but also depicting the intense, crush-
    ing industrial poverty of Norkus's home life: Jay W. Baird, 'From Berlin
    to Neubabelsberg: Nazi Film Propaganda and *Hitler Youth Quex*', *Jour-
    nal of Contemporary History*, vol. 18, no. 3, July 1983.

13  Ibid.

14  Ibid.

15  Ibid.

16  Christa Ronke's memoirs, curated by the Zeitzeugenbörse.

17  Ibid.

18  Gerhard Rietdorff's recollections, curated by the Zeitzeugenbörse.

19  Ibid.

20  Ibid.

21  As quoted in a fascinating monograph by David K. Yelton: '"Ein Volk
    Steht Auf"': The German Volkssturm and Nazi Strategy 1944–1945',
    *Journal of Military History*, vol. 64, no. 4, October 2000.

22  Ibid.

23  The account features in *Prague in Danger: The Years of German Occupa-
    tion, 1939–45. Memories and History* by Peter Demetz (Farrar, Straus and
    Giroux, 2009).

24  This is from a lengthy and sparky interview with the architect con-
    ducted by Rem Koolhaas and Hans Ulrich-Obrist for the highly
    specialized journal *Log*, issue 16, Summer 2009.

25  Ibid. Ungers was alive to the Kurt Vonnegut-like oddness of his war
    experiences.

26  Christa Ronke's memoirs.

27  Ibid.


## 3. The Revolutionary Agony

1  From *The Diaries of a Cosmopolitan: Count Harry Kessler, 1918–1937* (Weidenfeld and Nicolson, 1971).

2 There is a range of wonderful essays on the life of Rosa Luxemburg to be found in the archives of the *London Review of Books*, including those by Jacqueline Rose ('What More Could We Want of Ourselves!', 16 June 2011) and Edward Timms ('Rosa with Mimi', 4 June 1987). Some strikingly warm detailing is given by Susan Watkins in a review of *Rosa Luxemburg: An Intimate Portrait* by Mathilde Jacob (Lawrence & Wishart, 2000), published 21 February 2002.

3 From *Diaries of a Cosmopolitan*.

4 Ibid.

5 Ibid.

6 Quoted in 'Weimarama', a compelling essay by Professor Richard J. Evans for the *London Review of Books*, 8 November 1990.

7 Ibid.

8 An observation from Kessler's *Diaries of a Cosmopolitan*.

9 A fascinating analysis of the origins of the Freikorps movement – and others like it – can be read in 'Vectors of Violence: Paramilitarism in Europe After the Great War, 1917–1923' by Robert Gerwarth and John Horne, *Journal of Modern History*, vol. 83, no. 3, September 2011.

10 'The Fortress Shop: Consumer Culture, Violence and Security in Weimar Berlin' by Molly Loberg, *Journal of Contemporary History*, vol. 49, no. 4, October 2014.

11 'Refugees from the East' by Joseph Roth, first published in *Neue Berliner Zeitung*, 20 October 1920 (trans. Michael Hofmann for Granta Books).

12 'The Orient on Hirstenstrasse' by Joseph Roth, first published in *Neue Berliner Zeitung*, 4 May 1921 (trans. Michael Hofmann for Granta Books).

13 'Wailing Wall' by Joseph Roth, first published in *Das Tagebuch*, 14 September 1929 (trans. Michael Hofmann for Granta Books).

14 'Fluctuations in Infant Mortality Rates in Berlin . . .' by Jay Winter and Joshua Cole, *European Journal of Population*, vol. 9, no. 3, September 1993.

15 From *The Gift* by Vladimir Nabokov, trans. Michael Scammell and Dmitri Nabokov (Penguin Modern Classics, 2001).

16 Ibid.; the novel's first third is an immersive literary evocation of the texture of those 1920s Berlin streets (and the latter pages evoke the Berlin literary journals, the testy émigré politics, and the nudity).

17  Quoted in a beautifully illustrated architectural monograph 'Poe-
    lzig and the Golem' by Marco Biraghi and Michael Sullivan (trans.),
    published in the Architectural Association's journal *A A Files*, no.
    75, 2017.

18  From Speer, *Inside the Third Reich*.

19  'Skyscrapers' by Joseph Roth, first published in *Berliner Börsen-Courier*,
    12 March 1922 (trans. Michael Hofmann for Granta Books).

20  Ibid.

21  Gropius's manifesto, its echoes down the years and its influence upon
    other Weimar architects are explored in a monograph called 'Gropius
    the Romantic' by Wolfgang Pehnt, *The Art Bulletin*, September 1971.

22  Ibid.

23  As quoted in Speer, *Inside the Third Reich*.

24  Ibid.

25  *Albert Speer: His Battle with Truth* by Gitta Sereny (Macmillan, 1995)
    grips hard throughout; an extraordinary quest on Sereny's part, through
    face-to-face interviews, to try to penetrate to the core of Speer.

26  Quoted in 'The Display Window: Designs and Desires of Weimar
    Consumerism' by Janet Ward Lungstrum, *New German Critique*, no. 76,
    Winter 1999.

27  Ibid.

28  From Paenhuysen, 'Berlin in Pictures'.

29  Lungstrum, 'The Display Window'.

30  Refreshments vividly recalled by artist George Grosz in his memoir
    noted above; but there are also details in a wonderful anthology of Kurt
    Tucholsky's work (he was an extraordinary Berlin satirist, social obser-
    ver and melancholic prophet, as well as editor of *Die Weltbühne*) entitled
    *Germany? Germany! Satirical Writings: The Kurt Tucholsky Reader*, trans.
    Harry Zohn (Berlinica, 2017).

31  Ibid.

32  Joseph Roth's essay 'Berlin's Pleasure Industry', *Münchner Neueste Nach-
    richten*, 1 May 1930 (trans. Michael Hofmann for Granta Books), is an
    amusing and evocative tour of Berlin's wide-ranging drinking estab-
    lishments, with all their fads and crazes.

33  From *Going to the Dogs: The Story of a Moralist* by Erich Kästner, trans.
    Cyrus Brooks (NYRB Classics, 2013), first published 1931.

34  Speer, *Inside the Third Reich*.

35  Ibid.
36  Ibid.

## 4. Spilled Blood and Exultation

1   Klemperer, *The Language of the Third Reich*.
2   *The Times*, 9 February 1920; the article in question also relates, in a tone that suggests suppressed glee, the thieving exploits of the criminal underworld, and incidences of gangland slayings.
3   Ibid.
4   *Daily Telegraph*, 30 June 1922.
5   Ibid.
6   *Daily Telegraph*, 17 December 1925.
7   Kästner, *Going to the Dogs*.
8   Ibid.
9   Ibid., Afterword.
10  From Eric Hobsbawm's extraordinary and endlessly engaging memoir *Interesting Times: A Twentieth-Century Life* (Allen Lane, 2002).
11  From a vivid contemporary memoir, *Walking in Berlin: A Flaneur in the Capital* by Franz Hessel, trans. Amanda DeMarco (Scribe, 2016), first published in 1929.
12  Hobsbawm, *Interesting Times*.
13  Hessel, *Walking in Berlin*.
14  There is a monograph exploring how Goebbels, having fashioned his political soldiers, then grasped the power of martyrdom. 'Goebbels, Horst Wessel and the Myth of Resurrection and Return' by Jay W. Baird, *Journal of Contemporary History*, vol. 17, no. 4, October 1982.
15  As quoted in a perhaps surprisingly beguiling work – *Ulbricht: A Political Biography* by Carola Stern (Pall Mall Press, 1965).

## 5. The Road That Led into Darkness

1   Klemperer, *The Language of the Third Reich*.
2   From *The Origins of Totalitarianism* by Hannah Arendt (Schocken Books, 1951; repr. Penguin Classics, 2017).

3 From 'A Berlin Chronicle' by Walter Benjamin, written in 1932 but not published until 1970 and now to be found in a handsome Benjamin anthology, *Reflections* (Mariner, 2019). Benjamin's observations – ranging from immersive monographs to acutely observed paragraphs – offer dizzying intellectual perspective, focusing in on minutiae while at the same time exploring the labyrinth of philosophy and language and image.

4 Ibid.

5 From Walker Benjamin, 'The Storyteller' (1936), in *Illuminations* (Bodley Head, 2015).

6 Ibid.

7 Ibid.

8 From *Young Lothar: An Underground Fugitive in Nazi Berlin* by Larry Orbach and Vivien Orbach-Smith (I. B. Tauris, 2017).

9 Ibid.

10 Hannah Arendt, *Men in Dark Times* (Mariner, 1970).

11 This is cited in a hugely absorbing monograph focusing on Heidegger's *Black Notebooks* – 'Great Again' by Malcolm Bull, *London Review of Books*, 20 October 2016.

12 Ibid.

13 Hobsbawm, *Interesting Times*.

14 Ibid.

15 Ibid.

16 Ibid.

17 Ibid.

18 Ruth-Johanna Eichenhofer's recollections, curated by the Zeitzeugenbörse.

19 Brigitte Lempke's memoirs.

20 Ibid.

21 Orbach and Orbach-Smith, *Young Lothar*.

22 Ibid.

23 *The Times*, 10 November 1938.

24 Ibid.

25 Ibid.

26 Ibid.

27 *Daily Telegraph*, 10 November 1938.

28 Ibid.

29 Ibid.

30  *The Times*, 10 November 1938.

31  Reinhart Crüger's recollections, curated by the Zeitzeugenbörse.

32  Ibid.

33  Ibid.

34  Ibid.

35  Ibid.

36  Ibid.

37  The persistence of Holocaust denial in some corners of international discourse never fails to shock. Nor is it a recent phenomenon. Back in 1984, a monograph entitled 'The Holocaust Hoax: A Rejoinder' by Wallace Greene and published in *Jewish Social Studies*, vol. 46, Summer 1984, took on contemporary deniers by laying out coldly and plainly the documentation of mass extermination and the inability of the Nazis to wholly conceal what they were doing.

38  Reinhart Crüger's recollections.

39  Ibid.

40  Ibid.

41  Orbach and Orbach-Smith, *Young Lothar*.

42  Ibid.

## 6. The Projection of Dreams

1  Helga Hauthal's recollections, curated by the Zeitzeugenbörse.

2  Ibid.

3  There is an intriguing and illuminating monograph on Billy Wilder's surprising 1920s Berlin hinterland as a paid male dance partner: 'Billy Wilder's Work as *Eintänzer* in Weimar Berlin' by Mihaela Petrescu, *New German Critique*, no. 120, Fall 2013.

4  The film, still mesmerizing to watch 100 years on, is available on DVD and Blu-Ray in the 'Masters of Cinema' series from Eureka.

5  From '14 February 1924: *Die Nibelungen* Premieres, Foregrounds "Germanness"' by Adeline Mueller, in a vast and wonderfully detailed book *A New History of German Cinema*, ed. Jennifer M. Kapczynski and Michael D. Richardson (Camden House, 2012).

6  Ibid.

7  Ibid.

8  As relayed by Fritz Lang when interviewed by critic and film historian Alexander Walker in 1967; *Fritz Lang: Interviews*, ed. Barry Keith Grant (University Press of Mississippi, 2003).

9  A quote deployed by Eric Rentschler for his book *The Ministry of Illusion: Nazi Cinema and Its Afterlife* (Harvard University Press, 1996).

10  A quote attributed to actress Elisabeth Bergner.

11  There is an interesting piece from March 1951 exploring Krauss's career (and his denazified return to post-war Berlin in the teeth of protests): 'The Return of Goebbels' Film-Makers: The Dilemma Posed by Werner Krauss and Veit Harlan' by Norbert Muhlen, reproduced in the online journal *Commentary*: www.commentary.org/articles/norbert-muhlen/the-return-of-goebbels-film-makers-the-dilemma-posed-by-werner-krauss-and-veit-harlan/.

12  As quoted by Andrew Dickson in a publication by the British Library, which holds a rare still of that production in its archives; a grim historical record illustrating how theatre and literature were distorted towards National Socialism. From '"Deutschland ist Hamlet": Shakespeare in Germany': www.bl.uk/shakespeare/articles/deutschland-ist-hamlet-shakespeare-in-germany (March 2016).

13  Ibid.

14  Kapczynski and Richardson (eds.), *A New History of German Cinema*.

15  This troubling film – a giddy and richly visualized fantasy on so many levels but impossible to separate from its Nazi production – is available on DVD.

16  Quoted on a German website on a page focusing in on Kästner's rather swish apartment: www.zeitreisen.de/kaestner/adressen/roscher.htm.

17  From Knef's autobiography *The Gift Horse* (André Deutsch, 1971).

18  Ibid.

19  Ibid.

20  Ibid.

21  Ibid.

## 7. The Uranium Club

1  From a very interesting monograph on the earlier career of Professor Hertz and other distinguished scientists: 'April 1915: Five Future Nobel

Prize-Winners Inaugurate Weapons of Mass Destruction and the Academic–Industrial–Military Complex' by William Van der Kloot, *Notes and Records of the Royal Society of London*, vol. 58, no. 2, May 2004.

2 From *Einstein: A Life* by Denis Brian (John Wiley, 1996).

3 Kessler, *Diaries of a Cosmopolitan*.

4 Brian, *Einstein*.

5 Ibid.

6 Ibid.

7 Ibid.

8 Ibid.

9 There was a rather moving monograph published not long after the war entitled 'Max Planck and Adolf Hitler' by James C. O'Flaherty, *American Association of University Professors Bulletin*, vol. 42, no. 3, Autumn 1956.

10 'Lise Meitner: 1878–1968' by O. R. Frisch, *Biographical Memoirs of Fellows of the Royal Society*, vol. 16, November 1970.

11 From *Heisenberg's War: The Secret History of the German Bomb* by Thomas Powers (Cape, 1993).

12 Ibid.

13 Ibid.

14 Ibid.

15 Speer, *Inside the Third Reich*.

16 Ibid.

17 From *Von Braun: Dreamer of Space, Engineer of War* by Michael J. Neufeld (Knopf, 2007).

18 Ibid.

19 There is an unusually lavish website devoted to the life and works of Manfred von Ardenne at www.vonardenne.biz/en/company/mva/. There are also many photographs. His autobiography was published in German in 1971. His work in the field of electron microscopy is mentioned in innumerable academic scientific journals.

## 8. The Prophecy of Flesh

1 From a delightful monograph, 'Hot Swing and the Dissolute Life: Youth, Style and Popular Music in Europe 1939–49' by Ralph Willett, *Popular Music*, vol. 8, no. 2, May 1989.

2 Ibid.

3 Manfred Omankowsky's recollections, curated by the Zeitzeugenbörse.

4 Ibid.

5 From a wholly absorbing monograph entitled 'What is "Nazi Music"?' by Pamela M. Potter, *Musical Quarterly*, Autumn 2005.

6 Ibid.

7 The terrible dilemmas faced by Furtwängler are explored in a monograph entitled 'Political Pleasures with Old Emotions? Performances of the Berlin Philharmonic in the Second World War' by Sven Oliver Müller, *International Review of the Aesthetics and Sociology of Music*, vol. 43, no. 1, June 2012.

8 From a monograph entitled 'Furtwängler the Apolitical?' by Chris Walton, *Musical Times*, vol. 145, no. 1889, Winter 2004.

9 Ibid.

10 Ibid.

11 Ibid.

12 For the rise of Karajan, see 'Political Pleasures with Old Emotions?'

13 A gripping account of how the link was made between the bloody brawl at the Silesian station and *Die Dreigroschenoper* is in 'The Criminal Underworld in Weimar and Nazi Berlin' by Christian Goeschel, *History Workshop Journal*, vol. 75, no. 1, Spring 2013.

14 From the illuminating *The Jazz Republic: Music, Race and American Culture in Weimar Germany* by Jonathan O. Wipplinger (University of Michigan Press, 2017).

15 The racist mania that lay behind Nazi loathing of jazz and swing is explored in some detail in a monograph entitled 'Forbidden Fruit? Jazz in the Third Reich' by Michael H. Kater, *American Historical Review*, vol. 94, no. 1, February 1989.

16 Wipplinger, *The Jazz Republic*.

17 Ibid.

18 Ibid.

19 It is one of the more startling developments of the modern age that this particular hit can now be found on YouTube by searching for 'Charlie and His Orchestra'; even a Nazi ersatz swing band, it seems, will today have its own fan base.

20 From an absorbing monograph entitled 'Hitler's Very Own Hot Jazz Band' by Mike Dash, *The Smithsonian*, 17 May 2012.

21 Ibid.

22 Ibid.

23 Ibid.

24 Ibid.

25 The *lustmord* motif was one of the more unusual sub-genres of Weimar art, and an interesting overview of this undercurrent of sexual violence, with an exploration of Grosz's 'Interregnum' cycle, can be found in 'Torture and Masculinity in George Grosz's *Interregnum*' by James A. Van Dyke, *New German Critique*, no. 119, Summer 2013.

26 Orbach and Orbach-Smith, *Young Lothar*.

27 From a letter to Herbert Fiedler, February 1946.

28 There is a rather nice visual Grosz primer to be found on the website of art auctioneers Christie's, giving a flavour of the range of his work, as well as reactions to it: www.christies.com/features/10-things-to-know-about-George-Grosz-7883-1.aspx.

29 Grosz, *A Small Yes and a Big No*.

30 Ibid.

31 Van Dyke, 'Torture and Masculinity in George Grosz's *Interregnum*'.

32 The story was reported on German news website DW, among other publications, on 4 February 2020.

33 From a hugely illuminating monograph entitled '"Only the Real, the True, the Masculine Held Its Value": Ernst Röhm, Masculinity and Male Homosexuality' by Eleanor Hancock, *Journal of the History of Sexuality*, vol. 8, no. 4, April 1998.

34 Ibid.

35 Ibid.

36 Ibid.

37 Ibid.

38 All of this is explored compellingly in *Magnus Hirschfeld and the Quest for Sexual Freedom: A History of the First International Sexual Freedom Movement* by Elena Mancini (Macmillan, 2010).

39 Ibid.

40 Ibid.

41 From 'The German Invention of Homosexuality' by Robert Beachy, *Journal of Modern History*, vol. 82, no. 4, December 2010.

42 Orbach and Orbach-Smith, *Young Lothar*.

43 Ibid.

44  Ibid.

45  Ibid.

46  There is an interesting monograph, ' "Judge for yourselves!": The Degenerate Art Exhibition as Political Spectacle' by Neil Levi, *October*, vol. 85, Summer 1998.

47  Ibid.

48  From an illustrated monograph, 'Hitler the Artist' by O. K. Werck-meister, *Critical Inquiry*, vol. 23, no. 2, Winter 1997.

49  Ibid.

50  Helga Hauthal's recollections.

51  Ibid.

52  Ibid.

## 9. The Ruins of Palaces

1  The structure is now a much-visited attraction, and there are some nice pictures giving different angles of this unique house to be found at visitworldheritage.com/en/eu/cecilienhof-country-house-in-the-new-garden/4e8e31d3-7819-413f-a4ea-62f06fee36d1.

2  Referred to in *The Berlin Diaries 1940–1945 of Marie 'Missie' Vassiltchikov* by Marie 'Missie' Vassiltchikov (Chatto & Windus, 1985).

3  Ibid.

4  Ibid.

5  Ibid.

6  From a review of *Stauffenberg: A Family History 1905–1944* by Peter Hoff-mann (Cambridge University Press, 1995), by Peter Black, *Central European History*, vol. 30, no. 1, 1997.

7  From 'Plutarch in Germany: The Stefan George *Kreis*' by Lawrence A. Tritle, *International Journal of the Classical Tradition*, vol. 1, no. 3, Winter 1995.

8  There is a fascinating (and furious) piece by Matthew Olex-Szczytowski entitled 'An Alternative History' for *The Spectator*, 21 July 2018.

9  The idea of the *Eintänzer* is explored in rich detail in 'Social Dancing and Rugged Masculinity: The Figure of the *Eintänzer* in Hans Jano-witz's Novel *Jazz* (1927)' by Mihaela Petrescu, *Monatshefte*, vol. 105, no. 4, Winter 2013.

10  The floral spectacle (in that heavy Berlin heat) was reported by the *New York Times*, 5 June 1905.

11  This acidic observation was made by Lord Edgar Vincent D'Abernon, British ambassador to Germany 1920–26, in his memoir *The Diary of an Ambassador*, vol. 3: *Dawes to Locarno, 1924–26* (though collected into one volume – *An Ambassador of Peace*, Hodder and Stoughton, 1930).

12  Kessler, *Diaries of a Cosmopolitan*.

13  Cited in a riveting essay, 'What Do the Hohenzollerns Deserve?' by David Motadel, *New York Review of Books*, 26 March 2020.

14  Cited in Speer, *Inside the Third Reich*.

15  Ibid.

16  Vassiltchikov, *Berlin Diaries*.

17  There is further rich detail in 'Franz von Papen, the German Center Party and the Failure of Catholic Conservatism in the Weimar Republic' by Larry Eugene Jones, *Central European History*, vol. 38, no. 2, 2005.

18  From an absorbing monograph: 'Franz von Papen, Catholic Conservatives and the Establishment of the Third Reich, 1933–1934' by Larry Eugene Jones, *Journal of Modern History*, vol. 83, no. 2, June 2011.

19  Ibid.

20  Speer, *Inside the Third Reich*. One striking thing about this story is the way that he confesses that the incident 'didn't affect me any more than that'.

## 10. Suspended in Twilight

1  From *The Memoirs of Marshal Zhukov* by Marshal G. K. Zhukov (Jonathan Cape, 1971).

2  Ibid.

3  As reported in the *Daily Telegraph*, 3 April 1945.

4  There is a gripping historical monograph by a German journalist, Erich Schneyder, who was moving among government circles, and translated and abridged by an American journalist, Louis Lochner, which closely observes Goebbels and others at street level through the downfall. 'The Fall of Berlin', first published in *Wisconsin Magazine of History*, vol. 50, no. 4 (Summer, 1967).

5  A chilling detail from the magisterial *Berlin: The Downfall, 1945* by Antony Beevor (Viking, 2002).

6  Zhukov, *Memoirs*.

7  Ibid.

8  Florence, www.elinorflorence.com/blog/berlin-bombing/.

9  Ibid.

10 Ibid.

11 Marion Keller's account, curated by the Zeitzeugenbörse.

12 Ibid.

13 Ibid.

14 Ibid.

15 Ibid.

16 Ibid.

17 Brigitte Eicke's memoirs, curated by the Zeitzeugenbörse.

18 Ibid.

19 Ibid.

20 From Richard Strauss's diary, 8 May 1945, quoted in 'Music, Memory, Emotion: Richard Strauss and the Legacies of War' by Neil Gregor, *Music and Letters*, February 2015.

## 11. *The Screaming Sky*

1  From an often surprising monograph entitled ' "Germany is Our Mission – Christ is Our Strength!": The Wehrmacht Chaplaincy and the "German Christian" Movement' by Doris L. Bergen, *Church History*, September 1997.

2  Ibid.

3  Ibid.

4  Ibid. Bergen explores the ethical fissures that opened up as the Nazis increased their pressure on the chaplains to preach 'soldierly virtues' and 'self-sacrifice' as part of God's 'will for order on earth'; the painful meshing of different types of faith.

5  Zhukov, *Memoirs*.

6  Schöneck quoted at length in *Berlin Battlefield Guide* by Tony Le Tissier (Pen & Sword, 2014).

7  Knef, *The Gift Horse*.

8  Lutz Koch, as relayed by the *Daily Telegraph*, 17 April 1945.

9  Zhukov, *Memoirs*.

10 Ibid.

11  Ibid.

12  Ibid.

13  Speer, *Inside the Third Reich*.

14  Ibid.

15  Ibid.

16  Ibid.

17  Mechtild Evers's account, curated by the Zeitzeugenbörse.

18  Ibid.

19  Ibid.

20  Quoted at *Hitler's Girls: Doves Amongst Eagles* by Tim Heath (Pen & Sword, 2017).

21  Quoted at very great length by the *Daily Telegraph* on 17 April 1945; the mad, gothic intensity of the rhetoric, signalling its own kind of dissolution, must have made for mesmerizing reading across countless rationed-breakfast tables in Britain.

22  Ibid.

23  Ibid.

24  The diaries of Ruth Andreas-Friedrich were translated and published as *Battleground Berlin: Diaries, 1945–48* (Paragon House 1990); a volume covering earlier years depicted the courageous resistance to the regime.

25  Beevor, *Berlin: The Downfall, 1945*.

## 12. The Tears of All Mothers

1  There is a thoughtful monograph entitled 'Writing Through Crisis: Time, History and Futurity in German Diaries of the Second World War' by Kathryn Sederberg, *Biography*, vol. 40, no. 2, Spring 2017.

2  Ibid.

3  There are many newsreels of Hitler's birthdays in Berlin across the years which can now be viewed on YouTube. Some of these reports have a dated charm of their own. Particularly eyebrow-raising today is the entry from British Movietone News, covering a parade in the Tiergarten in 1936, and using insulting terms such as 'Fritz'.

4  Cited in a mesmerizing monograph: 'Wagnerian Self-Fashioning: The Case of Adolf Hitler' by Hans Rudolf Vaget, *New German Critique*, no. 101, Summer 2007.

5  Speer, *Inside the Third Reich*.

6  Ibid.

7  Dorothea von Schwanenfluegel's memoirs were published under the title *Laughter Wasn't Rationed: A Personal Journey Through Germany's World Wars and Postwar Years* (Tricor Press, 2001).

8  Ibid.

9  The career of Lutz Heck is explored in a hugely illuminating monograph: 'Green Nazis? Reassessing the Environmental History of Nazi Germany' by Frank Uekötter, *German Studies Review*, May 2007.

10  And yet one alligator did survive: indeed, Saturn, as the reptile was called, went on to live a long life in captivity, only passing away in 2020: 'Berlin WW2 Bombing Survivor Saturn the Alligator Dies in Moscow Zoo', BBC News; www.bbc.co.uk/news/world-europe-52784240.

11  Uekötter, 'Green Nazis?'

12  Ibid.

13  Ibid.

14  Ibid.

15  There is more in a left-field history entitled *The Zookeepers' War: An Incredible True Story from the Cold War* by J. W. Mohnhaupt, trans. Shelley Frisch (Simon & Schuster, 2019).

16  In the accounts offered to the Zeitzeugenbörse, and in memoirs too, the threat of air raids is always muffled by the fear of the attacks to come from the Red Army.

17  Von Schwanenfluegel, *Laughter Wasn't Rationed*.

18  There is an excellent novel, written in 1946, detailing the destruction of Berlin, which cited this and other official Goebbels speeches in full, weaving them in and around the fictional jeopardy faced by its characters. *Berlin Finale* by Heinz Rein, trans. Shaun Whiteside, first published 1947 (Penguin, 2017).

19  Von Schwanenfluegel, *Laughter Wasn't Rationed*.

20  Reported in the *Daily Telegraph*, 21 April 1945.

21  Knef, *The Gift Horse*.

22  Ibid.

23  Ibid.

24  Ibid.

25  Ibid.

26  Ibid.

27  Christa Ronke's memoirs.

28  Ibid.

29  Schneyder, working with Louis Lochner, cited this incident in a mono-graph called 'The Fall of Berlin', *Wisconsin Magazine of History*, vol. 50, no. 4, Summer 1967.

30  Hildegard Dockal's recollections curated by the Zeitzeugenbörse.

31  Ibid.

32  Ibid.

33  Günther Lothar's recollections curated by the Zeitzeugenbörse.

34  Ibid.

35  Ingeborg Seldte's recollections, curated by the Zeitzeugenbörse.

36  Alfred Czech was interviewed on a few occasions, one of the last being for the *Independent* on 16 November 2005: www.independent.co.uk/news/world/europe/downfall-the-story-of-a-nazi-boy-hero-520880.html.

37  Ibid.

38  Speer, *Inside the Third Reich*.

39  Ibid.

40  Via the ever-astonishing reach of YouTube, it is possible to listen to a 1929 recording of 'Blutrote Rosen', with some footage of late 1920s Berlin night-life. It can be found here: www.youtube.com/watch?v=4yauXRh5NW4.

41  Cited on a powerful website: Music and the Holocaust: holocaustmu-sic.ort.org/places/camps/central-europe/sachsenhausen/.

42  This and other extraordinary, haunting stories can be read at www.below-sbg.de/geschichte/april-1945-todesmarsch-und-waldlager/aussagen-von-zeitzeugen/.

43  From a fascinating study by Mordechai Altshuler in *Soviet Jews in World War II: Fighting, Witnessing, Remembering* (Academic Studies Press, 2014).

44  Ibid.

45  Schneyder, 'The Fall of Berlin'.

## 13. *Streets of Blood*

1  From *A Writer at War: Vasily Grossman with the Red Army, 1941–1945* by Vasily Grossman, ed. and trans. Antony Beevor and Luba Vinogradova (Pimlico, 2006).

2  Ibid.

3  Schneyder, 'The Fall of Berlin'.

4  Ibid.

5  Ibid.

6  Ibid.

7  Cited in an intriguing book, *Uncertainty: The Life and Science of Werner Heisenberg* by David C. Cassidy (W. H. Freeman, 1992).

8  Ibid.

9  From an illuminating monograph: 'Entering the Nuclear Arms Race: The Soviet Decision to Build the Atomic Bomb, 1939–45' by David Holloway, *Social Studies of Science*, May 1981.

10  Ibid.

11  Ibid.

12  Ibid.

13  There is more on the earlier noted Manfred von Ardenne website.

14  Ibid.

15  Holloway, 'Entering the Nuclear Arms Race'.

16  Ibid.

17  Ibid.

18  There is more, with related links, on the Manfred von Ardenne website.

19  Christa Ronke's memoirs.

20  Ibid.

21  Ibid.

22  Ibid.

23  Marion Keller's account.

24  Ibid.

25  Ibid.

26  Ingeborg Seldte's recollections.

27  Ibid.

28  Ibid.

29  Ibid.

30  Jalowicz-Simon, *Underground in Berlin*.

31  Ibid.

32  Ibid.

33  Ibid.

34  Ibid.

35  Ibid.

36  Ibid.

37  Anon., *A Woman in Berlin*.

38  Inge Deutschkron was later to become a journalist and author. She was interviewed many times and wrote a memoir: *Outcast: A Jewish Girl in Wartime Berlin* (Plunkett Lake Press, 2017).

39  Ibid.

40  Anon., *A Woman in Berlin*.

41  Zhukov, *Memoirs*.

42  Ibid.

43  Mechtild Evers's account.

44  Ibid.

45  Ibid.

46  Ibid.

47  Ibid.

48  Ibid.

49  Ibid.

50  Knef, *The Gift Horse*.

51  Ibid.

52  Ibid.

53  Ibid.

54  Ibid.

55  Cited in a deeply absorbing monograph, 'Philomela's Legacy: Rape, the Second World War and the Ethics of Reading' by Elisabeth Krimmer, *German Quarterly*, Winter 2015.

56  From an illuminating and moving monograph, 'A Question of Silence: The Rape of German Women by Occupation Soldiers' by Atina Grossmann, *October*, vol. 72, Spring 1995.

57  Ibid.

58  Christa Ronke's memoirs.

## 14. Oblivion

1  From a grimly fascinating monograph, 'Suicide at the End of the Third Reich' by Christian Goeschel, *Journal of Contemporary History*, vol. 41, no. 1, January 2006.

2 There is a recent, hypnotically bleak book on the subject of German civilians committing suicide: *Promise Me You'll Shoot Yourself: The Downfall of Ordinary Germans, 1945* by Florian Huber, trans. Imogen Taylor (Allen Lane, 2019).

3 Ibid.

4 Goeschel, 'Suicide at the End of the Third Reich'.

5 Ibid.; there are also many medical papers online, such as 'Cyanide Poisoning: Pathophysiology and Treatment Recommendations' by D. M. G. Beasley and W. I. Glass (reassuring in the event of mild poisoning); https://academic.oup.com/occmed/article/48/7/427/1514905.

6 Goeschel, 'Suicide at the End of the Third Reich'.

7 Ibid.

8 Huber, *Promise Me You'll Shoot Yourself*.

9 Ibid.

10 Goeschel, 'Suicide at the End of the Third Reich'.

11 Anon., *A Woman in Berlin*.

12 Knef, *The Gift Horse*.

13 Ibid.

14 Ibid.

15 Jalowicz-Simon, *Underground in Berlin*.

16 Ibid.

17 Ibid.

18 Marion Keller's account.

19 Zhukov, *Memoirs*.

20 Ibid.

21 Stern, *Ulbricht*.

22 Ibid.

23 Grossman, *A Writer at War*.

24 Ibid.

25 There is a warm and detailed biography of von Treskow (in his own way, quite a municipal reformer in Berlin back in the Wilhelmine era) that can be found on the website of Museum Lichtenberg; www.museum-lichtenberg.de/index.php/menschen/lichtenberger-persoenlichkeiten/694-sigismund-johann-carl-von-treskow.

26 Grossman, *A Writer at War*.

27 Vaget, 'Wagnerian Self-Fashioning'.

28 Goeschel, 'Suicide at the End of the Third Reich'.

## 15. 'The shadows on our souls'

1 Goeschel, 'Suicide at the End of the Third Reich'.

2 Ibid.

3 From the hypnotic *The End: Germany, 1944–45* by Ian Kershaw (Allen Lane, 2011).

4 Cited in *Time and Power: Visions of History in German Politics, from the Thirty Years' War to the Third Reich* by Christopher Clark (Princeton University Press, 2021).

5 Cited in 'How the Berlin Garrison Surrendered, 2 May 1945' by Igor Venkov, published in *Army History*, no. 17, Winter 1990/91.

6 Ibid.

7 Anon., *A Woman in Berlin*.

8 Discussed in the monograph 'Gazing at Ruins' by Stefan-Ludwig Hoffmann, published in the *Journal of Modern European History*, vol. 9, no. 3, 2011.

9 There is an illuminating article about Hans Fritzsche, his subsequent trial at Nuremberg and the nature of his broadcasts, to be found online at www.jewishvirtuallibrary.org/nuremberg-trial-defendants-hans-fritzsche. Although after Nuremberg he was 'denazified', he faced trial again in West Germany and was sentenced to nine years in jail, but released in 1950.

10 Ibid.

11 Ibid.

12 Ibid.

13 Hoffmann, 'Gazing at Ruins'.

14 Venkov, 'How the Berlin Garrison Surrendered'.

15 Anon., *A Woman in Berlin*.

16 Dieter Pfeiffer's recollections, as curated by the Zeitzeugenbörse.

17 Ibid.

18 Ibid.

19 Ibid.

20 Jalowicz-Simon, *Underground in Berlin*.

21 Grossman, *A Writer at War*.

22 *The Times*, 3 May 1945.

23 Ibid.

24 There is further vivid detail to be found in Anon., *A Woman in Berlin*.

25  There is more, sometimes terrible detail in 'Remembering/Forgetting' by Helke Sander, trans. Stuart Liebman, *October*, vol. 72, Spring 1995.

26  There are a number of nice articles about this key moment: one that is both interesting and well illustrated can be found here: https://about-photography.blog/blog/2019/10/12/the-story-behind-the-raising-a-flag-over-the-reichstag-by-yevgeny-khaldei-1945.

27  There is an absorbing monograph that includes the swift Soviet effort to restore art and culture on strictly party lines: 'Reconfiguring Postwar Antifascism: Reflections on the History of Ideology' by Clara M. Oberle, *New German Critique*, no. 117, Fall 2012.

28  Cited and discussed in *In a Cold Crater: Cultural and Intellectual Life in Berlin, 1945–1948* by Wolfgang Schivelbusch (University of California Press, 1998).

29  Ibid.

30  Ibid.

31  Marion Keller's account.

32  Ibid.

33  Ibid.

34  Ibid.

35  Ibid.

36  Ibid.

37  Peter Lorenz's recollections curated by the Zeitzeugenbörse.

38  Ibid.

39  Ibid.

40  Knef, *The Gift Horse*.

41  Ibid.

42  Grossman, *A Writer at War*.

43  Knef, *The Gift Horse*.

44  Orbach and Orbach-Smith, *Young Lothar*.

45  Discussed in a terrific monograph, 'Typical Russian Words in German War-Memoir Literature' by Katherina Filips, *Slavic and East European Journal*, vol. 8, no. 4, Winter 1964.

46  Ibid.

47  Explored in 'Street Names and Political Identity: The Case of East Berlin' by Maoz Azaryahu, *Journal of Contemporary History*, vol. 21, no. 4, 1986.

48  Ibid.

49  *Daily Telegraph*, 11 May 1945.

50  Mechtild Evers's account.

51 Knef, *The Gift Horse*.

52 Ibid.

53 As part of the unceasing wonder of the modern technological age, it is now possible to see this film online via the Jewish Film Institute: https://jfi.org/watch-online/jfi-on-demand/professor-mamlock.

## 16. Complicity

1 There is a terrific recent article by Alex Ross, 'The Haunted California Idyll of German Writers in Exile', *The New Yorker*, 9 March 2020, which explores the vast US community of German artists, including Mann, Alfred Döblin, Bertolt Brecht and many others. Also discussed in 'The Hannah Arendt Situation' by Richard Wolin, *New England Review*, vol. 22, no. 2, Spring 2001.

2 Ross, 'The Haunted California Idyll'.

3 *Essays in Understanding, 1930–1954* by Hannah Arendt (Shocken Books, 2005).

4 As reported in *The Times*, 3 June 1945.

5 Ibid.

6 Ibid.

7 Anon., *A Woman in Berlin*.

8 Stern, *Ulbricht*.

9 Oberle, 'Reconfiguring Postwar Antifascism'.

10 Ibid.

11 Ibid.

12 Ibid.

13 There is a wonderfully detailed monograph, 'The Hut on the Garden Plot: Informal Architecture in Twentieth-Century Berlin' by Florian Urban, *Journal of the Society of Architectural Historians*, vol. 72, no. 2, June 2013.

14 Ibid.

15 Oberle, 'Reconfiguring Postwar Antifascism'.

16 Ibid.

17 As analysed in an absorbing monograph: 'Johannes R. Becher and the Cultural Development of the GDR' by Alexander Stephan, *New German Critique*, vol. 2, Spring 1974.

18 Ibid.

19 Ibid.

20 Ibid.

21 From an article published in the Zeitzeugenbörse journal, 2005.

22 The Red Star is still there; each year's flowers tenderly nurtured.

23 The terminology, and philosophy, is discussed in Wolin, 'The Hannah Arendt Situation'.

24 Ibid.

25 Christa Ronke's memoirs.

26 The book that emerged from Trevor-Roper's investigations of those ruins was *The Last Days of Hitler* (first published 1947, and which can now be found under the imprint of Pan Books).

27 Margot Sharma's recollections, curated by the Zeitzeugenbörse.

## 17. 'Where was home?'

1 As recalled in a feature in the Zeitzeugenbörse journal, 2005.

2 Christa Ronke's memoirs.

3 Explored in detail in Hoffmann, 'Gazing at Ruins'.

4 A great deal has been written in recent years about Wilder's life and later Hollywood years; in this instance, there is an illuminating essay titled 'Billy Wilder's Cold War Berlin' by David Bathrick, *New German Critique*, no. 110, Summer 2010.

5 Ibid.

6 Ibid.

7 Quoted ibid.

8 Quoted ibid.

9 Knef, *The Gift Horse*.

10 *A Foreign Affair* is available on DVD, and the darkness of its comedy is frequently eyebrow-raising. The scene involving the mischievous little boy who cannot stop drawing chalk swastikas – and the exasperated father who does not realize his boy has drawn one on the back of his jacket – is simultaneously laugh-out-loud funny and chilling; a most unusual combination.

11 Bathrick, 'Billy Wilder's Cold War Berlin'.

12  As quoted in a beguiling essay, 'Fashion Amidst the Ruins: Revisiting the Early Rubble Films *And the Heavens Above* (1947) and *The Murderers are Among Us* (1946)' by Mila Ganeva, *German Studies Review*, vol. 37, no. 1, February 2014.

13  Knef, *The Gift Horse*.

14  There is an illuminating but very sad chapter, 'Repressive Rehabilitation: Crime, Morality and Delinquency in Berlin-Brandenburg, 1945–1958' by Jennifer V. Evans, in *Crime and Criminal Justice in Modern Germany*, ed. Richard F. Wetzell (Berghahn Books, 2014), which also explores how numbers of these young people fell into prostitution, utilizing areas such as the city's larger railway stations.

15  Ibid.

16  There is an abundance of chilling detail on the website www.sachsenhausen-sbg.de/en/history/1945-1950-soviet-special-camp/. The website chronicles the entire span of Sachsenhausen's existence.

17  As discussed in the essay 'The Postwar Restoration in East and West' by Stephen Brockmann, *New German Critique*, no. 126, November 2015.

18  Christa Ronke's memoirs.

19  The grim business of bodies in the forests around Berlin – fragments of which still emerge even now – is discussed in an article entitled 'Digging Up the Past in Halbe', which can be read at www.dw.com/en/digging-up-the-past-in-halbe/a-16762689.

20  There is a warm and compelling essay about the formation of the Berliner Ensemble and the pivotal role occupied by Helene Weigel, Brecht's wife: 'Gossip, Ghosts and Memory – Mother Courage and the Forging of the Berliner Ensemble' by Gitta Honegger, *TDR*, vol. 52, no. 4, Winter 2008.

21  Jalowicz-Simon, *Underground in Berlin*.

22  There is an absorbing article (and programme) that can be found at the news site Deutsche Welle: www.dw.com/en/how-jewish-life-developed-in-germany-after-the-holocaust/a-56604526.

23  Ibid.

24  Ibid.

25  As discussed in 'East Germany's Jewish Question: The Return and Preservation of Jewish Sites in East Berlin and Potsdam, 1945–1989' by Michael Meng, *Central European History*, vol. 38, no. 4, 2005.

26 Quoted on the news site Deutsche Welle, as above.

27 Meng, 'East Germany's Jewish Question'.

28 Ibid.

29 Explored in *Jews, Germans and Allies: Close Encounters in Occupied Germany* by Atina Grossmann (Princeton University Press, 2009).

30 Ibid.

31 As explored in *Visual Histories of Occupation: A Transcultural Dialogue* by Jeremy E. Taylor (Bloomsbury Academic, 2021).

32 Ibid.

33 Ibid.

34 Part of the ongoing miracle of the digital age, the British Pathé newsreel of this event can be seen on YouTube at www.youtube.com/watch?v=M17bEXksnBc.

35 As reported – with now amusing indignation – on page three of *The Times*, 2 September 1947.

## 18. The Islanders

1 There is an interesting exploration of the magazine, and of post-war satire in Berlin, in 'The *Ulenspiegel* and Anti-American Discourse in the American Sector of Berlin' by Cora Sol Goldstein, *German Politics and Society*, vol. 23, no. 2, Summer 2005.

2 This gruesome pencil work may be viewed on the website of the Museum of Modern Art at www.moma.org/collection/works/151564.

3 This atmospheric work can be viewed on www.meisterdrucke.uk/fine-art-prints/Gustav-Wunderwald/690135/Bridge-over-the-Ackerstraße-Berlin-North.html.

4 Part of a feature devoted to the street and its neighbourhood in the journal of the Zeitzeugenbörse, Summer 2006.

5 Dr Alfred Wege's recollections, curated by the Zeitzeugenbörse.

6 There is much fascinating social historical detail in *Inventing a Socialist Nation: Heimat and the Politics of Everyday Life in the GDR, 1945–90* by Jan Palmowski (Cambridge University Press, 2009).

7 Ibid.

8 The original 'long telegram' document has been digitized and can be read at digitalarchive.wilsoncenter.org/document/116178.pdf.

9 There is an arrestingly revisionist (and very absorbing) study, 'The Incomplete Blockade – Soviet Zone Supply of West Berlin, 1948–49' by William Stivers, *Diplomatic History*, vol. 21, no. 4, Fall 1997.

10 Ibid.

11 Ibid.

12 An area explored in Palmowski, *Inventing a Socialist Nation*.

13 As quoted in Stivers, 'The Incomplete Blockade'.

14 Ibid.

15 A horrid detail from a contemporaneous article, 'Life in Berlin Today', *The World Today*, December 1948.

16 Ibid.

17 Ibid.

18 As quoted in Stivers, 'The Incomplete Blockade'.

19 Ibid.

20 Ibid.

21 He has been interviewed many times, but there is an especially nice and detailed article by Kris Hendrix, Researcher in Aviation History at the RAF Museum, written in the wake of a visit from the elderly Gail Halvorsen, at www.rafmuseum.org.uk/blog/the-candy-bomber/.

22 Ibid.

23 British participation in the airlift is explored in 'The Role of Britain in the Berlin Airlift' by Emma Peplow, *History*, vol. 95, no. 2, April 2010.

24 All this was captured on British Pathé newsreels. This, and a range of other blockade filmed reports, are available to view at www.british-pathe.com/workspaces/df699ffd537d4e0c74710ad015dfd64d/fGjL01IJ.

25 'Life in Berlin Today'.

26 Stivers, 'The Incomplete Blockade'.

27 Ibid.

28 There is a (very faintly chilling) near contemporaneous study on the subject: 'Nutrition Lessons of the Berlin Blockade' by H. E. Magee, *Public Health Reports*, vol. 67, no. 7, July 1952.

29 Ibid.

30 Ibid.

31 'Life in Berlin Today'.

32 There is a rather nice appreciation of the production – and of Brecht's wife Helene Weigel's starring role, and of the influence and impact that

this particular production had (Brecht decreed Epic Theatre over Stanislavsky-style realism) in the years after – by Gideon Lester at americanrepertorytheater.org/media/a-model-of-courage/.

33  As reported, with some pleasure, by *The Times* on 23 August 1948.

34  Ibid.

35  Ibid.

36  There is a short tribute to presiding genius Günter Neumann, plus a recording of 'The Islanders' Song' at www.günter-neumann-stiftung. de/die-insulaner.

## 19. *'The crowd started howling'*

1  *The Times*, 21 January 1952.

2  *The Times*, 26 May 1952. Burianek – eventually posthumously rehabilitated in 2005 – had been previously described as a CIA-sponsored terrorist, who had been plotting arson and to destroy a railway bridge.

3  *The Times*, 3 June 1952.

4  Ibid.

5  Ibid.

6  *The Times*, 6 June 1952.

7  Ibid.

8  An interesting clip of British Pathé newsreel also shows Acheson on the same visit looking at a scale model of a proposed library that foreshadows the architecture of a new area – the modernism that straddled the Iron Curtain.

9  Stern, *Ulbricht*.

10  From an absorbing essay about the style and the aspirations of communist building in East Berlin: 'The Vernacular and the Monumental: Memory and Landscape in Post-War Berlin' by Paul Stangl, *GeoJournal*, vol. 73, no. 3, 2008.

11  Ibid.

12  Ibid.

13  Ibid.

14  Ibid.

15  From a beguiling diary, 'My Berlin' by Horst Koegler, *Dance Chronicle*, vol. 36, no. 1, 2013.

16  Ibid.

17  Ibid.

18  Ibid.

19  Ibid.

20  Discussed in 'Hero or Villain? Bertolt Brecht and the Crisis Surrounding June 1953' by Mark W. Clark, *Journal of Contemporary History*, vol. 41, no. 3, July 2006.

21  Cited in '"Keeping the Pot Simmering": The United States and the East German Uprising of 1953' by Christian F. Ostermann, *German Studies Review*, vol. 19, no. 1, February 1996.

22  Ibid.

23  Ibid.

24  Horst Kreeter, interviewed by Dr Richard Millington for the podcast 'Cold War Conversations', which can be found at https://coldwarconversations.com/episode6/.

25  Ibid.

26  As cited in Stern, *Ulbricht*.

27  There is an interesting essay analysing the nature of Brecht's humour: 'Bertolt Brecht, Politics and Comedy' by Marc Silberman, *Social Research*, vol. 79, no. 1, Spring 2012. That particular Brecht line is also possibly one of the world's most frequently quoted out of context.

28  As cited in Ostermann, '"Keeping the Pot Simmering"'.

29  Ibid.

30  Ibid.

31  Ibid.

32  Ibid.

33  Ibid.

34  Ibid.

35  Ibid.

## 20. The Widening Chasm

1  There is some wonderful archival material to be seen on the National Security Agency's website at www.nsa.gov/portals/75/documents/news-features/declassified-documents/cryptologic-histories/operation_regal.pdf.

2  Stern, *Ulbricht*.

3  *Daily Telegraph*, 16 January 1956.

4  Ibid.

5  Ibid.

6  The rising tension over the prospect of 'Russia' arming these groups was reported in the *Daily Telegraph*, 11 February 1956.

7  Discussed in a beguiling monograph: 'Rock 'n' Roll, Female Sexuality and the Cold War Battle Over German Identities' by Uta G. Poiger, *Journal of Modern History*, vol. 68, no. 3, September 1996.

8  Ibid.

9  For an amazing blast of 'Elvis in Germany' memorabilia, plus the fascination of 1950s popular magazine layout and typography, there is a highly specialized web page detailing Elvis's appearances in *Bravo* Magazine that can be found at http://www.elvisechoesofthepast.com/elvis-in-bravo-magazine-germany-1956/.

10  Poiger, 'Rock 'n' Roll'.

11  Ibid.

12  Ibid.

13  Ibid.

14  Elke Rosin's story – encapsulating the rise of the Berlin Wall – can be found at the haunting website www.berliner-mauer-gedenkstaette.de/en/elke-rosin-783.html.

15  Poiger, 'Rock 'n' Roll'.

16  Ibid.

17  *Daily Telegraph*, 28 January 1956.

18  Ibid.

19  Ibid.

20  Ibid.

21  Ibid.

22  A fascinating and chilling Stasi archival documentation on the case – retrieved and digitized – can be found at www.stasi-mediathek.de/themen/person/Elli%20Barczatis/.

23  *Daily Telegraph*, 7 February 1956.

24  Ibid.

25  John Peet's story is explored in depth in 'John Peet (1915–1988): An Englishman in the GDR' by Stefan Berger and Norman Laporte, *History*, vol. 89, no. 1, January 2004.

26  There is a nice and enthusiastic short biography – with the emphasis upon his motoring career – at media.daimler.com/marsMediaSite/en/ instance/ko/Biography-Manfred-von-Brauchitsch.xhtml?oid=45194996.

27  This fear of rearmament as a motive was picked up in numerous *Daily Telegraph* reports in the early weeks of 1956.

28  There are many interesting essays about the way that the Stasi was constructed to permeate all corners of society, and to reach beyond the GDR too; like this, from Deutsche Welle (11 June 2019): www.dw.com/ en/stasis-pervasive-footprint-across-two-berlins-revealed/a-49135973.

29  As reported on a near daily basis by *The Times* throughout 1960 and the early months of 1961; there were good colour pieces, such as that on 26 April 1960 involving the anxieties of craftsmen as well as 'intellectuals'.

30  Ibid.

31  Margot Schorr's recollections, as curated by the Zeitzeugenbörse.

32  Ibid.

33  As reported in *The Times*, as above.

34  Ulbricht made the demand many times that year; the first was reported by *The Times* on 2 January 1961.

35  Palmowski, *Inventing a Socialist Nation*.

36  To read that entire parliamentary session now – where Heath takes questions from across the House on matters pertaining to all corners of the globe – is not so much to fall into the old-age trap of imagining that parliamentarians back then were giants compared to the present day, as to reflect on a period where debates and questions were focused on the House, rather than on the twenty-four-hour news cycle. Visit hansard. parliament.uk/commons/1961-07-31/debates/e299acfa-8686-46cd-b1e7-6c0d807e1a26/ForeignAffairs.

37  *Daily Telegraph*, 11 August 1961.

38  *Daily Telegraph*, 12 August 1961.

39  Ibid.

40  A report from a young Nigel Lawson, a few years away from his stint as Chancellor of the Exchequer, in the *Sunday Telegraph*, 27 August 1961.

41  Dieter Weber, interviewed for a lively and informative site, filled with striking visuals: www.the-berlin-wall.com.

42  Ibid.

43  Ibid.

44 There is more on this, with links to archives, to be found online at www.wilsoncenter.org/publication/new-evidence-the-building-the-berlin-wall.

## 21. *There is a World Elsewhere*

1 President Kennedy's full speech can be read at the JFK Presidential Library and Museum, here: www.jfklibrary.org/archives/other-resources/john-f-kennedy-speeches/berlin-w-germany-rudolph-wilde-platz-19630626.

2 The idea of the Wall as 'Anti-Fascist Protection Barrier' – among its other meanings and uses – is bracingly discussed by historian and long-term Berlin habitué Neal Ascherson (before and after the Wall) in 'The Media Did It', *London Review of Books*, 21 June 2007.

3 Her story can be read here on this Berlin Wall memorial website: www.berliner-mauer-gedenkstaette.de/en/1961-299.html.

4 Elke Rosin's story, ibid.

5 Olga Segler's story on the Berlin Wall memorial website: www.berliner-mauer-gedenkstaette.de/en/1961-299.html.

6 Günter Litfin's story, ibid.

7 Ibid.

8 Udo Düllick's story on the Berlin Wall memorial website: www.berliner-mauer-gedenkstaette.de/en/1961-299.html.

9 As quoted in *Belonging in the Two Berlins: Kin, State, Nation* by John Borneman (Cambridge University Press, 1992).

10 Ibid.

11 As quoted in a finely illustrated essay, 'The Architecture and Message of the "Wall", 1961–1989' by Leo Schmidt, *German Politics and Society*, vol. 29, no. 2, Summer 2011.

12 This, and other haunting stories, can be read at the Berlin Wall memorial website: www.berliner-mauer-gedenkstaette.de/en/1968-316.html.

13 Cited in a monograph written at a time when the Wall still seemed permanent: 'Disquiet on the Western Front: Observations on the Twentieth Anniversary of the Berlin Wall' by John C. Palenberg, *The Fletcher Forum*, vol. 5, no. 2, Summer 1981.

14 Schmidt, 'The Architecture and Message of the "Wall"'.

15 Ibid.

16 Ibid.

17 Cited ibid. (originally from an article in *Der Spiegel* in 1981).

18 This, and other stories, can be read at the Berlin Wall memorial site: www.berliner-mauer-gedenkstaette.de/en/1981-326.html.

19 Ibid.

20 This story can be read at the Berlin Wall memorial website: www. berliner-mauer-gedenkstaette.de/en/1989-332.html.

21 Ibid.

## *Afterword*

1 Benjamin, 'A Berlin Chronicle'.

# Index

# DRESDEN
## SINCLAIR MCKAY

### The *Sunday Times* bestseller

In February 1945 the Allies obliterated Dresden, the 'Florence of the Elbe'. Bombs weighing over 1,000 lbs fell every seven and a half seconds and an estimated 25,000 people were killed. Was Dresden a legitimate military target or was the bombing a last act of atavistic mass murder in a war already won?

From the history of the city to the attack itself, conveyed in a minute-by-minute account from the first of the flares to the flames reaching almost a mile high – the wind so searingly hot that the lungs of those in its path were instantly scorched – through the eerie period of reconstruction, bestselling author Sinclair McKay creates a vast canvas and brings it alive with touching human detail.

Impeccably researched and deeply moving, McKay uses never-before-seen sources to relate the untold stories of civilians and vividly conveys the texture of contemporary life. Writing with warmth and colour about morality in war, the instinct for survival, the gravity of mass destruction and the importance of memory, this is a master historian at work.

'Powerful . . . grips by its passion and originality'

> Max Hastings, *Sunday Times*

'Beautifully crafted, elegiac, compelling . . . a masterpiece of its genre'

> Damien Lewis, author of *Zero Six Bravo*

'He makes Dresden come alive, before, during, and after the infernal 13th'

> John Lewis-Stempel, *Daily Express*